MARY BLAIR'S
HORS D'OEUVRE
◾ COOKBOOK ◾

A Complete Guide
to Hors D'oeuvre Cookery
and Festive Menus

---

by

MARY BLAIR

FREUNDLICH BOOKS
New York

Library of Congress Cataloging in Publication Data

Blair, Mary, 1922–
Mary Blair's hors d'oeuvre cookbook.

Includes index.
1. Cookery (Appetizers)   2. Cookery, International
3. Entertaining.   I. Title
TX740.B54   1985   641.8′12   84–25850
ISBN 0–88191–004–X

Published by Freundlich Books (A Division of Lawrence Freundlich Publications, Inc.)
80 Madison Avenue
New York, New York 10016

Distributed to the trade by
The Scribner Book Companies, Inc.

Manufactured in the United States of America

10 9 8 7 6 5 4 3 2 1

The author is grateful for permission to reprint the following material:

"Low Cal Mayonnaise" from *Haute Cuisine for Your Heart's Delight* by Carol Cutler. Copyright © 1973 by Carol Cutler. Used by permission of Clarkson N. Potter, Inc.

Recipe for "Devonshire Cream" used with kind permission of *Country Journal* Magazine.

"Veal and Ham Pâté en Croûte," "Orbec Sauce" and "Light Tomato Sauce" recipes from *Pâté—New Main Course for the 1980s* by Carol Cutler. Copyright © 1983 Carol Cutler. Reprinted with the permission of Rawson Associates.

"Raw Bar Cocktail Sauce" and "Shallot Seafood Sauce" reprinted from *The Grand Central Oyster Bar and Restaurant Seafood Cookbook* Copyright © 1977 by Jerome Brody and Joan and Joseph Foley; Used by permission of Crown Publishers, Inc.

"Cebiche" from *The Cuisines of Mexico* by Diana Kennedy. Copyright © 1972 by Diana Kennedy. Reprinted by permission of Harper & Row, Publishers, Inc.

"Ritz Cocktail Sauce," "Ritz Sponge Cake," "French Fried Almonds," "Delice d'Orient," and "Remoulade Sauce" adapted from *The Ritz-Carlton Cook Book and Guide to Home Entertaining* by Helen E. Ridley (J.B. Lippincott Company). Copyright © 1968 by Helen E. Ridley. Reprinted by permission of Harper & Row, Publishers, Inc.

"Cheese Crescents" and "Orange-Almond Dip" from *The Enchanted Broccoli Forest* by Mollie Katzen. Copyright © 1982. Used with Permission. Available from Ten Speed Press, Box 7123, Berkeley, CA 94707. $11.95 (paper), $16.95 (cloth) + $ .75 for postage and handling.

"Louis Dressing" and "James Beard's Shrimp Sauce" Adapted from *James Beard's New Fish Cookery* copyright 1954, Copyright © 1976 by James A. Beard. By permission of Little, Brown and Company.

"Sand Tarts" and "Chocolate Dipped Pirouettes" from *The Dione Lucas Book of French Cooking* by Mark Lucas and Marion F. Gorman. Copyright © 1973 by Mark Lucas and Marion F. Gorman. By permission of Little, Brown and Company.

"Viennese Balls," "Creamy Chocolate Glaze" and "Rich Tart Pastry" from *The Art of Fine Baking* by Paula Peck. Copyright © 1961 by Paula Peck. Reprinted by permission of Simon & Schuster, Inc.

"Southern Style Smithfield Ham," and "Beaten Biscuits" from *Four Great Southern Cooks,* published by DuBose Publishing.

"Farm Wife's Head Cheese," "Cold Avocado Soup," and "Spicy Iced Tea" courtesy of Stephen Greene Press.

"Eggless Herb Mayonnaise" and "Quick Tomato Sauce" adapted from *New Menus from Simca's Cuisine,* copyright © 1979, 1978 by Simone Beck and Michael James. Reprinted by permission of Harcourt Brace Jovanovich, Inc.

To my husband, William Blair, who encouraged me
in my culinary efforts by bringing all manner
of friends and colleagues to our house
to be entertained at home.

ACKNOWLEDGMENTS

I could not have compiled this book without the help of countless others.

First, I want to acknowledge our children: each one—Colin, Fiona, Sheila and Jonathan—cooks well, tries new recipes and shares them with me. And beyond them, my own original family: my mother, who loved to cook and showed me so many of her ways; my father, who only cooked in the country but was excellent with steaks and wild game, and my three sisters, who have given much from their lives in Montreal and from sojourns in Toronto, the Maritimes and Kenya.

In Vermont I want to thank Linda King, my partner in countless catering expeditions, for her constant good humor, her easy assurance and her help with testing. It has been a joy and we both learn something new at each party.

Then, too, I want to thank Neysa Hebbard, the knowledgeable friend who has typed and tidied the manuscript. Her organizing and planning abilities and her eye for detail have made the book possible.

Many of the parties I share with you here were old territory to me, well worn and comfortable, but others presented new territory to chart. To make them as authentic and flavorful as possible, I turned to friends who knew the terrain far more intimately than I.

For the Scots High Tea, Bette Fischer, who came from Scotland, reminisced for me, as did Anne Kanter, who grew up with family "teas" a part of her everyday life in the north of England. Sarah Alden Gannett, who fishes each year on the banks of the River Spey, added welcome up-to-date information and several local recipes.

My interest in the Réveillon party sprang naturally from my own upbringing in Montreal but was enriched immensely by a chance encounter with a French Canadian banker whose mother, Madame Constance Garneau, drew generously from her great knowledge of French Canadian cooking and customs to give real substance to this party. Her aid, and that of my Montreal sisters, affords this party an authentic ring I couldn't have managed without them.

The Greek party was in large part inspired by my acquaintance with Angie Viscardi, who owns the Colonial Restaurant in Old Greenwich, Connecticut, and who was full of encouragement and suggestions from her own Greek background. Alice Hoopis, a Vermont friend, added valuable current on-the-scene advice garnered from her frequent visits to relatives in Greece.

Due partly to my long-time love affair with Mexico—the result of many happy visits—and partly to an awareness of the growing interest in modern-day Mexican-American cuisine, I was anxious to include at least one party featuring a Mexican-American theme. Not completely confident with the American portion of this equation, I turned to my good friend Ida Sloane Snyder for help and she didn't let me down. Much of the Southwestern Sporting Breakfast party springs from her experience and recipes.

As I say elsewhere, one of my delights in working on this book—as in life —has been the opportunity to encounter new things and new ideas. Despite having lived in London, Montreal and New York, I was happy to find that our move to Vermont widened my horizons even further. Some of these new horizons are reflected in this book—first by the traditional Southern party, for which Jane McFadden, a near neighbor, and her mother, Mrs. Thomas McCutcheon, contributed both recipes and genuine background; my old friend Marion Yearley also helped with this. George and Laura Lewis, both on the staff at our local high school, did the same for my New Orleans jazz party, as did Carol Eaton for the Superbowl Sunday curry party, and Susan Ross for the auction preview party.

Many others provided both moral and more specific support. It was a special joy to have several area professionals share their expertise: Chuck Hornsby, a Brattleboro wine merchant and purveyor of gourmet food; Hi Kyung Brandt, who specializes in Chinese dishes, Angela Lea, a young Vermont pastry-maker; and Peter and Lillian Zilliacus, of both restaurant and accounting fame—all were most generous. Rhonda Burgess shared her knowledge of quantity cooking and Anne Canady helped keep our household going, as she does faithfully, book or no book. And a very special delight was a hand-up from our Vermont Senator Patrick Leahy, who sent me several choice political recipes.

Just as a party needs to be graced by decoration, so does a book. For help with this, I am indebted to several very talented artists: Hanson Carroll, who did the cover photography; Bob Grant, the interior photography; and Claude Martinot, the line art.

On a more practical level I am deeply indebted to the law firm of Kristensen, Cummings, Murtha and Stewart, and their staff, who most graciously made an office, and other services, available for my work; to Sara Fisher for the use of her IBM Selectric typewriter, and to all at Blair and Ketchum's *Country Journal* magazine for their many assists along the way.

CONTENTS

Come to the Party   *I*

CONVIVIAL YET CASUAL   5

1   TWO INTIMATE GATHERINGS   7
    Perfect for the Small Apartment   10
    On the Patio   13

2   A PAIR OF PORTABLE FEASTS   17
    Picnic for a Summer Day   21
    A Tailgate Picnic   28

3   WHEN BREAKFAST MEETS LUNCH   33
    A New England Sunday Brunch   35
    Southwestern Sporting Breakfast   41

4   SUPERBOWL SUNDAY   51

5   TWO VEGETARIAN SPREADS   63
    A Harvest-Time Fête   65
    A Winter Caper   76

6   THE PLEASURES OF TEA   85
    High Tea Family-Style   92
    A "Ritzy" Tea at Home   97

7   ENTERTAINING THE VISITING FIREMAN   105
    A Winter Welcome—Family Style   107
    An Alfresco Welcome à la Carte   116

8   FOR PARENTS AT A CHILDREN'S PARTY   123

9   WHEN TEENAGERS GET TOGETHER   129

10   A COUNTRY WEDDING   139

11 FESTIVELY FOREIGN: TWO PARTIES 157
    Réveillon de Noël 159
    Your Yearly Bash à la Grecque 166

ELEGANT YET PERSONAL 181

12 A SOUTHERN "AT HOME" THANKSGIVING PARTY 183

13 WHEN CONGRATULATIONS ARE IN ORDER 201

14 PICTURES AT THE EXHIBITION 217

15 AN OLD-FASHIONED SALON 229

16 BEFORE THE FOOTLIGHTS GO UP 237

17 AFTER THE NIGHT MUSIC 249

18 AN INTIMATE WINTER WEDDING 259

19 TWO EXTRA-SPECIAL WEDDINGS 269
    An Elegant Afternoon Wedding 271
    Candlelight Wedding Supper 281

FOR PLEASURE ... AND PROFIT 289

An Introduction 291

20 BROWN BAGS WERE NEVER LIKE THIS 297
    Box Lunch Suggestions 302
    Box Breakfast Eye-Openers 312

21 CHEERING THE CANDIDATE 315

22 THE EARLY BIRD ... 325

23 SPARKLING WINES AND SUGARPLUMS 335

24 "RIFFING" ON RAMPART STREET 349

25 A GALA CHAMPAGNE EVENING 359

BACK-UP BASICS FOR THE PARTY GIVER 381

Dressings, Dips, Marinades and Sauces 383

Basic Pastries 399

Fillings and Frostings 405

A Few More Punches 408

A Few Words on Cheese 412

All About Nuts 416

How Much for How Many 418

Hiring a Caterer 419

INDEX 421

MARY BLAIR'S
HORS D'OEUVRE
◪ COOKBOOK ◪

COME TO THE PARTY

A FEW PRELIMINARY WORDS

This collection of menus, recipes and parties is the result of forty years of delight.

I was born in Montreal, a beautiful city with elegant French food and design, tempered by English gardening and organization, and I have felt the pull of both these cultures ever since.

In my youth we enjoyed simple, well-cooked food at home in town and the same at our farm in the country. But one day my horizons were vastly widened with the arrival of an invitation to a French-Canadian "Cocktail." There, drinks were served with a resplendent buffet of pâtés, prosciutto and melon, hors d'oeuvre, delicate sandwiches, lobster-filled bouchées and more—bloater paste was gone from my repertoire forever.

Hospitality in its widest sense was the core of my mother's house. She was the youngest of eight children and loved to entertain. She sang beautifully but always with her audience in mind. A lovely woman, as she grew older she always took care to offer her guests a comfortable milieu for discussions of world and local events and for happy times. From this I learned to love parties and to consider my guests and their enjoyment. If there is one single most important ingredient to happy party-giving it must be this.

This was reinforced in New York City, where my husband and our family moved in 1965. Our home there was a gracious place to entertain. Our neighborhood around Gramercy Park was quiet, but nearby Third Avenue had excellent groceries and bakeries, and deliveries of liquor and soft drinks as well as ice. Specialty markets and flower shops abounded. And when we needed extra professional help, it was readily available. All that and our comfortably large apartment made entertaining possible and pleasant.

My husband's work meant that much of our entertaining was of authors and book people, and I still vividly recall, among many other happy associations, how striking Maya Angelou was sitting near the library fire in her multicolored dress and turban—and the time Norman Mailer brought two young Puerto Rican fighters needing sustenance before going on to the boxing arena. But not all the guests were illustrious: there were many beginning authors and young editors and they were always hungry. These parties made me even more aware of the importance of providing good food at a party and of the need for at least one hearty dish that can serve as a hungry guest's supper.

Hors d'oeuvre are a symbol of greeting and welcome; self-contained, they can be taken in one hand and eaten quickly, leaving one's mouth and thoughts free for socializing and conversation. So when my publisher suggested I focus my book on this aspect of entertaining it seemed a happy idea. But in addition to discussing hors d'oeuvre, I will share with you how I plan the various aspects of a successful party, including suggested menus (with alternate recipes) and emphasizing taste, texture, color and costs—both in money and in energy. The proper setting, plus the best food and wine, to serve requires a delicate balance, but it can be achieved—and a happy time as well. All it takes is practice and the desire to share with your friends. But always be prepared for a disaster. If it isn't the same one again, it will be another.

Poor planning can be a disaster of one sort. Be sure not to put everything out at once. Always hold back a few dishes so that the table looks as tempting toward the end of the party as it did at the beginning and so you can be sure hungry early arrivals don't shortchange any latecomers. And more dramatic things can happen: things can burn, or go limp when defrosted, or fall apart when unmolded; just be prepared and keep smiling.

This book will offer many recipes, spiced here and there with a hard-learned homily. The first I share with you here: always read the whole recipe through. Recently I did not: the result was a lemon pudding, not the delicate hot bread expected.

Second, these menus are not written in stone. They are merely outlines for you to adapt to your own taste, budget and time constraints.

Third, the wide availability of good produce and quality food items ensures the quality of the food you serve; but you must also consider the reason for the party, what your guests would enjoy, how large a budget is comfortable and how much time you can spend. Do not overextend yourself. One good new glamorous dish, surrounded with a simple but delicately balanced supporting cast, will do nicely.

The book is divided into three categories—each reflecting an important part of my own entertaining experience. The first, most informal, the parties we all encounter as we make our way through life. The second, more involved and usually more elegant, the parties that certain special occasions in our personal and business lives require. And third, a category combining pleasant entertaining with fund-raising for the various favorite organizations in our lives. Living in Montreal and London, then through Connecticut to New York City, and ending in Vermont has given me many opportunities to put all three types of entertaining into action—and even to learn to like it.

In the back of the book, in addition to the index, you will find a collection of basic recipes I've used throughout, such as the various pastries, and extra dips and dressings. There are also a few words on hiring a caterer, a section of simple Japanese designs for making flowers from vegetables, a collection of personal tips, or tricks—and more.

Remembering again that consideration for your guests is the most important ingredient, if you are planning a large party, do plan for some paid help. Service is a mark of consideration. You can hire a professional caterer but there are other excellent less expensive sources as well. College students, for one, are often trained to tend bar, refill platters and help in the kitchen. A good rule of thumb: for each 25 guests, one in help. If this is not possible, plan a smaller party or share the responsibility with a friend. It is not a successful party if you have no time for conversation with your guests.

True hospitality provides both good food and good drink—each to enhance the other and the pleasure of our guests . . . and ourselves. Enjoy!

MARY BLAIR

CONVIVIAL
YET
CASUAL

1
TWO INTIMATE GATHERINGS

Perfect for the Small Apartment
for 8 to 10

A SLICE OF PÂTÉ

CHERRY TOMATOES WITH CURRY AND
SEA SALT DIP

BROCCOLI-SCALLOP TERRINE

MARINATED MUSHROOMS

HOT CHEESE PUFFS

CHINESE SWEET NUTS

DRINKS OF CHOICE

On the Patio

for 8 to 10

CORNETS DE JAMBON

SHRIMP WITH PARSLEY CREAM CHEESE

GRACE'S CURRY AND CHUTNEY SPREAD

SLICE OF BRIE WITH FRESH FRUIT

NANCY DREWS

DRINKS OF CHOICE

TWO INTIMATE GATHERINGS

This is a wonderfully simple party—perfect for the working couple and single or older person who want everything done ahead so they can relax and enjoy their guests without fuss.

In putting this menu—or variations of your own choosing—into action, simply apply equal measures of quality, variety and ease. And, of course, a little style never hurts.

Many local delicatessens have excellent pâté. By all means use one of these if available, served with thinly sliced brown bread or water biscuits. If you have time and would like a pâté of your own creation, try the recipe for Broccoli-Scallop Terrine or one of the several pâté recipes listed in the index.

Cherry tomatoes are especially tasty if dipped in a mixture of curry powder and sea salt (I use roughly half and half, wetting the tomatoes so the sea salt will stick). They certainly brighten a winter party and I like to serve them with both green and ripe olives for an extra splash of color and taste. However, if the tomatoes are just too green, you can substitute crisp celery or endive slices stuffed with a lively ham or crabmeat spread, remembering, as with all parties, that some guests may be allergic to seafood. Both the Marinated Mushrooms and the Hot Cheese Puffs can be done ahead. For other nibbles I often opt for the Chinese Sweet Nuts or for one of the several Pepperidge Farm cocktail fishes. (Other nuts you might try are the Spiced Pecans on page 187 or perhaps the Hot Peanuts on page 377.)

The drinks for such a party could include a nice sherry (I like Tio Pepe or perhaps the somewhat sweeter Harvey's #28), a whiskey and gin or vodka with tonic, a good white wine such as a chilled chablis and, of course, a V-8 or other juice ready for the nondrinker.

Almost all of this can be set out ahead—the drinks on a tray with an ice bucket—on a gaily clothed serving table, or even on a large coffee table if the group is small, with the hot cheese puffs brought in at the last moment.

This type of party works equally well out-of-doors. I recently attended such a party given by a Swedish friend on a beautiful spring day. Her menu varied but it worked just as well. She set her smorgasbord on a table inside but adjacent to her balcony—a lovely spot which bridged a rushing mountain stream. The drinks were on a counter by the sink and the glasses ready on a tray. The first gentleman to arrive was asked to be bartender, a chore he seemed to relish.

Her menu included little ham cornucopias, cream cheese sprinkled with chopped parsley and surrounded with cocktail shrimp, a peach chutney spread, a slice of Brie accompanied by fresh fruit and a basket piled high with mixed Swedish crackers and dark brown bread, and a basket of Nancy Drews, a light cheese and pecan biscuit. The new twist was the delightful peach chutney spread, which came from a Cambridge, Massachusetts, friend. Little plates were available for individual portions and pretty napkins matched the cloth.

The seven of us enjoyed ourselves immensely as we watched the lovely sunset while listening to our hostess's many tales of Sweden.

BROCCOLI-SCALLOP TERRINE

The broccoli mousseline garnish in the center and over the top of this terrine adds a welcome splash of color and flavor as well. For a small party such as this, half of the recipe will be more than adequate; better still, make the whole, use half for the party and save the other half for another party or for supper some evening. When using as a supper dish, serve with the Fresh Tomato sauce in the back of the book. If using a food processor as the recipe suggests, be sure to pre–chill the bowl and blade.

FILLS A 2-QUART TERRINE

2 slices fresh white bread
½ cup milk
1 10-ounce package frozen chopped broccoli, thawed and well-drained
¾ pound fish fillets (preferably sole), skinned
Salt
Freshly ground black pepper

Dash of Tabasco
1 cup plus 2 tablespoons heavy cream
4 egg whites
1 shallot, chopped
⅓ cup dry vermouth
1½ pounds scallops

TO PREPARE MOUSSELINES

Remove and discard crusts and break bread into large pieces. Soak in the milk for 5 or 10 minutes. Squeeze out well and chill.

Place ¼ of the moistened bread, broccoli, and sole in chilled bowl of a food processor and process until coarsely chopped. Season with salt, Tabasco and cayenne pepper. With motor running, gradually pour in 5 tablespoons of the cream. Add 1 egg white and process until blended. Transfer to a mixing bowl and chill.

In a small saucepan, combine shallot and dry vermouth and boil over a high heat until reduced by about half. Remove from heat and chill.

Place chilled shallots, scallops and remaining moistened bread in the chilled bowl of a food processor, season with additional salt, and pepper, and process with on/off action until scallops are coarsely chopped. With the motor running, slowly add the remaining cream. Add 2 egg whites and process until smooth. Poach a spoonful to try, and adjust seasoning to taste. Transfer to a mixing bowl and chill.

TO FORM AND BAKE   PREHEAT OVEN TO 250°

Cut parchment or wax paper to fit bottom and top of a 2-quart terrine. Generously butter the terrine. Fit one piece of parchment or wax paper in the bottom of the terrine and butter again.

Spread ⅓ of the broccoli mixture in the bottom of the terrine and smooth with a spatula. Gently tap terrine to settle mixture and brush top with some of the remaining egg white.

Spread about ⅔ of the scallop mixture on top and smooth with a spatula. Using the back of a tablespoon, make a rounded trough about 1 inch wide down the center of the terrine. Brush hollow with more of the egg white. Spoon remaining broccoli mixture into the hollow and, using a spoon or fingers, mound the broccoli into a round core. Brush with egg white.

Spoon remaining scallop mixture along both sides and on top of broccoli core and smooth with a spatula. Gently tap terrine to settle mixture. Butter the top piece of parchment and place, buttered side down, on top of the terrine. Fit aluminum foil tightly over the top of the terrine and pierce several times with a fork. Place terrine in a water bath or a large baking pan filled with enough warm water to reach halfway up sides of the terrine.

Bake for 1½ hours or until terrine feels firm to the touch. Remove foil and let terrine cool in water bath for 30 minutes. Remove from water bath and weight terrine with a foil-wrapped brick or 2-pound can for about 2 hours. Refrigerate for 1 or 2 days before serving.

To serve, remove from refrigerator about an hour in advance, unmold onto a platter, removing parchment, and serve with crackers or small rounds of brown bread. A nice touch is to ring this terrine with a row of capers.

Note: Although I use the food processor for this terrine, I see no reason why a blender wouldn't work as well, again chilling the utensils as you go.

MARINATED MUSHROOMS

SERVES 8 TO 12

1 pound fresh mushrooms, as evenly sized as possible
1 cup lemon juice, freshly squeezed
¼ cup olive oil
¼ teaspoon cracked black pepper, or 6 to 8 turns on your grinder
½ teaspoon salt
1 tablespoon chopped fresh tarragon, or 1 teaspoon dry
1 tablespoon chopped fresh summer savory, or 1 teaspoon dry
2 cloves garlic, thinly sliced

Wipe mushrooms clean, leaving whole if size allows, and cut off dried parts of stems. Put prepared mushrooms in a fairly wide, shallow container which can be tightly covered.

Mix all other ingredients together and pour over mushrooms. The mushrooms must be completely submerged in the marinade so they will stay white. To accomplish this, if necessary place a weighted plate or ceramic lid directly on top of the mushrooms in the container.

Allow mushrooms to marinate in the fridge until needed (at least an hour) remembering to stir occasionally to ensure thorough marination.

HOT CHEESE PUFFS

The recipe for these comes to me from Amy Shapero, a Connecticut friend.

MAKES 50 PUFFS

½ pound sharp Cheddar cheese, grated
1 stick (8 tablespoons) butter, or ½ cup Crisco
⅛ teaspoon black pepper
1 cup flour

Mix grated cheese with butter or Crisco until fluffy. Add the pepper. Gradually mix in flour and knead until well mixed. Refrigerate dough 2 hours or so before baking.

TO BAKE   **PREHEAT OVEN TO 400°**

Form dough into balls about the size of an olive and place on ungreased cookie sheets. Bake for 10 to 15 minutes, or until golden brown.

Note: These puffs can be placed on a cookie sheet and frozen the night before. They also store well so leftovers can be saved and used the next day or so with soup or a salad.

CHINESE SWEET NUTS

This slightly sweet nut makes a very satisfying nibble. But have plenty: they disappear fast.

MAKES 1 ½ CUPS

> *1 ½ cups walnut meat halves* *½ cup sugar*
> *1 cup water* *½ cup oil*

Bring water to a boil and pour over nut meats in small bowl. Let stand 2 minutes and drain well. Add sugar and toss. Spread out and let stand overnight to dry.

Heat oil and fry nuts until golden, stirring to prevent burning. Drain well on paper towels and serve. (If you prefer, these nuts can be deep fried in a wire basket.)

Note: These nuts, tightly covered, keep well in the refrigerator for several weeks, but be sure to let them come to room temperature before serving.

ON THE PATIO

CORNETS DE JAMBON

Simple ingredients combine here to make an elegant canapé.

MAKES 24

> *24 thin slices boiled ham, about 3 ½* *1 tablespoon chopped chives*
> *inches long by 1 ½ inches wide* *Salt and pepper*
> *1 cup whipped cream (about ½ cup* *4 stuffed olives, each cut into 6 thin*
> *heavy cream)* *rings*
> *2 tablespoons grated horseradish,* *Parsley, for garnish*
> *squeezed dry of its vinegar*

Roll ham slices to form tiny cornucopias. Combine whipped cream, horseradish, chives, salt and pepper. Using a demitasse or other small spoon, or a small pastry bag, fill each cornucopia with the whipped cream mixture and top each with an olive ring. Place each cornet on a Melba toast round or cracker, arrange on a serving tray and garnish with parsley.

Note: If these are not used right away, be sure they are kept chilled, especially in the summer.

GRACE'S CURRY AND CHUTNEY SPREAD

MAKES 1½ CUPS

½ pound Cheddar cheese
6 ounces (2 small packages) cream
  cheese, softened
1 tablespoon chopped onion
2 tablespoons sherry

¼ cup chopped chutney (peach,
  pear or mango)
1 teaspoon curry powder
A few drops oil
A drop or 2 Tabasco sauce

Shred the Cheddar cheese on a grater or in a Mouli (you can use store-grated but it may not be fine enough) and mix well with the cream cheese. Blend in the chopped onion, sherry and chutney (I make my own chutney [see index] but Major Grey's or other good-quality store-bought varieties are fine). Warm your curry powder in a little hot oil and add to mixture (this is an especially good trick if there is any danger of your powder being a little stale). Blend well, add Tabasco and blend again. Taste and adjust as needed.
  Chill and serve with crackers of your choice.

Note: This spread will keep nicely refrigerated in a jar for several weeks—if well hidden.

NANCY DREWS

These biscuits are basically an icebox cookie made of good sharp cheddar cheese and nuts. Despite their name there is no mystery about them. They are easy to make and easy to keep. Best when served the day of baking, Nancy Drews are still very good if frozen after baking and used later.

MAKES 100 BISCUITS

1 pound sharp Cheddar cheese, grated
7 tablespoons butter or margarine, softened
1 cup unbleached flour
¼ teaspoon cayenne

½ teaspoon salt (omit if cheese is salty)
1 cup pecans, lightly chopped (walnuts or cashews can be used but will alter the flavor)

Mix cheese and butter or margarine thoroughly. Add flour, cayenne and salt (if using), and mix well. Add nuts and form into two rolls approximately 1½ inches wide by 6 inches long.

Wrap rolls in wax paper and refrigerate overnight, or chill in the freezer for several hours if time is of the essence.

TO BAKE   **PREHEAT OVEN TO 325°**

Slice chilled dough with a sharp knife as thinly as possible and place rounds fairly close together on an ungreased cookie sheet. Bake for 10 minutes.

Note: These biscuits can also be kept well in a tin for a week or so after baking.

2

A PAIR OF
PORTABLE FEASTS

Picnic for a Summer Day
for 10 to 12

COLD STUFFED VINE LEAVES

SLICED VEGETABLES AND
ASSORTED DIPS IN A BASKET

FRESH HERB TERRINE OR
SAVORY SANDWICH LOAF

PASTA SALAD

CHEESE BOARD

CRUSTY BREAD AND CRACKERS

FRESH FRUIT IN SEASON

COCKEYED CHOCOLATE CAKE

CHILLED WHITE WINE AND BEER

ICED TEA AND COFFEE

A Tailgate Picnic

for 8 to 10

MUSHROOMS NONPAREIL AND
CHINESE SPICED NUTS

PORKLESS PÂTÉ

BUTTERED FRENCH AND
BROWN ITALIAN LOAVES

CLAM CHOWDER ZELDA OR
U.S. SENATE BLACK BEAN SOUP

ASSORTED CHEESES

FRESH PEARS AND APPLES

SWEET TRAY OF PUMPKIN BREAD,
DATE BALLS AND
BUTTERSCOTCH BROWNIES

RED WINE AND BEER

CIDER AND HOT COFFEE

YOU CAN TAKE IT WITH YOU

Picnics have long been very much a part of American life—from the time-honored family beach picnic to the ever popular tailgate basket lunches marking one or another football rivalry. And today a good picnic often serves as the carrot to lead friends and neighbors to a country or city work-bee: wood stacking and house painting become light work when accompanied by good company and good food. In fact, picnics have become so popular that, even here in usually do-it-yourself Vermont, a lady in Woodstock has begun a "moveable feast" catering service.

You will have to supply the "Thou," but for our summer "Jug of Wine and Loaf of Bread" why not plan simple crudités and Mint and Rice Stuffed Vine Leaves, followed by an herbed terrine, Pasta Salad, fresh bread, cheese and fruit in season (when available, strawberries to be dipped in confectioners' sugar are my favorite). Then top it off with an easy-to-make-and-carry chocolate cake. For an even simpler summer menu, you might try the savory chicken and ham loaf, along with the salad, fruit and cookies. But remember: a picnic—summer or fall—is not meant to be a sitdown meal, rather a portable feast offering nourishing treats from the very beginning until after the very last swim or last piece of piled wood, and should always include a surprise or two.

For serving your picnic there are a myriad of new gadgets. The basket plate-trays to hold paper plates are a blessing and don't take much hamper room. Another is a fairly compact (about 12-inch) round red plastic ball which, when opened, contains 2 good-sized bowls, 6 plastic glasses, 6 fruit or salad bowls and 6 luncheon-sized plates. It is easy to carry and easy to store.

There are a vast variety of coolers and enough sizes to suit every excursion. Lightness and sufficient insulation are the crucial considerations: a little research will lead you to the perfect one for your needs. A good thermos jug is a necessity for soups and drinks, both hot and cold. Insulated mugs, too, are a great boon. A set of secondhand silverware or heavy-duty plastic eating utensils kept always ready in your picnic hamper is another good idea, and

I try not to leave home without my Swiss Army knife. It fills so many needs and even includes a corkscrew: there's nothing worse than a lovely bottle of cool white wine with no way to open it.

There is another aspect to picnics—especially the summer ones—we should consider. Lovely warm weather brings its hazards as well as its delights, and can result in food spoilage, even food poisoning, if not treated with respect. The simple rules of proper food hygiene must be observed. Always choose your picnic foods with the weather and the distance you will be traveling in mind. Simple plain food that can be assembled at the picnic spot avoids some of the problem. Mayonnaise premixed with fish or eggs can be especially treacherous if kept in the heat too long. Such items can be packed separately and then mixed when wanted. Pâté, too, when kept in a cooler and spread when ready to eat stands less chance of spoilage. Prewashed fresh fruits also bear up better if kept cool.

You can keep items very cold in clean wrapping paper or containers tucked into a cooler over lots of ice or by using one of the several synthetic ice packs now available. (Ice Paks, a sturdy and compact pack, is only one of many on the market. Once frozen—in about six hours—it holds its colder-than-water-ice temperature for up to 72 hours—longer than any picnic I can think of—and at a cost of about $2.50.) Hot foods, in turn, should be kept very hot with their thermoses heated with boiling water prior to filling.

Other summer picnic hazards are sunburn, insect bites and poison ivy and oak. Any well-filled picnic hamper should include a small first-aid kit, sun lotion, bug discouragers and the like.

Autumn is another tempting time for picnics, particularly here in our Northeast when the leaves turn their stirring red and yellow and the brisk air almost shrieks, "Take to the road: it's picnic time!"

In fall, especially for a work-bee, the food should be more substantial, with a piping hot soup or chowder to warm any chilled picnickers. We like a very special clam chowder we came upon in Rhode Island or sometimes the famous bean soup served in the U.S. Senate, the recipe for which came to me from our Vermont Senator Patrick Leahy. The rest of my menu for this picnic is a rather simple one with mushroom and nut nibbles, Porkless Pâté and cheese, fruits and sweets. Nice cheeses for this menu might be Morbier, Port Salut and one of the Vermont Cheddars. The Pumpkin Bread, Date Balls and Butterscotch Brownies happen to be favorites of ours and offer two definite advantages: they are easy to make and easy to pack. And what better way to round out the liquid refreshment for this fall picnic than with a great jug of fresh-made cider.

Whether summer or fall, you may want to plan your picnic menus as a way to use leftovers from your fridge or pantry. Here I hope the index will help: many of the party foods suggested for other sections of the book will work just as well for picnics. Just remember that they should carry well and of course be kept at the appropriate temperature.

© Robert Grant

On the Patio

NANCY DREWS
SHRIMP WITH PARSLEY CREAM CHEESE
GRACE'S CURRY AND CHUTNEY SPREAD

New England Sunday Brunch

GERMAN PANCAKES WITH APPLESAUCE
LINGONBERRIES AND MAPLE SYRUP

I guess it's hardly necessary to add that in planning your picnic—plain or fancy—as in all entertaining, be sure to plan for the particular guests that will be sharing it with you and remember that at picnics these guests often include children. The fanciest picnic hamper will not a happy picnic make if the children present cannot find something they like too, this being especially important for a portable feast, where there is no handy refrigerator to raid.

MINT AND RICE STUFFED VINE LEAVES

As opposed to the hot stuffed vine leaves used as part of the Greek party menu, cold stuffed vine leaves are usually meatless. They take time to make (several hours overall), but can be made a day ahead and kept cool until needed.

MAKES 30 TO 40

1 pound fresh tender vine leaves, or
* 1 (1-pound) jar pickled*
1 ¼ cups rice
½ cup pine nuts
½ cup minced scallions
½ cup chopped fresh parsley, or
* more to taste*
½ cup chopped fresh mint
¼ teaspoon cinnamon
1 ½ teaspoons salt
¼ teaspoon pepper

1 cup chopped fresh tomatoes or
* canned Roma tomatoes*
4 to 5 whole garlic cloves (optional)
1 cup olive oil
½ cup tomato juice, or more as
* needed*
½ cup lemon juice
1 lemon, cut in eighths, for garnish
1 tomato, sliced and skinned, for
* garnish*
Yogurt, as side dish

TO PREPARE VINE LEAVES

To prepare *fresh* vine leaves, first soften them by plunging them, a few at a time, into boiling water until they become limp. This will take a few minutes. Then drain well and dry. Tongs work well for this task.

To prepare *pickled* vine leaves, put them in large bowl and pour boiling water over them, making sure that the water penetrates well between the layers. Let soak for at least 20 minutes and drain. Then soak in cold water and drain again. Do not skimp on this: it is important to remove the excess salt.

TO STUFF THE LEAVES

First soak and stir the rice in boiling water for approximately 2 to 3 minutes. Rinse well under the cold water tap and drain well. Then, in good-sized bowl, mix the rice with the pine nuts, scallions, parsley, mint, cinnamon and salt and pepper.

Stuff the drained vine leaves with this mixture. To fill, place 1 leaf at a time on a plate vein side up. Heap 1 ample teaspoon stuffing in the center of the leaf near the stem end. Fold the stem end up over the filling, then fold both sides in toward the middle and roll the whole up like a small cigar. Squeeze each filled leaf lightly in your palm as you finish rolling, and don't worry: this technique will become easier and easier as you work.

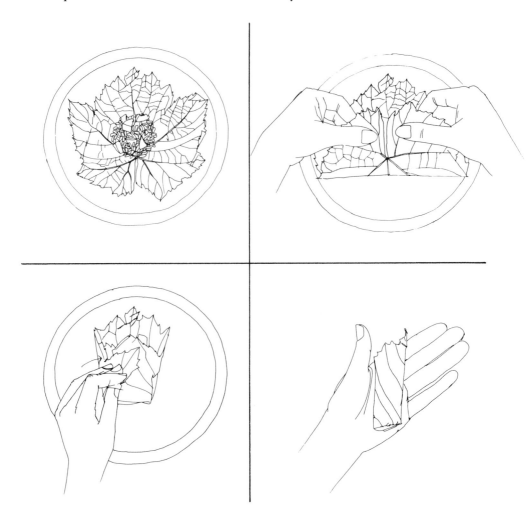

TO COOK AND SERVE

Place the stuffed leaves tightly together in a large baking pan, or large black frying pan, lined with the chopped tomatoes and and any torn leaves, and if you choose, tucking in an occasional garlic clove as you go.

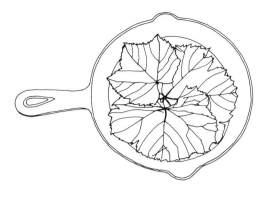

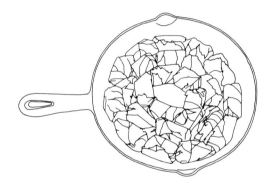

Mix the olive oil with the tomato juice. Add lemon juice and pour mixture over the tiny leaf rolls. Using a plate on top of the rolled leaves to keep them from unwinding, cover the pan and simmer very gently for at least 2 hours, until the rolls are thoroughly cooked. Add more tomato juice occasionally, ½ cup at a time, as the pan liquid becomes absorbed. Cool in the pan before turning out, draining thoroughly first.

Serve cold on colorful ceramic plates, with lemon pieces, tomato slices and yogurt.

Note: To rewarm from refrigerator, add sliced tomatoes (for moisture) and heat through gently. This will eliminate any congealed oil.

Variation: Add 2 tablespoons chopped dill and ¾ cup seedless raisins or currants to the filling.

FRESH HERB TERRINE

As they said in *Sphere* Magazine, where I first found it, this terrine is something of a dandy. However, it makes a perfect *pièce de résistance* for a moveable feast since it also travels well.

SERVES 6, OR MORE IF NOT TOO HUNGRY

1 pound boneless pork
½ pound boneless veal
4 ounces pork fat
¾ cup chopped onion
2 cloves garlic, minced
1 tablespoon butter or margarine
1½ cups packed chopped fresh
spinach, or well-drained frozen
3 tablespoons brandy
1 egg
1½ tablespoons snipped fresh basil,
or 1 teaspoon dried
1½ tablespoons snipped fresh
rosemary, or 1 teaspoon dried

1 tablespoon snipped fresh thyme, or
½ teaspoon dried
1¼ teaspoons salt
½ teaspoon crushed fennel seeds
¼ teaspoon freshly ground black
pepper
6 ounces sliced bacon
3 hard-cooked eggs
Sprig fresh thyme
Cornichons, for garnish
Marinated pearl onions, for
garnish

TO PREPARE

Cut pork, veal and pork fat into small pieces, passing all through fine blade of meat grinder twice or using steel blade of food processor. In a small skillet sauté the onion and garlic in the butter or margarine about 5 minutes. Add the spinach and cook, stirring, about 1 minute. Transfer to good-sized bowl and add ground meats, mixing well. Stir in remaining ingredients except the bacon, hard-cooked eggs, thyme sprig and garnishes.

Arrange bacon slices across bottom and up sides of 8½-by-4½-inch loaf pan. Fill the pan with half of the meat mixture. Arrange the hard-cooked eggs end to end down the length of the pan, pressing them lightly into the meat mixture. Cover with remaining meat mixture and wrap overhanging bacon pieces over the top, crowning all with the thyme sprig.

TO BAKE   PREHEAT OVEN TO 350°

Cover loaf with aluminum foil and set pan in a water bath holding enough hot water to reach ⅓ up the sides of the loaf pan. Bake about 1¼ hours or until the meat juices run clear. Remove from water bath and let loaf stand uncovered for 20 minutes, then pour off fat. Cover; place weight on top of loaf and refrigerate at least 24 hours.

TO UNMOLD AND SERVE

When ready to serve or pack for your picnic, run a spatula around edge of pan and unmold, trimming any excess fat. Serve in ½-inch slices garnished with the pickles and onions if desired. For a picnic, you could preslice the loaf; however, if you elect to slice at eating time, be sure you have a good sharp slicing knife along.

Note: This terrine can be stored in your freezer, wrapped in freezer paper, up to 1 month. To travel, overwrap the chilled or frozen terrine in newspaper and place in an insulated bag with a frozen refrigerant. Carry chilled terrine no longer than 5 hours; frozen, no longer than 10.

SAVORY SANDWICH LOAF

This tasty loaf has several advantages. It's fun, uses up bits of leftovers and is easy to prepare.

MAKES ABOUT 12 SLICES

1 long (1-pound) loaf French bread
2 cups (about 8 ounces) finely chopped cooked chicken or turkey
2 cups (about 8 ounces) finely chopped cooked ham
4 hard-cooked eggs, chopped
⅓ cup finely chopped scallions (including tops)

1 cup finely chopped dill pickles, drained
½ cup chopped parsley
1 recipe Caper-Mustard Dressing (see page 390)
Garlic salt to taste
Freshly ground pepper to taste

Cut a 1½-inch-thick slice from each end of bread loaf and set aside. With long serrated knife cut away and pull out the soft center, leaving an approximately ½-inch shell.

In a bowl, combine the chicken or turkey, ham, eggs, scallions, pickles and parsley, and set aside.

Prepare the Caper-Mustard Dressing, stir into the chicken mixture and season to taste with the garlic salt and pepper.

TO ASSEMBLE

Stand hollowed-out loaf on end and stuff with filling, using a long-handled wooden spoon to pack tightly. Set the end slices back in place and wrap in foil. Refrigerate for at least 4 hours (overnight is even better). Unwrap and cut into ¾- to 1-inch slices. Rewrap in foil and refrigerate until moveable feast starts to move, being sure, of course, to transport in a proper cooler.

Notes: The hollowed-out portion of bread can be dried out, diced fine, and used to stuff tomatoes or peppers, or cubed and used, spiced, for croutons. Also, this recipe is a good imagination stretcher. Certainly other meats could be used and the seasonings played with a bit.

PASTA SALAD

This good salad can be served either hot or cold. For this party we'll have it cold. It comes to us from George Crowell, who tosses a mean pasta. It is incredibly flexible: almost any combination of the following—and other ingredients not yet thought of—will work.

SERVES 6 TO 8

4 tablespoons butter
¼ cup olive oil
1 or 2 cloves garlic, chopped
¼ cup white wine
½ cup each sliced red onions, chopped broccoli, chopped red and green peppers, sliced mushrooms, whole pitted olives, or more to taste

½ pound whole bay scallops
1 (16-ounce) package pasta (thin noodles, spaghetti, linguini, or other thin pasta of choice)
½ to 1 pound cooked shrimp
1 cup tomato wedges
2 tablespoons fresh basil, or more to taste
Salt and pepper to taste

In a saucepan, make a sauce by combining the butter, olive oil, garlic and wine. Heat through. When blended, set aside.

Steam the prepared mixed vegetables until just tender.

Sauté the scallops in a little of the sauce for about 2 minutes or just until tender. Set aside to cool.

Prepare pasta according to package instructions. Set aside to cool.

When ready, combine the sauce, steamed vegetables, cooked shrimp and scallops with tomato wedges, basil and salt and pepper and toss lightly with the pasta.

Spoon into a large plastic container and transport to picnic covered.

Notes: Other vegetables may be added to this salad. George says he often adds zucchini, red and green cabbage and even asparagus, all prepared just to the point of tenderness before adding.

To prepare hot: Sauté all the vegetables in the hot sauce, simmering for about 7 minutes. Add the seafood, cooking about another 2 minutes, and toss with the pasta.

ONE-PAN CHOCOLATE CAKE

This is a very simple recipe that anyone can make quickly and easily. In the late 1940's a lemon cake made with oil instead of butter was served at the Montreal Ritz-Carlton and acclaimed as the first new cake in years. This is a chocolate variation, with the icing baked right on, and it's easy to carry!

SERVES ABOUT 12

1½ cups flour
3 tablespoons cocoa
1 teaspoon baking soda
1 cup sugar
½ teaspoon salt
5 tablespoons cooking oil
1 tablespoon vinegar

1 teaspoon vanilla
1 cup cold water
4 tablespoons butter, softened
⅔ cup brown sugar
2 tablespoons cream
⅓ cup chopped nuts or coconut

TO MIX

Grease a 9-by-9-by-2-inch square pan. Sift the flour, cocoa, soda, sugar and salt directly into the pan. Then make three holes in the dry mixture. Into one, pour the oil; into the next, the vinegar; into the last, the vanilla. Pour the water over the top of all and beat all with a spoon until nearly smooth and the flour can't be seen.

TO BAKE   **PREHEAT OVEN TO 350°**

Bake this "batter" for about 30 minutes, leaving it in the pan to cool on the counter, and not turning off the oven.

TO MAKE THE TOPPING

Mix the remaining ingredients together well. Then, when the cake has cooled a few minutes, spread the topping over the cake and put it back in the oven to cook. This only takes a few minutes; watch that it does not burn.

Let cool in the pan and serve—for your portable feast or wherever—right from the pan.

A TAILGATE PICNIC

MUSHROOMS NONPAREIL

It's hard to imagine a party that doesn't improve with mushrooms. If you don't want this quantity, cut in half but check seasoning.

MAKES 20 SERVINGS

¼ cup prepared mustard, preferably Dijon
6 tablespoons wine vinegar
1 teaspoon sugar
1 teaspoon salt
Freshly ground black pepper to taste

2 cups oil, half olive and half peanut
¼ cup minced shallots
3 pounds mushrooms, wiped clean and sliced thin
¼ cup minced parsley

Put the mustard, vinegar, sugar, salt and pepper into blender or food processor. Gradually pour in the oil, making sure it is thoroughly blended, then add shallots. Toss the mushrooms in this dressing and marinate at room temperature about 2 hours.

Before serving, turn mushrooms and marinade into serving bowl—or covered container for carrying—sprinkle with parsley and chill thoroughly.

CHINESE SPICED NUTS

Nuts have gotten to be pretty expensive but they do, especially when they are dolled up like this, make a wonderfully tasty addition to a picnic—or any—party menu. For this picnic, you may want to halve the recipe.

MAKES 20 TO 30 MODEST SERVINGS

2 tablespoons butter, melted
Liberal dashes Worcestershire sauce

Modest dashes Tabasco sauce
1 pound pecan halves

Make a sauce of the butter and seasonings. Stir in the nuts gently but thoroughly and place on baking sheet.

TO BAKE   **PREHEAT OVEN TO 300°**

Bake in slow oven until the nuts are brown and crisp. Drain on paper toweling if necessary and serve either cool or warm.

Note: It is really folly to try to predict how many this recipe will serve: I apologize. Sometimes it seems they disappear even before they reach the serving table. Any leftover shelled nuts should be kept frozen.

PORKLESS PÂTÉ

This is a relatively simple pâté using chicken livers rather than pork. It is best made at least a day ahead.

SERVES 10 TO 12

1½ pounds chicken livers
½ pound lard, ground, plus 10
  strips lard, sliced thin
2 eggs, lightly beaten
¼ teaspoon nutmeg
⅛ teaspoon ground clove
⅛ teaspoon cinnamon
1 teaspoon salt
¼ teaspoon pepper

2 tablespoons margarine or butter
3 cloves garlic
1 onion, chopped
¼ cup chopped red pepper
¼ cup chopped green pepper
5 sprigs parsley, chopped
leaves from 3 stalks of celery,
chopped
3 bay leaves

TO PREPARE PÂTÉ

Using blender or food processor, blend liver; then again with the ground lard. Add eggs, spices and seasonings, and blend until smooth.

In margarine or butter, sauté garlic, onion, peppers, parsley and celery. Blend well and combine with liver mixture.

**TO FILL MOLD
AND BAKE**   **PREHEAT OVEN TO 300°**

Line 6-cup terrine with single layer of lard strips, saving remainder for top. Fill with liver-vegetable mixture, top with bay leaves and remaining lard strips.

Place terrine in bain-marie (larger pan half filled with warm water) and bake for 2½ hours. Remove from oven and allow to cool at least an hour. Then refrigerate for at least a day, preferably 2.

Before serving, remove lard slices and bay leaves, and serve with French or brown bread and with little cornichons on the side.

CLAM CHOWDER ZELDA

The recipe for this clam chowder was given me by Margo Waite, my husband's right-hand everything when he and Dick Ketchum first started their Blair & Ketchum's *Country Journal* magazine. Margo and her husband have since left Vermont for Newport, Rhode Island, where he has started the Café Zelda restaurant, one of whose specialties is this excellent chowder.

SERVES 8

*¼ pound salt pork, or a little less,
    diced
1 to 2 onions, sliced
6 medium potatoes, peeled and diced
1 quart chowder clams, shucked
Flour, for sprinkling
Salt, for sprinkling
Freshly ground black pepper, for
sprinkling*

*2½ cups boiling water
4 cups hot milk
1 tablespoon fresh thyme, or 1
    teaspoon dried
Dash Worcestershire sauce
8 pats butter
Dill, for garnish*

Sauté diced salt pork until crisp. Remove and set aside pork pieces, pouring off some of the fat. Sauté onions in remaining fat until translucent; do not brown.

In soup pot make layers of the cooked onions, raw potatoes and clams, sprinkling each layer lightly with flour, salt and pepper. Add boiling water and simmer until potatoes are done.

Add hot milk, stir in pork bits and season with thyme, Worcestershire and salt and pepper as needed.

Serve with a pat of butter and snip of dill.

SENATE BLACK BEAN SOUP

This is the famous bean soup served in the U.S. Senate dining room, and one that I have enjoyed more than once when visiting in Washington. The recipe was sent to me by our Vermont Senator Patrick Leahy.

SERVES 8

*2 pounds small dried Michigan
    navy beans
4 quarts hot water
1½ pounds smoked ham hocks*

*1 onion, chopped
1 or 2 tablespoons butter
Salt and pepper to taste*

Wash beans thoroughly and run through hot water until beans are white. Put in soup kettle with 4 quarts hot water. Add the ham hocks and boil slowly approximately 3 hours in covered pot.

Toward end of cooking time, braise onion in butter until a light brown, and add to soup pot.

Salt and pepper to taste when ready to serve. (For our picnic purposes, this will mean taking along a free-running salt shaker and pepper mill.)

PUMPKIN BREAD

This recipe comes to me from Helene Druhl, one of this corner of Vermont's better cooks.

MAKES 1 LARGE LOAF

2½ cups sifted flour
2 cups sugar
1 teaspoon baking soda
1 teaspoon cinnamon
1 teaspoon ground cloves

1 cup chopped walnuts
1½ cups raisins
1 (14½-ounce) can pumpkin
½ cup salad oil

TO PREPARE BATTER

Mix all dry ingredients together in a good-sized bowl; add nuts and raisins, and blend thoroughly. Add pumpkin and salad oil, and mix well. Pour into a greased 8- or 9-inch bread or meatloaf pan.

TO BAKE AND STORE   PREHEAT OVEN TO 350°

Bake for 1 hour or until cake tester comes out clean when inserted in center.
  When cool, remove from pan and serve. Or, if you prefer, wrap in plastic wrap, and then foil, and freeze.

Note: Helene likes to double this recipe to fill 6 of the small (approximately 4- to 5-inch) foil baking pans, baking them about 30 to 35 minutes. She then wraps and freezes them to have ready for holiday or hostess gifts as needed.

BAKED DATE BALLS

Another simple and healthful sweet to offer picnickers or anyone—this one coming from Jean Allen, another fine Vermont cook.

MAKES ABOUT 2½ DOZEN

1 cup sugar
2 eggs
½ cup flour
½ teaspoon baking powder

¼ teaspoon salt
1 cup pitted dates, chopped
1 cup chopped pecans
Granulated sugar, for rolling

Beat sugar and eggs until fluffy. Add flour, baking powder, salt, and blend. Fold in the dates and nuts. Grease an 8-inch square pan and spoon batter into pan.

TO BAKE   **PREHEAT OVEN TO 350°**

Bake for 30 minutes. Remove from oven and stir with wooden spoon. Let cool enough to handle, then roll into 1-inch balls, coating each ball in granulated sugar as you work.

Note: If time is of the essence this recipe also works nicely just cut into small squares at the end of the 30-minute baking time. Sprinkle granulated sugar on top before serving.

BUTTERSCOTCH BROWNIES

Delicious and perfect for picknicking.

MAKES 32 SMALL BARS

1 cup brown sugar
4 tablespoons butter, melted
1 egg
1 teaspoon vanilla
½ cup flour, sifted

1 teaspoon baking powder
½ teaspoon salt
½ to 1 cup finely chopped nut
  meats

Stir sugar into melted butter. Set aside to cool slightly. Then add the egg and vanilla, beating in well. Combine the flour, baking powder and salt, and stir into the egg mixture. Add nuts and pour into greased and floured 8-by-8-inch baking pan.

TO BAKE AND SERVE   **PREHEAT OVEN TO 350°**

Bake for about 30 minutes. When cool, cut into small bars.

Note: Be careful not to scorch the brown sugar and butter. If you have to be away from stove, a "flame spreader" helps.

3
WHEN BREAKFAST MEETS LUNCH

A New England Sunday Brunch
for 8 to 10

BLOODY MARYS   SCREWDRIVERS
PITCHER OF FRUIT JUICE

KEDGEREE WITH TOAST POINTS
BASKET OF WARM HERB BREAD

GERMAN PANCAKES
WITH
APPLESAUCE, LINGONBERRIES
AND MAPLE SYRUP

OR

FRESHLY MADE OMELETTES
WITH
FILLINGS TO ORDER

SAUSAGES AND BACON

RHUBARB ROLLS OR
BLUEBERRY MUFFINS

BAKED FRUIT COMPOTE

COFFEE   TEA   SANKA

Southwestern Sporting Breakfast
for 8 to 10

TEQUILA SUNRISES   SANGRIA
FRUIT JUICE

COLD AVOCADO SOUP

HUSH PUPPIES   CHILE-QUESO SQUARES

HUEVOS RANCHEROS OR CHIMICHANGAS

CORN DOGS

BACON   SAUSAGE

BOLILLOS OR SWEET ROLLS

PAPAYA, GRAPEFRUIT AND
MELON PLATTER

COFFEE   TEA   MILK   BEER

WHEN BREAKFAST MEETS LUNCH

NEW ENGLAND STYLE

One newer form of entertaining is a sliding meal known as brunch. It is a great help to working couples and those for whom the weekend is an ideal time to cook and entertain. As with all entertaining, many menu choices are possible; some of the most interesting are those that reflect different regional and ethnic combinations. Variety here, as in so many things, is indeed the most essential spice.

For my brunch menus I have chosen one from New England and another from the Southwest, though I suppose the New England menu could be found almost anywhere. They are both planned for between 8 and 10 people.

The first menu can be easily assembled after church, jogging or reading the Sunday papers. This type of entertaining requires little attention to ambiance. However, I do recommend a large bowl of flowers or a vegetable arrangement in the center of your brunch table: they will divert your guests' attention from any basic household comforts not quite up to snuff. You can eat in the kitchen, dining room or wherever, but a spot to sit for each guest is essential; holding plates of hot food while standing is too much to ask of any guest, especially early in the day.

I suppose, if there is one brunch maxim to apply, it is to be ready for the first guests with the openers—in this case the Bloody Marys and Screwdrivers and a large pitcher of fruit juice together with something for the guests to nibble on. The Scotch Kedgeree can be served from a chafing dish with toast points, and for the nonfish folks a basket of warm and buttery herb bread can be ready, so your guests have something to accompany their drinks while they wait for their main course.

I am suggesting German Pancakes—a rather different and puffier pancake than the everyday American flapjack—for your main course. Individually prepared omelettes are another good brunch idea; but if this is your choice, be sure to have a good supply of grated cheese, chopped tomatoes, peppers, mushrooms or other fillings ready in bowls for the chef. The chef could be a member of the family or a friend who likes to show off his or her cooking talents and is willing to stay at the omelette station until everyone is served.

A large pot of good hot coffee is a must. If you don't own one, beg or borrow one of the 20- or 30-cup percolators; they make excellent coffee and clean easily. But be sure the pot is scrupulously clean (if you have any doubt, a good soaking in a baking soda solution will freshen the pot nicely). Be sure, too, to start with a good-quality coffee and cold water. If you do not have a large pot available you can make a good quantity of coffee ahead and fill several thermoses or candle-warmed carafes. And have a good-sized kettle of water on low for fresh tea, or Sanka.

If dishwashing or your china supply is a problem, there are attractive paper plates and bowls available now, though you will surely want the heavy-duty ones for pancake eaters. Mugs will suffice nicely for the tea and coffee (I draw the line at paper cups).

Your early-morning will prove well worthwhile. As Sunday begins to wind along, your brunch guests will slowly take their leave—after a pleasant and relaxed time, and glad for the opportunity for good conversation and good food.

VINCENT PRICE'S BLOODY MARYS

I suppose there are almost as many favorite ways to make Bloody Marys as there are Marys. This is a good—and fiery—one, and certainly the proportions are easy to remember.

SERVES 6

6 jiggers vodka
6 drops Tabasco sauce, or more to taste
6 tablespoons lemon juice
6 dashes Worcestershire sauce
½ teaspoon salt
½ teaspoon pepper
2 teaspoons sugar
2 (24-ounce) cans V-8 or tomato juice, or less to taste
Celery stalks, for garnish
Lemon slices, for garnish

Mix all ingredients together well in pitcher and keep ready to pour into ice-filled highball glasses as needed. Garnish with celery or a curled lemon slice if you like.

SCREWDRIVERS

Using a proportion of 1½ ounces vodka to 6 to 8 ounces fresh orange juice per 12-ounce highball glass (over ice), you can either serve your Screwdrivers one by one—or make up a small pitcher of the vodka-juice mixture to pour as you need it.

KEDGEREE

This is a simple and tasty fish dish to offer for openers. And cooked on a double boiler, it holds well with the heat turned down. Salmon is used here but any well-flavored flaked fish will do as well, and if you're feeling flush you can even substitute lobster.

SERVES 8

2 cups cooked rice
3 cups cooked flaked salmon
4 hard-cooked eggs, chopped
Salt and pepper to taste

4 tablespoons minced parsley
½ cup cream
2 tablespoons butter

Combine all ingredients in top of double boiler and heat thoroughly over hot water.

To serve, transfer to chafing dish or use a warming tray under a favorite pot. Have toast points nearby.

Note: One or 2 teaspoons curry powder is a nice addition to this recipe.

GERMAN PANCAKES

This recipe is based on a family recipe sent me by an old friend, Jan Zehnder. The original recipe serves only two at a time and calls for slow baking. I have revised it slightly for this brunch to allow quicker cooking time so more can be served in less time. You'll need an oven-proof frying pan; two will make your pancake production line go even faster. Each pancake should be made fresh.

SERVES 2

3 eggs
½ cup flour
½ cup milk

A few drops vanilla (optional)
4 tablespoons butter or margarine

TO PREPARE BATTER

Beat together the eggs, flour, milk and vanilla, if used, with an egg beater or wire whisk.

TO COOK AND SERVE   PREHEAT OVEN TO 400°

Melt the butter or margarine in oven-proof 8-to-10 inch frying pan and pour in batter. Allow batter to float in butter and cook, covered, over low to medium heat until it begins to set. Transfer pan to oven and bake until cake is puffed and firm, total cooking time about 7 minutes.

If you have two pans, while first cake is in oven, second cake can be mixed and started on stove. Perhaps one of your guests will make the batter while you or another guest supervise the cooking.

When the cakes are done, cut in half and serve immediately with home-made or store-bought applesauce, maple syrup or Swedish lingonberries.

Notes: Some German pancake fans prefer to separate the eggs, folding in the stiff-beaten whites just before cooking. This recipe cannot be doubled so consider using a mix if large quantities are needed. But remember, your brunch guests may want to eat at different times.

RHUBARB ROLLS

Rhubarb is rather like tomatoes and zucchini: you crave it all fall and winter and then when it comes—what to do with it? This good recipe comes from Sue Ross, a friend who passed it along to me, and offers another way to use at least some of this welcome harbinger of spring.

MAKES 1 DOZEN ROLLS

2 cups diced rhubarb	½ cup milk
¾ cup granulated sugar	6 tablespoons butter or margarine,
1½ cups flour	melted
1 tablespoon baking powder	½ teaspoon cinnamon
½ teaspoon salt	¼ teaspoon nutmeg
2 tablespoons shortening	½ cup brown sugar, firmly packed
1 egg, beaten	

TO PREPARE

Wash the rhubarb before dicing, cutting off the leaf and root ends. Combine the rhubarb with the granulated sugar, mix well and set aside. Sift flour, measure and sift again with baking powder and salt. Cut shortening into the flour mixture until mixture resembles cornmeal. Add egg and milk, stirring to make a soft dough. Roll out on lightly floured board until dough is about ¼ inch thick. Brush with 2 tablespoons of the melted butter and spread with rhubarb mixture. Sprinkle with cinnamon and nutmeg. Beginning with a long edge, roll up as for jelly roll, pinching the seams to seal. Cut into ½-inch-thick slices.

TO BAKE   **PREHEAT OVEN TO 425°**

Pour the remaining melted butter into an 8-inch square baking pan. Blend in the brown sugar. Place the slices flat in the pan. Bake for approximately 25 minutes or until richly browned.

Note: I have cut the sugar (both kinds) in this recipe in half. If your family has a sweet tooth you might want to put some or all of it back in.

BLUEBERRY MUFFINS

This recipe comes from a fellow cookbook author, Bebe Buszek of Annapolis Valley, Nova Scotia—who not only cooks with berries of all kinds, but raises them as well.

MAKES ABOUT I DOZEN MUFFINS

1½ cups flour
3 tablespoons sugar
3 teaspoons baking powder
Dash of salt

1 egg, lightly beaten
¾ cup milk
1½ cups blueberries
3 tablespoons melted shortening

Sift together dry ingredients. Combine beaten egg with milk. Stir into dry mixture. Add blueberries and shortening. Mix lightly just to dampen; expect a lumpy batter.

TO BAKE   **PREHEAT OVEN TO 400°**

Pour batter into greased muffin tins, filling about ¾ full, and bake about 20 minutes. They will be lightly brown.

Note: A good trick when baking with blueberries is to save out a little of the flour to lightly coat the berries; this way they don't sink when added to the batter. Another nice trick with these muffins is to sprinkle their tops lightly with a half-and-half mixture of granulated sugar and lemon rind just before baking.

BAKED FRUIT COMPOTE

This compote, although designed as a light dessert, can be used nicely in a winter breakfast.

SERVES 10

1 (1-pound) can sliced peaches, preferably Elberta

1 (10-ounce) package dried apricots, soaked

1 medium jar or can pitted sweet Bing cherries

1 orange, juice and rind

1 lemon, juice and rind

1 lime, juice and rind

1 pint sour cream

TO PREPARE AND BAKE PREHEAT OVEN TO 350°

Pour juices and fruit syrups over uncooked apricots and canned fruits in casserole. Mix in rinds and bake 1½ hours.

Serve still warm with sour cream.

Note: If you prefer a less sweet or less-caloric fruit dish, you can use the low-cal fruit brands or perhaps thin the fruit syrups by using half the syrups with an equal amount of orange juice instead of the syrups alone.

SOUTHWESTERN SPORTING BREAKFAST

Another approach to our brunch idea suggests itself from the southwest corner of our country—Texas, New Mexico and Arizona—where the culture and life style are very much influenced by the Mexican culture just "south of the border." In this warm-weather environment, weekend sporting —whether it's riding, tennis, hiking or golf—is much more comfortable in the early morning before it gets too hot. Then, after a swim or a shower, and a change of clothes, a companionable breakfast is in order.

Again it is good to have the first round of drinks ready before the guests assemble. Perhaps pitchers of well-chilled Tequila Sunrises and/or Sangria and fruit juice, with a chilled bowl of Cold Avocado Soup for those who would prefer that. To accompany these a chock-full basket of Hush Puppies and Chile-Queso Squares would be perfect.

When thirsts are slaked and appetites piqued, the main course of one or another filled-tortilla surprise can follow. One of my favorites, Huevos Rancheros—that wonderful combination of eggs, chilies and cheese—is a hot one, but crunchy warm Bolillos alongside will soften the blow. Or you might want to try Chimichangas, a sautéed tortilla filled with hot chili meat sauce, baked and served with sour cream, lettuce and avocado. A nice plus for this dish is that it can be prepared almost all the way through beforehand. If you're a purist or just very energetic, you can even make your own tortillas ahead: see the instructions for both corn and flour tortillas in this section.

There is a wide variety of fruits to choose from to round out this Tex-Mex brunch. Slices of papaya, melon and ruby red grapefruit, or something else from your garden or the fruit store—with or without dips—will make an attractive fruit platter to admire throughout the meal and to enjoy at the end.

One last thought for our Southwestern brunch: be sure to have mugs of cold beer available throughout. Beer is surely the area's favorite hot-weather drink. And I know of what I speak: when my husband was visiting Texas in the 1940's he was asked by the family he was with what he would like to drink. When he said a beer but was indecisive about the brand, his host hastened him to a special basement room where seven different refrigerators were kept full of beer of all brands—known and unknown. Need I go on?

TEQUILA SUNRISES

This is a very popular southwestern waker-upper but remember when using tequila that it doesn't keep as well as most spirits so should be used while still fairly fresh. For this brunch you'll want to have at least a small pitcher ready beforehand.

MAKES 1 SERVING

1 ½ ounces tequila	*6 to 8 ounces orange juice*
1 teaspoon grenadine	*Orange slice, for garnish*

For a single serving, pour the tequila and grenadine over ice cubes in a highball glass. Then fill with orange juice and stir. Garnish with a twisted orange slice. For a pitcher, combine tequila, grenadine and juice in their proper proportion and then pour over ice as needed.

SANGRIA

I am told that, next to cold beer, Sangria is the most popular Texas summertime drink. It can be served either in a bowl or from a pitcher. The recipe doubles, triples and more, as needed, and can be enhanced by adding fresh fruit in season as you choose.

SERVES 6

2 oranges	*½ cup sugar*
1 lemon	*1 (7.5 ml) bottle Burgundy wine*
1 lime	*8 to 10 ounces club soda*

Cut 1 orange and the lemon and lime into quarters. Squeeze juices from fruits into a pitcher, straining if necessary, and add the rinds and sugar. Stir with wooden spoon to combine juice and sugar, pressing rinds with spoon to muddle. Add Burgundy and soda, mixing well.

If serving from a pitcher, pour into tall, ice-filled glasses, garnishing each glass with a slice of the second orange. If serving from a bowl, keep chilled over large ice block, using the second orange as garnish.

Note: Sangria is available ready-made in many stores. If you have a favorite and want to save a little fuss, by all means use that, though I suspect it may be a little less expensive to start from scratch.

COLD AVOCADO SOUP

Avocados make a refreshing and tasty cold soup.

MAKES 8 SERVINGS

2 or 3 avocados
5 cups chicken stock (more if you prefer a thinner soup)
2 scant tablespoons lemon or lime juice

¼ teaspoon Tabasco sauce
2 teaspoons grated onion
Salt to taste

Halve avocados and scoop out pulp to make 3 cups. Place all ingredients, including avocado, in blender and purée well. Chill soup thoroughly in blender jar or other container. Serve chilled.

Note: I like to garnish this soup with a nice bright yellow-orangish blossom. Nasturtium and squash blossoms are great favorites of mine but use what is available to you, making sure, of course, that whatever you choose is completely edible.

HUSH PUPPIES

Hush puppies, it seems, are as much a part of the Oklahoma landscape as the oilwells on the Capitol steps. When I wrote my friend Ida Sloane Snyder of Norman for suggestions for an Oklahoma brunch, she sent me six different recipe versions. Here are two.

MAKES 12 TO 16

1 cup cornmeal
1 cup flour
2 teaspoons baking powder
1 teaspoon sugar
½ teaspoon salt

1 pinch baking soda
1 cup buttermilk
1 egg
1 medium onion, finely chopped
Fat for deep frying

Mix and sift all dry ingredients except baking soda. Add the baking soda to the buttermilk. Combine egg, onion and buttermilk and add to dry ingredients. Mix well. Heat fat to 350°; drop batter from end of spoon into fat, pushing off desired amount from end of tablespoon. Fry until golden brown. Dry on paper towels. Serve at room temperature.

HUSH PUPPY BALLS

These hush puppies are formed into balls rather than dropped off the end of a spoon.

MAKES ABOUT 2 DOZEN BALLS

2 cups cornmeal
2 teaspoons baking powder
1 teaspoon salt
½ cup flour

1 cup finely chopped onions
1 teaspoon Tabasco sauce
1 (6-ounce) can tomato juice
Fat for deep frying

Combine all ingredients and mix well. Form into balls about the size of a walnut. Heat fat to 350° and fry until golden brown. Dry on paper towels. Serve at room temperature.

CHILE-QUESO SQUARES

These lively bites will serve nicely as something for the guests at this Tex-Mex brunch to nibble on until the main dishes are ready.

MAKES ABOUT 70 SQUARES

4 cups (1 pound) grated Cheddar
  cheese
10 canned jalapeño peppers, seeded,
  rinsed and finely chopped

6 eggs, well beaten
1 (4 ounce) jar pimientos, drained
  and coarsely chopped

Generously grease a 1½-quart shallow baking dish. Evenly distribute 2 cups of the Cheddar over the bottom of the dish and sprinkle with the chopped jalapeños. Spread the remaining cheese on top. Pour the beaten eggs evenly over the cheese and sprinkle with the chopped pimientos.

TO BAKE AND SERVE   PREHEAT OVEN TO 350°

Bake on the center rack of a preheated oven for 30 to 40 minutes, until the egg has set and the top is light golden brown. Let cool briefly before cutting into small squares. Serve warm or at room temperature.

HUEVOS RANCHEROS

For Huevos Rancheros, or ranch-style eggs, the eggs may be poached, fried or scrambled. I prefer them poached as in the following version.

8 SERVINGS

2 cans (4 ounces each) green chilies
2 cans (16 ounces each) tomatoes
1½ tablespoons bacon drippings or
    vegetable oil
1 cup finely chopped onions
1 teaspoon finely chopped garlic
1 teaspoon salt
Freshly ground black pepper

1 tablespoon finely chopped fresh
    cilantro (optional)
8 eggs
⅓ cup vegetable oil
8 corn or flour tortillas
12 ounces sharp Cheddar cheese,
    diced or grated

Reserving the juices, thoroughly drain tomatoes and chilies and finely chop. In a large heavy skillet, heat the drippings or oil. Add the onions and garlic and sauté until softened. Add tomatoes and chilies and their reserved juices. Stir in salt, pepper and cilantro and simmer over moderate heat about 10 or 15 minutes, until reduced to a thick sauce.

Make eight indentations in the sauce with the back of a spoon and break an egg into each indentation. Cover the skillet and cook slowly for 2 to 5 minutes, until eggs are poached to desired doneness.

Meanwhile, heat 2 tablespoons of the oil in an 8-inch skillet. Fry the tortillas one at a time for 1 to 2 minutes, or until lightly browned on each side, adding more oil to skillet as needed. Drain tortillas on paper towels.

Arrange tortillas on serving plates, top each with an egg and spoon the sauce over the top. Sprinkle with the cheese and place plates under the broiler briefly to melt the cheese. If desired, sprinkle with additional chopped green chilies and serve.

CHIMICHANGAS

These chili-cheese-beef tortilla fold-ups are very good but also very rich. With all the other things planned for this brunch, this recipe making 12 should be ample for 8 to 10 guests.

MAKES 12 PORTIONS

12 (7-inch) flour tortillas
1 teaspoon salt
2 pounds lean ground beef
2 cloves garlic, crushed
2 teaspoons ground cumin
1 teaspoon oregano, crushed
½ cup chopped canned green chilies
1½ cups bottled taco sauce

1½ cups sour cream
4 tablespoons cider vinegar
2 sticks (½ pound) butter or
*   margarine*
1 cup shredded Cheddar cheese
3 cups shredded lettuce, well crisped
2 ripe avocados, peeled and sliced

TO PREPARE TORTILLAS

If you prefer to make your own tortillas (always fun, but work), see recipe below, and make them ahead. Otherwise, buy.

TO PREPARE FILLING

Sprinkle salt in medium-sized skillet. Place over medium heat. Add beef, garlic and seasonings. Cook, crumbling with fork, until meat loses its pink color. Stir in chopped chilies, ½ cup taco sauce, ½ cup sour cream and vinegar, mixing well. Remove from heat and cool.

TO STUFF TORTILLAS

Melt the butter or margarine in an 8-inch skillet. Dip both sides of each tortilla, one at a time, into melted butter or margarine and drain well. Mound ⅓ cup filling in center of each tortilla and fold envelope-fashion. Place seam side down in large ungreased baking dish. (If you don't have a single dish large enough, two 7-by-11-inch baking pans will hold them nicely.)

Recipe can be made to this point and then refrigerated, covered, up to 24 hours. (If you are holding the Chimichangas in the fridge at this point, this is a good time to wash, dry and shred the lettuce, tucking it, well-dried, into a plastic bag and then into the refrigerator to crisp up thoroughly overnight; but whatever the timing, be sure the lettuce is well dried and crisped before serving.)

TO BAKE AND SERVE   PREHEAT OVEN TO 500°

When ready, bake Chimichangas, uncovered, until crispy, about 15 minutes. Sprinkle with shredded cheese and return to oven just long enough to melt cheese (it doesn't take long).

Serve hot topped with the remaining sour cream and taco sauce, with crisp lettuce and avocado slices on the side; or offer toppings in separate bowls from which your guests can help themselves.

CORN TORTILLAS

Although tortillas can be made with flour, the traditional and more familiar tortilla has, from the very earliest times, been made from maize. Dried kernels of maize were boiled in water with a little charcoal or lime added to loosen the skins, which afterward were removed by rubbing the kernels between the hands. The kernels were then crushed with a stone roller to form a paste, with extra water added as necessary. Finally this dough was kneaded and slapped into thin round cakes and cooked on a special hotplate, a *comalli,* rested over the fire. Thus, the grain for tortillas was actually cooked twice, giving a considerable difference to the final result.

By now, of course, all this has changed. Although some tortilla lovers may still start from scratch, most tortilla makers have access to the already prepared *masa harina,* a corn flour sold by the pound. And, of course, ready-to-use tortillas can be found on most supermarket shelves.

MAKES 16 TO 18 6-INCH TORTILLAS

> 2 cups instant masa harina   1 cup water
> ½ teaspoon salt

TO PREPARE

Place the masa and salt in a mixing bowl and slowly add the water, working the mixture with your fingers to make a smooth dough. If dough is dry and crumbly, add a few tablespoons more water. If dough seems sticky, work in a little more masa. Form the dough into a ball, cover with a damp towel and let stand for half an hour. Divide the dough into 16 or 18 pieces and shape each piece into a ball. Place each ball between two sheets of plastic wrap or wax paper. If you have a tortilla press, place one ball at a time on press and close firmly. Or, place ball on a flat surface and roll out with a rolling pin to form a 6-inch circle about 1/16-inch thick. If necessary, flatten dough further with your fingers or a pie plate.

TO COOK   **PREHEAT GRIDDLE**

Heat an ungreased griddle or heavy skillet. Carefully peel plastic from tortillas, place on the griddle and cook for about a minute. Flip tortilla and cook the other side for another minute, until tortilla is browned or begins to puff. Place browned tortillas in a cloth-lined basket, cover and keep warm until serving. (Or prepare in advance, let cool and reheat just before serving.)

FLOUR TORTILLAS

These have a different flavor and texture from the more traditional corn tortillas above. Still, they are good and, these days, frequently used.

MAKES 16 TO 18 6-INCH TORTILLAS

> *3 cups flour, plus extra for*
>   *sprinkling*
> *1 teaspoon salt*

> *3 teaspoons baking powder*
> *¼ cup lard or shortening*
> *¾ to 1 cup warm water*

TO PREPARE

Combine flour, salt and baking powder in a medium bowl. Add the lard or shortening and work it into the flour with your fingers until well mixed. Gradually add water, stirring in just enough to make a soft dough. Turn out onto a lightly floured board and knead 3 to 5 minutes, until the dough is no longer sticky. Cover and let rest for about 20 minutes. Divide dough into 16 or 18 equal pieces and shape each into a ball. Smooth a little lard or shortening over each ball of dough, place them in a large mixing bowl, cover with a towel and let stand 15 minutes. Flatten each ball slightly with the palm of your hand and sprinkle both sides with flour. On a lightly floured board, roll out each ball to a 6-inch round about ¼-inch thick.

TO COOK   **PREHEAT GRIDDLE**

Heat an ungreased griddle or heavy skillet and brown each tortilla lightly on both sides, about 1 or 2 minutes per side. Place in a cloth–lined basket or bowl, cover and keep warm until ready to serve.

CORN DOGS

These frankfurters on a stick are a hit almost everywhere—at fairs, carnivals, rodeos and at home, especially with children.

MAKES 10 SERVINGS

1 egg
1 ¼ cups milk
1 tablespoon melted butter
4 teaspoons dry mustard
¾ cup cornmeal
1 tablespoon brown sugar
1 ¾ cups flour

1 ½ teaspoons baking powder
½ teaspoon salt
10 frankfurters (one 1-pound package)
4 cups vegetable oil or shortening
10 round wooden sticks

In a large mixing bowl, beat the egg with the milk, melted butter and mustard. Stir in the cornmeal and brown sugar. Sift together the flour, baking powder and salt, and gradually stir into the egg mixture, beating until the batter is very smooth.

Pat the frankfurters dry with paper towels and drop them into the batter. Chill in the batter for 2 hours or overnight.

TO FRY AND SERVE   PREHEAT OIL TO 375°

Remove franks from the batter and gently slide them into the hot oil, being careful not to splatter oil. (If necessary, fry in two batches to prevent dogs from sticking together.) Fry until golden brown, turning once. Drain on paper towels, insert stick in the end of each frank and serve with mustard or hot sauce.

Note: Corn dogs may be made in advance and frozen. To reheat, do not thaw: bake the frozen dogs in a 400° oven for 10 to 15 minutes. Having these ready ahead of time will make it possible to delight any child without a lot of last-minute fuss.

BOLILLOS

Bolillos are delicious Mexican yeast rolls. Their crust is hard and crunchy, much like a French bread, while the inside is moist and rich.

MAKES 20 TO 24 ROLLS

4 tablespoons butter or lard
2 tablespoons sugar
1 ½ teaspoons salt
1 ¾ cups boiling water

1 envelope (1 tablespoon) active dry yeast, dissolved in ¼ cup warm water
6 cups flour

In a large mixing bowl, combine the butter or lard, sugar and salt with the boiling water, stirring until the sugar dissolves. Let stand until the butter has melted and the mixture cools. Combine softened yeast with the cooled butter and water mixture.

Stir in 2 cups of the flour. Add remaining flour 1 cup at a time to make a stiff dough. Turn dough onto a lightly floured surface and knead until smooth and elastic, about 10 minutes. Add additional flour if dough is sticky.

Grease a large mixing bowl. Place dough in bowl, turning to grease all sides. Cover and let stand in a warm place until dough doubles in bulk, about 1½ hours. When doubled, punch down the dough. Divide into 20 to 24 balls, shaping each into an oval. Place on a greased baking sheet about 2 inches apart. Cover with a damp towel and let rise until doubled, about 30 minutes.

TO BAKE   **PREHEAT OVEN TO 400°**

Make a shallow, lengthwise cut in the top of each roll with a sharp knife. Bake at 400° for 10 minutes; reduce heat to 350° and bake for 20 minutes longer, or until golden brown.

Note: Bolillos can be baked in advance and frozen. To reheat, bake at 350° for 15 minutes.

4

SUPERBOWL SUNDAY

A TV Curry Party for 12 to 20

PAPPADUMS SAMOSAS

GINGERED VEGETABLES

JUMBO SHRIMP

MARINATED CHICKEN STRIPS

LAMB CURRY

PLAIN OR SAFFRON RICE

CURRY TOPPINGS

CUCUMBER RAITA

FRESH BANANA RAITA

FRESH CHUTNEY

FRESH PEAR SHERBET OR
GINGER PEAR ICE CREAM

COLD AND HOT BEVERAGES

SUPERBOWL SUNDAY

Is there an American "with soul so dead" who doesn't know that, in America, all conversation during the last half of January is consumed by football and that all paths lead to the Superbowl—if not to the stadium at least to the television set?

Come game time—usually late afternoon—all else ceases. What a good opportunity for a well-planned continual meal—one that guests can get up and help themselves to as time-outs and commercials permit.

Such a party needs a menu that can be put together ahead of time for the most part, and is fun to eat and share as well. A good curry offers just this. The main dish can be served from a Crock-Pot, the rice kept warm over a candle or in a chafing dish, and guests can help, if they like, by bringing one of the meal's various parts.

The nibbles I'm suggesting are varied and come from different regions of India. The crunchy Pappadums, thin southern Indian dough wafers, which swell when they are fried, are known as *papars* in the north. Alas, they must be reheated in hot oil at the last moment, but surely at least one guest will be willing to undertake this task, if only during time-outs. The wafers can be bought from Indian grocery stores or mail-order houses (there is information on how to go about this a few paragraphs on).

Cocktail shrimp are universally popular and well worth the expense. For this party, I'd suggest stir-frying the shrimp after dipping them in blended spices, then serving them with toothpicks. The Samosas and Marinated Chicken Strips are other authentic nibbles you can add; and, if you like, all sorts of nuts and fruits can be scattered about in little bowls.

The main dishes for this continuously available meal speak for themselves. The basic thing here is simplicity, which, as any seasoned hostess knows, means careful thought and preparation ahead of time. And share the labor; your guests will enjoy the party all the more.

Be adventurous: my menu is only a suggestion. In India, people eat by the season. They enjoy mushrooms during the monsoons and melon during the summer and so on, so do try different things at different times. If you, and your guests, are not used to hot foods vary the degree of spice and balance the hot foods with cooling ones. The marinated chicken fingers, for instance, are mild to begin with but even more so with the cayenne left out completely.

Try to prepare as much of the meal ahead as possible: even if you're not crazy about football, your guests will enjoy themselves all the more if they know you are free to share the party with them. The lamb curry can be started the day before and various of the curry condiments as well. The same holds true for most of the hors d'oeuvre, the *raita* and the ice cream and sherbet, though you'll want to make your rice fresh.

I can't imagine such a party without beer: either a special international one or a domestic favorite. You might also want to have some cool wine, some coffee, and milk too, if any children are to be included.

And remember, Superbowl Sunday is just an arbitrary designation for this ad hoc, fix-it-yourself party: it could be assembled just as easily for any occasion where the central focus is on a TV or video screen, or even home movies —any time when the enjoyment of the food and companionship will not interfere with the enjoyment and concentration of others.

A practical footnote: You'll find that most of the spices among the ingredients for the recipes given here are readily available in American supermarkets. However, a few are not: *garam masala,* for one. This is a spice mixture obtained by blending black pepper, cardamom, cinnamon, cloves and cumin. Send for the real thing if you have time; otherwise, you can experiment with these ingredients to make your own favorite blend.

For those of you who want to order Indian specialty items by mail, Madhur Jaffrey's *An Invitation to Indian Cooking* (published by Random House under their Vintage Books imprint) has an excellent state-by-state mail-order source list. Foods of India at 120 Lexington Avenue in New York City (zip code: 10016) is only one example. Many of these stores have a minimum order requirement: at Foods of India it is $10.00. All will label their shipments, especially if you remind them—and do remind them, as many Indian spices look very much the same until you get used to them.

SAMOSAS WITH SOOKHE ALOO FILLING

Samosas are deep-fried patties filled with various mixings, in this case a potato filling. They can be cooked in a wok or electric fryer if you have one, but whatever you have for deep-fat frying will be fine.

MAKES 50-PLUS SMALL PATTIES

1 cup white flour
1 cup whole wheat flour
2 tablespoons peanut oil
Pinch of salt
¾ cup water

1 recipe Sookhe Aloo Filling (see below)
Vegetable oil for frying, ample for 3 to 3½ inches in a pot

TO PREPARE AND FILL PATTIES

Combine flours and oil and rub together. Add salt and mix. Add water, a little at a time, until you have a firm dough. Knead well for 7 to 10 minutes until smooth, and form into a ball. Brush with a little oil and cover with a damp cloth. Set aside until ready for use.

Make Sookhe Aloo Filling. When filling is ready, divide dough into 2 long rolls; slice each into 14 equal slices (each slice makes 2 Samosas). Flatten each slice and roll it out on a floured surface until it is 3½ to 4 inches in diameter. Cut each round in half. Then, taking 1 semicircle at a time, moisten ½ the length of the cut edge with a finger dipped in water. Form a wide cone from the semicircle, overlapping the moist section about ¼ inch and pressing it firmly to hold the cone together. Then fill the cone about ¾ full with the filling, moistening the inside edges of the cone opening and pressing it shut. Seal together with the tip of a fork as you would a pie crust.

Keep filled Samosas covered with plastic wrap until ready to cook.

TO FRY PATTIES   HEAT OIL TO MEDIUM HEAT

I like to use an electric fryer for this task, but any deep-fry equipment should work well.

When you think oil is ready, drop in a trial Samosa to test the temperature: it should start sizzling immediately. Fry the pattie 2 to 3 minutes or until it looks a warm brown. Remove with slotted spoon and drain on paper toweling. Repeat for all Samosas. If they brown too fast, lower the heat.

TO SERVE

Place on a platter and serve warm or hot. They thrive with a light chutney dip of some sort: I often liquefy the Fresh Chutney given for this menu in my blender and use that.

Notes: Samosas may be made a little ahead and reheated in a 300° oven when ready to serve. Samosa dough may be made in a food processor.

Sookhe Aloo Filling

YIELDS ENOUGH FOR 50-PLUS SAMOSAS

2 medium onions, peeled and
coarsely chopped
1½ pieces fresh ginger, 2 inches
long and 1 inch wide, peeled
and coarsely chopped
½ cup plus 3 tablespoons water
3 tablespoons vegetable oil
1 stick cinnamon, about 2 inches
long
4 whole cloves
4 black peppercorns

1 bay leaf
Dash cayenne, to taste
1 tablespoon ground coriander
1½ teaspoons curry powder
1 large canned tomato or 2 small,
coarsely chopped
2 pounds cold boiled potatoes,
skinned and finely chopped
¾ to 1 teaspoon salt, to taste
1 tablespoon lemon juice

Place chopped onions and ginger in blender with 3 tablespoons water and blend to smooth paste (about 1 minute). Set aside.

Heat oil in 10- to 12-inch skillet over medium heat. When hot, add cinnamon, cloves, peppercorns, bay leaf and cayenne. Add paste from blender, turning your face in case of splatters. Fry for about 10 minutes, adding a sprinkling of water if mixture sticks to bottom. Add coriander and curry, and fry another 5 minutes. Add chopped tomato, frying another 2 to 3 minutes. Then add potatoes and salt. Fry on high heat about 5 minutes, browning as much as you can. Add lemon juice and ½ cup water. Bring to boil and cover. Lower flame and let simmer for 1 hour, or more.

To use as stuffing, Sookhe Aloo should be cooked until almost dry, with no extra liquid left. If the bay leaf and cloves are still whole, they should be plucked out; and if any fat has accumulated, it should be scraped away. When dry and cool enough to handle, stuff the Samosas.

Note: Be sure to use fresh, good-quality curry for this–and all–Indian recipes.

GINGERED VEGETABLES

Peel or scrub carrots (or try zucchini, turnips, rutabaga) and cut into fairly large julienne strips. Make a vinaigrette sauce with white vinegar and white sugar with a lot of grated ginger (see page 383 in back of book for Basic Vinaigrette recipe). Cook vegetables until tender but not soft and chill immediately in sauce. Drain well before serving when using as a cocktail hors d'oeuvre.

JUMBO SHRIMP

If you don't mind bending the budget a bit, this is a wonderful way to serve the ever-popular shrimp.

ENOUGH FOR 8 MODEST HELPINGS

5 cloves garlic, peeled and chopped
1 piece fresh ginger, about 1-inch cube, peeled and chopped
7 tablespoons water
1½ pounds jumbo shrimp, peeled and deveined

3 tablespoons vegetable oil
3 tablespoons tomato paste
½ teaspoon ground turmeric
1 tablespoon lemon juice
¾ teaspoon salt
⅛ to ¼ teaspoon cayenne

Put the garlic and ginger in electric blender or food processor container along with 3 tablespoons water. Blend or process at high speed until you have a smooth paste.

Wash shrimp well and pat them dry. Set aside.

Heat oil in a 10- to 12-inch skillet over medium heat. When hot pour in the ginger-garlic paste and fry, stirring constantly, for 2 minutes. Add tomato paste and turmeric, and fry, stirring, another 2 minutes. Add 4 tablespoons water, the lemon juice, salt and cayenne. Cover, and simmer gently for 2 to 3 minutes. (If you like, this much can be done in advance.)

Five minutes or so before serving time, lift cover off the sauce pot, put in the shrimp and turn heat to high. Stir and fry for about 5 minutes or until shrimp just turn opaque.

Place on a serving platter and serve hot with a toothpick in each piece.

MARINATED CHICKEN STRIPS

These lightly but definitely spiced chicken strips are very versatile. And, if you ask your butcher to do the boning and skinning, they are also easy to prepare. Hot or cold, they can be served as an appetizer or part of the main course. For the purposes of this party, they can either go on the table with the main dishes, or if your guests are great nibblers, can be set out on the cocktail table in front of the entertainment. The chicken can be marinated the day before it is prepared.

SERVES 6 TO 8

5 tablespoons olive or vegetable oil

4 tablespoons red wine vinegar

1 medium-sized onion, peeled and chopped

6 to 8 cloves garlic, peeled and chopped

1 piece fresh ginger, about 1-inch cube, peeled and chopped

1 tablespoon ground cumin

Seeds from 7 or 8 cardamom pods

1 teaspoon ground cinnamon

8 whole cloves

20 black peppercorns

½ teaspoon cayenne

2 teaspoons salt

3 tablespoons tomato paste

3 pounds boned and skinned chicken breasts

TO PREPARE CHICKEN STRIPS

Combine all ingredients except the chicken in a blender or food processor container. Blend at high speed until you have a smooth paste.

Wipe the chicken pieces dry. Divide breasts in 2 sections and cut into strips about 1½ or 2 inches long by ½ inch wide. Combine the chicken with the marinade, mixing well. The fingers work nicely to thoroughly rub the marinade into the chicken. Cover and refrigerate a minimum of 4 to 5 hours; overnight is better.

TO BROIL AND SERVE   PREHEAT BROILER

Line a baking tray with aluminum foil, spreading the marinated chicken in one layer on the tray (unless you have a large broiler, this recipe will likely require two go-rounds). A good deal of the marinade will cling to the chicken.

Turn broiler to 450° and broil chicken 10 minutes on the first side; turn over and broil again another 10 minutes, or until the chicken is lightly browned. The pieces will not be uniformly dark-brown, only in spots. Remove broiled pieces with a spatula and keep in a warmed serving dish until ready to serve.

Serve on a warm platter if part of the main course, or on toothpicks as an appetizer.

Note: The spices for this marinade are measured for a mildly hot dish. You can add or subtract according to taste.

LAMB CURRY

Although this curry recipe calls for lamb, beef or chicken would work equally well for another menu. For this party, prepare the lamb the day ahead, adding the spices just shortly before the party. Otherwise, it may get too strong.

SERVES 16 OR SO

4 pounds lamb, cut in 1-inch cubes	*2 tablespoons coriander*
Pinch of turmeric	*1 to 2 tablespoons cayenne*
8 tablespoons cooking oil, more or less	*Several pinches cinnamon*
	Several whole cloves
2 cups water, or more as needed	*Several whole cardamom seeds*
6 cloves garlic, peeled and chopped	*Several peppercorns*
2 large onions, sliced	*2 bay leaves*
1 (2-inch) piece fresh ginger, diced	*1 teaspoon salt*

Brown lamb with a pinch of tumeric in 4 or more tablespoons of the cooking oil; add water and simmer over low heat until lamb is tender, about 40 to 45 minutes. Set aside to cool; then refrigerate until the other preparations are under way.

Shortly before serving, sauté the garlic, onions and ginger in 2 or 3 tablespoons of the remaining cooking oil. Keep at a gentle simmer while preparing the spices.

Grind the spices and seasonings together and add to the simmering garlic-onion-ginger mixture, adding more water or lamb juices as necessary to keep simmering. Simmer about 45 minutes and then add cooked lamb. Heat through and keep warm until ready to serve.

Serve with a bowl of plain or saffron rice and surround with dishes of chopped apples, chopped cashew nuts, raisins, shredded coconut and a variety of chutneys from which your guests will serve themselves.

Notes: Some curries call for chopped tomatoes (1 or 2 added toward the end might make a welcome addition). Yogurt is another ingredient often found in curries; ¼ to ½ cup could be added to this recipe when the cooked lamb is added.

CUCUMBER RAITA

A curry party menu almost begs for a cool, refreshing yogurt dish of some sort. This one calling for grated cucumbers meets this requirement and is easy to prepare as well.

MAKES 3 TO 4 CUPS

16 ounces plain yogurt
2 to 3 good-sized cucumbers, peeled and grated
1 teaspoon salt
⅛ teaspoon freshly ground black pepper

⅛ teaspoon coriander powder (optional)
⅛ teaspoon paprika, for garnish

Empty the yogurt into a serving bowl and beat well with a fork until it is smooth and pastelike. Add the cucumber, salt, black pepper (reserve a pinch for garnish) and coriander, if desired, mixing well.

Sprinkle with paprika and refrigerate until ready to serve, at least one hour.

Notes: If you prefer, the cucumber could be sliced and then marinated in a well-blended mixture of the other ingredients, making it more of a salad dish than a relish.

FRESH BANANA RAITA

This banana raita compliments curry very nicely and is a pleasant variation on the more usual cucumber.

MAKES ABOUT 2 CUPS

2 ripe bananas, chopped
½ teaspoon powdered cardamom
Pinch of cinnamon

Dash cayenne pepper
1 tablespoon sugar
1 cup yogurt

Mix all together gently and serve.

FRESH CHUTNEY

A pleasant combination and a welcome bland contrast to the other spicy dishes on this curry menu.

MAKES ABOUT 4 CUPS

2 cups freshly grated coconut (the
dried is too sweet)
1 cup finely chopped green pepper
1 cup finely chopped seeded and

drained fresh tomatoes or canned
Romano
1 tablespoons sugar
Salt and pepper to taste

Mix ingredients together well and let blend for several hours before serving.

Note: If you want to offer more than one chutney, Major Grey's commercial chutney is always a good addition—or alternative.

FRESH PEAR SHERBET

A wonderful treat when pears are in season and even when they aren't.

SERVES 8 AMPLY

5 or 6 fine ripe pears, peeled, cored
and cut into chunks, to make
about 2 cups
Juice of 2 lemons, to make 4
tablespoons

¾ cup sugar, preferably instant
superfine
1 egg white
3 to 4 tablespoons Poir Wilhelm IV
or comparable pear liqueur

Wash the pears and lemons before using. Prepare the pears. Grate the rind of 1 of the lemons into large mixing bowl; add the strained lemon juice and toss in the pear chunks with a sprinkling of the sugar. (The lemon juice and sugar will prevent the pears from darkening.) Purée the mixture, add the remaining sugar and purée until all the sugar crystals are completely dissolved. If you are using a food processor, add the egg white to the pear purée and purée a moment more. Otherwise, beat the egg white in a small bowl until it forms soft peaks and fold into pear purée.

TO FREEZE

Prepare ice cream freezer, using 1 part salt to every 4 parts crushed ice. Pour pear mixture into freezer container, and at last minute, pour in pear liqueur (this to prevent the liqueur from darkening the fruit). Freeze the sherbet about 25 minutes, then pack in a well-sealed container and keep in the freezer about 4 hours to cure (it will take this long for full flavor to develop).

TO SERVE

Twenty to 30 minutes before serving, remove the sherbet from the freezing compartment and place in refrigerator. Then, when ready to serve, spoon out into goblets and garnish with mint or perhaps a cookie.

Note: This sherbet can also be made from scratch in your freezer. Just be sure, when it begins to freeze around the edges, to beat very well before returning to freezer to firm up completely.

GINGER ICE CREAM

This recipe, which blends the peppery–sweet taste of preserved or candied ginger with sweet smooth cream, is a splendid finale for our curry party.

MAKES ABOUT 1 QUART

4 to 6 egg yolks, slightly beaten
½ cup sugar
⅛ teaspoon salt
2 cups scalded milk
2 cups heavy cream

1 tablespoon vanilla
½ cup candied ginger, finely
chopped
2 to 3 tablespoons ginger syrup
(optional)

Mix egg yolks, sugar and salt. Pour into milk while stirring constantly. Then cook in double boiler until mixture coats spoon. Cool and strain; add cream, vanilla, ginger and ginger syrup, if using, and freeze. Allow to season several hours or more before serving.

Notes: Do not use *fresh* ginger for the *candied*: it will curdle the mixture. If you want the extra flavor and do not have ginger syrup available, you can soak a small piece of fresh ginger in rum or sherry and use 2 to 3 tablespoons of the resulting liquid.

5
TWO
VEGETARIAN SPREADS

A Harvest-Time Fête

A party for 25 or so

CRUDITÉS WITH GADO GADO SAUCE

DEVILED EGGS PLATTER

CAPONATA OR BABA GHANOUSH
WITH DARK BREAD

CHERRY TOMATOES
STUFFED WITH CRAB
OR TUNA MOUSSE

TABBOULEH AND HUMMUS
WITH TOASTED PITA BREAD

MINT AND RICE STUFFED VINE LEAVES
WITH GREEN YOGURT DRESSING

TIROPITAS

FRIED SQUASH BLOSSOMS

STUFFED FRESH APRICOTS

CHINESE SWEET NUTS

POPPYSEED CAKE

CHEESE CRESCENTS   DATE BALLS

WINE   BEER   CIDER

A Winter Caper

A party for 25 or so

SEA SCALLOP SEVICHE

SMOKED MUSSELS

ROQUEFORT-STUFFED ENDIVE

TABBOULEH AND HUMMUS
WITH PITA TRIANGLES

GINGERED CARROTS

SPINACH BROWNIES   ONION TART

HERB-STUFFED BROILED MUSHROOMS

CHILI CON QUESO WITH NACHOS

APRICOT WALNUT BARS

OLD-FASHIONED GINGER COOKIES

CARDAMOM COOKIES

WINE   BEER

HOT CIDER   MULLED WINE

A HARVEST-TIME FÊTE

Most of the world's cultures have celebrated the harvest season. It certainly seems the perfect time to plan a party. I have planned two: one to follow the immediate harvest time and another to celebrate the "put away" harvest from your cupboard and freezer some winter day when thoughts of spring and gardens and another harvest are about all that pull us through.

The idea of a harvest party is especially appealing to me just now, perhaps because as I write this the memory of the past summer's garden delights are still fresh on my tongue. Beyond that, interest in vegetables is mushrooming (that, too!) and has led to both a greater and a better selection in the markets and to a deepening commitment to "growing your own." Each year, more and more people plant at least a small vegetable patch of their own.

New vegetable varieties are being introduced, including those with shorter growing seasons. For example, tomatoes, which are so very good when freshly picked, can now be grown in wooden maple sugar buckets or plastic or earthenware jars—right at the edge of your porch or on an apartment windowsill. This past summer we tried some of the yellow pear-shaped cocktail tomatoes in tubs. They do need regular watering, easy drainage and full sun —and to be moved toward the house as the nights get cooler—but the harvest was plentiful and we felt rewarded. I'm sure there will be more such varieties for us all to try as time goes along.

Another reason vegetables have become so popular is that many people have substantially reduced their red meat intake. Do be creative. You'll find a Hummus and a Tabbouleh among the recipes here, but don't stop there. Try the many interesting things to be made with tahini, bean curd, bulgur and the others.

As with any party you'll want your table for these harvest-time spreads to be gay and colorful. With a vegetable menu this is perhaps easier than with other party menus: the color is already there. Today much is being done with vegetables as decoration; if you have the time and talent, try something a little out of the ordinary. Failing that, put together a big bowl of fresh vegetables in the summer, and perhaps gourds and squashes in the winter, and you can't go wrong.

The menu for the summer party features vegetables taken right from your own garden or perhaps from a nearby farmer's market or one of the many supermarkets now offering good selections of truly fresh vegetables. The menu for the winter party draws more heavily from your cupboard, freezer and from your grocer's shelves.

As with the other menus for this book, I've set the food out roughly in the order it will be served—always with a good portion of it ready when the guests arrive. For the summer party the Crudités, Deviled Eggs, Caponata or Baba Ghanoush, stuffed tomatoes, Hummus, Tabbouleh and cold vine leaves can be set out shortly ahead, and even the sweets. The rest can come along as the guests arrive.

You'll find hints for preparing and serving the Crudités, Deviled Eggs and stuffed tomatoes later in the chapter. There are now many variations of cold vine leaves—most of them delicious. My favorite is given in the Picnic for a Summer Day on page 21, with the recommended Green Yogurt Dressing (page 391). However, be sure these stuffed leaves are served dry enough to be eaten easily.

Caponata, too, comes in many costumes these days. I have tested almost more than I can remember, and that doesn't count the Baba Ghanoush also suggested here, or the various eggplant caviars. For this menu choose either the Caponata or the Baba Ghanoush—whichever appeals to you more, or try them both at different times. Both are good, relatively easy to make and reasonable in cost.

The Hummus and Tabbouleh are also relatively easy and inexpensive—and transfer nicely to the winter party as well. They are very good served with the numerous good pita breads available in the markets.

The Tiropitas and Fried Squash Blossoms need to be served warm. You'll find the Tiropitas recipe on page 169 in the Greek party chapter. It gives the details both for making them fresh and for freshening them if frozen. They are among the most popular hors d'oeuvre I serve: leftovers are rarely a problem. Remember that they should be served warm, but not too hot: the stuffing can burn the tongue. Should they begin to cool off, 1 or 2 minutes in a microwave will heat them through (if you use a regular oven, be careful: you don't want to dry them out).

I have saved the Fried Squash Blossoms until last; partly because they can be done only when blossoms are available but also because they must be done at the very last minute or while the party is in session. You may decide you'd rather skip them: however, they are a fun new twist and lovely in appearance and taste.

Not everyone agrees with me, but I think that a few sweets at every party are not only pleasant but necessary. The Stuffed Fresh Apricots, Date Balls and Chinese Sweet Nuts (page 13) provide sweetness and the extra bonus of not being too rich. The Poppyseed Cake and Cheese Crescents will satisfy the cake and cookie eaters among your guests, and again, are not too rich.

CRUDITÉS

The custom of using raw or partially cooked vegetables accompanied by a spicy dip is a regular part of almost any cocktail party these days. They are delicious, good for you and low in calories (if you go lightly on the dip). The vegetables that can just be washed, sliced and put out work especially well, and there are more of them than you might think. We're all used to mushrooms, celery, red and green peppers, cucumbers and carrots, but how about fennel and celeriac and the various squashes? Other of the vegetables —such as cauliflower, broccoli and Brussels sprouts—are better blanched several minutes, then quickly chilled with cold running water and refrigerated, even as long as 24 hours, before serving. Others—for instance the beans, snow peas and asparagus—need to be peeled or the strings pulled off and then quickly blanched and drained. This last group is best prepared the same day as your party.

Gado Gado Sauce

This is an Indonesian sauce used originally as a dressing for vegetarian dishes. More recently it has become a favorite for dipping. For nonvegetarian parties I especially like it with Pork Teriyaki (page 208) and nibble-sized Benne Chicken Fingers (page 191). But, be careful—it's very hot!

MAKES APPROXIMATELY 50 SERVINGS

1 cup chopped onions	*¼ teaspoon cayenne*
2 cloves garlic, crushed	*3 to 4 tablespoons fresh lemon juice*
2 tablespoons sesame oil	*½ teaspoon freshly grated ginger*
1 cup good freshly made peanut	*1 tablespoon cider vinegar*
butter (crunchy or plain)	*½ teaspoon salt*
¼ cup tahini	*Dash tamari sauce*
1 tablespoon molasses	*Dash hot pepper oil*

Sauté onions and garlic in sesame oil until onions are crispy brown. Using a food processor or blender, blend all ingredients together until smooth. Refrigerate in covered jar to blend flavors thoroughly before serving.

Note: Commercial peanut butter does not work well for this recipe. The oil tends to separate out.

DEVILED EGGS PLATTER

Deviled eggs are another perennial party favorite—and with good reason. They, too, can be done ahead and are almost foolproof. Two dozen—or 48 individual servings—should be ample for this party. Their basic preparation is simple: just make certain the eggs are at least several days old and start them in cold water, cooking them gently so they don't break open. Anyone having trouble hard-cooking eggs should spend a few minutes with Julia Child in *From Julia Child's Kitchen,* page 78, where she recommends salting already-simmering water and pricking the eggs before lowering them into it.

Simmer the eggs 12 to 14 minutes. Crack them gently and chill under cold running water. Peel and cut them in half lengthwise. Then carefully remove the yolks and place in a separate bowl.

To make the filling, sieve the yolks and mix them together with mayonnaise, heavy cream or soft butter. Then season lightly with salt and pepper. With this base, exercise your creativity. Divide the base into parts; then add a little mustard to one, a little Worcestershire to another, and perhaps a little curry or chopped chutney to a third batch. Or add a little canned shrimp or crabmeat, draining and washing the seafood before it's used (and perhaps adding a teaspoon of gin to kill any "canny" taste). Give each filling a special garnish to alert guests to each different flavor—paprika for one, parsley, chives or perhaps capers for the others.

CAPONATA

This Sicilian specialty—known as the "poor man's caviar"—makes a tasty appetizer, especially when complemented by a well-flavored dark bread.

MAKES ABOUT 3 CUPS

4 to 5 small, long eggplants (preferred)	3 to 4 anchovies (optional)
1 cup pitted black olives	2 tablespoons lemon juice
1 tablespoon chopped white onion	4 tablespoons olive oil
1 to 2 cloves garlic	Salt and pepper to taste (watch the salt if you use the anchovies)
1 "deadly" ripe tomato, skinned, seeded and drained	

TO PREPARE EGGPLANTS PREHEAT OVEN TO 400°

Line a jelly-roll pan with aluminum foil. Pierce the eggplants thoroughly with a fork, place on the foil and bake 30 to 35 minutes or until they collapse. Remove from oven. Pull off skins, remove cores and discard.

TO FINISH AND SERVE

Place baked eggplant together with remaining ingredients in blender or processor bowl and blend or process for 2 to 3 turns (may be chopped or mashed by hand but it will take more doing to get the same result). Taste for seasoning and refrigerate in a glass or plastic container for at least a day.

Serve with dark bread and garnish with parsley, black olives and capers.

Note: Caponata, if kept in a covered jar, will hold well in fridge for about a week.

BABA GHANOUSH

This rich mixture of eggplant, tahini and yogurt is reputed to have made a grown man faint with delight.

SERVES 25 TO 30

3 large eggplants (about 2 pounds each)
Salt to taste
2 to 4 cloves garlic
1 cup tahini or less, depending on size of eggplants
Juice of 3 lemons, or more to taste
½ teaspoon ground cumin (optional)

¼ cup yogurt
2 tablespoons finely chopped parsley
A few black olives, thinly sliced, for garnish
1 or 2 tomatoes, thinly sliced, for garnish

TO PREPARE EGGPLANTS

Peel the eggplants, squeezing out as much juice as possible (it tends to be bitter). Then mash, or put through fine blade of vegetable mill.

Crush the garlic cloves with salt to taste. Beat into eggplant, beating to a smooth, creamy purée. Then add tahini and lemon juice alternately, beating well or blending after each addition. Taste and add more salt, lemon juice, garlic or tahini as needed, and, if you like, the cumin.

Serve with yogurt in a bowl and garnish with chopped parsley, and the olive and tomato slices. It goes well with thinly sliced dark bread or with the Arab pita bread.

CHERRY TOMATOES
STUFFED WITH CRAB OR TUNA MOUSSE

Three or 4 dozen cherry tomatoes should do nicely for this party. First prepare 1 recipe Crab or Tuna Mousse (see below). When this is ready, prepare the tomatoes. Wash and then cut a thin slice off the top of each tomato. Using a demitasse spoon, or small melon-baller, remove the bulk of seeds and juice. Then drain by turning upside down over a dish drainer or on paper toweling. When dry, using the same spoon fill the tomatoes and decorate with a sprig of parsley or sprinkling of chives.

Variation: For a less expensive alternative, fill with seasoned chopped eggs.

Crab or Tuna Mousse

Although this recipe makes a very good fish mousse, I like to use it to fill the little cherry tomatoes so many of us have in our gardens each summer.

AMPLE TO FILL 3 OR 4 DOZEN CHERRY TOMATOES

1 tablespoon (1 envelope) unflavored gelatin
¼ cup cold water
¼ cup boiling water
¾ cup mayonnaise
1 cup flaked crabmeat or tuna
½ cup finely chopped parsley

¼ cup finely chopped cucumber
¼ cup finely chopped water chestnuts
Salt as needed
¼ teaspoon paprika
1 tablespoon lemon juice

Soak the gelatin in the cold water and then dissolve in the boiling water. Combine with mayonnaise, blending well. Add remaining ingredients, mixing all together well. Fill an 8- or 9-inch mold and chill until firm. (If not using this mousse to stuff tomatoes, use a ring or fish-shaped mold if you have one; they look so much prettier.)

TABBOULEH

This popular dish is Lebanese in origin and can be used as either an hors d'oeuvre or an appetizer. Couscous is a cracked uncooked wheat resembling semolina.

SERVES 8 TO 10

1 cup couscous
1¾ cups salted boiling water
2 cups chopped parsley
1 medium cucumber, peeled, seeded and chopped
1 clove garlic, or more to taste finely chopped and pressed

½ cup fresh lemon juice
3 tablespoons olive oil
1 tablespoon dried peppermint leaves or 3 tablespoons chopped fresh mint
Salt and pepper to taste

Pour water over couscous in a bowl and let stand until the water is absorbed. Cool and add the remaining ingredients. Then chill for several hours.

To serve, place in a shallow bowl or on a platter. Garnish with more parsley and chopped cucumbers.

Notes: Tomato pieces may be added if you like. Do try to use fresh mint if you can; to my taste, it adds much more.

HUMMUS
(CHICK PEAS IN SESAME OIL SAUCE)

Known as *Hummus bi Taheeni* in the Middle East, our Anglicized *hummus* is becoming very popular in the West. It is a delicious dip for pita bread or crackers and makes an excellent sauce for certain lamb dishes.

MAKES 6 CUPS

2½ cups chick peas, soaked overnight with ½ teaspoon baking soda, or use canned
1 cup sesame seed paste (available at health food stores)
1½ cups lemon juice or more to taste

1½ teaspoons salt
5 cloves garlic, crushed
2 tablespoons chopped parsley
Drizzle olive oil

Wash soaked peas well and pick over. Put in pot with salt and water to cover. Bring to boil and then simmer for about an hour or until quite soft. (If you have a pressure cooker, cook for 20 minutes under pressure.) Press all but a few cooked peas through sieve or food mill, or purée in food processor or blender. To the pea purée slowly add sesame seed paste and lemon juice alternately. Add salt and garlic. Sauce should be thick and smooth but "dippable." If too thick, thin sauce with a little stock or water. Pour sauce into serving bowl and garnish with parsley and the reserved whole cooked peas. Drizzle a little olive oil over the top and chill.

Notes: The sesame seed paste (or *tahenni,* as it is called in the Middle East) is much like old-fashioned peanut butter and separates when not in use. Be sure to mix well before using and to keep any unused portion in fridge. Dried chick peas are available in many health food stores but the canned are simpler to use.

FRIED SQUASH BLOSSOMS

A guaranteed conversation maker, these appealing and provocative party bites also serve to diminish an overabundant squash crop—something almost every home gardener relishes as the summer growing season gets into full gear.

MAKES 12

¼ cup minced fresh parsley
1 teaspoon minced fresh garlic
12 fresh squash blossoms, allowed to
*   close*
12 strips Fontina cheese, cut 1½ by
*   1 inch*

½ cup yellow cornmeal
½ teaspoon salt
⅛ teaspoon pepper
2 large eggs
¼ cup milk
Vegetable oil for frying

Mix together the parsley and garlic and stuff mixture inside the blossoms along with 1 cheese strip each. Gently twist the blossom tips to seal.

   Mix the cornmeal, salt and pepper together and separately beat together the eggs and milk. Dip each blossom first in the egg mixture and then in the cornmeal, shaking to remove excess.

TO FRY   HEAT OIL TO 365° OR 370°

Using about 3 to 4 inches of oil, fry the blossoms, 4 or 5 at a time, for 1 to 2 minutes, holding them under the fat with a slotted spoon for about 30 seconds. Drain well and serve hot, decorated with thyme sprigs or other garnish.

STUFFED FRESH APRICOTS

Kirsch-flavored cream cheese makes a delightful filling for fresh apricots. To fill about 2 dozen you'll need an 8-ounce package softened cream cheese and about ⅛ cup kirsch, or a little more if you like a stronger flavor. Beat the cheese until fluffy; mix together well with kirsch and stuff each apricot half with about a teaspoon of the mixture.

POPPYSEED CAKE

This cake comes to me from my friend, Calista Kristensen, and combines a lovely crunchiness with a delicate sweetness.

SERVES 8 TO 10

2 cups sifted cake flour	1½ cups sugar
2 teaspoons baking powder	1 cup milk
7 tablespoons poppyseeds	4 large egg whites
1 stick (8 tablespoons) butter, softened	¼ teaspoon salt
	Confectioners' sugar
2 teaspoons vanilla	

TO MIX

Sift together the flour and baking powder; mix in the poppyseeds and set aside.

Beat together the butter and vanilla, gradually adding 1¼ cups of the sugar and mixing well after each addition. Add in the flour-seed mixture alternately with the milk.

Combine the egg whites and salt and beat until they stand in peaks. Gradually beat in the remaining ¼ cup sugar and carefully fold whites into the batter.

TO BAKE AND SERVE   PREHEAT OVEN TO 350°

Turn batter into a well-greased and lightly-floured 9-by-3½-inch tube pan, and bake 55 minutes. Cool in pan about 10 minutes and then turn out on rack. Dust with the confectioners' sugar—perhaps using a lace-like paper doily to make a decorative pattern.

CHEESE CRESCENTS

MAKES 40 OR SO

2 sticks (½ pound) sweet butter, softened	½ cup ground nuts
2 cups flour	2 teaspoons cinnamon
1 cup firm cottage cheese	½ cup honey, jelly or fruit preserves

TO MAKE DOUGH

Using a pastry cutter, electric mixer or food processor, blend the butter, flour and cheese together to make a uniform dough. When thoroughly blended, divide into 4 equal balls; wrap well and refrigerate about 1 hour.

TO ASSEMBLE AND BAKE PREHEAT OVEN TO 350°

Combine ground nuts and cinnamon and set aside.

Roll out each dough ball, one at a time, aspiring to make a near-perfect ⅛-inch-thick circle.

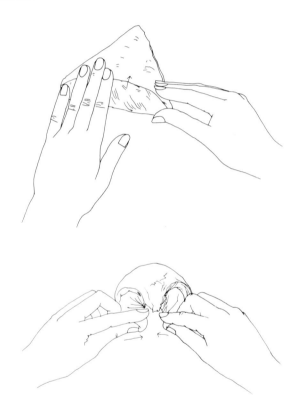

Spread lightly with honey or preserves and sprinkle with ¼ of the cinnamon-nut mixture (it will be ample). Cut circle into 10 to 12 pie-shaped pieces and roll each wedge toward its point, pressing lightly but firmly to hold the crescent shape. Place completed crescents on ungreased baking sheet and bake about 25 minutes or until nicely browned. Repeat for each dough ball.

Note: If you are using preserves, choose a nonlumpy variety; the crescent will roll more easily.

DATE BALLS

This is a quick and simple recipe which fills the bill for that extra sweet.

MAKES ABOUT 30

2 cups bran, wheat or corn flakes
¾ cup pitted dates, chilled
½ cup pecan meats
2 tablespoons honey
1 tablespoon butter, softened

2 teaspoons lemon juice
1 egg yolk, if needed
Confectioners' sugar, sifted, to roll in
About 30 pecan halves, for topping

Put cereal, dates and ½ cup pecans through meat grinder or the steel blade of a food processor (if using processor, give the dates a few jolts before adding the cereal and nuts). Add the honey, butter and lemon juice. Knead, or continue to process, until well blended.

Shape into about 30 1-inch balls (if balls don't hold well, add 1 egg yolk), roll in sugar and top each with a pecan half.

Note: Be sure the dates for this recipe are the sticky variety, not dry. Otherwise, the mixture won't hold well.

A WINTER CAPER

When planning this out of the cupboard or freezer winter vegetarian party, your choices may be limited by the fresh produce available but not by the number of menu possibilities. Here again I have tried to balance hot and cold, spicy and bland, rich and light. Feel free to amplify or simplify this menu to suit your own budget and time schedule, and the "druthers" of your guests. But be sure to balance your menu and have it include several prepared-ahead dishes. Then you can set enough things out to allow you to greet your guests with grace and with the relaxation necessary to enjoy your party as much as your guests do.

Rather than offer both fish dishes, you might want to choose just one. The seviche I'm suggesting is made of sea scallops and is delicious. Although scallops are in season during the winter, they are expensive so you may wish to skip them, or try the Cebiche made of fish fillets (see page 366). The smoked mussels can come either from a can or from your neighborhood deli, which couldn't be simpler.

In recent days, stuffed Belgian endive has become one of my pet vegetable nibbles: its combined tenderness and crispness make it both easy to eat and simple to stuff. At the same time it blends well with all sorts of fillings beyond the Roquefort cheese suggested here.

The Tabbouleh and Hummus have been moved over from the summer vegetarian party and the Gingered Carrots from the Gingered Vegetables in the Superbowl Sunday curry party (see page 57).

The Spinach Brownies and Onion Tart on this menu are a hostess's delight: they are relatively inexpensive, easy to make, and can be made ahead and frozen to be reheated shortly before party time. One or the other should be sufficient, though winter parties—especially if they follow winter sports—sometimes bring big appetites so you might want them both.

The Herb-Stuffed Broiled Mushrooms can be stuffed shortly ahead but do need last-minute attention at the moment of broiling. If that is a problem, no mushrooms are no doubt better than burnt mushrooms, or see the index for other ways to prepare them.

The Chili con Queso adds a wonderful bit of zip to any party and especially to a winter gathering, but it can be tricky. I have made this numerous times, usually with great success, though the cheese can separate. However, don't let this possible pitfall put you off. If you work carefully, using a double boiler, you should have no trouble. Should the cheese ever separate, just do what a host at a recent party I was at did: simply encourage your guests to dip into first one separated portion and then the other. It tasted good regardless and nobody cared.

The sweets I have suggested combine the sweet with the spicy. Apricots for the Apricot Walnut Bars are a little expensive, but they are very good. If you want a wider choice, do consult the index: there are a number of other cookies, bars, cakes and tarts there.

The Hot Cider is a nice touch for a blustery-day winter party. And you might want to consider Mulled Wine to replace or augment the chilled wine on the menu. Just in case: I include one that our family enjoys from time to time. Sköl!

SEA SCALLOP SEVICHE

MAKES ENOUGH FOR 12 OR SO

1 cup (about ½ pound) sea scallops *2 tablespoons chopped green pepper*
Juice of 4 limes *3 tablespoons olive oil*
2 tablespoons chopped onion *Salt and freshly ground black*
1 tablespoon chopped parsley *pepper to taste*

Cut the raw scallops into quarters and cover with lime juice. Marinate at least 2 hours in the refrigerator. Drain well.

Combine the onion, parsley and green pepper with the scallops. Add olive oil, mix well and season with salt and pepper.

TO SERVE

Drain again and serve with little rounds of French bread or with toothpicks and napkins handy.

Variation: You can use good small fish fillets to vary this recipe and to make it more reasonable in cost.

SPINACH BROWNIES

This recipe from a Vermont friend, Hildegarde Hawkes, has served many happy partygoers in our part of Vermont and has helped to make money for the Vermont Cancer Fund by being a part of its fund-raising cookbook, *Vermont: A Collection of Outstanding Recipes.* Beyond that, these "brownies" are simple to prepare—and tasty.

MAKES ABOUT 40 SMALL SQUARES

- 1 (10-ounce) package frozen chopped spinach, thawed
- 1 (1-pound) package Cheddar cheese, shredded
- ½ cup chopped onion
- 1 teaspoon salt
- 1 teaspoon baking powder
- 1 cup flour
- 2 eggs, beaten
- 4 tablespoons butter, melted
- 1 cup milk

Drain spinach in colander and squeeze out moisture; combine cheese, spinach and onion in large bowl, mixing well. Stir salt and baking powder into flour, then mix with spinach. Mix together beaten eggs, melted butter and milk, and stir into other ingredients.

TO BAKE   **PREHEAT OVEN TO 350°**

Line a 13-by-9-by-2-inch baking dish with aluminum foil, spray with Pam (or similar product) to ensure a nonstick result and pour in the spinach mixture. Bake about 35 minutes, until lightly browned.

TO SERVE

When cool, remove from the foil lining and cut into 2-inch squares.

    These brownies can be prepared ahead and frozen until wanted. Simply lift them still uncut out of their baking pan, aluminum foil liner and all, and wrap for the freezer. To serve, thaw and reheat.

Note: Although it wasn't in the original recipe, on the theory that spinach and nutmeg were made for each other, I usually add about ¼ teaspoon nutmeg along with the other dry ingredients.

ONION TART

Many years ago, when we moved to Connecticut, I was enticed by a friend to join a cooking course given by Dione Lucas. The course was utter joy from beginning to end. Dione Lucas's hands were a marvel to watch: I can still see her fluting a mushroom and smiling while we all gasped. Her knowledge of cooking was tremendous and her comments witty. One in particular I still quote with regularity: if an ingredient in itself tastes pleasant (i.e., butter, cream or sherry), be generous; on the other hand if it tastes sharp or salty (i.e., lemon, vinegar or salt), be sparing. One can always add, she went on, whereas compensating for too heavy a hand is difficult, if not impossible.

This onion tart was from our first lesson and soon became my chief party hors d'oeuvre.

8 TO 10 SERVINGS

1 (10-inch) pâte brisée tart shell, unbaked (see page 401)
¼ cup breadcrumbs
1 cup grated Parmesan cheese
2 large Bermuda onions, thinly sliced
1 clove garlic, finely chopped
¼ cup bacon fat, or 4 tablespoons butter
¾ cup light cream, scalded
2 whole eggs plus 1 yolk, well beaten

½ cup grated Swiss cheese
1 teaspoon prepared mustard, preferably Dijon
½ teaspoon Worcestershire sauce
½ teaspoon nutmeg
Salt and pepper to taste
A drop or 2 Tabasco sauce, if needed
Paprika, to sprinkle on top

TO PREPARE SHELL AND FILLING

Place unbaked shell on baking sheet, piercing the shell lightly with a fork, but not all the way through. Sprinkle with breadcrumbs and 2 tablespoons of Parmesan, and set aside.

In saucepan, slowly soften the onions and garlic in bacon fat or butter; cook slowly so onions don't brown. Then add scalded cream to beaten eggs, mixing well. Add Swiss cheese, ½ cup Parmesan and onions to egg mixture; then add mustard, Worchestershire and nutmeg. Taste and add salt and pepper as needed; cheese may be salty so go light on salt until you're sure. If taste is bland, add another spoonful or 2 Parmesan and a drop or 2 Tabasco sauce.

TO BAKE AND SERVE   PREHEAT OVEN TO 350°

Pour cheese, onion and egg mixture into prepared shell, sprinkle with 2 to 3 tablespoons Parmesan, dust with paprika and bake 20 to 30 minutes, or until done. Test for doneness by inserting knife: it should come out clean. This tart will keep hot for about ½ hour. If you need to keep it longer, cover and return to a 120° oven until wanted.

Serve as is, or, to make a very special appetizer, with the Onion Ring Garnish below.

Onion Ring Garnish

24 small onion rings, freshly cut   *Oil for deep-fat frying*
Flour for dusting   *Parmesan cheese, for sprinkling*
1 egg, beaten   *1 tablespoon chopped fresh parsley*
¼ to ½ cup breadcrumbs

Dust onion rings with flour, dip in beaten egg and coat with breadcrumbs. Heat oil for deep-fat frying to 375° and fry onions until golden brown. Drain on paper towels. When dry, overlap rings on baked tart. Sprinkle with Parmesan cheese and fresh parsley, and serve warm.

HERB-STUFFED BROILED MUSHROOMS

There is something about broiled mushrooms at a party that spells SPECIAL.

20 OR SO, DEPENDING ON SIZE

1 pound good-sized fine mushrooms,   *½ teaspoon dried basil*
washed and patted dry   *½ teaspoon dried tarragon or thyme*
5 tablespoons butter   *¼ teaspoon salt*
1 small onion, skinned   *A few grains cayenne*
½ cup fine breadcrumbs   *3 or 4 tablespoons grated cheese*

Once they are clean and dry, separate the mushroom stems from the caps. Chop the stems fine and set aside. Using 2 tablespoons butter either sauté the caps lightly or brush them and broil them lightly.

Chop the onion fine, mix with mushroom stems and sauté in remaining butter. Add the remaining ingredients, except for cheese, and cook through.

Press the stuffing into the mushroom caps firmly, sprinkle with grated cheese and set aside until ready to broil.

Just before serving, tuck the stuffed mushrooms under the broiler to melt the cheese and heat through.

Variations: There are many alternate possibilities for this mushroom stuffing. The herbs can be adjusted in both amount and content; 1 or 2 teaspoons sherry or other spirits can be added; ¼ cup finely chopped pecans or other nuts, or perhaps water chestnuts, can be tried—and other variations of your own concoction.

CHILI CON QUESO

If you and your guests like things really spicy, you might try hot green chilies for the chilies indicated, but be careful. Not only can chilies burn your tongue, they can burn your skin and eyes.

MAKES ABOUT 1 CUP

1 medium onion, chopped fine
3 to 4 fresh green chilies or small drained canned chilies
1 tablespoon oil
1 ripe tomato or 2 canned plum tomatoes, chopped and drained

½ cup grated Monterey Jack, Meunster or mild Cheddar cheese
¼ cup milk
Salt to taste

Sauté onion and chilies in oil; add tomato and mix. Add cheese and milk and whisk until melted.

Serve as soon as possible, with Nachos (see recipe below) or chips. To reheat, use a double boiler.

Note: To be on the safe side, I often use a double boiler all the way through for this recipe.

Nachos

Nachos are only one of the many good things we have adopted from our Mexican neighbors in recent years. Their lively, almost nutty flavor and sturdy crispness make them ideal to use with Chili con Queso and other dips.

First, quarter as many tortilla rounds as you think you will need (if you want to start from scratch, see the recipe on page 49 in the Southwestern brunch party). Fry the quarters in deep fat until crisp, draining them well. Then top with grated Cheddar cheese and thin slices of green chilies, and broil until the cheese melts.

For those who don't want the fuss, or haven't the time, the already prepared corn chips in most markets can be used to much the same effect.

Note: To use with Chili con Queso, you may want to go light on the cheese and chili topping.

APRICOT WALNUT BARS

This recipe comes from Alice Tobin—a long-time Bostonian and apricot lover.

MAKES 20 TO 25

1 cup dried apricots
1 cup flour, for crust, plus ⅓ cup, sifted, for topping
¼ cup granulated sugar, for crust
1 stick (8 tablespoons) butter or margarine

2 eggs
1 cup light brown sugar
½ teaspoon baking powder
¼ teaspoon salt
½ teaspoon vanilla
¾ cup chopped walnuts

TO PREPARE FRUIT AND CRUST

Well beforehand, cover apricots with water in saucepan and bring to boil. Simmer 10 minutes, drain, cool and chop.

When ready, sift 1 cup flour and granulated sugar together. Cut butter or margarine into mixture until coarse like cornmeal. Press firmly into bottom of greased 8-by-8-inch baking pan to make crust.

TO PREPARE TOPPING AND BAKE   **PREHEAT OVEN TO 350°**

When oven is heated, bake crust 25 minutes.

Meanwhile, combine eggs, brown sugar, sifted flour, baking powder, salt, vanilla, nuts and apricots. When ready, spread apricot mixture over baked crust and bake another 35 minutes. Cool in pan; top will be soft.

Note: This can be cut in small squares, as it is quite sweet and rich, and the recipe may easily be doubled.

OLD-FASHIONED GINGER COOKIES

MAKES ABOUT 3 DOZEN

1 stick (8 tablespoons) butter
½ cup brown sugar, well packed down
½ cup molasses

2 cups flour
1½ teaspoons ground ginger, or more to taste

Cream the butter and sugar well. Add the molasses and beat thoroughly. Sift the flour and ginger together, and add. Mix all well and form the dough into 2 rolls about 2 inches in diameter. Wrap in wax paper and chill overnight.

TO BAKE   **PREHEAT OVEN TO 350°**

When ready to bake, cut dough into thin cookie slices, approximately ⅛ inch, and bake on ungreased foil covered cookie sheets for about 5 minutes, watching to be sure they don't get too brown.

Note: These are especially good with sherry and other full-bodied wines.

CARDAMOM COOKIES

These cookies have a lovely subtle flavor.

MAKES 5 TO 6 DOZEN

2 sticks (½ pound) butter, softened	1 teaspoon cardamom seeds, crushed
1 cup sugar, white or light brown	¼ teaspoon salt
2 eggs	Grated rind of 1 lemon
4 cups flour	

Cream butter and sugar. Add other ingredients, mixing well. Roll out thin on floured board. Cut in circles, diamonds, or shapes of your choice.

TO BAKE AND STORE   **PREHEAT OVEN TO 400°**

Place cookies on ungreased cookie sheets and bake for 10 to 12 minutes, or until golden brown.

Store in airtight container.

HOT CIDER

Cider is, of course, wonderfully refreshing when left in its untampered–with state. But on a cold afternoon or evening, it is awfully good served hot with a touch of spice.

SERVES 10

2 quarts cider	*3-inch stick cinnamon*
¼ teaspoon salt	*Ground nutmeg, to taste*
1 teaspoon whole allspice	*Orange slices, for garnish*
1 teaspoon whole cloves	

Add salt to cider in good-sized pot and heat slowly. Tie whole spices in cheesecloth to make a secure packet. Add to cider mix and slowly bring just to boil. Cover and simmer gently 20 minutes; remove spice bag and dash liberally with nutmeg.

Serve hot with orange slices floating in serving bowl or kettle.

MULLED WINE

This warm wine drink is a welcome addition to many winter parties.

MAKES ABOUT 2 QUARTS

1 cup sugar	*lemon, orange, pineapple, apple,*
½ cup water	*cranberry, etc., to taste)*
2 sticks cinnamon	*1 (7.5 ml) bottle red wine*
½ lemon, cut in slices	*Slices of lemon, orange and*
24 cloves	*pineapple, for garnish*
4 cups hot fruit juice (mixture of	

Combine the sugar, water, cinnamon, lemon slices and cloves, and boil 5 minutes to make syrup. Strain and add fruit juices. Separately heat, but do not boil, wine and add to fruit juice mixture. Keep hot over gentle heat, and when ready serve with fruit slices.

Note: The ingredients and proportions for this mulled drink may be varied almost at will. One suggestion: if you use many sweet fruits and juices, cut the sugar a little.

© Robert Grant

Vegetarian Spreads

CRUDITÉS WITH GADO-GADO SAUCE
ONION TART
STUFFED ENDIVE
TABBOULEH

Pleasures of Tea

SCONES WITH JAM
STRAWBERRY TART
APPLE AND DATE TEA LOAF
KIPPER

6

THE PLEASURES OF TEA

High Tea Family-Style
A Scottish summer Sunday supper for 6 to 8

SALMON MOUSSE   COLD CHICKEN

COLD MEAT PLATTER

SLICED TOMATOES

BREAD AND BUTTER

APPLE AND DATE TEA LOAF

RICH SCONES WITH JAM

BLUEBERRY-APPLE TART

SCOTS' SEED CAKE
OR SCOTCH SHORTBREAD

TEA   MILK

A few winter alternates

KEDGEREE   CREAMED OYSTERS

STEAK AND KIDNEY PIE

KIPPERED HERRING

A "Ritzy" Tea at Home

Afternoon tea for 10 to 12

CUCUMBER AND SMOKED SALMON
TEA SANDWICHES

WATERCRESS ROLLS

LEMON AND APRICOT-PECAN BREADS

CINNAMON STICKS

RICH SCONES WITH JAM

STRAWBERRY CREAM TART

TEA   COFFEE   WINE   SPICY ICED TEA

A summer substitute

STRAWBERRIES AND DEVONSHIRE CREAM

THE PLEASURES OF TEA

When I wrote my friend Bette Fischer—a Scot and an alumna of many early-day High Teas—telling her I was thinking of including a segment on teas in this book on party giving, her reply was immediate and overflowing with reminiscence and an urgent plea: "Do bring back High Tea!" So this section is as much in answer to that plea as anything.

If High Tea is indeed revived it will mark the revival of an old custom. When most people worked close to their homes and outdoor lighting was minimal, dinner was served at midday. Then in the early evening the family gathered for a simple meal served with tea around the kitchen or dining room table, with a guest or two easily included. My Scottish friend writes that she still harbors visions of the family "teas" of her childhood and especially those on the weekend, when they were more relaxed and her mother—once things were pretty well prepared—would take her place at the table, allowing the children and other volunteers to take over the serving.

For this traditional family tea, each place was set with a knife, fork, tea-spoon, dessert spoon and a small knife, often ivory handled, for buttering and cutting cheese. A good-sized plate would be used for the main course, a small one for the cakes. The main dishes would be spread out on the dining table with either a side table or tea cart for the dessert cakes and puddings. The tea things would be by her mother's side: it was always her job and joy to pour.

For these teas, the menu included a light main course—perhaps cold meats, a loaf of some sort and a salad—followed by scones, fruit breads, cakes and, naturally, tea, with a more substantial main course in winter.

Today, with so many men taking a large business lunch at noon and children having a hot lunch at school, perhaps the time to revive family High Teas has come. And children, of course, particularly enjoy this type of pick-up meal. Try the traditional menu given here. Begin with the Salmon Mousse suggested; it is delicious. However, other mousses can be found aplenty in the index along with a page reference for Kedgeree and a lovely fruit tart. It's a wonderful meal offering simplicity and warmth, and ample opportunity for good fellowship and good conversation.

In a different vein, another friend wrote from Scotland about the hotel and inn High Teas she found there on a recent vacation. Though some country hostelries are still serving a High Tea catering to the hearty late-afternoon appetites developed from a long day's fishing or hiking, she reports with regret that these teas are getting harder and harder to find and are usually by reservation only. The menus for these Scottish country teas include such dishes as haddock fillets in bread cups with peas and "chips" (the English French fry), plaice (a wonderfully good and not too expensive flat fish) with cheese and mushrooms, or a mixed grill with fried tomatoes and, again, "chips." In the summer, cold sliced ham or roast beef and salads replace the more substantial winter meal, but all is always followed by scones with butter and jam, an assortment of cakes and tarts, and of course tea.

Farther south in England's West Country one finds Devonshire Cream, a local delight made from the very rich milk found there, which would surely find its way to the tea table, to be served on strawberries, spread on buns or just eaten plain if no one was watching. Other areas no doubt offer their own special tea-time delights; here in Vermont our own local maple butter would qualify.

Scotland and England are not alone in offering these country inn High Teas. A recent issue of the Boston *Globe* reports that High Tea is still served at some of the Irish Bed & Breakfast inns. And closer to home, I note a 1983 guide to American Bed & Breakfast homes lists a number that provide their guests an afternoon tea as well as breakfast (it may not be High but it is a tea).

There remains the elegant 4 o'clock Afternoon Tea still available today in some of the world's most prestigious hotels and department stores and which my Scottish correspondent reminds me should not be confused with High Tea. The Empress Hotel in Victoria, British Columbia, is one place these teas can still be enjoyed, as are the Ritz-Carlton in Boston and the American Stanhope in New York, and in England such a tea is still served at Harrod's department store, and many other places.

Recently friends and I decided to reacquaint ourselves with the Boston Ritz-Carlton's renowned Afternoon Tea. On the chance that you have not had the pleasure, let me share it with you here.

At tea time, the Ritz reserves its delightfully appointed mezzanine for a luxurious and relaxing tea or aperitif. Deep, well-upholstered armchairs ring small linen-covered tables, each perfectly set with flowered china and a delicate floral piece. The tea is, of course, made in a pot, with an extra pot of piping hot water right at hand and with individual strainers for each participant. The menu offers either a full tea with assorted sandwiches, scones, tea breads and fruit tart, or a chance to order à la carte. As we had had an adequate lunch, we chose one item each: a selection of tea sandwiches, crustless and elegantly thin with a variety of fillings—watercress, smoked salmon, ham and cheese; a plate of scones served with butter and a pot of jam, and, lastly, a strawberry tart. The tart was a confection almost without equal, with a thin layer of chocolate somehow tucked amongst the pastry, strawberries and real cream. We shared the variety of tastes and each drank her own pleasure (Lapsang Souchong and Earl Grey tea and a pot of French Roast coffee). The service was quiet and discreet, and the whole tea time a delightful and welcome respite.

This would be an excellent tea to re-create at home—perhaps to greet a special friend or around which to have a small bridal or baby shower. With this in mind, you might follow the menu I have suggested or perhaps use some of these tea-time recipes with which to embroider your own tea menu. Other ideas can be found in the index, or where better to look than in the Ritz-Carlton's very own *Ritz-Carlton Cook Book,* by Helen Ridley.

Obviously a special tea like this would merit your very best china and silverware, a lovely teapot and accouterments—and fine tea napkins. You might even want to get out the old family tea service. And there are other fun things to use. Perhaps you have an old-fashioned three-tiered cake stand or one of the special serving dishes for muffins (in this case, scones)—a silver dish kept warm by hot water in a separate dish nestled below. Keep a lookout for such stands and dishes at your local flea market and antique shops: they would make a fun, and noteworthy, addition to your tea party.

Let the season dictate the flowers. Perhaps just a lovely single blossom on the tea tray itself, or a potted plant from the garden, to lend that special air.

VARIETIES OF TEA

Tea was first introduced into England in the early 17th century as a drug. Since then the consumption of tea in England has increased to nearly 10 pounds per person annually. At first it was used as a cure for almost everything from migraine to gallstones, but as it grew more plentiful and cheaper many people found it an improvement over many of the gins they drank and it became an important part of English daily life. It of course followed the English to the American colonies where, as we know, it became subject to heavy taxes.

Nowadays, a great variety of tea is available in the United States, and it has become an interesting and relatively easy challenge to experiment with the different teas at different times of the day. To help in this, Twinings Teas has an excellent and fun-to-read guide to the various teas (obtained by writing Twining Teas, East 210 Route 4, Paramus, New Jersey 07652).

Their *Gunpowder Green* tea, for example, originated in China and is the world's oldest known tea type as well as the lowest in caffeine. The leaves, unfermented and neatly curled into pelletlike rolls, give off a slightly astringent flavor which goes well with Chinese and Japanese dishes.

English Breakfast tea is a combination of Ceylon and Indian teas which are black in color and produce a stronger, darker liquid. This tea serves nicely as an all-round tea to be served with either milk or lemon.

Lapsang Souchong, my personal favorite for afternoon, is from the province of Fukien in China and is a large-leaf tea. It is usually served clear with a slice of lemon in the afternoon.

Russian Caravan, despite its name, comes from China's Anhwei Province. It is a fragrant blend of fine-quality China black and Oolong brown teas, and was indeed widely used in Russia, kept ready in a samovar for all occasions. It also makes an excellent iced tea.

The teas perhaps most common on today's supermarket shelves are *Orange Pekoe,* a general-purpose tea with a delicate flavor originating in Ceylon that can be served with or without milk or iced with lemon; *Darjeeling,* an Indian tea with a hint of muscatel flavor, used to accompany curry dishes and going well with either milk or lemon, and *Earl Grey,* a secret blend of China and Darjeeling teas, another fine all-purpose tea and good when iced.

MAKING GOOD HOT TEA

Put fresh water in tea kettle and bring to a full boil (no cheating, please). Heat the teapot by first swirling piping hot water in it, catching all corners. Then empty completely and measure out your tea: 1 teaspoon per person and 1 extra for the pot (if the tea becomes too strong you should have ample hot water ready from which to add more). Pour boiling water on the tea leaves and let tea steep (5 minutes used to be the magic number; if you're using small-leaf tea or tea bags, 3 minutes).

Serve in cups or thin mugs with lemon, milk and sugar available. Tea is much better fresh, so make a new pot if other people join in later on.

MAKING GOOD ICED TEA

FOR 8

Hot Water Method

Pour boiling water over tea leaves (1½ to 2 teaspoons tea per serving, depending on variety and personal preference) or tea bags (I use 10 bags for my almost-full 2-quart whistling tea kettle) and let steep 10 to 15 minutes. Remove bags (or strain) and cool. Then fill glass jars, juice or cider bottles, and chill in the fridge. Serve over ice with superfine sugar or honey and a slice of lemon and sprig of mint. If this tea becomes cloudy you can clear it by stirring in a little boiling water.

Cold Water Method

In 2-quart pitcher or jar, place desired quantity of tea and fill with freshly drawn cold water. Cover tightly and keep in cool place from 6 hours to overnight, mixing occasionally. Strain and pour into glasses or refrigerate in covered jars until needed. Iced tea made this way does not get cloudy and can be stored in the refrigerator for several days.

Some people make iced tea in this same fashion but by steeping it most of the day in direct sunlight. This method, too, produces a noncloudy tea.

SALMON MOUSSE

This delicious and attractive salmon mousse comes to me through the kindness of Joan Bibby. It originated at The Cooking School, a popular cooking center in Halifax, Nova Scotia.

SERVES 6 TO 8, OR 12 TO 16 AS HORS D'OEUVRE

*1 pound salmon fillets, skinned and
  ground*
¼ cup heavy cream
6 large eggs
1 teaspoon paprika
Salt and pepper to taste

*1 pound fresh peas, shelled,
  parboiled and drained*
*¼ cup very finely chopped sorrel or
  spinach*
1 cup finely chopped fresh parsley
2 tablespoons finely cut fresh chives

TO PREPARE MOUSSE

Place salmon in bowl with ⅛ cup cream, 3 eggs, the paprika and dash of salt and several pepper grindings. Beat well and poach a teaspoon of the mixture in water to check seasoning. (Fresh salmon can vary in saltiness, so you may need to add a little more salt here.) When adjusted to your taste, set aside.

Purée the peas in food processor or blender. Add the sorrel or spinach, parsley, chives and remaining cream. Again season with salt and pepper. Beat well to form a smooth mousse, gradually incorporating the remaining 3 eggs, and set aside.

TO BAKE   PREHEAT OVEN TO 350°

Butter a 6-cup heatproof terrine. Put in ½ the salmon mixture, cover with pea mousse and add rest of salmon. Cover terrine with buttered foil, place in a bain marie (baking dish partially filled with hot water) and bake for 1 hour. Cool and refrigerate.

TO SERVE

This makes a lovely hors d'oeuvre served with a light Dill and Sour Cream Dressing (see page 388), or just plain with toast points or Melba toast nearby to spread it on.

APPLE AND DATE TEA LOAF

This loaf recipe, as does the scone recipe that follows, comes to me from Mary Law, of Fochabers, Scotland, who has shared her fine Scottish cooking with many Americans over the years and who also shared with me her great enthusiasm for the old-fashioned High Tea.

10 TO 12 SLICES

½ pound cooking apples, peeled, cored and sliced
Juice and grated rind of 1 lemon
½ cup dates, chopped
1 stick (8 tablespoons) butter or margarine

½ cup brown sugar
2 eggs
1 cup flour
1 teaspoon baking powder
½ teaspoon salt

Cook the apples with the lemon juice and 1 tablespoon water, if needed. Add lemon rind and cover pan. When apples are soft, mash with a fork and add dates.

Cream the butter or margarine and sugar; beat in eggs and flour, baking powder and salt. Add apple mixture and blend all together well. Turn into greased 1-quart loaf pan.

TO BAKE AND SERVE   PREHEAT OVEN TO 350°

Bake for 1 hour and cool on wire rack. Remove from pan and wrap well and keep for 1 day before serving.

RICH SCONES

MAKES 6 (2½-INCH) SCONES

1 cup flour
1 teaspoon baking powder
1 teaspoon salt
3 tablespoons butter or margarine
2 tablespoons sugar
2 tablespoons currants, sultanas or raisins

1 egg, beaten, keeping a little aside to brush tops
Milk to make a soft dough (about ⅓ to ½ cup)

TO MAKE AND CUT DOUGH

Mix flour, baking powder and salt in bowl. Rub butter or margarine in with fingers. Mix in sugar and fruit. Stir in egg and then milk to make a nice soft dough.

Roll dough out to approximately ½-inch thick and cut with 2½-inch scone cutter (any comparable cutter is fine; I have a fluted-edged round one and a diamond-shaped one that I use). Place on greased baking sheet and brush tops with remaining beaten egg.

TO BAKE AND SERVE   PREHEAT OVEN TO 425°

Bake near top of oven for 10 to 15 minutes or until golden brown. They can be served cool or warm, as long as there is lots of butter and pots of jam.

Note: I like to plump currants and raisins before using them. This is easily done by soaking in about ¼ cup fruit juice or a favored liqueur or brandy for about 20 minutes before using them. But be sure that any excess moisture is blotted off.

SCOTS' SEED CAKE

This fruity cake happens to be a favorite of my Scots husband. The true Scots recipe I borrowed from here indicates caraway seed, but I prefer the somewhat more subtle poppyseed.

MAKES 20 SLENDER SLICES

1 stick (8 tablespoons) butter
½ cup sugar
3 eggs
2 cups flour
2 teaspoons baking powder
½ teaspoon cinnamon
½ teaspoon nutmeg
⅓ cup milk

2 tablespoons minced candied orange peel
2 tablespoons minced candied lemon peel
¼ cup minced citron
⅓ cup blanched, chopped almonds
2 teaspoons poppyseeds

Cream the butter and sugar until fluffy. Beat in the eggs one at a time. Sift the flour, baking powder, cinnamon and nutmeg together and add alternately with the milk, beating well each time. Stir in the minced fruits and almonds.

TO BAKE   PREHEAT OVEN TO 350°

Grease a deep 10-inch round pan, line with wax paper and grease again. Turn the batter into pan and sprinkle with the poppyseeds. Bake for about 30 minutes or until done.

This cake may also be baked in a loaf or Bundt pan if you prefer.

SCOTCH SHORTBREAD

This is another good one from Helene Druhl.

MAKES ABOUT 40 SMALL SQUARES

2 sticks (½ pound) butter
2 cups flour

½ cup confectioners' sugar, plus
extra for sprinkling on top
¼ teaspoon salt

Cream butter. Sift dry ingredients together and blend with butter. Then press dough into small jelly-roll pan. It should press out to about ¼-inch thickness.

TO BAKE AND SERVE   PREHEAT OVEN TO 350°

Bake for 30 to 35 minutes or until golden in color; do not let brown. Remove from oven and cut into small squares. When cool, sprinkle with confectioners' sugar.

Note: This dough may also be rolled, again to ¼-inch thickness, and cut into cookie shapes. This is fun to do, especially if children will be at the party. The baking time is the same.

CREAMED OYSTERS

Clean and shuck the oysters. For each dozen, make a cream sauce combining ½ cup cream, 1 tablespoon vermouth, and dashes of salt and pepper. Heat sauce to boiling; add oysters and simmer until edges curl, about 3 minutes.

STEAK AND KIDNEY PIE

SERVES 6 TO 8

2 pounds sirloin, cut in 1-inch
cubes
2 to 3 tablespoons bacon fat or
vegetable oil
4 lamb kidneys or piece of beef
kidney, cut in ¼-inch cubes
2 onions, sliced
2 tablespoons flour

2 cups canned beef stock
1½ tablespoons Worcestershire
sauce
2 tablespoons chopped parsley
(optional)
¼ cup sherry
Salt and pepper to taste

Thoroughly brown sirloin cubes in bacon fat or oil and remove. Sauté kidneys and remove. Sauté onion until clear. Place onions and meats in heavy oven casserole or deep pie dish. Add flour to pan drippings and simmer with beef stock, Worcestershire, parsley, if using, sherry, and salt and pepper until slightly thickened. Add sauce to meats and top with a lard crust (see Lard Pastry Dough on page 404).

TO BAKE   **PREHEAT OVEN TO 350°**

Cut steam vents in crust and bake pie for 45 minutes or until crust is golden brown.

Notes: It is traditional to place a black ceramic pie bird in this pie. Also, when I have time, I like to decorate the crust with dough leaves and other designs, securing them to crust with a bit of water.

KIPPERED HERRING

To prepare Kippered Herring, wrap in foil with a pat of butter and heat through thoroughly in medium oven, about 15 minutes. This method of preparation eliminates any strong cooking odor.

A "RITZY" TEA AT HOME

CUCUMBER SANDWICHES

These delicate little sandwiches come from a time long ago when Afternoon Tea was an elegant repast served in the drawing room with good china.

MAKES ABOUT 40 LITTLE SANDWICHES

2 long Dutch seedless cucumbers, or fresh garden cucumbers in season
2 tablespoons kosher salt
1 teaspoon dried dill weed
Salt and freshly ground black pepper to taste

1 loaf thin-sliced white or whole wheat bread, preferably day-old
Butter, softened, for spreading
Mayonnaise to spread
Watercress or dill, for garnish

Peel the cucumbers and thinly slice into a good-sized bowl and add ice. Add kosher salt, sprinkle with dill and mix. Refrigerate at least 3 hours, or better still overnight, to crisp.

Shortly before serving time, rinse and drain the cucumbers well and add black pepper and salt to taste.

TO MAKE THE SANDWICHES

Taking two slices of thin bread at a time, first spread one slice with butter and the other with mayonnaise, being sure to cover the corners as the combination of flavors is essential. Pile with enough slices of cucumber to cover well, pressing down the top slice slightly to contain the filling. Cut off the crusts and slice sandwich into fours diagonally. Repeat for remaining bread and cucumbers.

Arrange the sandwiches on a plate decorated with touches of watercress or fresh dill. A nasturium or two in the center adds a lovely bit of color and can be eaten if desired. Then cover until needed.

Notes: I find the thin-sliced white and whole wheat bread that the Arnold and Pepperidge Farm bakeries sell perfect for these sandwiches. However, any brand will do as long as the bread is firm, and of course, tasty. For sandwich mayonnaise, I prefer Hellmann's.

Variations: There are many variations for these delightful little sandwiches. In addition to the Watercress Rolls and Smoked Salmon already given for this menu, you might try deviled ham instead of the butter, or a little liverwurst creamed with a bit of Dijon mustard. Thin slices of ham or a nice cheese also make inviting tea sandwiches.

SMOKED SALMON TEA SANDWICHES

Smoked salmon is expensive but the amount needed for these little sandwiches is very modest (perhaps ½ pound for 20 or so tea-sized sandwiches) —and worth it. These sandwiches can be served either open-face or in the more typical closed fashion. In either case, the bread should be thinly sliced and of high quality and the salmon also sliced very thin. If open-face, lightly butter (with sweet butter) and decrust the bread, cutting each slice into quarters, or more elaborate shapes if you like. Put a slice of salmon on each piece, top with a few capers and serve with enough lemon twists to go around. Most will want to add a sprinkling of lemon. To make the closed version, simply cover the salmon and capers with a second piece of lightly buttered bread.

Smoked salmon trout from Norway is now available and makes a delicate sandwich.

WATERCRESS ROLLS

Whenever I think of watercress I think of the cress that grew, wild by the time we got there, along a nearby Connecticut brook. How nice it was just to go out the kitchen door and pick a great bunch of that wonderfully crisp and authoritative green.

MAKES 56 ROLLS

2 sticks (½ pound) sweet butter, softened
2 tablespoons minced fresh parsley leaves
1 cup watercress leaves, blanched, drained, squeezed dry and minced, plus 1 bunch watercress, rinsed, patted dry, coarse stems discarded and separated into 2-inch sprigs

1 tablespoon minced fresh tarragon, or 1 teaspoon crumbled dried
1 teaspoon Dijon mustard
1 teaspoon Worcestershire sauce
1 teaspoon fresh lemon juice
Salt and pepper to taste
28 slices very thin homemade-type bread, decrusted

TO PREPARE THE WATERCRESS FILLING

In a small bowl cream the butter until light, blend in the parsley, minced watercress, tarragon, mustard, Worcestershire sauce, lemon juice and salt and pepper to taste, and let stand in a cool place for an hour or so.

TO MAKE THE ROLLS

Roll the bread slices as thin as possible with a rolling pin and spread with the prepared herb butter. Then arrange the watercress sprigs along one edge of each slice—four sprigs works well for me—so that bits of the green will protrude from each end when the bread is rolled. Beginning with that end, carefully roll up each sandwich and place each, seam side down, on a baking sheet or other flat surface. Chill, covered, for about an hour. When ready to serve, halve each roll crosswise.

 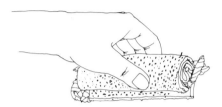

Note: I like to use the very thin Arnold or Pepperidge Farm breads for these sandwiches—mixing whole wheat and white on the platter—and maybe piling a few cherry tomatoes or even strawberries in the center for color.

LEMON BREAD

This bread makes a wonderful sweet-sour addition to almost any party menu.

MAKES 1 LOAF

1 cup sugar, plus scant ¼ cup for glaze
6 tablespoons shortening
Rind and juice of 1 lemon, reserving juice for glaze
2 eggs

1 ½ cups flour
½ teaspoon salt
1 teaspoon baking powder
½ cup milk
½ cup nuts, chopped

Cream 1 cup sugar and shortening in a medium size bowl. Add the lemon rind and beat in the eggs. Sift the flour, salt and baking powder together, and add alternately with the milk, beginning and ending with the flour. Stir in the nuts.

TO FINISH AND SERVE   PREHEAT OVEN TO 325°

Pour the batter into a small greased loaf pan and bake for 35 to 45 minutes, until done. Dissolve the scant ¼ cup sugar in the lemon juice and pour over the bread while still hot. Allow to cool in pan.

When cold, slice the bread and serve with sweet butter.

Notes: I like to test quick breads for doneness with a cake tester, which should come out clean, though you can usually tell easily without one: the top will crack slightly and the cake will pull away from the sides of the pan slightly. If you have trouble with bread sticking to sides of pan, line pan with greased aluminum foil.

APRICOT-PECAN BREAD

This is perhaps my favorite of all the quick breads I make. It is a little more work than some but worth it.

MAKES 18 TO 20 SLICES

1 ½ cups dried apricots
1 ½ cups boiling water
2 tablespoons butter
1 cup sugar
1 teaspoon salt
1 ½ cups pastry flour

1 teaspoon baking soda
1 cup whole wheat flour
1 cup pecans, chopped
1 egg, well beaten
1 teaspoon orange extract

TO PREPARE BATTER

Finely chop the apricots (this may be done by hand or in a food processor). Add the boiling water, butter, sugar and salt to the apricots and mix well. Sift together the pastry flour and baking soda and add to apricot mixture. To this, add the whole wheat flour, pecans, egg and orange extract, again mixing well.

TO BAKE AND SERVE   PREHEAT OVEN TO 350°

Pour batter into buttered 9-by-5-inch loaf pan. Allow to rest 20 minutes and then bake for 1 hour or until cake tester comes out clean. Cool on wire rack. Remove from tin, wrap in aluminum foil and store at least 24 hours (the longer the better) before slicing.

To serve, slice thin and use as is or for tea sandwiches.

CINNAMON STICKS

This recipe comes to me from Sarah Gannett, a Vermont friend and a most helpful resource for this section on teas.

TO MAKE 15 TO 20 STICKS

*3 to 4 slices 4- or 5-day-old white
   sandwich bread*
*½ cup cinnamon-sugar mixture (3
   parts sugar to 1 part cinnamon)*

*4 tablespoons melted butter, or more
   as needed*

First set out pastry brush and 3 flattish dishes: 1 for the bread, 1 for the cinnamon-sugar and 1 for the butter.

Trim crusts from bread (it's important that the bread be able to hold its shape). Then, holding 1 slice of bread at a time in the palm of your hand, brush both sides with butter. Working as you go and using kitchen scissors, cut each buttered slice into 4 or 5 strips, each between ½ and ¾ inch, setting them on the "bread" dish as finished. Spread each strip with more melted butter, dip into the cinnamon-sugar mixture and place on ungreased cookie sheet.

TO BAKE   **PREHEAT OVEN TO 350°**

When all strips are done, bake for 5 to 10 minutes, watching to be sure they aren't getting too brown, turn and bake on other side another 5 or so minutes —still watching.

Serve in lined basket.

STRAWBERRY CREAM TART

I don't have as elegant a strawberry tart as the Ritz-Carlton offers in my recipe box, but this one is very good and very pretty. Made as a single tart here, it could be made in individual shells as well, and to resemble the Ritz-Carlton tart more closely, could be laced with a little Creamy Chocolate Glaze (see page 344).

SERVES 8 TO 10 MODESTLY

*1 recipe Max's Pastry (see page
   402).*
2 pints top-quality strawberries
*2 to 3 tablespoons Grand Marnier,
   Cassis or other liqueur of choice*

*1 recipe Classic Soft Custard (see
   below)*
Soft Custard (see below)

TO PREPARE SHELL   **PREHEAT OVEN TO 450°**

Roll pastry to ⅛-inch thickness between layers of wax paper. Peel off top layer of paper. Invert pastry over 8- or 9-inch fluted flan pan with removable bottom. Peel off remaining sheet of wax paper and gently push pastry into bottom and against sides of pan. Using pastry roller or other tool over rim of flan cut pastry edges cleanly and remove excess. Prick pastry well and weight it with dry beans or pie beads. Then bake for 10 to 12 minutes and let cool completely.

TO FILL AND FINISH TART

While crust is cooling, prepare Classic Soft Custard. Then slice best of the strawberries lengthwise and toss gently in bowl with 2 tablespoons of the liqueur.

When ready, remove shell from pan, spoon the custard into the shell evenly, and arrange strawberries over the top in a pattern of your choice. Then melt the currant jelly with the remainder of the liqueur and brush thoroughly over the entire tart.

Serve as soon as possible. This tart has a happy life of 1 to 2 hours if kept well chilled. Kept any longer its crust is apt to become soggy.

Variations: Many other fruits work nicely for this tart—peaches, blueberries, kiwis, oranges, plums, etc. However, I like to vary the glaze with the fruit; for peaches and pears, the Apricot Glaze (see page 00) makes a nice match.

Classic Soft Custard

The custard may be made several days ahead.

AMPLE FOR AN 8- OR 9-INCH TART

2 cups light cream	*Pinch salt*
3 or 4 egg yolks, lightly beaten	*1 teaspoon vanilla or liqueur of*
¼ cup sugar	*choice (to match tart flavor)*

Scald cream in top of double boiler, slowing adding eggs, sugar and salt when cream is ready. Then place mixture over, *not in,* boiling water. Stir constantly until mixture begins to thicken. Remove from heat, continuing to stir to release heat. Add flavoring and chill.

Note: This custard will keep several weeks if chilled and tightly covered. It's always nice to have a little soft custard ready in the fridge.

DEVONSHIRE CREAM

This recipe was researched and updated by Jo Ann Gardner, a farm wife and guest house hostess from the Canadian Maritimes, and it first appeared in the May, 1983, issue of *Country Journal* magazine.

Two gallons of milk yield about 1½ quarts Devonshire Cream (or more, depending on the cow and her forage)

Using the morning milk (whole milk from a first milking; any good milker will do), strain it into a wide-mouthed pot. This type of pot allows the milk to heat more evenly. Let the pot sit, covered, at room temperature for about 12 hours in the winter or 6 in the summer. (If the weather is very warm, reduce the time somewhat.)

Then set the pot, uncovered, to heat on "low," or, in the winter, at the side of a woodburning stove, watching it carefully to be sure it doesn't boil. When the surface of the milk barely begins to wrinkle, or you notice small rings and undulations, remove the pot from the heat at once, cover it and refrigerate if possible. (Otherwise, place it in a very cool cellar for 12 hours, or until the cream has risen to the top. If the cellar temperature is not cold enough, the cream will be on the thin side, but it will thicken once refrigerated.) Skim off this cream with a large spoon and refrigerate.

Devonshire cream should be slightly tangy and thick enough to cut with a knife.

Note: This cream will keep about 2 weeks in the refrigerator and is delicious on berries all summer or slathered on blueberry pie and apple crisp as the summer tails off.

SPICY ICED TEA

I found this deliciously different iced tea in Beatrice Vaughan's *The Ladies' Aid Cookbook* some time ago and have been serving it ever since. Beatrice Vaughan, a fellow upcountry cook, is gone now but her fine Vermont country cooking lives on.

MAKES A GENEROUS 3 QUARTS

1 teaspoon whole cloves	⅔ cup bottled lemon juice
1½ quarts boiling water	1½ quarts cold water
6 tea bags of choice	Mint sprigs, if available
1 cup sugar	

Combine cloves and boiling water and simmer 5 minutes. Remove from heat and immediately add tea. Let stand until cool, then strain. Stir in sugar, being sure it is thoroughly dissolved. Then add lemon juice and cold water.

Serve over ice cubes with sprigs of mint.

7
ENTERTAINING THE VISITING FIREMAN

A Winter Welcome–Family Style
serves up to 10

WHITE WINE   SHERRY   HIGHBALLS

V-8 OR TOMATO JUICE

BABY HOT DOGS IN BLANKET

WATER CHESTNUTS IN BACON

PAPRIKA CHEESE ROLL OR
CHEESE & PISTACHIO ROLL

CORN CHOWDER OR
SOUTHERN BAKED CHICKEN

GARDEN CASSEROLE

HOT BISCUITS WITH HERBED BUTTER

TOMATO ASPIC OR TOSSED SALAD

APPLE CRISP
OR
LILLIAN'S CHEESE CAKE

WINE   BEER   COFFEE

An Alfresco Welcome à la Carte

serves up to 10

SESAME-CHEESE FINGERS

BROCCOLI BALLS

VEGETABLE PLATTER
WITH FETA WALNUT DIP

GAZPACHO OR CHICAGO CUCUMBER SOUP

BARBECUED FLANK STEAK
OR BARBECUED CHICKEN

BARBECUED ONIONS

COAL-ROASTED SWEET POTATOES
AND/OR
CORN ON THE COB

SLICED TOMATOES WITH BASIL
OR TOSSED LETTUCE SALAD

BLUEBERRY-APPLE TART

CHOCOLATE BROWNIES

WINE   COFFEE   BEER

A WINTER WELCOME—FAMILY STYLE

An almost unique characteristic of American hospitality that I've noticed on my travels is the custom of inviting the visiting business acquaintance or foreigner into one's home for the evening meal or overnight, and often on very short notice—a practice only rarely seen in other countries. Perhaps somewhat less done these days when so many people commute and so many families are two-worker families, this "home brew" hospitality is still a common practice. But it always poses the question: what to serve?

The answer, of course, depends on who is coming and also on just how much warning you have. It's important when planning this menu—since you likely will not know the guest well—to find out if there are any special foods to avoid for cultural, religious or health reasons. This is something whoever extends the invitation should try to ascertain beforehand.

But just as important, whatever the particulars of the menu, do plan that it be an "American" one, or in the case of an American visitor, one with a "regional" flavor. Your foreign visitor will welcome an opportunity to get a better idea of what American cooking is like as well as a chance to eat some excellent food, and the American visitor will enjoy becoming more familiar with food from another section of the country. Here in Vermont it's the rare visitor who doesn't have to sample our maple syrup in one form or another at some point.

The charm of a home visit is the opportunity it gives the visitor to see how one lives as an American, a Westerner, Southerner, or whatever. Remember that a well-placed bowl of flowers on the coffee table and candles in the dining room will focus attention—both on and away. Since various members of your household may have other activities already planned, the meal should be kept simple and available at a time convenient to all.

As I myself frequently tend to run a little late I always try to have the hors d'oeuvre ready and the drinks and ice on a tray (drinks, too, vary from culture to culture, but a simple choice will certainly suffice, with at least one juice on hand for nondrinkers). If you don't have time to prepare the hors d'oeuvre we're suggesting, Mrs. Rudkin of Pepperidge fame has saved us all with her Farm's selection of cocktail fishes. And don't forget: nuts, olives and other nibbles can come quickly out of the cupboard when you need them.

If you choose a fairly light main course, such as the corn chowder here, you may want to pad out the hors d'oeuvre a bit. One way to do this, if you have time to hard-cook and cool a few eggs, would be to offer a platter of deviled eggs (I've already discussed this in the vegetarian chapter). You can perk them up with a bit of curry powder or a dollop of lumpfish or red caviar if you happen to have a jar handy. To accompany the Southern Baked Chicken, I've suggested the Zucchini Casserole.

Although I am suggesting the very American Apple Crisp, or perhaps the very special Lillian's Cheese Cake, for this menu's dessert, by all means vary this with your own favorite apple, or other, dessert—or with Mrs. Smith's also Very American apple pie from your grocer's freezer if need be. The idea, whether for the winter or the summer menu, being that you combine a fairly simple and typical American, or regional, dinner with a few special additions. The impromptu invitation is a reflection of the informal, yet gracious, atmosphere of your home and this meal requires no apologies for its simplicity. The important thing is that you not feel pressed so you can fully enjoy your guest and make him or her feel truly at home.

BABY HOT DOGS IN BLANKET

Depending on the number to be fed, buy 1 or 2 packages of the little beef cocktail "dogs"; the canned ones are permissible, but to my taste second best. Then dress them up in coverlets made from the prepared Pepperidge Farm or Pillsbury Bakery crescent roll dough, usually kept in the grocer's dairy case (again, 1 or 2 packages). This is easy: simply roll the individual dough pieces out very thin and cut to fit the baby hot dogs with just a little excess. Brush one side of the pastry with mustard, put a baby frank on top and roll up, sticking the pastry tails together with a little water. Brush each roll with melted butter and bake at 375° until brown.

Serve with hoisin or barbecue sauce or a favorite of your own.

Note: These rolls can be made ahead and frozen (Freeze before cooking). If frozen, put the rolls directly in the preheated oven upon taking from freezer. Give the "dogs" a chance to warm through and the pastry a chance to puff up (this usually takes about 10 minutes).

WATER CHESTNUTS IN BACON

This recipe is a revision of one from Marjorie Hamilton, a cookbook author in her own right.

MAKES 24 ROLLS

8 strips bacon
1 (8-ounce) can whole water
  chestnuts

¼ cup soy sauce
¼ cup molasses

Partially cook bacon strips; they should be no more than halfway done. Drain excess fat, cut in thirds and wrap each piece around a water chestnut, securing with a toothpick.

Combine soy sauce and molasses, and marinate wrapped chestnuts for several hours.

TO BROIL AND SERVE   PREHEAT BROILER TO 375°

When ready to serve, drain and place on broiler rack in oven. Broil about 10 minutes, or until bacon is crisp.

Serve warm, perhaps over a candle warmer or on a hot tray.

Variation: Bacon can be wrapped around a piece of chicken liver and a water chestnut in the same way. Prepare bacon as above, wrap and marinate (in soy sauce and sherry) and broil in same fashion. The Japanese call this *rumaki.*

PAPRIKA CHEESE ROLL

One of the first hors d'oeuvre I learned to make—taught to me by my oldest sister. If you are feeling fancier, search out the Pistachio & Cheese Roll that follows.

20 PORTIONS

1 (8-ounce) package cream cheese
1 (8-ounce) package wine Cheddar
  cheese

1 clove garlic, crushed
Several spoonfuls paprika

Soften both cheeses and mix well in a bowl with the crushed garlic. Refrigerate until workable. Then spread ample paprika to cover a 5- to 6-inch roll on a good-sized sheet of wax paper. Shape the cheese into two rolls and roll in the paprika until well covered, shaking off any extra. Wrap cheese rolls in wax paper and refrigerate until needed. These rolls will keep chilled for a week.

Serve with slices of party rye or dark pumpernickel.

Note: Be sure to spread the paprika on the wax paper before you begin to roll the cheese. Once your hands start working with the cheese everything else becomes untouchable.

CHEESE & PISTACHIO ROLL

Even though I have more than once sworn I would never do anything to Brie but serve it plain, I have served this and it is delicious.

20 OR MORE PORTIONS

½ pound Brie
½ pound Gorgonzola cheese
1 tablespoon heavy cream

¾ cup coarsely chopped pistachio nuts

TO PREPARE

Trim off and discard the rind from both cheeses. Let each come to room temperature and cut into 1-inch cubes. Place in a blender or food processor with the cream and blend until smooth. Transfer to a mixing bowl and refrigerate until manageable. Shape the chilled cheese mixture into a round loaf and roll it in the chopped nuts until coated on all sides. Roll nutted loaf in wax paper and refrigerate until needed. Allow to soften slightly before serving and serve with breads or crackers.

Note: Although for this party you will probably need only ½ the above recipe, why not make the whole amount and save what you don't need for another party. It will keep in the refrigerator for several weeks and can be frozen for up to 2 months.

CORN CHOWDER

It's hard to imagine anything much more American than corn chowder and this is a very good one.

S E R V E S 8

6 *largish potatoes, peeled and diced*
4 *medium onions, finely chopped*
2 *cups chopped celery*
½ *pound bacon, cut into ¼-inch bits*
4 *tablespoons butter*
1 *cup heavy cream*
3 *cups milk*

2 *(16-ounce) cans corn niblets, with juice, or fresh*
6 *to 8 tablespoons chopped parsley*
Salt and freshly ground pepper, to taste
Several dashes paprika, for color and taste
8 *pats butter, for topping*

Cook the potatoes and half of the chopped onions in lightly salted water. Drain well. Do the same with the celery. Put in separate bowls and set in oven to keep warm. Fry the bacon, pouring off half the fat when partly cooked; add the remaining onions and brown lightly. When browned, this mixture should also wait in the oven.

Put the butter in the top of a double-boiler immersed in an inch or so of boiling water. When the butter is melted, pour in the cream and two cups of the milk. Purée half the diced potato mixture with the remaining cup of milk and add to the heating cream and milk. When this is piping hot, add the corn and cook 3 or 4 minutes (if fresh corn is used this would take at least twice that). Then put in the remaining potatoes, celery, bacon-onion mixture and parsley, keeping the chowder over the heat as you work. Season with the salt and pepper. Mix well and serve in well-heated bowls (if possible), sprinkling each bowlful lightly with paprika and topping each with a generous pat of butter.

SOUTHERN BAKED CHICKEN

When our children were all in school and I returned to work part time, we had a marvelous housekeeper, Miss Lizzie. She brought many wonderful qualities with her: good solid rules of behavior, an abiding faith in God and a talent for cooking. She came from Virginia, and loved to adapt her old southern recipes to the New England palate. One was her way of cooking chicken. This is it.

Take 2 or 3 cut chickens, wet wipe and dry the individual pieces, sprinkle with salt, paprika and a whisper of flour and place in a wide baking pan. Pour in ½ cup of Vermouth and bake in a preheated 350° oven for about 1 hour. If the chicken didn't brown to her liking, she brushed it with a little oil or butter. The slow cooking time drew out the chicken fat and left a lovely, crisp brown chicken.

ZUCCHINI CASSEROLE

This is a quick and easy vegetable dish and just the right size for a family supper like this. You can use half-squash, half-zucchini if you want.

MAKES ABOUT 8 SERVINGS

6 or so small fresh squash, about 6 to 11" long, or an equal amount of zucchini or combination of the 2

2 or 3 onions, sliced (the ratio of onions to squash should be about 1 to 3)

1 or 2 tablespoons fresh marjoram or 1 to 2 teaspoons dried

Salt and pepper to taste

4 or 5 pats of butter, for top

⅛ cup or so grated Parmesan or Cheddar cheese, to sprinkle on top

Wash the squash or zucchini thoroughly; top and tail. Slice the remains into ¼-inch slices and drain if there is too much liquid.

Butter a medium-sized casserole and fill with alternating layers of squash or zucchini and onion, ending with the squash layer and sprinkling each layer with some of the marjoram and seasonings.

TO BAKE   PREHEAT OVEN TO 350°

Top the casserole with a few small pats of butter and sprinkle with cheese (I prefer Parmesan but Cheddar is fine). Cover and bake for 30 minutes or so, a little less if vegetables are fresh from the garden.

Don't worry if other dishes are cooking in the oven: squash and zucchini are very accommodating, a few degrees one way or the other won't matter; just don't overcook.

HOT BISCUITS WITH HERBED BUTTER

These biscuits are snow white and 2 inches high. The Herbed Butter is a nice addition.

MAKES 14 TO 16, VARYING WITH CUTTER SIZE

2 cups flour
3 teaspoons baking powder
½ teaspoon salt

4 to 6 tablespoons butter
½ to ¾ cup milk

Mix flour, baking powder and salt. Cut butter into mixture until finely crumbed (I prefer to use my fingers). Make a well and add milk, as needed, to make soft dough, stirring lightly only to incorporate liquid. Turn dough onto lightly floured surface and knead gently with heel of hand (no more than 10 times). Roll or pat dough out to about ¾-inch thickness. With lightly floured cutter or glass, cut out biscuits about 2 inches in diameter (cut straight down; do not twist) and place on lightly greased cookie sheet.

TO BAKE AND SERVE   PREHEAT OVEN TO 425°

Brush biscuit tops lightly with milk and bake 10 to 12 minutes or until risen and lightly browned.
    Serve with Herbed Butter.

Herbed Butter

Mix 1 stick softened butter with ½ teaspoon dried thyme and ½ teaspoon marjoram, dill weed or dried calendula petals—or your own mix. Serve in little butter pots.

TOMATO ASPIC

This aspic is another favorite from Helene Druhl. The vegetables chosen can of course vary with the season, but Helene usually includes carrots and celery with some green pepper and a little onion, and a nicely sliced avocado tucked in at the very end.

SERVES 6 TO 8

1 package lemon Jell-o
1 cup boiling water
1½ cups V-8 juice
2 to 3 cups assorted vegetables,
  finely chopped

Cherry tomatoes, cucumber, broccoli,
radishes, for garnish, if desired

Dissolve the Jell-o in the boiling water, stirring until thoroughly dissolved. Add the V-8 juice and vegetables. Then set in the fridge to firm.

To serve, unmold onto a bed of coarsely shredded lettuce with a dressing (or several) of choice nearby. (Helene prefers one made by blending horseradish to taste with 1 cup of mayonnaise.) If your mold is ring-shaped, the center can be filled with cherry tomatoes, or perhaps with cucumber chunks or radish or broccoli buds.

Note: Plain gelatin may be used in place of the lemon Jell-o, following the directions on the package to soften, and perhaps adding a little lemon juice to taste.

APPLE CRISP

There are few desserts more American than this. With good apples it's also one of the very best.

MAKES 6 OR SO SERVINGS

3 pounds tart cooking apples (7 or 8 large), peeled, cored and sliced

1 stick (8 tablespoons) butter, plus 2 to 3 tablespoons

1 to 2 tablespoons lemon juice, to taste

1 teaspoon grated lemon rind, to taste

1 cup flour, or ¾ cup flour and ¼ cup regular oatmeal

1 cup brown sugar, or less to taste

½ teaspoon salt, if using sweet butter

1 teaspoon cinnamon

½ teaspoon nutmeg

Light or whipping cream, for topping (optional)

Place sliced apples in 7-by-7-inch pan. Dot with 2 to 3 tablespoons butter (if apples are moist you won't need as much); sprinkle with lemon juice and rind (less if apples are very tart); set aside.

Work remaining butter, flour, brown sugar, salt (if needed), and spices together like pastry (work lightly so mixture doesn't become oily). Spread mixture over apples (topping may crumble).

TO BAKE AND SERVE   PREHEAT OVEN TO 375°

Bake about 30 minutes, or until apples are done. Serve plain, with cream, with lightly sweetened whipped cream, or with a tasty hard sauce.

Note: The apples can be quickly sliced using a food processor with the slicing disk and the topping quickly mixed with the regular blade.

Variation: If you want to expand this recipe a bit, 3 to 4 cups sweetened rhubarb or pitted cherries may be added before the pastry topping goes on, and I often add about 2 tablespoons brandy.

LILLIAN'S CHEESE CAKE

This delicious cheese cake came to me from Lillian Zilliacus. It was served for a number of years at The Hermitage, a restaurant in Dover, Vermont, which she and her husband ran, and came originally, Lillian tells me, from still another restaurateur. It makes a lovely full-sized dessert cake but it also works well halved to make two shallower cakes for the "must" sweet at cocktail-type parties.

MAKES 1 DEEP OR 2 SHALLOW CAKES, OR UP TO 20 OR SO SLENDER SLICES

5 egg whites
1 cup sugar, plus 2 tablespoons
3 (8-ounce) packages cream cheese, at room temperature
3 teaspoons vanilla
Butter, to grease pan(s)

½ cup finely rolled graham cracker crumbs, more or less
1 pint sour cream
¼ cup slivered or grated almonds (½ cup for two-cake version)

Using electric mixer beat egg whites until stiff. Gradually add 1 cup sugar while continuing to beat, being sure well blended. Add cream cheese, broken in pieces, then 2 teaspoons vanilla. Again, beat until well blended.

TO BAKE **PREHEAT OVEN TO 350°**

Lavishly butter 8- or 9-inch spring form pan (for 1 cake), or 2 removable-bottom sponge cake pans (for 2 cakes), and sprinkle lightly with graham cracker crumbs. Fill with cream cheese mixture and bake 35 to 45 minutes or until center rises. (Cake(s) will not show real color change.) Raise oven temperature to 450°. Top cake, or cakes, with mixture of sour cream blended with 2 tablespoons sugar and 1 teaspoon vanilla. Sprinkle almonds over top(s) and return to oven for 10 minutes or so to set.

Cool cake(s) on rack before removing from pan(s) and refrigerate overnight if possible.

Serve as is for a supper dessert or add a little fresh or frozen fruit; for a party sweet, slice thin.

Note: I usually use Philadelphia or Borden's cream cheese to make my cheese cakes, though I have made them very successfully with bulk cream cheese purchased at our local food co-op.

AN ALFRESCO WELCOME

The summer version of our visiting fireman menu moves outdoors to the barbecue. Surely there's nothing more American than a barbecue. Barbecuing has become an integral part of the American life style: these days even at the farmhouse door one sees a Weber Bar-B-Q-Kettle. This type of cooking has greatly enlarged the variety of summer foods and encouraged alfresco dining. And even if it rains, the cooking can be done in a sheltered spot, with the eating transported indoors.

There are many ways of barbecuing—from the open pit to the hibachi to the kettle; and many kinds of fuel to choose from—wood, charcoal, briquets, and even gas.

Today many barbecue models have the ability to open and close the drafts and even to raise and lower the cooking surface, and some have covers so they can be used like an oven. But whatever you have—old or new, plain or fancy —the important thing is that your barbecue chef thoroughly know its operating quirks and requirements. If yours is new, it's wise to practice a bit before inviting guests.

For this menu I suggest an alfresco à la carte. The recipes are either found in this chapter or through the index, though I leave the green salad to you. By all means substitute your own favorites, remembering of course to balance the flavors, colors and textures as always, and again to select American or regional dishes as much as possible. There are several excellent barbecue books on the market to help you with your choices: I especially like the Betty Crocker *Outdoor Cookbook* and one that *Sunset* magazine publishes.

And don't forget: it's far more fun for all if you are free to have a good visit with your visitor rather than spend most of your time in the kitchen.

SESAME-CHEESE FINGERS

These are delicately flavored pastries similar to those found in some shops. If you have an adventurous palate you can almost double the spices.

MAKES ABOUT 60

1 cup flour
½ teaspoon salt
1/16 teaspoon cayenne
½ teaspoon dry mustard
½ teaspoon ground ginger
½ teaspoon sugar
½ cup sharp Cheddar cheese, grated

⅓ cup sesame seeds, toasted (see Note below)
1 large egg, lightly beaten
6 tablespoons butter or margarine, softened
1 tablespoon water

First mix the 6 dry ingredients. Add the cheese and toasted sesame seeds. Combine the remaining ingredients, add to first mixture and stir. Form dough into ball, wrap in wax paper and chill for several hours (the dough can be chilled overnight but allow time for it to soften a bit before rolling out and baking).

TO ROLL AND BAKE   PREHEAT OVEN TO 350°

On a lightly floured board roll dough out to ⅛-inch thickness. Cut into strips about ¾ by 2 inches and place on ungreased baking sheets. Bake for 15 minutes or until brown. When cool store in air-tight tin. Any leftovers will keep well frozen.

Note: To toast sesame seeds, use a shallow baking pan or cookie sheet to heat the seeds in a 350° oven for about 20 minutes, stirring occasionally to ensure even toasting. Watch them carefully: they seem to take forever and then presto are done.

BROCCOLI BALLS

Fortunately not many party-goers would agree with Roy Blount, Jr. when he opined: "The local groceries are all out of broccoli . . . Loccoli." My thanks to Linda Clews for this recipe.

MAKES 20 TO 24 BALLS

10 tablespoons margarine or butter, melted
6 eggs, lightly beaten
½ teaspoon pepper
¼ teaspoon salt or Seasonall

2 to 3 cups herbed stuffing
1 cup grated Parmesan cheese
2 (10-ounce) packages frozen broccoli, thawed, drained and chopped well

Mix all ingredients together thoroughly and shape into balls about the size of a walnut.

TO BAKE   PREHEAT OVEN TO 350°

Place balls on a lightly greased baking sheet and bake for 20 to 25 minutes, until lightly browned. If excess grease runs off the balls, tip or dab this away to keep balls light and nonsticky.

Note: I use Pepperidge Farm herbed stuffing, but your own favorite is fine.

GAZPACHO

This is an excellent way to use extra summer garden produce—and it's good too. Modify it freely to suit your own garden. For outdoor parties, I like to serve it in mugs.

MAKES ABOUT 2 QUARTS

2 pounds very ripe fresh tomatoes, seeded and finely chopped
1 large green pepper, seeded and finely chopped
1 small cucumber, peeled, seeded and finely chopped
1 red onion, peeled and finely chopped
1 clove garlic, peeled and finely chopped

Small bunch fresh summer savory, finely chopped
Small bunch fresh oregano, finely chopped
¼ cup red wine vinegar
½ teaspoon sugar, or more to taste
2 cups water or tomato juice
¼ cup olive oil
Salt and pepper to taste

Combine all ingredients, blending well.

Chill well, overnight if possible, and serve in chilled mugs or bowls, garnishing with finely chopped, seeded and peeled cucumber, green pepper, tomatoes or other vegetables of choice—and croutons.

CHICAGO CUCUMBER SOUP

The ingredients for this fine cucumber soup may be altered to expand both its quantity and its flavor. The fresh dill is the most important herb in this version and we love it. But if you and your guests prefer another, feature that.

SERVES 8 TO 10

4 tablespoons butter, melted
4 tablespoons flour
2 cups chicken broth
4 cups peeled, sliced and seeded
 cucumbers
½ cup finely chopped celery leaves

½ cup chopped chives
2 sprigs fresh dill, or ½ teaspoon
 dried dillweed
2 cups light cream
Salt and pepper to taste
Chopped dill, for garnish

Mix the butter and flour thoroughly and add to the chicken broth, stirring well. Add cucumbers, celery, chives and dill, and bring to a boil. (If store-bought cucumbers are used, simmer the peeled slices 10 minutes in chicken broth before adding other ingredients; garden-fresh cucumbers are fine just as is.) Remove from heat and gradually stir in cream and salt and pepper to taste.

Serve well chilled with a side dish of chopped dill for those who want more.

PREPARING THE BARBECUE

The preliminary planning. Meats under 2 inches thick can be cooked on a hibachi; thicker meats and vegetables require a larger grill. What you have will determine when you have to start your fire and whether or not you can manage with a single grill (if you only have more than one, don't worry: you can always do one or more of the dishes inside). For this menu, if you serve the roasted sweet potatoes, you'll need hot coals about 1 hour ahead; chicken takes about the same time and onions almost. The corn and flank steak require considerably less lead time.

Lighting the fire. Be sure to start early. If you use briquets, be sure they are dry (briquets absorb water); they should be stored indoors to prevent their getting damp. Be wary of the liquid fire starter: it is dangerous and can flavor the food. Electric fire starters work well, but are not necessary. Once well lit, sprinkle old herbs over the coals; they add flavor and a wonderful aroma.

Cooking the flank steak. First marinate steak in Teriyaki Sauce (see page 394) for several hours, trimming away excess fat (to help eliminate splattering from the coals) and slashing steak edges. When coals and you are ready, grill about 3 to 4 inches above hot coals until done to your liking.

Barbecuing the chicken. Unless you use a prepared barbecue sauce, first make up about 1 cup of your favorite. When ready, place basted chicken pieces bone side down on grill about 5 inches from medium-hot coals. Cook 20 to 30 minutes, then turn and baste with hot barbecue sauce and continue to cook another 30 minutes or so, watching carefully so that chicken doesn't burn. It is done when the juices at the joints run clear. If you are using a covered grill, the cooking will take less time.

Roasting the onions. Wash 1 large onion of uniform size for each guest. Put directly on low coals or on grill 3 to 4 inches above coals. Cook, turning occasionally, 30 to 45 minutes or until tender. To serve, squeeze roasted onions; the yellow hearts will "pop" out ready to eat.

Roasting the sweet potatoes. Choose one medium-sized potato for each guest, scrub well and rub with salad oil or butter. Wrap each potato in heavy-duty foil and roast on medium-hot coals 45 to 60 minutes, or on grill about 1 hour. The potatoes are done when a fork will pierce potatoes easily.

Potatoes may also be placed directly on the coals to roast, after scrubbing. This method takes about 45 minutes and allows only the potato innards to be eaten.

Roasting corn on the cob. To grill over the coals, remove outer husks, turn back inner husks and remove silk. Spread corn with soft butter, replace inner husks, binding with fine wire. Roast about 3 inches from coals 15 to 20 minutes, turning often.

To roast on coals, again remove outer husks, turn back inner husks and remove silk. Butter corn and replace inner husks. Wrap well in foil and roast on coals 10 to 15 minutes, turning at least once.

BLUEBERRY-APPLE TART

I put this custard-less fruit tart together quite by accident one day but we all liked it so much, I share it with you here. Almost any combination of fruits can be used and a currant jelly glaze substituted for a change. But always check the sweetness of the fruit you're using. If it's a little tart, you'll need a little more sugar; if it's on the sweet side, a little less.

SERVES 6 TO 8

1 (9-inch) tart shell, unbaked (see page 00)
1 egg yolk, beaten
2 tablespoons Cassis or other fruit liqueur
1 pint blueberries, washed and drained
3 large Cortland, Northern Spy or any firm cooking apples, peeled, cored and thinly sliced

Juice of 1 lemon (about 2 tablespoons)
½ to ¾ cup sugar, more or less to taste
1 teaspoon cinnamon
2 tablespoons flour
Pinch salt
Apricot Glaze (see below)

TO PREPARE SHELL   **PREHEAT OVEN TO 425°**

Sprinkle chilled shell with enough grains of rice or dried beans to cover bottom; this keeps pastry flat. Place shell in oven for about 8 minutes; take shell from oven, remove rice or beans, then brush with egg yolk. Return to oven for another 2 minutes; remove and cool.

TO PREPARE FRUIT AND GLAZE

In medium-sized bowl, combine liqueur with blueberries and set aside to marinate for 20 to 30 minutes.

Meanwhile, in separate bowl, sprinkle prepared apples with lemon juice. Gently add in sugar, cinnamon, flour and salt, combining well.

Make Apricot Glaze, following recipe below.

TO FILL AND BAKE   **REDUCE OVEN TO 375°**

Fill partially baked shell with marinated blueberries. Then ring outer edge of filled tart with prepared apples. Finally, brush liberally with warm Apricot Glaze and bake 30 minutes or so until apples are soft but not mushy.

Cool and serve as soon as possible.

Apricot Glaze

This glaze not only adds a little extra sweetness, it gives the tart a lovely sheen.

MAKES AMPLE FOR 9-INCH TART

1 cup apricot jam, sieved
2 to 4 tablespoons Cognac,
applejack or other liqueur

In saucepan, combine jam with liqueur and heat until boiling. Remove from heat and spoon over tart while still warm.

Note: I like to use the midget Mouli grater to sieve the jam for this glaze. It is much easier to use and to clean than a sieve.

CHOCOLATE BROWNIES·

Of all the chocolate brownies I have made these are my favorite. Beyond that, if you cut them fairly small, they go a long way.

MAKES UP TO 54 BARS

4 ounces unsweetened chocolate
1 stick (8 tablespoons) butter
4 eggs
¼ teaspoon salt

2 cups sugar, sifted
1 teaspoon vanilla
1 cup flour, sifted
1 cup nut meats, coarsely chopped

Melt chocolate and butter together in double boiler and set aside to cool. Beat the eggs and salt together until light. Gradually add the sugar and continue to beat until light and creamy. Fold in chocolate mixture and vanilla. Add flour and beat just until smooth. Fold in nuts.

Foil line and grease 9-by-13-inch baking pan (use unsalted shortening). Pour in batter.

TO BAKE AND SERVE   PREHEAT OVEN TO 325°

Bake for about 30 minutes or until cake tester comes out clean. When completely cooled, cut into small squares or oblong bars. If freezing, leave whole and cut into pieces as needed.

8

FOR PARENTS
AT A CHILDREN'S PARTY

A party for 12 to 16 kibitzers

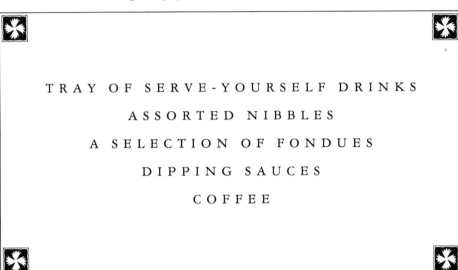

TRAY OF SERVE-YOURSELF DRINKS

ASSORTED NIBBLES

A SELECTION OF FONDUES

DIPPING SAUCES

COFFEE

FOR PARENTS AT A
CHILDREN'S PARTY

W̲hen children are quite young—and party time comes along—a short
bit of game playing, a little ice cream, a quick piece of cake and off
home they go again. Then, if any parents are on hand to either pick up or
watch for a while, a tray of drinks and a few well-chosen nibbles set out ahead
will suffice. But, as the children get older and the parties run a little longer
—sometimes including a makeup free-for-all, puppet show, scavenger hunt or
other lively nonsense—their parents, too, may be on hand for a while: some
may even *want* to be invited to watch the shenanigans. For this linger-longer
party you'll want to offer a little more substantial adult fare.

This party and its menu would also work well for the neighborhood family
party one has from time to time as the years go by—informal but fun for all
ages. I think immediately of the Easter Sunday egg hunts our family used to
plan after church each Easter morning. Children of all ages would hunt the
eggs we had tucked here and there around our yard and along the brook while
the parents watched, chatted and partook of the informal party food and drink
we had put out. Other families might plan a Halloween costume and dunk-for-
apples do or perhaps an annual Christmas trim-the-tree party, and I know
another family—the father a frustrated thespian if truth were known—that
gathered whatever neighbors they could at Christmas time each year for an
animated rendering of Dickens' *A Christmas Carol.*

So this is meant as a party where the central focus is on fun for the children
but where the hosts and guests of all ages enjoy themselves too. I leave the
children's refreshments to you (obviously they would be dictated by the
occasion, the season and the numbers) and turn my attention to the adult
menu—something tasty and fun, but something that can be prepared ahead
and that, for the most part, the guests can tend to for themselves. I like the
idea of fondue for this: it's light and a little different—and can be set out ready
to go with only a little care from the hostess and not too much from the guests.

To organize this parents' linger-awhile fondue party, you will want to
prepare the fondue ahead. Then shortly before you become too busy to think

about anything else, set out a tray of glasses, a bottle of sherry, some chilled wine and whatever liquor you wish to offer, along with a bucket of ice, tongs, mixers, soft drinks and openers—and finally, the fondue and its accouterments. As long as you have arranged for a fireproof tray, a strong stand and a secure method of controlling the cooking oil's heat, this is a relatively trouble-free way to feed an elastic number of guests quickly and painlessly. An electric fondue pot is a godsend, as the sterno burners work well but require closer watching. Long wooden-handled forks are essential for spearing and cooking the meat and you'll want lots of napkins and a good thick potholder handy, as well as bowls for the dipping sauces.

The essence of this fondue menu is advance preparation and easy service allowing the hosts to keep the "little" guests busy and the "big" guests happy.

NUTS AND BOLTS

Any of your favorite nibbles will serve well as the opener for this party—these are a perennial favorite. The recipe came to me from Priscilla Richardson, who has made nuts and bolts as one of her Christmas offerings for years.

4 ½ TO 5 POUNDS

2 cups salad oil
2 tablespoons Worcestershire sauce
1 tablespoon garlic salt
1 tablespoon seasoned salt
2 pounds salted peanuts

1 (12-ounce) box Wheat Chex
1 (6½-ounce) box Rice Chex
1 (10-ounce) box Cheerios
1 (12-ounce) box thin pretzel sticks

Combine the salad oil, Worcestershire sauce, garlic salt and seasoned salt, and mix well. In a large roasting pan, pour the oil mixture over the combined cereals, nuts and pretzels, again mixing well.

Roast in a 250° oven for about 2 hours, stirring every 15 minutes or so.

To store, drain well on paper toweling and put in airtight containers until ready to use—or give away.

PREPARING THE FONDUE

Oil for fondue. The oil can be either vegetable or peanut oil. The pot should be filled at least 2 inches deep and not more than ½ full. For both beef and chicken fondue, the oil should be brought to 425° (if using an electric pot, this is simple—and preferable for a casual party). Keep a salt cellar handy: an occasional sprinkling of salt helps keep the fat from splattering.

For beef fondue. The meat should be at room temperature and cut into ¾-inch cubes. Allow between ⅓ and ½ pound per person. Cook the beef about 15 seconds for rare and about 1 minute for well-done.

For chicken fondue. Cut the meat into 1-inch pieces and marinate for several hours in Teriyaki Sauce (see page 394) or another of your own choice. Bring meat back to room temperature, and cook between 2 and 3 minutes.

Seafood and vegetable fondue. Some seafood and bite-sized vegetables may also be used for fondue. A lower, 375° temperature is required (difficult for this particular party if also serving beef and chicken). The vegetables are usually predipped in an egg and crumb batter. Crabs, oysters and scallops do not work well as they cook too quickly.

Sauces for fondue. The range of sauces for fondue is wide. You might try a hoisin, or Herbed Cream Cheese, or the spicy Gado Gado for the beef; and perhaps the Bernaise or Orange-Almond for the chicken.

9
WHEN TEENAGERS GET TOGETHER

A party for 20 to 30

SANGRIA-STYLE FRUIT PUNCH

CHILI CON QUESO WITH NACHOS

PENNSYLVANIA DUTCH-STYLE
POTATO CHIPS
WITH
GUACAMOLE AND BLUE CHEESE DIP

TACOS AND FIXINGS

FRUIT SALAD MELON BASKET

MAKE-YOUR-OWN SUNDAES

MILK   SOFT DRINKS   COFFEE

WHEN TEENAGERS GET TOGETHER

Perhaps most important of all for this teenage party is that the young—both host and guests—be involved in its planning and menu. Since Tex-Mex is very popular and a lot of fun, I am suggesting a taco party. A great pot of chili set in the midst of bowls of cheese, chopped mushrooms, onions and sour cream is one idea; a pile of enchiladas rolled around chicken, pork or other meat fillings, and baked—with a choice of sauces—another. A look at one of the several excellent books on Mexican cooking will give your particular young people even more ideas. I especially like Diana Kennedy and *Good Food from Mexico,* by Ruth Watt Mulvery and Luisa Maria Alvarez, and have found the more recent *Cooking Texas Style,* by sisters Candy Wagner and Sandra Marquez, very helpful. On the other hand—if Tex-Mex is not on your neighborhood's Top Ten—there's always pizza.

Along with deciding the theme, do encourage your young people to help plan the menu details, as well as the decorations, games, music for dancing, or whatever activity your party will focus around. They might even want to do some of the shopping and cooking.

Once the theme and menu are decided—and second only to good overall organization—the most essential element for any young people's party must be a mammoth supply of soft drinks, both "lite" and "regular."

In addition to plenty of chilled soft drinks, you might want to offer a sangria punch. The recipe here includes an optional amount of wine, which will add flavor with very little "punch."

The Chili con Queso, which I've suggested as one of the "befores," is a little different and can be made on the mild side if you think the youngsters might not relish its native zip (you'll find the recipe for this on page 81 in the winter vegetarian party, along with that for the Nachos). It can be made ahead and kept warm in a chafing dish or in the top of a double boiler. A bowlful of the Pennsylvania Dutch-style potato chips makes a nice change if you can find them. These chips, from Pennsylvania Dutch country, are made with lard and are less salty. They also hold together well for dipping. You may wish to add other dips—Tex-Mex or otherwise (there are a number to choose from in the index).

The "main event" for this party meal will be your basket of taco shells surrounded by taco fillings and toppings in individual serving bowls. The taco shells can be one of the very good already-made brands available at most markets or you can start from scratch if you like, using the Taco Shells recipe that follows. For the fixings you will want shredded lettuce and cheese, chopped peppers, onions and tomatoes, sliced mushrooms and olives and a large bowl of Beef Taco Filling or hamburger meat gently sautéed with a bit of onion. The sauce can be one of the several ready-made varieties or the Salsa Picante or Hot Sauce following (or one from the Dips section at the back of the book). Why not offer both a "hot" and a "not-so-hot" version to cover all taste buds?

A bowl of fresh fruit will lend a cooling balance to this fairly "hot" menu. Try the Fruit Salad Melon Basket here: not only is it refreshing, the kids would enjoy making it. Then, to top things off, Make-Your-Own Sundaes— with a variety of ice creams, sauces, nuts, etc. And, if a special occasion calls for it, a decorated cake. You'll find recipes for several ice creams and sherbets to try—and cakes, too—in the index.

Other things you'll need for this party are ample gay paper plates, cups, napkins and bowls. I also like to use the woven basket plate-trays.

No doubt your young people will have the decorations and entertainment well in hand but urge them to plan outlets to absorb at least some of the high spirits that go hand in hand with most teenage gatherings. The party might be geared around a special occasion or school event, or perhaps dancing, skating, or a softball or other sports game. Such activities help make social mixing easier and allow the still-shy young person a chance to shine at something. And so, we're back full circle to the most important thing of all for this teenage party: that the young people involved participate and have fun!

SANGRIA-STYLE FRUIT PUNCH

For this refreshing sangria-type punch, the wine is optional and the proportion way down.

SERVES 30 OR SO

2 bottles dry red wine, or cranberry or cranapple juice

2 quarts fresh or frozen orange juice

2 cups fresh or reconstituted lime juice

2 cups fresh or reconstituted lemon juice

1 cup sugar, or more to taste

3 to 4 quarts sparkling water, to taste

Orange slices, for garnish

Combine all but the sparkling water and orange slices, cover and chill. Just before serving, stir in the sparkling water, pour into your punch bowl over a solid block of ice and garnish with the orange slices.

Note: If you choose to serve this punch full strength, the wine should be doubled to 4 bottles and the sparkling water cut to 2 quarts. If fresh lime and lemon juice is a problem, you can use the small cans of frozen lime and lemonades but with considerably less sugar and the greater amount of sparkling water. Taste to be sure you have the mix you want.

GUACAMOLE

There are most likely as many Guacamole recipes as there are avocados but this one makes a very pleasant dip.

ENOUGH TO SERVE 25

2 ripe medium-large avocados, mashed
4 tablespoons lemon juice
2 to 3 cloves garlic, crushed
½ teaspoon salt, or to taste
Chili powder to taste
Freshly ground black pepper to taste
4 to 6 tablespoons plain yogurt, sour cream or mayonnaise

Optional additions (one, more or all):
1 green or red pepper, minced
1 small red onion, finely minced
1 small cucumber, chopped
1 hard-cooked egg, chopped
1 medium tomato, diced
½ cup olives, chopped

Mix all together well, and chill. Serve with tortilla chips, corn chips or crispy pita bread triangles.

BLUE CHEESE DIP

MAKES ABOUT 1½ CUPS

¼ pound blue cheese
¼ pound cream cheese (½ large package)
3 tablespoons dry vermouth, or 2 tablespoons lemon juice

1 small clove garlic, mashed or minced
Sour cream, to thin (¼ cup or so)

Bring blue cheese and cream cheese to room temperature. Combine first 4 ingredients, blending well. Add enough sour cream to make dip thin enough for dunking potato chips.

TACO SHELLS

Taco shells are corn or flour tortillas fried in a U-shape. You have several ways to arrive at this end.

Prefried shells are available already packaged in most markets. They should be heated before serving.

Flat, baked tortillas, not yet fried, are also available packaged. These flat tortillas will need to be fried and shaped.

Or, you can *start from scratch* by making your own tortillas (see recipes for making Corn Tortillas on page 47 or Flour Tortillas on page 48).

TO PREPARE UNFRIED SHELLS

Heat ½ inch oil in small skillet. Using tongs immerse half of tortilla in hot oil and fry just until crisp. Roll the other half into oil and fry.

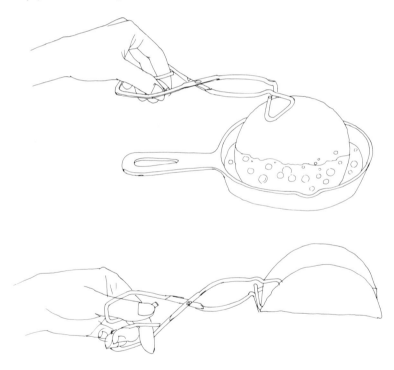

Use tongs to hold top edges of fried tortilla apart to make a 1- to 1½-inch opening at the top of the U. Set on paper toweling to drain and dry.

TO SERVE

Transfer prepared or purchased shells to large basket, perhaps wrapped in a gay cloth, and serve surrounded by Beef Taco Filling (below) or another filling of your choice, and all the fixings.

BEEF TACO FILLING

This is only one of several beef fillings for tacos. They vary widely in ingredients and spiciness: some add spinach and cheese, some, like this one, just a few spices. You'll need at least to double this recipe for this number of guests, depending on whether you also serve the chicken filling variation and on the appetites of your teenagers.

MAKES 12 TO 14 SERVINGS

1 tablespoon vegetable oil　　　*1 teaspoon cumin*
1 small onion, finely chopped　　*1 tablespoon flour*
1 clove garlic, finely chopped　　*1 teaspoon salt*
1½ pounds lean beef, ground　　*Freshly ground black pepper to taste*
1½ tablespoons chili powder　　*1½ cups beef bouillon*

Heat the oil in a large skillet. Add the onion and garlic and sauté until softened. Add the ground beef and sauté until browned, crumbling meat with a fork. Drain off excess fat. Stir in chili powder, cumin, flour, salt, pepper and bouillon and simmer over moderate heat until mixture thickens, stirring occasionally to prevent sticking. Serve immediately or prepare in advance and reheat gently just before serving.

Variation:　To make a chicken filling, for each 2 cups or so of boned chicken (in strips), you'll need about 3 tablespoons oil, 1 chopped onion and 1 minced clove garlic, plus about 1½ cups each canned tomatoes and green chilies with their juices and about ½ teaspoon cumin, and salt and pepper to taste. Simply sauté chicken, onion and garlic together in heavy skillet, shredding chicken as you go. Then cook over medium heat until chicken begins to brown and crisp around edges. Add remaining ingredients, breaking up tomatoes as they are added, and continue cooking until cooked almost dry—about 10 minutes. Watch to be sure mixture doesn't stick.

SALSA PICANTE

This hot sauce is easy to make and can be cooled down or heated up by adding fewer or more chilies.

MAKES 2 CUPS

2 to 3 serrano chilies, or other small　　*½ teaspoon salt*
*　　hot chilies*　　　　　　　　　　*¼ teaspoon sugar*
1 small onion
1 (16 ounce) can tomatoes,
*　undrained*

In a blender or food processor, blend the chilies and onion until finely chopped. Add the tomatoes and their juice, salt and sugar and blend until puréed. Transfer to a small saucepan and bring to a boil. Reduce heat to low and simmer gently for 20 to 25 minutes. Remove from the heat and let stand for an hour or two before using.

Note: Serrano peppers are hot, especially with the seeds and membrane left in. For a milder sauce, reduce the number of chilies, or remove seeds and membranes. This sauce can be made several weeks in advance and refrigerated in a sealed container until needed.

HOT SAUCE

MAKES 2 CUPS

1 small onion	*4 large ripe tomatoes (1 pound),*
3 fresh jalapeño peppers, peeled	*peeled and stemmed*
1 large clove garlic	*½ teaspoon salt*
1 tablespoon fresh cilantro leaves	*1 tablespoon vegetable oil*

In a blender or food processor, combine the onion, peppers, garlic and cilantro, and blend until finely chopped. Add the tomatoes and blend just until finely chopped but not puréed. Transfer to a non-metal bowl and stir in the salt and oil. (If the tomatoes are not ripe and juicy, it may be necessary to add another tablespoon of oil.)

This sauce will keep safely up to 1 week in the refrigerator.

Note: Because the seeds are left in the *jalapeños,* this sauce is extra-hot. For a milder version, remove the seeds and the white membrane from the peppers before processing them.

FRUIT SALAD MELON BASKET

For a summer fruit basket, cut a good-sized watermelon in half lengthwise and scoop out the fruit from one half. Remove the seeds and make melon balls or chunks from the fruit. Serrate the melon's rim to make an attractive edge. Prepare other fruits in small pieces to combine to fill melon shell: other melons, peaches, pears and berries make a good combination. If any of the fruit needs sweetening, sugar lightly and store separately until just before serving.

In winter a large bowl will do nicely as a container. Oranges, bananas, apples, grapes and pineapples are good wintertime fruit choices. Whole berries from the freezer case make a welcome out-of-season addition.

Apples, bananas, peaches and plum slices can be kept attractively fresh by dipping them in a mixture of lemon juice and water or fruit syrup, or ascorbic acid.

Small pieces of candied ginger (⅓ to ½ cup) give fresh fruit a nice shot in the arm.

Note: When I serve this fresh fruit to adults, I often add 2 or 3 tablespoons of Triple Sec or other orange liqueur.

10

A COUNTRY WEDDING

A summer celebration for 100 or so

PAPRIKA MEATBALLS

KIELBASA WITH BARBECUE SAUCE

COUNTRY CHEESE WITH CRACKERS

CURRY-STUFFED EGGS

BAKED HAM COUNTRY STYLE
WITH
MUSTARD AND PICKLES

POTATO AND LENTIL OR
PEPPER PASTA SALAD

BROCCOLI MOUSSE

SLICED TOMATOES WITH BASIL

HOMEMADE BREADS

FRESH FRUIT WATERMELON BASKET

WEDDING BELL BUTTER COOKIES

APPLESAUCE WEDDING CAKE
WITH
FLUFFY BUTTER CREAM FROSTING

WINE AND FRUIT PUNCHES BEER

CHAMPAGNE FOR TOASTING

COFFEE

A COUNTRY WEDDING

Simplicity, cooperation, affordability—and of course good food and fellow-ship—are the hallmarks of a delightful country wedding and make it the ideal way for a young couple and their families to have a joyful celebration without completely decimating their bank accounts.

This particular wedding was planned for 100 people but could easily be adjusted to fit your particular guest list and budget.

First, of course, the wedding service must be arranged. Will it be at church, at home, or perhaps in a garden or at some favorite scenic spot (an adventurous choice if there is no rain-out escape)? Certainly a home wedding, if the space and facilities allow, is the loveliest of all, but that is not always possible. What time is best? If family and friends are coming from any distance and will not be staying over, midday or early afternoon perhaps, as it will allow the guests to enjoy a relaxed time and still not be too late getting home again (and in the *real* country, allow the farmers to get home to the cows).

Once the time and place for the service are set, the rest soon falls into place. Next is the reception. What type and where should it be? Will it be in a church hall or other public place, or do you dare risk a lawn party? If you want to chance an outdoor party, the risk can be diminished by arranging a tent. Many local organizations have these for a reasonable rent: a fire department near us rents theirs for $250 a day (putting up and taking down included). Even if it doesn't rain, a tent often proves a good investment: the food and some of the guests may well do better out of the sun.

If the reception is to be held at a church hall, many times the church ladies will prepare the meal at modest cost, while the church men take care of the beer and punches—with their profit going to enhance their church coffers.

The meal itself can be as simple or complicated as you like—from an almost picnic-style meal on the lawn, to an informal buffet, with the odd table and chairs available for those who would like them, to a more formal sitdown meal. The last will require considerably more planning and expense. Tables and chairs will have to be arranged for and set properly, and much more silver and dinnerware secured—which, even if borrowed, can prove a nuisance. I myself tend to opt for the simpler buffet. Not only are buffets less expensive, they are less taxing and, in my experience, are apt to be more fun.

But whatever you decide—no matter how simple or formal—it should be done prettily. Tables should have little vases of flowers or greenery. They needn't be fancy: flowers picked fresh from the wild or the garden do very nicely indeed. Most churches have at least some little vases; friends will have others. Tables dotted with little nosegays of daisies, wild phlox, Queen Anne's lace, black-eyed Susans or even green ivy make all the difference. Perhaps this is an area one of the guests could help with. Most guest lists harbor at least one garden club member or gardening enthusiast who would like nothing better than to do the flowers for you: just give him or her a rough color scheme and let your helper go to town.

Another place you will need help is with the food. Unless the reception is to be in a public room or managed by a church or other group you will need at least one person to oversee the food in the kitchen, another to oversee the service at the buffet table and to be sure the platters are kept filled, and another to oversee the punches, coffee, and champagne when its time comes. A fourth as an all-round dog's-body would be a wonderful plus: a good guideline is one helper for each 25 or so guests. These can be paid help or dependable friends or relations—but they are essential. The wedding party and close family should be free to greet and enjoy the guests—and the occasion!

And do have music if you possibly can: it lends such a festive air! A full dance band is great fun, but expensive. Often informal music can be provided by friends of the wedding party for relatively little or sometimes just an invitation. And with today's sophisticated sound systems, dance music can be piped in from a nearby player when the party gets to that point.

Recipes for most of this wedding menu follow here. The Paprika Meatballs have long been a favorite dish at my parties, as has the Kielbasa with Barbecue Sauce. For the country cheese, I suggest a homemade Boursin, and a good Cheddar or Havarti.

Using shallots, herbs and curry is just one of the many ways I like to stuff eggs. You'll find other ideas in the index, but by all means plan to use what's easiest for you or whoever might be stuffing them for you.

As to the meal itself, I like to baste my ham with beer; it clears away the gelatinous liquid used to process hams and brings out the true ham taste. One could hardly have a country meal without potato salad; adding a lentil or pasta salad lends a nice variety. These salads can be made ahead, and in fact taste better that way. However, because they are time-consuming, they are a good item to put your friends to work on if they are willing. The Broccoli Mousse will look pretty, is simple to do and has a lovely delicate flavor, and the tomatoes add a bright touch of color. To round out this part of the menu you will find ample recipes for the homemade breads in the index, though chances are your friends will have their own ideas for this.

The fresh fruit basket for this party can be a variation of the Fruit Salad Melon Basket found on page 136; however, you'll need several refills. For the Wedding Bell Cookies, I include a butter cookie recipe, though your own favorite will do nicely. For the cake, I prefer this simple Applesauce Cake— it is a light and delicately flavored cake and makes a lovely pièce de résistance for a wedding party. (If you decide to opt for a professionally made cake, many bakeries will make a test cake for you. It costs a little but you'll be sure to get what you want.)

For the punches for this very special party, I share my family's favorites— plain and fancy—but again, you'll find others to choose from in the index. And on page 262 in the Intimate Winter Wedding section you'll find a few words on choosing and serving the champagne.

I recently planned a wedding very similar to the country wedding I have been outlining for you here: it was a joy! Let me share some of the particulars with you: perhaps this will give you some additional ideas—and confidence —as you plan your own country wedding.

By the time I became involved plans for the one-o'clock wedding service were already well in hand. It was to be at a local church with the maid of honor to sing and the whole wedding party to conclude the service with a joint chorale.

However, the reception plans were still in limbo. We found a nearby hall with lovely grounds and a good kitchen but with a $200 fee. Settling for this meant doing without much professional help and asking friends to prepare some of the food.

As it transpired the hall worked out beautifully. On the day of the wedding the bride's father supervised the setting up of a lovely buffet table and took charge of the buffet's featured ham, to be sliced by the store where it had been purchased (many supermarkets are happy to slice any ham bought from them after you have baked and decorated it at home).

The salads were prepared the day before at the hall and mixed just at noon. The watermelon fruit basket, cut in the shape of a whale, was made by a friend. The cake, made professionally but frosted at home, was embellished with natural flowers just before the reception. (Care must be taken when decorating with natural flora that whatever is used is nonpoisonous.) Paper plates on lightweight basket-woven plate-trays held the food nicely and gave the party a warm picnicky feel. And later, other pretty paper plates were set out for the fruit cup and cake.

The two punches were different colors and poured over decorated ice shapes made to keep the punches cold without weakening them—and at the same time to give the party a gay look.

While the buffet was being prepared at the hall, friends and church members were decorating the church and hall with wildflowers and more domesticated flowers from many of the town gardens.

The music for this wedding was mostly singing and a guitar, but its very simplicity added all the more to the charm and warmth of the occasion. And, to everyone's further delight, when all the tabs were in, the wedding turned out to be quite reasonable as well—under $1000 for everything.

You can, of course, adapt this country wedding plan to meet your own wishes—and budget. But, if the food is good, the work shared and the fellowship warm, it will be a joyous celebration whenever and wherever it happens.

PAPRIKA MEATBALLS

These "never fail" meatballs are browned in the oven, rather than in a skillet, which helps keep them from falling apart. They can be made well ahead, freezing the meat and sauce portions separately and combining just before serving. However, when freezing the sauce, be sure to withhold the sour cream, waiting to add that at the last. To make larger amounts, increase the recipe in equal measures to reach the number of servings desired.

MAKES 30 MEATBALLS

1 clove garlic, minced	*2 tablespoons finely chopped parsley*
1 small onion, chopped	*⅓ cup fine dry breadcrumbs*
1 tablespoon butter	*1 beef bouillon cube*
1 pound lean beef, ground	*½ cup V-8 juice*
1½ teaspoons salt	*1 tablespoon paprika*
Dash cayenne	*1 cup sour cream*

TO MAKE MEATBALLS   PREHEAT OVEN TO 350°

Using a skillet, cook the garlic and onion in the butter until the onion is transparent. In a bowl, combine with the beef, 1 teaspoon salt, the cayenne, parsley and breadcrumbs and shape into 1-inch balls.

Put the meatballs in a baking pan and brown in oven for 10 to 15 minutes, draining the fat as necessary but reserving ¼ cup for the sauce. *If freezing,* freeze the meatballs at this point after cooling them. I usually line the bottom of an airtight plastic freezing container with aluminum foil before putting in the meatballs.

TO MAKE THE SAUCE

In the top of a double boiler or in a saucepan set in a water bath (to be sure sour cream doesn't separate), combine the reserved fat, bouillon cube and V-8 juice and cook for 5 to 6 minutes. *If serving soon,* add the meatballs, cooking long enough to heat them through. Then combine the paprika, remaining salt and sour cream and add, heating only until hot. *If freezing,* do not add the paprika, salt and sour cream; freeze the cooked sauce. (after it cools) in a proper freezing container. Prior to serving, thaw the meatballs and sauce and combine, cooking over low heat until well heated. At this point, add the sour cream, paprika and salt mixture and heat through.

Note: Larger quantities of these meatballs, once done, can be kept warm in a large chafing dish.

KIELBASA WITH BARBECUE SAUCE

Kielbasa is a spicy Polish sausage made of pork and beef and smoked over maple or hickory chips. There are special kinds that are especially delicious made for the Christmas and Easter holiday seasons. The spices for these are a special blend that varies somewhat from maker to maker. Kielbasa freezes well, so that any you buy can be kept safely until you have need for it.

This particular recipe is very easy and popular. The sausage must be cooked before serving to remove the excess fat.

SERVES ABOUT 50

> 3 pounds kielbasa
> Pieces of several celery stalks, and 1
> or 2 onions and carrots, for the
> poaching liquid

> 2 (18-ounce) bottles Open Pit
> Barbecue Sauce (or your own
> favorite)

Slice the whole sausages on the diagonal about ¼ to ⅓ inch thick, trying to keep the slices a uniform width. Cover with water in a pot large enough to hold all the slices together. Add the celery, onion and carrot and bring to boil. Simmer for about 45 minutes or until the pieces are just tender. Drain and let cool.

To serve, the kielbasa slices can be reheated in the oven covered with the barbecue sauce and then turned out into a serving dish and served with toothpicks. If you prefer, the sausage can be reheated in a large black skillet over low heat. The meat should be gently crisped without letting it burn and served with sauce for dipping nearby. Either way the sausage should be served warm or hot, not cold.

COUNTRY CHEESE
A HOMEMADE BOURSIN

Genuine Boursin is a triple cream cheese from Normandy made from cow's milk and containing between 70 and 75 percent fat. It is rindless and flecked with herbs. The version I make is by no means authentic but it is good and very serviceable.

MAKES 2 CUPS

2 sticks (½ pound) sweet butter
8 ounces cream cheese
1 tablespoon each summer savory
and tiny leafed oregano or finely

chopped dill or sage or minced
calendula petals and cracked
black pepper, or almost any
combination of these

In a bowl, blend butter and cream cheese together well. Then blend in whichever combination of herbs you wish to try, starting slowly (and conservatively), then adding more to taste (it shouldn't be *too* lively). When the mixture is as you like it, set aside in the fridge to rest for 24 hours or so before serving.

Note: In blending your herbs, remember it's always easy to add but difficult to subtract.

CURRY-STUFFED EGGS

This stuffed-egg variation can be made ahead and kept in the refrigerator overnight until needed. Refrigerate scooped-out egg whites and stuffing separately; stuff shortly before serving.

MAKES 24 HALVES

2 tablespoons butter
4 shallots or scallions, minced
12 eggs, hard-cooked (see rule for
hard-cooked eggs on page 68)
2 tablespoons finely chopped parsley
and chervil, mixed (if dried, use
half the amount)

½ teaspoon good madras curry
powder
1 to 3 tablespoons heavy cream
Salt to taste
Freshly ground black pepper to taste
Paprika or chopped parsley, for
garnish

Melt the butter in a skillet, add the minced shallots or scallions and cook slowly until they are tender but not colored, stirring from time to time with a wooden spoon.

Cut the eggs evenly in half lengthwise and mash the yolks with the shallots, parsley and chervil and curry to make a paste.

Stir cream in by spoonfuls, being careful not to let the mixture become runny, and season lightly with salt and pepper. Fill the egg with the mixture, making a dome, then refrigerate until needed.

When ready to serve, sprinkle lightly with paprika or chopped parsley.

BAKED HAM COUNTRY STYLE

Today's hams are billed as "ready to eat," but I find they need additional care.

Choose a ham with the bone left in; it is more flavorful. Bake about 15 minutes a pound in a 325° oven after first drenching with a can of beer. The beer cuts away the gelatinous liquid found on prepared hams today. For a very large ham, 10 minutes a pound should be enough.

While the ham is cooking, mix together 2 tablespoons dry mustard, about 1 cup brown sugar and ¼ cup wine to make a glaze. When ham is cooked remove any excess skin, score the top and thoroughly "paint" the top with the mustard-sugar mixture. Bake another 10 minutes or so in a 450° oven, and serve either warm or cool.

To serve the ham presliced, take it back to your butcher if you wish (most markets will do this for you).

POTATO SALAD FOR A CROWD

You can prepare this basic salad the day before and then refrigerate it overnight, adding the mayonnaise and other ingredients the afternoon of the reception. Remember that the general rule of thumb is 15 pounds of potatoes for each 50 people and a proportion of about 8 to 1 for potato to onion and about 85 percent potato to 15 percent fillers.

AMPLE FOR 100

30 pounds good boiling potatoes, well-scrubbed
Salt as needed
2 quarts Basic Vinaigrette Dressing (see page 383)
1 quart commercial mayonnaise
1 cup sour cream, as needed, to thin

2 cups chopped scallions (optional)
1 cup coarsely chopped celery
1 cup well-chopped pimiento
12 hard-cooked eggs, cut in wedges (optional)
Freshly ground pepper to taste

Using two or more pressure cookers, cook the potatoes in their skins with a pinch or two of salt until done, but not soft. Under cold water cool cooked potatoes enough to handle, but without allowing them to get cold. Peel and chop coarsely. Place in large plastic bowls and mix with enough vinaigrette to be sure each piece is covered. (I like to use my hands as the potatoes are less apt to break.) When cool, cover and refrigerate.

Shortly before serving, mix in the mayonnaise, thinned with sour cream. Keeping some for decoration, mix in the remaining vegetables and eggs, again taking care that the potatoes are treated gently. Taste and season with additional salt and pepper as needed.

Transfer to serving bowls or platters, decorate and again refrigerate until ready to serve, covering with wax paper or plastic wrap.

Note: If you are leery of serving raw onion in this salad, you can flavor the salad a bit by cooking the potatoes with the still-whole onions and then removing them when the cooking is done.

LENTIL SALAD

This salad has a Middle Eastern flavor, which is nice for a change, but you can tone it up or down as you choose with more or less garlic and spice.

SERVES ABOUT 50

3 pounds (6 cups) dark brown dried lentils
Salt to taste
1½ cups salad oil
6 to 8 cloves garlic, crushed

Freshly ground black pepper to taste
2 teaspoons allspice
1 cup plus 2 tablespoons finely chopped parsley

After checking the package directions, if necessary soak the lentils overnight. Drain, place in pot half covered with water and bring to boil. Boil until barely tender, about 1 to 1½ hours. Salt lightly toward the end of the cooking time. Drain well.

Make a dressing of the remaining ingredients, except for the parsley, and pour over lentils while still hot. Mix well and chill (it does not have to be super cold). When ready to serve, dust with the chopped parsley.

Bash à la Grecque

GREEK CHRISTMAS BREAD
TIROPITAS (IN PROGRESS)
DOLMADES

© Robert Grant

Southern "At-Home"

BENNE CHICKEN FINGERS
CAVIAR PIE
SEAFOOD BOUCHÉES
CAROLINA WHISKEY CAKE
LEMON CHESS TARTS

PEPPER PASTA SALAD

This is a pleasantly different pasta salad.

SERVES 24 TO 30

3 cups Lemon-Garlic Mayonnaise
(see page 385)
6 red peppers
3 green peppers
40 to 50 (about 2 large jars) pitted
black olives, drained, and
rinsed if too salty

2¼ pounds penne pasta
1 tablespoon chopped fresh thyme or
basil

After making the Lemon Garlic Mayonnaise, roast, peel and slice the peppers and set aside. (If you prefer, wash, remove pepper seeds and veins, slice and parboil 1 to 2 minutes.) Test the olives, drain, rinse if necessary and set aside.

In a large kettle, cook the pasta 8 to 10 minutes or until just done. Drain well and transfer to large bowl. Toss the peppers and olives and thyme or basil with half the dressing and combine with the pasta, mixing gently. Cover and chill overnight in the fridge.

When ready to serve, gently toss in the remaining dressing.

Notes: The salad is also very nice with about 1½ pounds of sliced fresh mushrooms tossed in with the other vegetables.

BROCCOLI MOUSSE

This mousse comes to me from my niece Joanne Hodgson. For this party, triple the recipe. However, because gelatin is tricky, make in 3 separate lots.

MAKES ABOUT 12 TO 15 SERVINGS

1 large bunch fresh broccoli, or 2
(10-ounce) packages frozen
1¼ cups chicken stock
2 tablespoons (2 envelopes)
unflavored gelatin, softened in ½
cup water
3 tablespoons Worcestershire sauce

2 tablespoons lemon juice
½ teaspoon salt
¼ teaspoon black pepper
¼ teaspoon cayenne
4 hard-cooked eggs, chopped
(optional)
¾ cup mayonnaise

If using fresh broccoli, wash and trim. Then cook broccoli until tender, and drain. Reserve 6 flowerlets from the cooked broccoli and chop remaining to make 2 cups.

Bring the chicken stock to a boil, add the softened gelatin and stir until dissolved. Remove stock mixture from the heat and add the broccoli, Worcestershire, lemon juice, salt and peppers and the chopped egg, if using.

Chill mixture until it begins to thicken. At that point, fold in the mayonnaise and pour mixture into a lightly greased 1½-quart mold. Then chill again until needed. When ready, unmold, garnish with the reserved broccoli flowerlets and serve with a side dish of mayonnaise or other dressing of choice.

WEDDING BELL BUTTER COOKIES

These old-fashioned butter cookies can be shaped as bells, hearts, love knots or whatever your fancy dictates.

MAKES ABOUT 100 COOKIES, DEPENDING ON SIZE

2½ sticks butter, softened	*1 teaspoon salt*
2 cups sugar	*4 teaspoons baking powder*
2 eggs, well beaten	*1 teaspoon nutmeg*
4½ cups flour, or more as needed	*½ cup milk*

Cream butter and sugar together; add eggs and beat until fluffy.

Stir together dry ingredients; add alternately with the milk to the creamed ingredients. If dough is too sticky, add additional flour only until dough can be handled (too much flour will make cookies tough). Wrap in plastic wrap or foil and chill in refrigerator about an hour until ready to bake.

TO BAKE   **PREHEAT OVEN TO 375°**

When ready to bake, roll dough out (using a little dough at a time, from center to edge as for pie crust) to about ⅛-inch thickness. With a lightly floured cookie cutter, cut into shapes. Reroll dough as little as possible; it makes dough tough.

Bake on ungreased cookie sheet until cookies are a delicate light brown, about 8 minutes. Watch carefully so cookies don't burn.

To store, use a container with loose-fitting lid. Cookies can also be frozen wrapped in plastic wrap, but allow time for cookies to thaw, in unopened container, before serving.

APPLESAUCE WEDDING CAKE

This is a wonderfully pleasant cake which over the years has become my basic 3-tiered wedding cake recipe. I find it easier to make the batter (and bake the cake) in two batches (one to fill a 6-inch and a 9-inch pan and the second to fill a 12-inch pan). If you prefer, you can put it all together into one big batch and do it that way. I often replace the brandy with Grand Marnier.

SERVES 100 OR MORE

	To fill *1 6-inch and* *1 9-inch pan*	*To fill* *1 12-inch pan*
Cups raisins	4	6
Cups brandy or Grand Marnier	1 ⅓	2
Cups butter	2	3
Cups sugar	4	6
Eggs (optional)	4	6
Cups applesauce	4	6
Teaspoons baking soda	4	6
Cups flour	7	10½
Teaspoons salt	1	1½
Teaspoons ground cloves	1	1½
Teaspoons nutmeg	1	1½
Teaspoons cinnamon	4	6
Cups chopped nuts (optional)	2	3

TO PREPARE BATTER

First, put raisins to soak in brandy or Grand Marnier and set aside.

Cream butter and sugar together thoroughly and add eggs, if desired, beating in well. Add the applesauce, again stirring in well. Sift together the baking soda, flour, salt and spices and add to creamed mixture. Add the raisins and chopped nuts, if using.

Pour batter into well-greased and floured pans until about ⅔ full—a little higher on the sides as the center will rise more. Then follow steps for baking, assembling and decorating in Wedding Cake Guidelines on page 153. I bake the 6-inch and 9-inch layers at one time and the 12-inch layer at another, using the Apricot Custard Filling and Fluffy Butter Cream Frosting.

Note: This cake does not require eggs, so it is a good choice at parties where some guests may have egg allergies.

Apricot Custard Filling

AMPLE FOR 3-TIERED CAKE FOR 100 TO 120

4 pounds dried apricots	*½ cup flour*
3 quarts water	*½ teaspoon salt*
¾ cup lemon juice	*14 egg yolks*
1½ cups orange juice	*2¼ teaspoons grated lemon rind*
3¼ cups sugar	*(optional)*

First, wash the apricots thoroughly and make an apricot pulp by cooking the apricots together with all but 1½ cups of the water. Simmer them about 35 minutes and then bring to boil to evaporate excess moisture. Watch carefully so they don't go beyond a nice soft pulp. When ready, remove from stove and set aside to cool. You will need 1½ to 2 cups pulp.

Combine all remaining ingredients except about ¾ cup sugar in top of large double boiler or bain-marie (bowl set in large pan of water). Stir and cook until thick. When thickened, add apricot pulp and as much of the remaining sugar as needed to reach the sweetness you want. Then set aside to cool.

Note: If you would prefer a simpler filling, see the Apricot Glaze Filling on page 265.

Fluffy Butter Cream Frosting

This butter cream, from Linda King, is a flexible frosting and very easy to work with. I prefer vanilla or orange flavoring with this applesauce cake.

AMPLE FOR 3-TIERED CAKE FOR 100 TO 120

4½ pounds confectioners' sugar, sifted	*4 to 5 teaspoons vanilla, orange, lemon or almond extract, or*
2¼ sticks sweet butter	*a combination of ½ vanilla*
1⅛ cups shortening (Crisco is fine)	*and ½ another, to taste*
1¼ cups milk or cream	

Beat all ingredients together well until very fluffy and no graininess remains. If frosting is not quite moist enough to spread easily, add a little more milk, but don't let it get wet: it should stay nice and fluffy. You may want a little more flavoring, but again remember that one can always add but not always subtract.

Note: If you want a truly white vanilla frosting, add just a drop or two of blue food coloring—being careful not to overdo. (This, of course, would not work with the colored flavoring extracts.)

WEDDING CAKE GUIDELINES

Most of these suggestions come to me from Marjorie Blanchard, who for many years wrote the cooking column in my husband's and Richard Ketchum's *Country Journal* magazine. Others have been learned from Linda King, who provides the wedding cakes for much of southern Vermont and many points beyond. The suggestions here are geared to a cake serving 100 to 120: smaller and larger cakes obviously require different pans and different cooking times.

For this size cake, three tiers are sufficient: use one 6-inch; one 9-inch and one 12-inch pan. Both Marjorie and Linda advise securing use of commercial-sized pans (3 to 3½ inches deep). Pans can be improvised from cake tins but proper pans are easier and safer. They should be well greased and well floured.

To make batter. It is a good idea to divide the recipe and make the cake in two batches—one batch for the two smaller tins and a second for the largest. If you have adequate equipment and a commercial-sized oven, one batch is fine; otherwise, ⅔ is easier.

To bake. Preheat oven to 350° and fill tins about ⅔ full—and slightly higher at the sides. After 20 minutes reduce heat to 325°. Different batters and different-sized pans require different baking times, but as a rule for the smallest layer the times will vary from perhaps 15 minutes under an hour to 10 minutes past an hour. In general, each larger size requires an additional 15 minutes or so. However, test for doneness in each case. In fact, Linda likes to make a small test layer of any wedding cake batter before she bakes the full recipe just to be sure how it will act: there is ample batter in most recipes for a test.

Cool layers in pans on racks about 15 minutes, then turn them out to continue cooling. Chill or freeze the layers before using: this prevents their crumbling into the icing as you frost the cake.

To assemble. Most wedding cakes require cardboards between the layers and wooden doweling for the layer above to rest on: this keeps the top layers from sliding. The cardboards should be cut the same size as the layer above and wrapped in plastic wrap or aluminum foil. The dowels (you *can* use skewers or chopsticks) should be ⅜ inch in diameter and cut the height of the layers, including the filling: you'll need 3 for each layer (6 in all for 3 tiers). The dowels are placed in 3-legged-stool fashion down through the layer below to support the layer above. Don't skimp on this unless you're sure: especially in warm weather, cakes will slide. (If you prefer, rather than precut the dowels, you can spin your choice of "dowelling" down through each layer, snipping off each dowel at the right spot as you go.)

Place chilled 12-inch layer directly on serving platter (or board) or on sturdy flat cardboard prewrapped in plastic wrap or foil. Add second and third tiers in appropriate order, inserting the dowels and spreading the filling and frosting between each layer sandwich style as you go. (Elevating the layers is also possible but is of course more difficult, requiring longer doweling and the skill to fill the area between the layers attractively and safely.)

To frost. When layers are in place, frost sides first and then the top. Then using a pastry bag, decorate with scallops, fleur-de-lis or other patterns of your choice (see art here for ideas). Courage and pastry bags are truly all that's needed when you use a good, flexible frosting. (However, unless you love it and have the time, try to find a friend to tend to this task for you.)

To decorate. When the frosting is complete—as fancy or as plain as you like—shortly before serving finish the cake off with a flourish of fresh flowers (for a winter wedding they could be silk). Circles of scented geranium leaves or myrtle can be ringed around the two bottom layers and tucked on the top to make a base for any number of suitable fresh flowers: cosmos, daisies, clover, calendulas, roses, asters, sweet peas, lilies-of-the-valley, carnations, bridal wreath and baby's breath are fairly long-lasting; pansies and violets and most single-petaled flowers need to go on at the last minute.

A last word. If there are leftover batter and trimmings, you can make cupcakes. The children will love them.

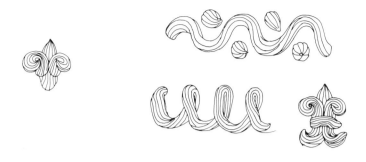

WHITE WINE FRUIT PUNCH

Be sure to allow time for the elixir for this punch to "mellow."

MAKES 80 TO 100 CUPS

2 cups Punch Elixir (see below)
2 (1½ litre) bottles dry white wine
  (I prefer Chablis)
2 bottles soda water

Fruit slices of choice, for garnish
½ pint berries, for garnish
  (optional)
Mint, for garnish

Pour elixir, wine and soda over large ice blocks (made in heart shapes would be fun), mixing well but gently. Add fruit slices, berries (if using) and mint, and serve.

If you would like a milder punch, add up to 2 cups cold tea with several slices of cucumber, or add a little more soda water.

Punch Elixir

TO MAKE 1 QUART (4 CUPS)

1 quart fresh strawberries, or peeled
and pitted fresh peaches
1 cup Triple Sec liqueur

½ cup lemon or orange juice
Brandy to make 1 quart

TO MAKE ELIXIR

Purée the fruit and liqueur in blender (if this is too much for your blender, do ½ at a time). Add fruit juice and enough brandy to make quart. Chill and let meld for at least 2 to 3 hours.

Note: If you wish to make this elixir in the nonfresh-fruit season you can use frozen strawberries or peaches, but try to find the nonsugared type; otherwise, cut the Triple Sec so mixture won't be too sweet.

STRAWBERRY RHUBARB PUNCH

This is a lovely nonalcoholic summertime punch.

SERVES 35 TO 40

3 cups sliced fresh rhubarb
1 cup sliced strawberries
3 cups water
¾ cup sugar

1 (10-ounce) can frozen pink
lemonade
Whole strawberries, for garnish
Mint, for garnish

To make the fruit syrup, mix the rhubarb, sliced strawberries, water and sugar, and boil until rhubarb is soft. Strain the mixture, pressing fruits with back of spoon firmly to get as much juice as possible; discard pulp. Keep syrup cool until needed, or freeze.

When ready to serve, pour portion of syrup over ice (ice blocks or shapes work best; cubes melt too quickly). Add an equal amount prepared lemonade and garnish with whole berries and mint.

Note: You may substitute carbonated lemon drink for the lemonade if you prefer.

11
FESTIVELY FOREIGN: TWO PARTIES

Réveillon de Noël

A 1780's-Style Christmas Eve Party for 40 or so

TUREEN OF BOUILLON

CRETONS

MONTREAL PÂTÉ DE MAISON

TOURTIÈRES

STUFFED PORK TENDERLOIN

FARM WIFE'S HEAD CHEESE

FRUIT TART   TARTE AU SIROP D'ERABLE

TEA

Your Yearly Bash à la Grecque

A special party for 50 or so

TIROPITAS
(SPINACH AND CHEESE TRIANGLES)

BAKED KEFTEDES
(GREEK MEATBALLS)

LOUKANIKA
(HOT GREEK SAUSAGE)

DOLMADES
(HOT STUFFED VINE LEAVES)

SKORDALIA (A GREEK DIP)

TARAMASALATA (GREEK ''CAVIARS'')

GREEK CHEESE PLATTER

GREEK-STYLE MARINATED MUSHROOMS

MARINATED GREEK OLIVES

KOURAMBIEDES
(GREEK WEDDING COOKIES)

GREEK SWEET BREAD RINGS

GREEK CHRISTMAS BREAD

LEMON CHEESE TARTS   BAKLAVA

SIKA GEMISTA
(NUT-STUFFED FIGS)

GREEK WINE   DRINKS OF CHOICE

RÉVEILLON DE NOËL

As an English Canadian in Montreal I was always curious about the French customs all around me and particularly about the traditional foods and holiday celebrations.

The celebration of Christmas in our home was very British—with early church on Christmas Day, then stockings opened, then breakfast, and finally the candles lit on the Christmas tree and the presents opened. Dinner followed a few hours later and included a large turkey, plum pudding, mince pies and hard sauce.

I envied my friends who went to midnight Mass on Christmas Eve and celebrated *Réveillon*—a late supper after Mass—even though their presents, traditionally, waited for New Year's Day. The mystery and excitement of a late-night service and the family supper following appealed to me and I yearned for their *tarte au sirop d'erable,* made with maple syrup.

In researching this festival I was lucky on a trip to Montreal to find a young banker whose mother, Madame Constance Garneau, loved the old French-Canadian celebrations and was good enough to write me a lovely long letter sharing her knowledge.

The French peasant women who came to the New World many years after the first soldiers and sailors brought their customs and recipes with them, and gradually these traditions were taken up by the townspeople as well.

To mark the birth of Christ and the New Year, the family pig was slaughtered, with every edible part used, including the head, and the raw materials for all the traditional dishes assembled. Chickens and game were prepared and stored in an outdoor cupboard called a *tambour,* where the meat froze solid and was taken out as needed during the winter. (Madame Garneau writes that a thaw in those days would have been as disastrous as a power outage in these, but that she never heard of a thaw.)

The *Réveillon* menu started with a strong homemade drink called Caribou. It was a kind of *alcool* or "firewater," and only the men drank it. For the women there was always a large pot of tea on the stove. The first course after the long trek home from Mass was a hot beef or chicken bouillon, followed by *cretons,* a minced pork and kidney dish much like rillettes, and a *pâté de maison* (the exact recipe dictated by the section of France from which the hostess came).

French-Canadian pork and veal pies called *tourtières* were one of the features of this celebration. It seems this pie derived its name from a bird, the *tourtre,* now extinct. However, at one time it was plentiful and "the skies were darkened by clouds" of them. In fact, at a fish and game club near Montreal a stuffed *tourtre* is one of their present-day treasures. It was a brown bird not unlike a partridge in size.

A stuffed pork tenderloin and head cheese would have been other features of the menu—both from the family pig. My Montreal sister feels sure that beans in some form would have been part of this menu too. And no doubt there would have been breads.

The desserts would have included fruit tarts, *croquignoles* (hot soft, caky doughnuts, yet "firm and thin") and the *tarte au sucre.* (You'll find a recipe for the *tarte,* along with others, here, but I have been unable to find an authentic *croquignole* recipe; perhaps one of you readers will have one.)

All kinds of game would have been added to this menu—plus chicken and turkey—depending on the hunting that autumn and on what was available in the *tambour* or in the market.

Nowadays, the celebration is more ecumenical. Oysters and pâté de foie gras as well as mixed drinks are served, though in most cases *cretons* and *tourtières* would still be on the menu.

My niece, who lived in France for a number of years, tells me that Réveillon is still de rigueur and very much a part of the French family Christmas. There, the first course would include the pâté and oysters but the rest would vary with the section of France. The north prefers turkey, farther south it is more likely to be goose, while in Provence, they might offer a homemade ravioli stuffed with beef and swiss chard. Simple country vegetables are added everywhere, making it more like our New England Christmas dinner. However, the *bûche de Noël,* a Christmas log, and the sweet, rich pastry differ from our plum pudding and pie.

In southern France, there is also the lovely tradition of including a bowl of thirteen different kinds of fruits and nuts in season—these to represent Christ and the Twelve Apostles. And today, one American custom has taken hold even in France: the children receive their presents on Christmas.

I have expanded this family party menu to accommodate the number of guests more usual at today's holiday parties, but the recipes for the menu's traditional French-Canadian dishes are, for the most part, as they have long been.

Réveillon literally means "wake up." I hope these party recipes will wake up your and your guests' taste buds, as well as your holiday spirits; you can add others of your own choosing to fill up your holiday party table.

CRETONS

This is the recipe of Lady Lacoste, a famous Quebec hostess whose daughter began the Berthe Dansereau Catering Company in Montreal, now run in turn by her daughter.

MAKES 40 OR SO SERVINGS

1½ pounds lard
2 pounds lean pork round
2 pork kidneys
3 medium onions, finely chopped (about "a soup plate full")

12 whole cloves
Salt (about 1 teaspoon) and pepper to taste

Mince all ingredients (if you use a food processor, do so with a pulsing motion to preserve the shape of the meat). Cover with water and simmer for 3 hours, stirring often, particularly during the last hour, to keep meat from sticking to pan bottom.

Rinse molds (several small 1½ cup molds work best) in cold water and fill with minced mixture.

Note: Truffles and herbs may be added if desired.

MONTREAL PÂTÉ DE MAISON

This pâté is best made several days in advance.

SERVES 12 TO 16

1 pound lean pork, lightly ground
1 pound pork liver, chopped
2 cloves garlic, finely chopped
6 scallions, finely chopped
1 teaspoon each salt, pepper and dried thyme

Pinch nutmeg
3 eggs, beaten
½ pound sliced bacon (more as needed)
½ to ¾ cup white wine, apple juice or cider

Grind or process meat if you want a smooth pâté. I prefer mine not too smooth so I go lightly here.

Combine all ingredients except bacon and wine. Line a 1½-quart terrine or casserole (or two small baking dishes) with bacon strips and fill with pâté mixture. Pour wine or apple juice over and cover with more bacon strips.

TO BAKE   **PREHEAT OVEN TO 325°**

Cover casserole and set in a roasting pan. Pour hot water to reach halfway up pan's sides and bake for 2 hours.

Remove pâté from oven, uncover and top with foil. Weight with heavy can or stone—or an iron—and let cool. Remove weight and chill. There will be a thin layer of fat on and around the meat, which helps keep it from drying out.

Serve with French bread or crackers of choice. For some, little cornichons are a must.

PORK TOURTIÈRE

A mainstay of French-Canadian holiday fare, *tourtières* come in many variations. The two in this chapter—this one using only pork and the next adding beef—will give you some idea of the possibilities.

MAKES 1 PIE

1 pound pork, ground
1 onion, diced
1 clove garlic, minced
½ teaspoon salt
½ teaspoon savory
¼ teaspoon celery powder
¼ teaspoon ground cloves

½ cup water
¼ to ½ cup breadcrumbs
Double crust for 1 (9-inch) pie,
unbaked (see Lard Pastry Dough,
page 404)
1 egg white, for glaze

Mix all ingredients except breadcrumbs, crust and egg, and bring to boil. Simmer, uncovered, for 20 minutes. Remove from heat. Add a few tablespoons breadcrumbs and let stand 10 minutes. If fat is sufficiently absorbed, no further crumbs are needed. Otherwise, repeat. Let cool.

TO BAKE   **PREHEAT OVEN TO 500°**

Pour meat mixture into unbaked pie crust. Cover pie with upper crust, slit several vents and glaze with egg white. Bake until crust is golden brown about 10 to 15 minutes. Serve hot.

PORK AND BEEF TOURTIÈRE

MAKES 2 PIES

2 tablespoons shortening
1 onion, sliced
1 pound beef, ground
½ pound pork, ground
4 potatoes, cooked and mashed
1 cup water
2 teaspoons salt
1 teaspoon pepper

1 teaspoon cinnamon
½ teaspoon ground cloves
½ teaspoon nutmeg
Double crusts for 2 (9-inch) pies,
unbaked (see Lard Pastry Dough,
page 404)
1 egg white, for glaze

Heat shortening in skillet. Sauté onion. Mix meats and add. Break up with fork and brown. Stir in potatoes, water and seasonings. Mix well.

TO BAKE   **PREHEAT OVEN TO 375°**

Turn meat mixture into pastry-lined pie pans. Cover with top crusts, slit several vents in each and glaze with egg white. Bake about 45 minutes or until golden.

FARM WIFE'S HEAD CHEESE

This recipe for head cheese, which comes to us from Janet Greene by way of her *Putting Food By* (certainly one of the best books on preserving and "putting by" anywhere), may not be exactly like the French farmers would have made it for Réveillon but it is good—and interesting to try. Jan adds that you may season it with herb seasoning but recommends trying it in its simple form first. She likes it as is in a sandwich or for a cold meat platter.

If you live in the country you may already know where to find a slaughterhouse: they will have a hog's head there, and if you ask, will trim it to your needs. In the suburbs or the city, your butcher can be pressed into service: he will either obtain one for you or tell you where you can find one.

FILLS SEVERAL STANDARD LOAF PANS

1 hog's head, thoroughly trimmed
and quartered

Salt and pepper to taste

In a large kettle cover the well-scrubbed quarters with water. Simmer until the meat falls from the bones—about 3 hours. Remove from heat and let cool until meat can be handled, but without allowing fat to congeal. Drain off the liquid and strain it well. Return it to the kettle, and over high heat reduce quantity by ⅓ or ½.

Carefully pick meat from the bone and gristle, put in a wooden chopping bowl and chop very fine. Add enough reduced broth to make a wet mixture and season to taste with salt and pepper. Pack several 7- or 8-inch loaf pans about ¾ full. Nest one pan on top of the next, with wax paper between each layer. Then weight the top pan to press all the meat thoroughly. If extra juice is pressed out, it can be saved for stock. Refrigerate the stack overnight. In the morning slide each loaf from its pan.

If you are using immediately, keep in the fridge until needed. Otherwise wrap it in freezer paper and freeze until needed.

TARTE AU SIROP D'ERABLE

This is a traditional maple syrup pie. However, please note that the pastry will need 2 hours to chill before you can put the tart together.

SERVES 6

> *1 recipe Tarte au Sirop d'Erable*
> *Pâte Brisée (see below)*
> *1 cup maple syrup*
> *1 cup whipping cream*

> *3 tablespoons cornstarch*
> *Cold water to moisten cornstarch*
> *Maple sugar, for sprinkling*

TO PREPARE
AND BAKE PASTRY   **PREHEAT OVEN TO 400°**

Roll out pastry to fit 9-inch pie pan. (See directions for preparing open-face tart on page 00.) Bake 10 to 12 minutes until lightly golden. Set aside to cool.

TO PREPARE FILLING

Mix maple syrup and cream together in saucepan and bring to boiling point. To cornstarch add just enough cold water to moisten and blend into maple syrup and cream mixture. Simmer for 2 minutes, stirring constantly.

Let cool and pour into baked pie shell. Sprinkle with maple sugar and serve lukewarm.

Tarte au Sirop d'Erable Pâte Brisée

½ cup vegetable oil
¾ cup flour

½ teaspoon salt
3 tablespoons cold water

Blend oil and flour. Add salt. Add water all at once and mix gently. Form into ball and chill for 2 hours before using.

YOUR YEARLY BASH À LA GRECQUE

After a joyous holiday celebrating the twelve days of Christmas—sharing gifts, love and good food—the decorations come down and are put away. January is here. What a good time, with spare moments by the fireplace or woodstove, to read recipes and think about what you will do in this new year to thank your friends. Remembering how crowded your calendar was during December—and what fun, if tiring, it all was—how best, you wonder, can you spread the pleasure of collecting your friends and sharing new drinks, foods and ideas out into the New Year.

Not everyone has to have a party: for many, just the thinking and scheming will be enough—at least for a while. But for many, it will be a time to plan your annual bash. Why not?

My choice is a Greek party. Just now that the bleak winter is about to set in, how appealing the thought of sunny Greece with its gaiety and color! And how much less fuss now that its many fine foods are becoming well known on this side of the Atlantic and available in so many markets.

In Greece, weather permitting, most people stop daily for outdoor refreshment and are served tidbits of some sort with their glass of wine, ouzo and water, or coffee. A multitude of olives, pistachio nuts, fried zucchini slices and various bits of fish, including squid, arrive almost as soon as the customer. The Greek principle that food enhances drink, and drink the food, is mine as well, and it is only a short jump from this daily Greek refreshment to ideas for a great welcoming cocktail party with new things to make.

Surely the menu should encompass the stuffed vine leaves (or *dolmades*) of which the Greeks are so fond, and *loukanika,* a hot sausage, steamed and then browned and served with lemon. Other hot hors d'oeuvre could include the delicate *keftedes,* meatballs flavored with parsley, allspice and mint, and we mustn't forget *tiropitas,* that fine spinach delicacy found throughout so much of the Mediterranean. Cheeses could include the widely known *Feta* and the lesser-known *Kasseri,* a goat cheese served at the table fried or broiled with bread.

And this is only the beginning. Greek breadstuffs are now widely available in Greek and specialty stores, or you can bake the ones you'll find here or in one of the many fine bread books on the market. Sweets can include the traditional *kourambiedes,* a butter cookie, the always popular *baklava* and perhaps *sika gemista,* a Greek nut-stuffed fig.

Greek wines are often matured in barrels with resin, which adds a different taste. Many of these wines—red, white and rosé—are now imported from Greece. The listing which follows will help you with your choices if you plan to add these wines to your party. And don't hesitate to consult your wine merchant: he will know what best meets your requirements and what's available.

Adjust the suggested menu to your own needs and fancies. Some of the recipes following are traditional Greek family recipes passed along to me by friends or just absorbed over the years. Others are from a favorite Greek restaurant in Old Greenwich, Connecticut, and others from a Hempstead, Long Island, church cookbook, *The Regional Cuisines of Greece* (a delightful, informative and well-illustrated book). Some may sound a little difficult, but after a little practice, they won't be. I will warn you about those that are perhaps a little tricky.

If you should have trouble obtaining ingredients for any of the recipes, there are a number of mail-order sources. Bloomingdale's (59th Street at Lexington Avenue, New York, New York 10022) is only one of them. A comprehensive nationwide listing is found in *Regional Cuisines of Greece.*

What fun, as you begin the New Year, to share something new and different with your friends!

GREEK WINES AVAILABLE IN THE UNITED STATES:
AN ABBREVIATED LISTING FROM PERSONAL TASTING

White Wines (serve well chilled)

Demestica—a light, clean, very fine wine

Mantina—a well-balanced, full-bodied wine

Aphrodite—a fine, dry vintage wine from Cyprus

Hymettus—a popular dry wine from the mountain area also producing Greece's best honey

Rosé Wines (serve chilled)

Roditys—a light, dry, very popular all-purpose wine

Rosella—a more robust version of Roditys from Cyprus

Red Wines (serve at room temperature)

Castel Danielis—a vintage wine of great quality and depth

Pendeli—a fruity, dry, full-bodied estate-grown wine from the southern slope of Mt. Pendeli

Mt. Ambelos—a big, dry wine with a smooth finish

Othello—a subtle, velvety wine from Cyprus

Dessert Wines

Mavrodaphae—one of the more famous

Commanderie St. John—a Keo wine from Cyprus

Muscat—from Samos

Retsina

This is a generic name applying to any wine (usually white or rosé) flavored with pine resin, a practice dating back to ancient times when resin was used as a preservative. Resinated wines do not improve with age and should always be drunk cold.

This listing has been drawn in part from the excellent listing given in *The Regional Cuisines of Greece* put together by the Recipe Club of St. Paul's Greek Orthodox Church of Hempstead, Long Island, and refined by my own experience.

TIROPITAS
(SPINACH AND CHEESE TRIANGLES)

Folding these takes a little practice, but is far easier than you might think.

MAKES 30, 40 OR 80, DEPENDING ON SIZE

3 tablespoons olive oil
1 medium onion, finely chopped
1 (10-ounce) package frozen chopped spinach, thawed and well drained
¼ teaspoon freshly grated nutmeg
½ pound Feta cheese, washed and drained
6 ounces pot cheese
¼ cup chopped parsley

1 teaspoon dried dill weed
½ teaspoon salt
⅛ teaspoon freshly ground pepper
3 eggs, well beaten
¼ cup cornflake crumbs
½ pound frozen phyllo dough (about 10 sheets), thawed (see below)
1 stick (8 tablespoons) butter, melted

In a saucepan, heat oil and sauté onion until wilted. Add spinach and simmer, stirring, until the moisture evaporates. Season with nutmeg.

Crumble the Feta cheese into medium-sized bowl. Blend in pot cheese, parsley, dill, salt, pepper and beaten eggs. Add spinach mixture and cornflake crumbs. Blend thoroughly and set aside.

Phyllo dough should be thawed just enough to allow sheets to separate (if completely frozen, about 2 hours). Working quickly, lay single sheet on wax paper, brush lightly with melted butter; top with second sheet and butter again. For hors d'oeuvre-sized triangles, cut into 4 strips. (Keep remaining sheets of dough covered with damp cloth. This will keep them from drying out before you get to them.)

Center ample teaspoon of spinach-cheese mixture about 1 inch above bottom edge of dough strip. Fold filled strip from side to side, flag-fashion, to make triangle (see art), sealing carefully with a little melted butter. Brush finished triangle with melted butter and set aside. Repeat with new strips of dough until filling is used up.

If you want to make larger (luncheon-sized) triangles, cut phyllo sheets into thirds and use a tablespoon of filling for each strip.

To make even more hors d'oeuvre, cut each quarter strip in half horizontally and fill as above, using a little less filling and being careful triangle is properly sealed. This will double the number.

TO BAKE   **PREHEAT OVEN TO 425°**

Place filled triangles on baking sheet and bake for 20 to 25 minutes, turning once, until light brown. Watch them carefully as they burn easily.

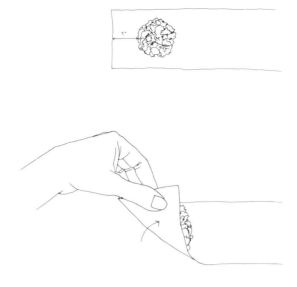

Note: It is a good idea to make these triangles when you have a free day and then freeze unbaked. Freeze them first on a flat surface, then pack in plastic freezer bags and store in freezer until needed (will keep nicely for several days). When ready to serve, put triangles on baking sheet, brush them lightly with melted butter and bake at 425° until done. Leftover baked triangles can be reheated: brush lightly with melted butter and put in 450° oven for 2 to 3 minutes.

BAKED KEFTEDES

Hot meatballs are always a great favorite for parties. The mint in this Greek version adds a special taste.

MAKES 75 COCKTAIL–SIZED MEATBALLS

½ cup fine, dry breadcrumbs
½ cup milk
2 medium onions, finely chopped
2 tablespoons butter
1½ pounds beef, ground
2 eggs

2 tablespoons chopped parsley
1 tablespoon chopped fresh mint
¼ teaspoon each cinnamon and
   allspice
Salt
Freshly ground black pepper

TO PREPARE

Soak the breadcrumbs in the milk for about 10 minutes; squeeze out excess milk. Sauté onions in the butter until softened. In a large mixing bowl, combine the beef, eggs, parsley, mint, basil, cinnamon and allspice, and season with salt and pepper. Add the breadcrumbs and sautéed onions and mix until thoroughly blended. Refrigerate for several hours. Roll into balls about ½ to ¾ inch in diameter and place on a cookie sheet lined with aluminum foil.

TO BAKE AND SERVE   PREHEAT OVEN TO 350°

Bake balls for about 15 minutes, turning during baking to brown on all sides and prevent balls from flattening out. Drain off excess fat during cooking if necessary.

Pile into a chafing dish and serve warm with sturdy wooden picks and yogurt dip or with the Skordalia dip in this party menu.

Note: Baked Keftedes may be prepared in advance, frozen and reheated for use later. Bake the meatballs and let cool. Freeze on cookie sheets for at least 12 hours; then transfer them to plastic freezer storage bags. Reheat on a foil-covered cookie sheet for about 15 minutes.

DOLMADES
(HOT STUFFED VINE LEAVES)

Dolmades (called by different names in different countries) are a delightful delicacy. There are numerous variations, but as a general rule, ground meat is used to make hot *dolmades* while cold *dolmades* are meatless. These do take time to prepare (as much as 60 minutes perhaps and then another 60 to cook), but they can be done ahead and reheated when ready to serve. The leaves used are usually grape.

MAKES 40 TO 50

100 or so tender vine leaves or 1 (16-ounce) bottle pickled vine leaves
1½ cups uncooked long-grained brown rice
2 cups ground lamb or beef
½ cup ground sausage (optional)
1½ teaspoons salt
½ teaspoon pepper
½ teaspoon cinnamon
2 cups cold water

1 medium fresh tomato, or 1 whole canned, chopped
2 whole cloves garlic, peeled
½ teaspoon dried mint, or 2 teaspoons fresh, and more for sprinkling
8 cloves garlic, crushed (optional)
½ cup pine nuts (optional)
½ cup fresh lemon juice, and more for sprinkling
Tomato or vegetable juice, as needed

TO PREPARE

Soften and blanch fresh vine leaves a few at a time in boiling salted water; if using pickled, rinse well in cold water at least 3 times. Cut any overly large leaves in half. Set aside.

Wash rice and mix with ground meat, 1 teaspoon salt, pepper, cinnamon and ½ cup cold water.

TO STUFF AND COOK

Stuff one leaf at a time, putting 1 teaspoon of stuffing in center of each leaf. Fold bottom edge of leaf up over the stuffing, then fold in from each side to the middle and roll tightly to form a cylinder about 1½ inches long and ½ inch thick. (See illustration for folding Mint and Rice Stuffed Vine Leaves, page 22.) Place the rolls in a large iron skillet lined with broken pieces of vine leaves or extra tomatoes. Cover this with a layer of the chopped tomatoes, whole garlic and mint, and sprinkle with crushed garlic and pine nuts (if using), remaining salt and lemon juice. Add layers in same fashion. Add rest of remaining water and cover with a weighted plate to keep the *dolmades* tightly rolled. Bring to a boil and then simmer gently to cook. Check carefully during cooking to be sure there is ample liquid, adding tomato or vegetable juice as needed, and sprinkling with more lemon juice and mint as you go. Cook for 60 minutes or until rice is thoroughly cooked.

TO SERVE

For hors d'oeuvre, drain well and serve warm with a yogurt dip, or the Skordalia dip given here. Have sturdy toothpicks nearby.

Notes: The ground sausage makes an excellent addition, so include it if you can. The use of garlic in *dolmades* varies across Greece. Some areas do not use it at all.

SKORDALIA

This dip is also often used as a sauce.

MAKES ABOUT 1 CUP

5 *cloves garlic*
¼ *cup chopped almonds*
2 *slices bread*
¼ *cup chopped parsley*
Juice of ½ lemon

2 *egg yolks (optional—to make dip more mayonnaise-like)*
½ *cup olive oil (green Sicilian or Greek preferred)*
Salt (optional)

Peel and chop garlic and pulverize with the almonds in food processor with steel blade or in blender. Remove crusts and soak bread in water for 1 second; then squeeze out the moisture. Beat the garlic-almond mixture, bread, parsley, lemon juice and optional egg yolks together either by hand or in mixer or food processor. Gradually beat in the olive oil. Season with salt, if you wish.

TARAMASALATA

This spread is made from *tarama,* the Greek name for carp roe. It can be found in bottles in Greek and Middle Eastern groceries.

MAKES 8 GENEROUS SERVINGS

4 slices white bread	*2 tablespoons lemon juice*
3 tablespoons bottled tarama	*1 teaspoon grated onion*
¾ cup olive oil	

TO PREPARE

Remove and discard crust from bread, break into pieces, moisten with a little water and squeeze dry. Place the tarama in a small mixing bowl and mash with the back of a wooden spoon to split the roe. (A mortar and pestle is the best tool for this if you have one.) Add the softened bread and continue to mash together until thoroughly blended, about 5 minutes. Using an electric mixer, gradually beat in olive oil and lemon juice, adding small amounts of each alternately. Add the onion and mix well. The spread should have the consistency of a thick mayonnaise.

Serve in the center of a tray surrounded with slices of fresh raw vegetables for dipping, or spread on small squares of buttered toast.

Tarama Salata Lianide

This *tarama* variation is by the well-known chef Leon Lianide, proprietor of The Coach House in New York City, and one that James Beard collected for the Cuisinart recipe book that accompanied my food processor. It is a little more complicated than the preceding recipe but well worth the trouble.

MAKES ABOUT 3 ½ CUPS

1 medium onion, quartered	*1 cup light olive oil*
1 clove garlic	*Juice of 3 lemons*
1 parsley sprig	*3 Greek black olives*
1 cup bottled tarama	*1 small lemon, thinly sliced*
8 slices firm white bread, soaked in water and squeezed dry	*1 ½ tablespoons pistachio nuts, chopped*

With the food processor's metal blade in place, add onion, garlic and parsley to the beaker. Process, turning on and off, until onion is evenly chopped. Add *tarama* and bread. Process again until evenly mixed, about 10 seconds. Continue processing, slowly drizzling the olive oil and lemon juice through the feed tube.

Transfer to serving dish and chill at least 2 hours.

To serve, garnish with the black olives, lemon slices and chopped nuts. The lemon can be sliced in your processor using the slicing disk and the nuts chopped with the metal blade.

Note: Although this recipe is designed for use with a food processor, it would work just as well mixed in a blender or by hand.

GREEK-STYLE MARINATED MUSHROOMS

The Greeks have given us another wonderful way of preparing mushrooms.

SERVES ABOUT 30

1 ½ pounds whole small mushrooms, cleaned	*4 sprigs fresh thyme*
	2 bay leaves
1 cup olive oil	*½ cup minced parsley*
2 cups water	*1 teaspoon coriander seeds, lightly crushed*
Juice of 1 lemon	
2 tablespoons red wine vinegar	*1 teaspoon fresh rosemary*
2 cloves garlic, pressed	*8 peppercorns*
1 rib celery, coarsely chopped	*1 teaspoon salt*

In a large saucepan, combine all ingredients and bring to a boil. Simmer for about 5 minutes, stirring occasionally. Pour into a medium-sized glass bowl and marinate in the refrigerator overnight or longer. Drain amd serve on toothpicks.

Variations: This hot marinade can be used for other vegetables too. *Peeled onions:* Cut a cross about ¾ inch deep in the root end to discourage the onions from bursting, then arrange in heavy-bottomed pan. Pour marinade about halfway up onion sides, adding water if necessary. Simmer for 20 to 30 minutes. Dip out with slotted spoon and put in serving dish. Boil marinade down rapidly until syrupy and check seasoning. Pour over onions and serve hot or cold. *Celery hearts:* Cut into 1- to 1 ½-inch pieces. Cover with marinade and simmer until tender but not floppy. Serve chilled.

MARINATED GREEK OLIVES

MAKES 12 TO 18 SERVINGS

*2 pounds small, pointed black
    Greek olives, drained*
2 lemons, thinly sliced
4 to 5 ribs celery, coarsely chopped

1 cup wine vinegar
2 cups olive oil
1 tablespoon dried oregano
2 to 3 cloves garlic, finely minced

Using a hammer, gently crack the olives open to remove pits. Pack olives into sterilized jars, arranging them in alternating layers with lemon slices and chopped celery. Combine vinegar, oil, oregano and garlic and pour over the olives. (If liquid does not cover, add water to cover.) Seal jars and let marinate for 2 to 3 weeks before serving. Olives will keep well up to 6 months in this marinade.

KOURAMBIEDES
GREEK WEDDING COOKIES

Served at all festive occasions, these traditional Greek favorites are considered good luck and are a must at marriages.

MAKES ABOUT 4 DOZEN

*1 pound sweet butter, at room
    temperature*
1 cup confectioners' sugar
1 egg yolk

2 tablespoons Cognac
4 to 4½ cups cake flour, sifted
Whole cloves (optional)

TO PREPARE

Cream the butter with a fork or an electric mixer until thick and fluffy. Gradually sift in ¾ cup of the confectioners' sugar, beating well between each addition. Add the egg yolk and beat for about 3 minutes. Add the Cognac. Gradually add the flour, mixing on low spead or by hand until dough is soft and will roll easily in the palm of the hand without sticking. If it seems too sticky, add a little more flour or refrigerate for about an hour before shaping.

TO FORM AND BAKE   PREHEAT OVEN TO 350°

Shape dough into 1½-inch diameter balls or ½-inch thick crescents. Stud each with a whole clove, if desired. Place on an ungreased baking sheet and bake until pale golden, not brown, about 15 minutes. Cool and dust with the remaining confectioners' sugar.

GREEK SWEET BREAD RINGS

No Greek holiday celebration is complete without at least one of their festive egg-rich yeast breads. These sweet rings, called *Koulourakia,* are known as "cookies" but are actually breads.

MAKES ABOUT 4 DOZEN

7 cups sifted flour
¼ cup warm water
½ cup warm milk
2 yeast cakes, or 2 (¼-ounce) envelopes dry yeast
1 teaspoon salt
1 stick (8 tablespoons) butter, melted

3 eggs, lightly beaten
⅓ cup cold milk
¾ cup sugar
1 tablespoon vanilla
2 tablespoons brandy
1 cup light cream

TO PREPARE

Sift 2 cups flour into large bowl. In a small bowl, combine the warm water and warm milk. Dissolve the yeast in this liquid and add to the 2 cups flour. Mix thoroughly to make a loose dough. Let rise in a warm place for about 1½ hours.

After the first rising, sift together the remaining flour and salt. Add the melted butter, mix until evenly blended and set aside.

In another bowl combine the eggs, cold milk, sugar, vanilla and brandy, and mix well. Add egg mixture to the risen dough, mixing with a heavy spoon until smooth. Add the flour and butter mixture and knead together for 10 minutes or until very smooth.

Cut off pieces of dough about the size of large walnuts and roll between the hands to form 3-inch-long ropes. Seal rope ends to form circles and place 2 inches apart on greased cookie sheets. Brush tops with cream and let rise for 1½ hours.

TO BAKE   PREHEAT OVEN TO 350°

Bake rings for 35 minutes and serve, plain or with butter.

GREEK CHRISTMAS BREAD

You'll need to allow at least 4 hours from start to finish for this holiday treat, but happily, it can be made the day ahead.

MAKES 2 (2-POUND) LOAVES

1 cup sugar
1 ½ teaspoons anise seeds, crushed
1 teaspoon salt
2 tablespoons (2 envelopes) dry yeast
About 7 ¾ cups flour

2 cups milk
2 sticks (½ pound) butter or
  margarine
3 eggs
16 red candied cherries

TO PREPARE DOUGH

In large bowl of mixer, combine sugar, anise seeds, salt, yeast and 2 cups flour. In 1-quart saucepan, over low heat, heat milk and butter or margarine until very warm (120° to 130°). Butter or margarine does not have to melt completely. With mixer at low speed, gradually beat liquid into dry ingredients until just blended. Increase speed to medium and beat 2 minutes, occasionally scraping bowl with rubber spatula.

Separate 1 of the 3 eggs, reserving the white for brushing loaves before baking. Gradually beat single egg yolk into flour-milk mixture, then gradually continue to beat in remaining 2 eggs and 2 cups flour to make a thick batter. Continue beating 2 minutes, scraping bowl often. Then with wooden spoon, stir in 3 cups flour to make a soft dough.

Turn dough onto well-floured surface and knead until smooth and elastic, about 10 minutes, working in more flour while kneading (about ¾ cup). Shape dough into ball and place in large greased bowl, turning dough over so that top is greased as well. Cover and let rise in warm place (80° to 85°), away from draft, until doubled, about 1 hour. (Dough is doubled when 2 fingers pressed lightly into dough leave a dent.)

When doubled, punch down. Then turn out again onto lightly floured surface; cover with bowl and allow to rest for 15 minutes (this makes for easier shaping). Meanwhile, grease 2 cookie sheets.

TO SHAPE LOAVES

When ready, cut dough in half, cutting off and reserving ½ cup dough from each half. Shape each half into 6-inch-round loaf, placing shaped loaves on cookie sheets. Roll 1 piece of reserved dough into 2 12-inch-long ropes, cutting a 3-inch-long slash into each end of the 2 ropes. Place ropes on top of first loaf to make a cross; do not press down. Curl slashed ends of each rope, placing a cherry in each curl (see illustration). Repeat with remaining reserved dough for second loaf. Cover loaves with towels and let rise in warm place until again doubled, about 45 minutes, or until 1 finger pressed very lightly against dough leaves a dent.

TO BAKE   **PREHEAT OVEN TO 350°**

Beat reserved egg white with fork, and using pastry brush, brush evenly over both loaves. Place cookie sheets, each with one loaf, on separate racks in the oven; bake 15 minutes. Switch cookie sheets between upper and lower racks so loaves brown evenly. Bake another 15 to 20 minutes or until loaves sound hollow when tapped lightly with fingers. (If loaves start to brown too quickly, cover loosely with foil.)

Remove loaves from cookie sheets and cool on wire racks.

LEMON CUSTARD TARTS

The dough for these tarts should set 24 hours before baking.

MAKES 4 TO 5 DOZEN 2-INCH TARTLETS

4 cups flour
Pinch salt
1 cup shortening (Crisco is good)
2 eggs, beaten with 1 to 2
  tablespoons ice water

1 recipe Lemon Cheese Filling (see below)

Mix flour with salt and cut in shortening. Add beaten eggs and blend well. Knead dough on a lightly floured surface with the heel of hand a few times to work the dough. Then store in refrigerator at least 24 hours before making shells.

TO BAKE   **PREHEAT OVEN TO 400°**

When ready to bake, roll out dough to thickness of about ⅛ inch and line tartlet or muffin tins 2 inches in diameter to a depth of about ½ inch. Fill with cooled Lemon Cheese Filling and bake for 7 to 8 minutes. Do not brown. Serve plain or dusted lightly with confectioners' sugar.

Lemon Custard Filling

4 tablespoons butter	*Juice and finely grated rind of 2*
1 cup sugar	*large lemons*
	2 eggs, well beaten

Melt butter and sugar together in top of double boiler. Add lemon juice and rind and heat slowly until sugar is dissolved. Add eggs and stir constantly until thick. Cool before filling shells.

This filling will keep about 2 weeks well covered in the refrigerator.

BAKLAVA

This traditional Greek dessert is a bit tricky to make but is delicious. Remember that when working with phyllo dough it is best to get all your ingredients ready ahead so when it comes time to lay out the dough you can work quickly.

MAKES 24 TO 30 SERVINGS

1 pound almonds, blanched and	*2 sticks (½ pound) butter, melted*
chopped fine	*1 cup water*
½ teaspoon freshly grated nutmeg	*1 cup honey*
1 pound phyllo dough (about 20	*Juice of 1 lemon*
sheets)	

TO PREPARE PASTRY

Combine chopped almonds and nutmeg, mix well and set aside.

Line a buttered 9-by-14-inch baking pan with 1 sheet phyllo dough and brush lightly with melted butter. (Keep the remaining phyllo dough covered with a slightly damp towel as you work so that it doesn't dry out.) Repeat dough-butter process two more times and cover with a thin layer of chopped almond mixture, about 3 to 4 tablespoons. Cover the nut layer with another phyllo sheet, brush with butter and repeat with layer of dough and then a layer of nuts. Repeat this pattern until all the ingredients are used, ending with 2 or 3 whole pastry sheets on top.

After the final pastry sheet is buttered, score top sheets (don't go all the way through) with a sharp knife to make small, bite-sized diamond shapes. This makes for easier cutting when cool.

TO BAKE   **PREHEAT OVEN TO 300°**

Bake for 1 hour or until golden brown.

TO PREPARE SYRUP AND COMPLETE

While pastry is baking, combine water and honey, and boil about 10 minutes. Add lemon juice and boil another minute. Watch to make sure syrup doesn't boil away while the pastry finishes baking. (If you are going to be distracted, keep the syrup hot in the top of a double boiler.)

When pastry is done, remove from oven and gradually pour the hot syrup over it. Continue to add syrup as long as it is absorbed by pastry (you may not need all of it). Cool and cut the scored pieces through.

Allow ample time for the syrup to be completely absorbed before serving.

If stored in an air-tight container, this pastry keeps nicely for several weeks.

Notes: Baklava can be frozen. Simply freeze the assembled pastry, *unbaked* and before the syrup is added. When ready to use, place the still frozen pastry directly in a 300° oven and bake, allowing an additional 10 minutes' baking time—or however long it takes to reach the flaky golden brown you are aiming for. Then follow the recipe as above. Pistachio nuts—combined with a little sugar—are often used in Baklava.

SIKA GEMISTA
(NUT-STUFFED FIGS)

These figs are easy to prepare and an appropriate sweet touch for this Greek menu.

ABOUT 24 PIECES

1 (12-ounce) package dried whole
 figs, about 24
1 cup orange juice
1 tablespoon grated lemon rind

1 tablespoon lemon juice
3 tablespoons sugar, plus sugar for
 rolling
24 pecan or walnut halves

Remove stem end from figs and place fruit in a saucepan along with the orange juice, lemon rind, lemon juice, and sugar. Heat to boiling and simmer, covered, until fruit is tender, about 45 minutes. Drain well and cool.

Insert knife in stem end of each fig to form a pocket. Fill each pocket with nut half. Roll figs in sugar until well coated and let dry overnight.

II

ELEGANT YET PERSONAL

12
A SOUTHERN "AT HOME" THANKSGIVING PARTY

for 60 or so

OPEN BAR CAROLINA EGGNOG WINES

SPICED PECANS

WILLIAMSBURG CHEESE STRAWS

HOT PEPPER JELLY WITH CREAM CHEESE

SOUTHERN-STYLE SMITHFIELD HAM
WITH TINY BEATEN BISCUITS

CAVIAR PIE WITH MELBA ROUNDS

BENNE CHICKEN FINGERS
WITH GADO GADO SAUCE

CHINESE PEAPOD, BELGIAN ENDIVE AND
PLUM TOMATO PLATTER

BROCCOLI MOUSSE

HOT BRIE WITH ALMONDS

SEAFOOD BOUCHÉES

SMOKED OYSTERS

Coffee and Dessert Sideboard

LEMON CHESS TARTS BOURBON BALLS

HOT MINCE TARTS WITH HARD SAUCE

OLD-FASHIONED POUND CAKE

CAROLINA WHISKEY NUTCAKE

LIQUEURS

SOUTHERN THANKSGIVING
"AT HOME"

This is a splendid Thanksgiving weekend party to give when all the young people are home and families are united. It combines a wide variety of traditional delights with some of today's newer party foods.

In many parts of the South, Thanksgiving weekend marks the beginning of the winter social season as well as the beginning of the hunting season. Many southern families would begin this party day with a hunt breakfast—perhaps at a house in the country—with friends and family stopping by to cheer the hunters on even if they don't join in the hunt. A typical hunt breakfast might include a dish of baked peeled and quartered apples, bacon, sausage, hominy, cheese biscuits and coffee.

A different evening party for this particular weekend might feature a hunt dinner offering the spoils of that day's or an earlier hunt. A casserole of duck or dove breasts or marinated quail in white sauce perhaps—or maybe a roast of venison matured in pineapple juice and well marinated in the "Marinade for Wild Boar" made famous by Mapi, the Countess of Toulouse-Lautrec. All to be followed by a chess pie or a rum cake.

However, since my emphasis for this book is on hors d'oeuvre and all that it implies, I have focused on a very elegant party with beautiful flowers and quiet, attentive service. It could easily be planned to precede one of the balls marking the opening of the social season and will include all ages and a generous buffet. Some at the party may then go on to the dancing, while others will linger for even more of an evening meal.

The pièce de résistance for this party menu is a baked Smithfield ham, sliced very thin and presented on tiny biscuits with a little butter. Sometimes served from a lovely silver standing holder, the ham by its very presence evokes a sense of hospitality, holiday and family. For this party it is cooked following an old southern recipe requiring five days. The beaten biscuits that accompany the ham are from an equally traditional recipe, though I am told by a South Carolina friend that tiny cheese biscuits are a great favorite too.

The drinks may include an eggnog along with a wide range of wines, and the host will have a well-stocked bar to suit every fancy. The Spiced Pecans and Williamsburg Cheese Straws, set out in easily reached small serving dishes, will accompany the drinks, and a plate of the Hot Pepper Jelly will offer a little tingle. The Caviar Pie—gay in yellow and black—comes to me from a favorite southern hostess, while the Broccoli Mousse (from the Country Wedding party) and elegant vegetable platter add even more color and a welcome contrast in texture.

Tomato roses, or other of the vegetable "flowers" scattered about on the serving platters will add a luxurious touch, accompanied by bouquets of whatever flowers are in season—camellias perhaps—to add their own elegance.

As the party progresses other dishes are brought in. A plate of Brie melted under the broiler and sprinkled with almonds arrives smelling marvelous and tasting divine and little bouchées filled with crab or lobster circulate, along with plates of smoked oysters and biscuits.

An antique sideboard would be the perfect place for the desserts and coffee to be set out, with a tray each of the Lemon Chess and Hot Mince Tarts, a bowl of the Bourbon Balls and somewhere on the buffet a traditional whiskey cake side by side with a large Old-Fashioned Pound Cake glittering with white sugar icing and nonpareils.

For those who arrive late or linger on into the evening, casseroles of game, cheese grits and wild rice are brought out from the kitchen along with perhaps a smoked turkey to satisfy all appetites.

With coffee and liqueurs available throughout, all will combine to complete a memorable evening of southern hospitality.

CAROLINA EGGNOG

This is a lovely smooth—but very rich—eggnog.

MAKES 1 GALLON

12 eggs, separated
1 ½ cups sugar
⅘ quart whiskey
1 quart light cream

6 ounces Jamaican rum, or more to
taste
1 pint heavy cream

With an electric mixer, beat egg yolks until lemon-yellow. Beat in 1 cup sugar. Then very slowly add in whiskey and light cream. Beat egg whites with ½ cup sugar until stiff and fold into whiskey-cream mixture. Add rum and mix gently but well. Keep chilled until ready to serve. For the best flavor, the eggnog should be allowed to "ripen" at least several days.

When ready to serve, whip heavy cream and fold in.

Note: I like to add a little freshly grated nutmeg at the last moment, or have a grater handy so guests can do it themselves.

SPICED PECANS

These southern spiced pecans, from an Atlanta, Georgia, friend, Marion Yearley, are sweeter and spicier than the Chinese version given earlier.

MAKES 4 CUPS

1 egg white, lightly beaten
2 tablespoons cold water
½ cup sugar
¼ teaspoon ground cloves

¼ teaspoon ground allspice
¼ teaspoon cinnamon
½ teaspoon salt
4 cups pecan halves

Combine all ingredients except pecans, mixing well. Set aside 15 minutes. Add pecans and mix.

TO ROAST **PREHEAT OVEN TO 250°**

Spread seasoned nuts evenly on 2 greased cookie sheets. Roast 1 hour. Loosen nuts from baking sheets immediately; cool and store in airtight container.

WILLIAMSBURG CHEESE STRAWS

MAKES ABOUT 5 DOZEN

1 cup sifted flour
½ teaspoon salt
¼ teaspoon dry mustard
⅛ teaspoon cayenne
⅔ stick (5⅓ tablespoons) butter or
  margarine

1 cup grated sharp Cheddar cheese
1½ tablespoons water
1 teaspoon celery seeds

Sift the first 4 ingredients into mixing bowl. Add butter or margarine and ½ cup grated cheese and cut into a coarse crumb consistency. Add water and toss lightly.

Shape into ball. Roll to ⅛-inch thickness. Sprinkle 1 side of dough with ¼ cup of the cheese. Fold dough over and sprinkle with remaining ¼ cup cheese. Roll to ⅛-inch thickness. Cut into 4-inch strips about ½ inch wide. Sprinkle with celery seeds.

TO BAKE   **PREHEAT OVEN TO 350°**

Bake on ungreased cookie sheet for 12 to 15 minutes or until lightly golden. Cool on rack and store in airtight container until ready to serve.

Note: If you want to make these straws ahead they will freeze nicely—baked or unbaked.

HOT PEPPER JELLY

This particular jelly—which may well have had its origins elsewhere—is today very much at home at southern parties.

MAKES 6 CUPS

5 cups sugar
1½ cups cider vinegar
¾ cup seeded and finely chopped
    green bell pepper

½ cup seeded and finely chopped
    fresh jalapeño pepper
1 (6-ounce) bottle liquid fruit
    pectin

In a large pot, combine sugar and vinegar. Bring to a boil; add peppers and bring to boil again. Stir in pectin and boil another minute. Strain liquid through a colander into large bowl. Pour directly into hot sterilized jars and seal.

Serve with cream cheese and water biscuits or melba rounds.

Note: It's the seeds of the jalapeño pepper that are hottest, so be sure to seed the peppers as the recipe suggests or you'll have a super-hot jelly.

SOUTHERN-STYLE SMITHFIELD HAM

This is a recipe from Ruth Jenkins of Atlanta, Georgia, found in *Four Great Southern Cooks.* It is a lot more demanding than working with a processed ham as I do, but the ham it produces is beautifully tender and tasty. Although constant attention is not required till the fourth day, one does have to start this ham five days ahead.

THINLY SLICED, AMPLE FOR 60 OR MORE

1 Smithfield ham, 15 to 18 pounds.
Water to cover
40 to 50 whole cloves

1 cup brown sugar
¼ cup medium-dry sherry

TO PREPARE HAM

Scrub the ham thoroughly. Place in large enamel roasting pan or kettle and cover with water. Let the ham soak for 3 days, changing the water twice a day, morning and night.

On the fourth day, cover the ham with fresh cold water. Place on top of stove over high heat and bring to boil. Reduce heat, cover the pan or kettle and simmer until done, allowing 25 to 30 minutes per pound. The ham is done when the small bone at the hock end can be pulled out.

Remove pan or kettle from heat and let ham cool in its stock overnight at room temperature.

TO BAKE HAM   PREHEAT OVEN TO 400°

On the next day, remove the ham from its stock and pull the skin free, leaving a thin layer of surface fat. Score the remaining fat with a small sharp knife and insert cloves where the scores intersect. Place studded ham in shallow roasting pan.

Stir the brown sugar and sherry together to make a glaze, being sure the sugar is completely dissolved. Brush glaze over ham and bake for about 30 minutes, or until the ham is nicely browned. Place on rack to let drain before serving.

TINY BEATEN BISCUITS

This old southern recipe is from Beatrice Mize of Atlanta, Georgia. To get the crisp biscuit she wants takes pounding the dough for at least 30 minutes with a hammer or mallet.

MAKES 5 TO 6 DOZEN BISCUITS

3¾ cups flour
1 teaspoon salt
Pinch baking soda
¼ cup vegetable shortening

½ cup milk, more or less, as needed
½ cup water, more or less, as needed

TO PREPARE BISCUIT DOUGH

Sift the flour, salt and baking soda together into a large bowl. Cut the shortening into the flour until mixture resembles coarse crumbs. Add milk and water gradually to make a very stiff dough.

Knead the dough until smooth and place on wooden chopping block. Pound with wooden mallet or hammer until flat; then form into ball and pound again. Repeat until dough blisters and pops; this takes about 30 minutes. The dough should be firm but not sticky.

Roll out dough to about ¼-inch thick and cut with small biscuit cutter, pricking each biscuit at least 3 times with fork.

TO BAKE **PREHEAT OVEN TO 350°**

Place on lightly greased cookie sheets and bake 30 to 35 minutes or until crisp. The biscuits should be a very pale brown.

Serve immediately with butter—and of course the ham.

CAVIAR PIE

Passed along to me by her daughter, this recipe is actually the treasure of Mrs. Thomas English McCutcheon of Columbia, South Carolina.

SERVES APPROXIMATELY 30

1 (8-ounce) package cream cheese, *1 or 2 tablespoons mayonnaise*
at room temperature *3 ounces black caviar*
½ cup sour cream *1 or 2 hard-cooked eggs, finely*
2 scallions, finely chopped, green *chopped*
parts and all

Mix the cream cheese, sour cream, scallions and mayonnaise together well and form into a round mold about 1 inch high, using a foil collar to contain the shape, or divide the mixture into 3 smallish (5- to 6-inch) molds. Then chill.

When ready to serve, spread the caviar gently over the mold to cover and sprinkle with the chopped eggs.

Note: Contrast red caviar with the black to make a gayer display. Either way, this recipe makes an attractive and tasty dish. Lumpfish roe may be substituted for a more economical version.

BENNE CHICKEN FINGERS

Benne is a traditional name for sesame in much of the South.

MAKES 4 DOZEN OR SO

*2 pounds chicken breasts, boned,
 skinned and cut into 2-by-¾-inch
 fingers*
1 large egg white, beaten
1 tablespoon cornstarch

1½ tablespoons soy sauce
A few drops hot sesame oil
*¾ to 1 cup sesame seeds, hulled or
 unhulled*
Oil for frying

Mix egg white, cornstarch, soy sauce and hot sesame oil to make a foamy, but not runny, sauce. If mixture is too thick, it can be thinned with a little chicken broth or sherry, but don't let it become too thin or it will be hard to handle and use up too many of the seeds. If too thin, add extra cornstarch.

Dip chicken fingers in sauce and then in sesame seeds. Set aside to dry a bit. Then, in an electric fryer set at 375°, deep fry 2 or 3 minutes until light brown; do not overcook or chicken will be tough.

Serve as is or with Gado Gado Sauce (see page 67).

Variation: Finely chopped peanuts can be substituted for the sesame seeds for a different—but equally good—taste.

CHINESE PEAPOD,
BELGIAN ENDIVE AND PLUM TOMATO PLATTER

Fresh stuffed Chinese peapods, Belgian endive and fresh plum tomatoes will make just the right combination for this special party.

I like to stuff the Chinese peapods with the Crabmeat Bouchée Filling (page 193). The filling can be made ahead but the later it's stuffed into the peapods the better. The peapods should be strung, seeded and blanched (2 to 3 minutes) first.

Softened blue cheese makes a lovely filling for endive. Simply fill the end of the cleaned and trimmed endive with a generous dab just before serving.

Guacamole (page 133) is a tasty and colorful filling for the little plum tomatoes. The tomatoes, of course, need to be hollowed out and drained thoroughly before stuffing.

LOBSTER SALAD BOUCHÉES

Good canned lobster is almost impossible to find and fresh lobster is difficult to deal with so I suggest the frozen, which is abundant in most markets. An alternate recipe follows for crabmeat, also an excellent filling.

MAKES 4 TO 5 DOZEN

2 recipes *Puff Pastry* (see page 400)
1 cup peeled and diced firm apples
Juice of ½ lemon
¾ pound frozen lobster, thawed
3 tablespoons butter
1 ½ tablespoons peanut or vegetable oil
1 cup chopped onions
2 tablespoons flour
1 cup juice (lobster drippings, prepared clam juice and 2 tablespoons sherry)
1 teaspoon curry powder
½ cup heavy cream
Salt
Freshly ground black pepper
Tabasco sauce to taste
1 recipe *Dorure* (see page 406)

Put prepared pastry in refrigerator to firm.

Sprinkle the apples with the lemon juice to keep them white.

Drain thawed lobster, reserving juice, and chop coarsely.

Heat the butter in a skillet, add the lobster and sauté for 30 seconds. Remove with a slotted spoon and set aside. Add the oil to the pan, heat briefly and add the chopped onions; cook gently until the onions are soft and lightly colored. Add the apples and cook until tender. Sprinkle with the flour and stir for about a minute to cook the flour; add the juice and continue to stir until smooth. Add the lobster, the curry and the cream. Season with the salt, pepper and Tabasco and set aside to cool.

**TO ASSEMBLE
AND BAKE**   **PREHEAT OVEN TO 400°**

Prepare the Dorure.

Roll the chilled dough out to a thickness of ⅛ inch. Cut into 4-inch rounds (two recipes of the pastry should make close to 60 rounds; you can use a saucer if you don't have a proper cutter). Place the rounds on baking sheets, separating any layers with waxed paper, and refrigerate to firm again.

When pastry has become firm, put about 1 teaspoon of the lobster mixture in the center of each pastry round, moisten the edges with cold water and fold over to make half-moons. Press the edges firmly with a fork to seal them and

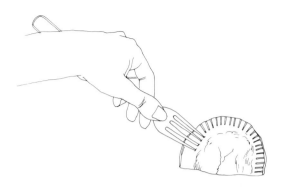

glaze the bouchées with the Dorure. Then refrigerate again for a few minutes before baking.

Bake for 12 to 15 minutes until nicely browned, and serve hot.

Note: Although I suggest using the Puff Pastry recipe found later in this book, if you are pressed for time, or just prefer, one of the excellent already prepared pastries, such as Pepperidge Farm's, will do.

Variation: For an especially attractive hors d'oeuvre, you can use both this lobster salad filling and the crabmeat filling that follows in Phyllo Baskets (see recipe page 214).

Crabmeat Bouchée Filling

FILLS 2 TO 3 DOZEN

½ cup good mayonnaise
½ cup whipped or sour cream
⅓ cup chili sauce
1 tablespoon chopped onion

1 (7½-ounce) can or ½ pound fresh crabmeat, flaked and looked over for shell
2 to 3 teaspoons gin (optional)

Mix the first 4 ingredients together to make a sauce. Add in as much of the crabmeat as you need to make a smooth but not runny filling for the bouchées. If the crabmeat is canned add the gin to kill any tinny flavor.

With a demitasse or small teaspoon, fill the bouchées and seal. Then bake following the instructions for the preceding lobster recipe.

GAME DISHES

If you want to make this buffet an even more complete meal, include one or more of these game dishes.

Duck Breasts in Casserole. Flour, season and sear duck breasts in cooking oil. Add 1 can consommé, ½ cup orange juice, 2 tablespoons dehydrated onion soup, 1 bay leaf and red wine to cover. Cook in slow (300°) oven for 2 hours.

Breast of Dove on Wild Rice. Simmer 12 dove breasts covered with water about ½ hour. Remove and place in 2-quart casserole. Add ¼ teaspoon salt and dash pepper, dot with butter and pour in ¾ cup sherry. Cover and cook in 350° oven for 30 minutes or so, basting often. Save liquid to use for gravy. While doves are cooking, prepare 1 cup wild rice according to directions on package. When ready, serve doves on bed of rice. If you want, make gravy from cooking liquid and sprinkle slivered almonds over all.

Marinated Quail in Wine Sauce. Place 18 cleaned quail in roasting pan. Pour 1¼ cups each red wine vinegar and red wine and ¼ cup olive or other oil over birds to marinate for 12 hours, turning birds to marinate thoroughly on all sides. Remove from marinade, saving liquid. Sprinkle birds with salt and pepper and secure legs to body with toothpicks. Make sauce from 2 tablespoons chicken drippings or bacon fat, 2 cups chicken broth, 1 cup Cognac, 2 tablespoons grated orange rind and enough marinade to make as much sauce as you need. Salt and pepper to taste; cover birds with sauce and bake, covered, at 350° until done, about 30 to 45 minutes.

LEMON CHESS TARTS

The methods in this recipe are culled from several different sources, but the filling is traditional. Rumor has it that this tart was named after a Southern military man.

MAKES 24 TO 30

1 recipe Rich Tart Pastry (see page 401)
2 cups sugar
2 tablespoons white cornmeal
4 eggs

¼ cup milk
¼ cup lemon juice
Grated rind of 1 lemon
4 tablespoons butter, melted

Prepare Rich Tart Pastry. Then, using a cookie sheet to rest them on, set out small (2-inch) greased tartlet pans touching one another in rows of 4 or 6 for as many rows as you'll need or have pans.

Next, between sheets of wax paper, roll out pastry ¼-inch thick to a size slightly larger than the total area covered by the tartlet pans. Peel off top sheet of paper. Invert pastry over tartlet pans. Peel off second sheet of paper. Let pastry stand about 10 minutes to settle into pans (this stretching won't harm pastry). Cover pastry-lined pans with wax paper and run rolling pin over the tops. This will cut pastry to just the right size. Gather up surplus pastry and pinch off a ball about the size of a walnut. Dip ball into flour and use to press pastry firmly into pans. Then chill pastry-lined pans well before baking. Repeat as needed to use up dough and as pans are free to fill again.

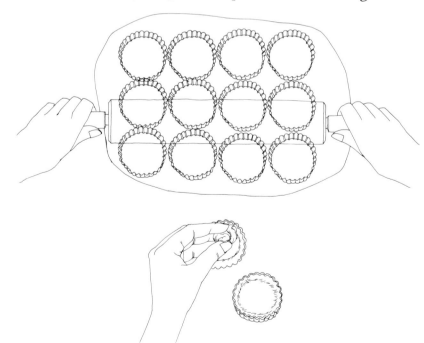

TO BAKE SHELLS **PREHEAT OVEN TO 350°**

When ready, place chilled shells on baking sheet and bake on second rack from bottom about 10 minutes, or until a light brown. Prick the shells several times with a fork during the first 5 minutes of baking when air bubbles start to appear. Cool baked pastry before filling.

TO MAKE FILLING

Combine sugar and cornmeal. Beat together eggs, milk, lemon juice and lemon rind. Stir in butter. Combine sugar-cornmeal mixture with egg-lemon mixture and pour filling into tartlet shells to about ¾ full.

TO BAKE FILLED TARTS **OVEN AT 350°**

Place tarts on baking sheet and bake about 20 minutes, until filling is set and pastry is golden brown.

Allow to cool slightly and remove tarts from pans. If pastry should stick, use point of small knife to loosen one side.

Serve at room temperature as soon as possible.

BOURBON BALLS

MAKES ABOUT 24

1 cup vanilla wafer crumbs
1 cup finely chopped pecans
½ cup bourbon
1½ tablespoons light corn syrup

2 tablespoons cocoa
Confectioners' sugar, to dust and roll

Mix all ingredients but sugar together in a food processor or blender. With hands dusted in confectioners' sugar, form walnut-sized balls from the dough, rolling them in additional confectioners' sugar.

Bourbon balls should mellow 24 hours before serving but can be made well ahead.

HOT MINCE TARTS

To make a plateful of tasty mince tarts, simply combine 1 jar Cross & Black-well Mincemeat with ½ cup brandy, mixing well, and use to replace the lemon filling for the Lemon Chess Tarts just preceding. The two tarts are put together using the same method. However, serve these hot with a dollop of Hard Sauce (see below).

Hard Sauce

MAKES 1 CUP

1 cup confectioners' sugar
5⅓ tablespoons (⅔ stick) butter, at room temperature

⅛ teaspoon salt
1 teaspoon brandy, or more to taste

Sift sugar. Cream butter until soft and add sugar gradually, beating until well blended. Add salt and brandy. Beat until sauce is very smooth, and chill.

Serve sauce in little dollops on the tarts, using a coffee or demitasse spoon.

OLD-FASHIONED POUND CAKE

The recipe for this glorious pound cake was given to me by George Lewis, an accomplished baker on top of his many other talents. Along with his recipe came these instructions: "Read through, follow the sequence, allow no substitutions, and let all ingredients come to room temperature."

SERVES 20

1 pound good-quality butter
3½ cups twice-sifted flour
¼ teaspoon baking soda
½ teaspoon ground mace
3 cups sugar
1 or more lemons, to make 3 tablespoons juice (use rind and 1 teaspoon remaining juice for glaze below)

1 tablespoon vanilla
10 eggs, separated
¼ teaspoon salt
1 teaspoon cream of tartar

TO PREPARE PAN AND MAKE BATTER

Grease a 10-inch tube pan with 2 tablespoons of the butter, using fingers to give a good even coat. Dust with flour (*not* from recipe amount), shaking to remove excess.

Lightly spoon twice-sifted flour (do *not* use cake or self-rising flour) into measuring cup. Level top with spatula. Put 3½ cups into sifter. Add baking soda, mace and 1½ cups sugar and sift all into large bowl.

Add remaining butter and blend in well with the fingers.

Stir 3 tablespoons lemon juice and vanilla into egg yolks. Add small amount of egg yolk mixture at a time to the butter and flour mixture, blending well with fingers each time (using the fingers is truly the best way).

Beat the egg whites and salt together until whites stand in glossy peaks, but are not dry. Gradually add remaining 1½ cups sugar, beating after each addition until all is well blended; gently fold in cream of tartar.

Drop beaten egg whites on batter, folding in gently with hands until whites are evenly distributed throughout the batter. Spoon batter into pan, smoothing the top. Set pan down hard on counter top to remove air bubbles.

TO BAKE   **PREHEAT OVEN TO 300°**

Bake about 2¼ hours, or until done. Cake is done when it shrinks from sides of pan and the surface springs back when lightly pressed.

Turn off heat and leave cake in oven for 30 minutes. Remove from oven, letting cake stand in pan (on rack) another 30 minutes. Then loosen sides and remove cake to rack.

When cool make Pound Cake Glaze and drip over cake. Decorate with a sprinkling of multicolored nonpareils, or with candied cherries and angelica if you prefer.

Pound Cake Glaze

3 tablespoons water
2 cups 10X sugar

Grated rind of ½ lemon (use lemon from Pound Cake recipe above)
1 teaspoon lemon juice

Mix water, sugar, lemon rind and juice together and beat until smooth. Dribble over cake.

CAROLINA WHISKEY NUTCAKE

I suggest making two of this lovely cake—one to have on the buffet and the other ready in the kitchen.

SERVES 10

1 stick (8 tablespoons) butter
¾ cup sugar
3 eggs, separated
1 teaspoon vanilla
1½ cups ground pecans
1½ cups ground apricots
1 cup flour

1 teaspoon baking powder
¼ cup orange marmalade, more or less
⅓ cup plus 3 tablespoons whiskey
Confectioners' sugar, for dusting
Grated orange peel, for garnish

TO MAKE BATTER

Cream the butter, sugar and egg yolks together until light and fluffy. Beat in vanilla, pecans, apricots, flour, baking powder, marmalade and whiskey. Whip the egg whites and gently fold into the batter.

TO BAKE   PREHEAT OVEN TO 350°

Pour batter into buttered and floured 8-inch round cake pan and bake 30 to 35 minutes. Test for doneness and when done turn out on cake rack to cool.

To serve, sprinkle top and sides with confectioners' sugar. Then top with a light dusting of the grated peel.

13
WHEN CONGRATULATIONS
ARE IN ORDER

A cocktail party for 100 to 125

COCKTAIL QUICHES

KIELBASA WITH BARBECUE SAUCE

SHRIMP WITH LOUIS DRESSING

PORK TERIYAKI WITH GADO GADO SAUCE

CHIPPED BEEF IN SWEDISH RYE ROUND

MEETING HOUSE LANE SEVICHE

CURRIED SHRIMP AND CRABMEAT BALLS

PÂTÉ AND CAVIAR PIE

VEGETABLE PLATTER WITH HERB DIP

TOMATOES IN KOSHER SALT

BABY BAKED NEW POTATOES À LA MODE

ASSORTED CHEESES, CRACKERS AND
FRUITS

LEMON PUFFS   PHYLLO FRUIT TRIANGLES

SPRITZ COOKIES   DATE BALLS

OPEN BAR   COFFEE

FOR THAT VERY SPECIAL PERSON

The challenges that come our way in life are sometimes well met, and when a promotion, new book or a special anniversary merits it, our imaginations are piqued to celebrate the occasion.

While we were living in New York my husband's career offered fascinating chances for this type of celebration. My parties often involved authors and many mixed business and pleasure. I once gave a party for a writer who was retiring from her work in China to take up a new career at the New School. Several of her friends helped compile a guest list of both old and new friends and we planned a menu to include many Chinese delicacies. It was a great success and happily brought her luncheon engagements for at least a year, making her feel very much at home again.

Now, in Vermont, another set of chances has come along. Individual musicians or a whole chorus have been celebrated with a party; and many others as well, some leading me to use banks, lawyers' offices and even a mountain-top as the locale to congratulate a very special person.

One of our well-known local bankers arranged that when he died "a drink was to be offered anyone with the stamina to go to the church for his funeral." Indeed, his wishes were followed fully; right after the service, "his" bank closed and a simple lunch with adequate liquid refreshment was offered to one and all. Many tales were told as we all celebrated his life.

While writing this book, a thoughtful local law firm made an extra room available to me rent-free. Then, when they wanted to welcome a new associate and celebrate their tenth anniversary, I was asked to oversee the affair and was delighted to accept.

Together with the lawyers, several of us planned the whole party from the first flower to the last ice cube. There was a large guest list and an ample budget, which allowed an interesting menu and some professional help. The location was to be the law offices themselves, which include the remains of a church kitchen, encompassing two large sinks, an icebox and running water. We added portable equipment—a microwave oven, a Crock-Pot to plug in, and a convection oven. The flowers were donated by a partner's wife, who made lovely spring baskets of moss, grape hyacinths and daffodils.

Our menu was much like the one I'm suggesting here, with most of the food served at room temperature and some kept warm in a Crock-Pot, oven, or over a warmer. Due to the traffic flow we had two complete bars set up, one with a professional bartender, the other manned by a waitress who could arrange platters, help refill the wine and serve drinks. Another helper in the kitchen kept an eye on the ovens and decorated the plates of fresh foods continually being brought out to the guests. The secret for this party was to offer a surprise dish every so often.

The younger staff at the law firm were asked to pass the hors d'oeuvre, watch to see that the guests could find a fresh drink when they wanted, and just mingle.

If you should be asked to be part of the planning for a similar party, you can follow pretty much the same scheme or initiate one of your own. Most of the recipes for this suggested menu follow right here. A few others are tucked away throughout the book: the index will lead you.

Be sure to have ample help—both at the bar and in the kitchen. Most bartenders will organize their own bars, including getting the supplies, but leave purchasing the liquor to you. However, if the entire setup should fall to you and you feel at all insecure, see the list of bar needs in the back of the book. Remember ashtrays and wastebaskets for the inevitable trash, and—most important—be sure to check that there are ample plugs for all that you are planning (we once almost blew the entire Brattleboro Museum building plugging in things for a large gala there). Beyond all that, there should be someone to tidy up before and after—and to arrange for the flowers and any other decoration.

Of course if your special person party is at home or in a public room, many of these concerns will fade away—but there is always something needing tender loving care.

Music is not usually an addition to these parties: the din is too great. But if your guest of honor is involved in the musical world, a little background music might be a delightful touch—perhaps a strolling minstrel of delicate tempo and tone who would not be offended if people didn't listen too carefully.

Music is only one way to make these parties a little more special. If there is a way to do it gracefully, you and whoever is planning the party with you might want to think of some type of special presentation to mark the occasion. Although I did not plan it, I recently attended an afternoon reception honoring Ambassador and Mrs. Ellsworth Bunker for their many years of service in the diplomatic corps. It was a simple but lovely party—made especially memorable by a lighthearted short musical skit touching bases with bits of their personal history and a few equally short but pithy remarks.

Another memorably unique—though quite different—party recently put on by a suburban Connecticut town honored a place instead of a person: the new town dump. The old dump had been reclaimed and the townspeople were invited to gather there to toast the new with champagne.

And I know of yet another party where a historian was honored by a menu of foods taken from "his" period of history.

Such twists are not always possible, but when they are, they do add, and make a special occasion even more special.

COCKTAIL QUICHES

Combine the Quiche Pastry below with the Spinach and Ham or Crabmeat filling, or both, to make a good supply of this delicious hors d'oeuvre.

Quiche Pastry

The dough for these bite-size quiches must be a little heavier than for a full-size quiche as it tends to break apart easily. A double recipe of the pastry should accommodate 1 recipe of each filling.

MAKES ABOUT 60 1-INCH QUICHES

> *1 stick (8 tablespoons) butter, softened*
> *4 ounces cream cheese, softened*
>
> *1¼ cups whole wheat pastry flour*
> *Salt to taste*

Mix butter and cheese well. Add flour (the flour must be *pastry* flour; otherwise the dough will not be light enough) and salt (the amount added will depend on the type of butter used and on the filling planned) and blend well until smooth. Chill dough for several hours before forming quiche shells.

TO FORM QUICHE SHELLS

Grease little cupcake tins (or small quiche molds if you have them) well with margarine, butter or lard. Pinch off pieces of dough about the size of a walnut. Roll each piece in your hands to soften, then using your thumb spread the dough gradually and firmly to form a shell, spreading the dough right to the top of the tin and making the "cup" as even as possible. When all the cups are filled, prick each several times to allow any excess air to escape. Then chill whole tin for a half hour or so.

While shells are chilling make filling(s).

TO FINISH AND BAKE   PREHEAT OVEN TO 425°

Once the filling is made bring out one chilled tin at a time and fill each cup ¾ full with a spoon or by pouring from a glass measuring cup.

Bake for 5 minutes then lower oven to 350° for 15 minutes. The quiches are ready when puffed up and brown. Allow quiches to cool to tepid before removing from pan. If time is of the essence you can use narrow spatula to circle each quiche before lifting out.

These quiches freeze well. Slide them into the freezer on a flat cookie sheet until frozen and then transfer them to plastic freezing boxes (small are best; then you can pluck out just as many as you need for a small party). Reheat in 425° oven for 10 to 12 minutes.

Spinach and Ham Filling

1 (10-ounce) package chopped spinach, thawed and drained	Salt and pepper to taste
	3 large eggs
4 ounces sliced ham, finely chopped (leftovers from a baked ham would be even better)	1 cup cream, more or less, as needed
1 tablespoon butter	¼ cup grated cheese (Swiss or Cheddar)
1 tablespoon finely sliced shallots or scallions	Parmesan cheese, finely grated, for topping
⅛ teaspoon freshly grated nutmeg	

In medium-sized pan, sauté spinach with ham in butter. Add shallots or scallions and toss lightly. Season with the nutmeg, salt and pepper, but taste first as the ham may have enough salt. Let cool.

Beat eggs and add enough cream to make 1½ to 1¾ cups liquid. Season lightly, add grated Swiss or cheddar cheese, and blend together well with spinach mixture.

After using to fill prepared quiche shells, top with grated Parmesan. (If you are going to freeze the quiches and reheat, use less Parmesan; you'll put more on just before reheating.)

Crabmeat Filling

2 tablespoons minced shallots or scallions	2 tablespoons Madeira or dry white vermouth
3 tablespoons sweet butter	3 large eggs
1 cup (¼ pound) cooked frozen or fresh crabmeat	1½ cups whipping cream or half and half
½ teaspoon salt	¼ teaspoon thyme (optional)
2 pinches pepper (three turns of the grinder)	1 tablespoon tomato paste

Cook the shallots or scallions in the butter for several minutes over moderate heat but do not brown. Add the crabmeat and stir gently for several minutes. Add ¼ teaspoon salt and 1 pinch pepper and then the wine, and bring to a boil. Allow to cool.

Beat together the 3 eggs with the cream, additional seasonings and tomato paste. Gradually blend in the crabmeat mixture.

Note: Shrimp or lobster can be substituted—in equal measure—for the crabmeat in this filling. You might also want to substitute ¼ teaspoon curry powder for the thyme.

SHRIMP WITH LOUIS DRESSING

Shrimp are ever-popular with the partygoers of this world. There are many ways to prepare them. You can boil them in the more traditional fashion (about 3 to 5 minutes in a Court Bouillon; see page 398) or stir-fry them with a little seasoning and oil, shelling and deveining them first, of course. Whichever way you choose, do as many as your budget can manage and serve chilled with the Louis Dressing given here, or a shrimp dip of your own choice.

Note: For a tangier shrimp you can prepare them as we did the Jumbo Shrimp for the Superbowl Sunday party, with ginger and tomato paste, and serve hot—without the dressing.

Louis Dressing

This delicious dressing goes with many seafood dishes and, with shrimp, I much prefer it to the more usual cocktail sauce.

MAKES ABOUT 1¾ CUPS

2 tablespoons grated red onion	*2 tablespoons chopped fresh parsley*
1 cup mayonnaise	*A few grains cayenne*
¼ cup chili sauce	*⅓ cup whipped cream*

Mix the first 5 ingredients and let meld for several hours. Fold in the whipped cream well; dressing should be thoroughly blended. Taste for seasoning.

Notes: You can make this dressing a day or two ahead, adding the whipped cream just before serving. If really pressed for time, try Marie's Blue Cheese commercially-made dressing: it's delicious too.

PORK TERIYAKI

The cut of pork for this teriyaki should be a tenderloin, which will then be marinated and broiled. If this cut is hard to find ask your butcher to bone the shank end of a pork loin and make it into three rolls about 1 ½ to 2 inches in diameter tied together well. (They usually run 5 to 7 inches in length.) This will give the same result. (Even more ideal: find a Chinese butcher with the meat already prepared for slicing and eating.)

When cooked, slice the meat thinly and serve with a dipping sauce. The Gado Gado Sauce on page 67 seems just right.

A ½ PORK TENDERLOIN WILL SERVE THIS PARTY EASILY

Teriyaki Marinade

AMPLE FOR ½ PORK TENDERLOIN

1 tablespoon finely chopped fresh ginger
2 cloves garlic, finely minced
1 medium onion, finely chopped
2 tablespoons honey, or maple syrup (for Vermont-style teriyaki)

½ cup dry sherry
1 cup light soy sauce
2 tablespoons catsup (optional, for color)

The first three ingredients can be chopped in a blender or food processor. Then add the liquids and mix well. Cover the tenderloin rolls with the marinade in a good-sized baking pan and refrigerate for 8 hours or so, if time allows—and at least 2 or 3—basting as regularly as possible.

TO COOK   **PREHEAT OVEN TO 350°**

Lift the pork out of the marinade and put on a wire rack, or use a barbecue pan. Brush well with the marinade and place under the broiler. Cook for 45 to 60 minutes turning and basting regularly so that all sides get nicely browned. To test for doneness, prick meat with a fork or skewer: the juices should run yellow.

Remove pork from oven and baste again. Let cool; refrigerate, wrapped in aluminum foil, if it will not be used immediately.

Any remaining marinade can be used again if the solid parts are strained out and it is stored in a covered jar in the refrigerator.

TO SERVE

Remove the cooked pork from the refrigerator about 1 hour before serving and slice into strips about ¼ to ½ inch thick. Arrange on a plate with toothpicks and the Gado Gado Sauce. Surround with fresh watercress sprigs and slices of salty rye bread.

CHIPPED BEEF IN SWEDISH RYE ROUND

This dark bread round when filled makes an attractive addition to any buffet table.

SERVES 25 OR SO

1 pint sour cream
1 ¾ cups mayonnaise (Hellmann's preferred)
1 ½ teaspoons celery seeds
2 teaspoons chopped parsley

2 teaspoons dill weed
1 (5-ounce) jar chipped beef (more or less by jar size), shredded
1 loaf round dark Swedish rye

To make the filling, combine the sour cream, mayonnaise, seasonings and chipped beef. Blend together well and put in refrigerator to chill until ready to use.

Cut the top of the loaf off horizontally to keep for a lid. Scoop out the insides leaving a good inch attached to the crust to form a "bowl" for the filling. If not using right away, slide the "lid" back on to keep the "bowl" moist.

If you are using right away, cut the scooped-out bread into bite-sized pieces which will be used to dip into the chipped beef filling. If not, or if you are transporting to assemble at another place, wrap the bread insides in foil or plastic wrap to keep them from drying out. Cut just before using.

When ready to serve, fill the bread bowl with the chipped beef filling and surround with the bite-sized bread.

If you are making more than one to serve for a large party, prepare the various parts ahead but do not stuff the bowl or cut the bread until just before serving; this will keep everything fresh.

To stretch this hors d'oeuvre even further, after finishing the dip and bread pieces, the loaf itself can be cut into bite-sized pieces: it too will be moist and delicious.

Note: Chipped beef is now also available in plastic pouches.

Variation: To make an equally good Spinach Pumpernickel Loaf, following the same procedure as above, combine 1 (10-ounce) package frozen chopped spinach, 1 package Knorr Leek Soupmix, 1 pint mayonnaise, 1 pint sour cream, and chopped scallions to taste, to make a filling for a hollowed-out pumpernickel loaf.

MEETING HOUSE LANE SEVICHE

This particular seviche came to me from Donna Borofsky who served it at a museum benefit we both helped hostess. Not only are the scallops delicious, served between their accompanying red tomato and green avocado dipping sauces, they are very festive as well.

MAKES ABOUT 80 PIECES

2 pounds scallops, large or bay
1 large onion, thinly sliced
4 bay leaves
1 tablespoon white wine vinegar
Generous pinches of dried red pepper, crushed peppercorns, tarragon and chopped garlic

1 cup lime or lemon juice
½ cup orange juice
Parsley and celery leaves, chopped, for garnish
1 each, small green and red pepper, thinly sliced

Wash and drain scallops. (If you are using the large scallops, which I prefer, cut them into bite-sized pieces.)

Put scallops into preferably enameled saucepan with onion, bay leaves, vinegar and herbs. Add citrus juices and bring mixture to boil. Remove from heat, cool and then chill for at least 6 hours.

When ready to serve, drain scallops thoroughly so they won't drip and put into shallow serving dish, banking them with the Seviche Tomato Dip and the Seviche Avocado Dip below. Then garnish with the chopped leaves and pepper slices. If you have a divided three-way serving dish available, this makes a charming display.

Note: The scallop marinade, strained, will keep a good while in the fridge so you can use again another time.

Seviche Tomato Dip

MAKES ABOUT 1¼ CUPS

1 tablespoon butter or oil, plus 1 teaspoon butter
1 teaspoon tomato paste
½ tablespoon minced garlic
1 tablespoon fresh basil, or 1 teaspoon dried

2 teaspoons potato flour
Salt and pepper to taste
1 cup clam juice, more or less

Heat 1 tablespoon butter or oil in saucepan, stir in tomato paste, garlic, basil and potato flour to make paste. Season with salt and pepper. Add clam juice and 1 teaspoon butter, watching so that sauce doesn't get too thin. Heat and stir until sauce is smooth and the consistency you want. If too thick, add a little additional clam juice.

Seviche Avocado Dip

MAKES ABOUT 1½ CUPS

2 ripe avocados, peeled and seeded	¼ cup mayonnaise
3 tablespoons lemon juice	¼ cup sour cream
1 tablespoon grated onion	Dash Tabasco sauce
½ teaspoon salt	

Put avocados in blender with lemon juice and purée. Add remaining ingredients and blend until smooth and creamy.

If dip is too thick, thin with milk or light cream.

Note: This dip also makes a good dressing for summer salads. I like it just as is for a fruit salad and with a minced clove of garlic added for a vegetable or green salad.

CURRIED SHRIMP AND CRABMEAT BALLS

These tasty bites are easy to make and not as heavy as when prepared in pastries.

MAKES 24 TO 30 BALLS

¾ cup minced canned shrimp	2 large egg yolks
½ cup minced canned crabmeat	2 tablespoons heavy cream
1 tablespoon gin	¼ cup fine, dry breadcrumbs
½ teaspoon curry powder	3 tablespoons untoasted sesame seeds
¼ teaspoon celery salt	Oil for frying
⅛ teaspoon ground black pepper	

Combine first 8 ingredients. Chill overnight (10 to 12 hours). When ready, shape into 1-inch balls. Roll the balls in combined breadcrumbs and sesame seeds.

Fry in 1 inch of hot (375°) oil until golden brown, about 2 minutes. Don't worry when the seeds don't brown. A Fry Baby works nicely for this chore, though you'll need the oil a little deeper.

Serve warm on toothpicks.

PÂTÉ AND CAVIAR PIE

This recipe came from an election night party some years ago now. At that time two of the husbands—Chet Huntley, the newscaster, and Oliver Quayle, the pollster—were analyzing the election results on television while the wives prepared the collation, each wife bringing a favorite recipe.

Mrs. Huntley brought this very decorative and delicious dish. The recipe had been given to her by a friend who asked that anyone wishing a copy of the recipe pay a dollar to be given, in turn, to a favorite charity. I did—and will again for use here—this time to my current favorite charity, the Brattleboro Museum & Art Center.

MAKES ENOUGH FOR 30 OR SO SERVINGS

I tablespoon (I envelope) unflavored gelatin
¼ cup water
I (10-ounce) can clear consommé
Dashes celery salt, onion salt, garlic salt, curry powder, cayenne and Worcestershire sauce

I (8-ounce) package cream cheese, softened
I (3-ounce) can domestic liver pâté
2 heaping tablespoons mayonnaise
4 ounces domestic caviar
Parsley sprigs, for garnish

Dissolve gelatin in the water and set aside. Heat the consommé, adding a dash of all spices. Add gelatin and again set aside. In a small bowl, mix together the cream cheese, pâté, mayonnaise and another dash of all the spices. Set aside, keeping at room temperature.

Oil a 12-inch round glass pie plate. Spread the caviar over the bottom of the dish. Spoon about half of the consommé-gelatin mix over the caviar and refrigerate about an hour. When set, spread the cream cheese-pâté mix over the caviar-consommé base; add the remaining consommé mix and again refrigerate.

When ready to use, invert on serving dish, garnish with parsley and serve with water biscuits or thin-sliced bread.

Note: This pâté pie will keep nicely in the fridge for several weeks.

BABY BAKED NEW POTATOES À LA MODE

Almost everyone loves a good baked potato. These little baked new potatoes are no exception, especially when surrounded by all manner of tempting garnish.

Allow I potato per person. Wash and arrange in single layers on as many baking pans as you need. Bake at 350° until tender.

Pictures at an Exhibition

ASSORTMENT OF ENGLISH TOFFEE BARS, PECAN TASJES,
PETIT FOURS AND OTHER SWEETS
SALMON AND PEA MOUSSE
FRUITED CHICKEN WINGS
CHEESE AND FRUIT TRAY

© Robert Grant

After the Night Music

GIU-MA BANG
QUEEN MOTHER CAKE
FLORENTINES

To serve, spread on a tray or heap in a bowl and surround with various toppings of your choice: sour cream, chopped ham, scallions, grated cheese and chopped parsley are some of my guests' favorites. Keep napkins handy.

Note: When purchasing the potatoes for this hors d'oeuvre buy the smallest, most uniform and most blemish-free new potatoes you can find.

LEMON PUFFS

This tempting sweet combines a *pâte à chou* pastry with a lemon filling.

MAKES ABOUT 3 TO 4 DOZEN

1 recipe Pâte à Chou (see page 399)

1 recipe Lemon Puff Filling (see below)

TO BAKE AND FILL   PREHEAT OVEN TO 400°

Pâte à chou dough should be stiff enough to stand in peaks when spoon is withdrawn. When dough is ready, drop by the teaspoonful or press through a pastry tube onto lightly greased baking sheet. (If using a pastry tube, the #7 tube works well.) Keep little rounds as high as possible. Bake about 10 minutes, or until done. Puffs should be golden brown with no beads of moisture showing. At this point, using the sharp point of a knife, poke side of each puff and turn oven off. Leave in closed oven another 10 minutes. This allows interior steam to escape and helps prevent later sogginess.

When ready to serve, fill puffs with Lemon Puff Filling using small spoon or pastry tube.

Note: These puffs may be made up to baking stage and then kept in refrigerator several days before baking. They also freeze well after baking: place on cookie sheets, wrap properly and freeze until needed; when ready to use, reheat puffs briefly just before filling.

Lemon Puff Filling

This is the wonderful filling that the English call lemon curd.

MAKES A LITTLE OVER 1 CUP/FILLS 3 TO 4 DOZEN PUFFS

5 egg yolks
½ cup sugar

Juice and grated rind of 2 large lemons
4 tablespoons sweet butter

In heavy saucepan or top of double boiler, over low heat combine egg yolks and sugar. Add lemon juice and rind. Stir, adding butter little by little. Cook until thick, stirring constantly.

Pour into clean jar. Unless you're using right away, cover top of cooled mixture with a thin layer of melted paraffin. Store in refrigerator. It keeps well —up to a month.

Note: Lemon curd is available in 12-ounce jars in specialty shops. It too keeps well.

PHYLLO FRUIT TRIANGLES

To make these fluffy sweet pastries, combine phyllo pastry as used to make the Tiropitas on page 169 with a filling of not-too-sweet good-quality preserves: cherry, blueberry or a sieved ginger marmalade are only a few possibilities. Or try mincemeat laced with a little brandy—anything that isn't too moist. They are folded and baked in the same manner as the Tiropitas.

Variation: To make Phyllo Fruit Baskets instead, use four layers of the phyllo sheets, buttered and sprinkled with finely ground nuts between each layer, and cut into 2-inch squares. Using miniature quiche pans, press a phyllo square into each mold, turning each with your thumb to anchor securely. Bake quickly, about 5 to 6 minutes. Store cooled baskets in airtight tin until needed. When ready to serve, warm baskets in low oven for several minutes. Then fill with marmalade, lemon curd, mixed fruit, etc.

If you wish to fill with a savory filling (cheese, spinach mousse, etc.), omit the ground nuts when putting the baskets together.

These baskets may be made larger, baking longer, for a dessert treat, but I like the miniature variety.

Note: Morello cherries, half chopped and half left whole, marinated in Kirsch are another good filling for these baskets. Fill with chopped cherries and top with whole.

SPRITZ COOKIES

This basic cookie recipe is fun for large parties because it can be adapted in so many ways. Various shapes can be achieved simply by changing the cookie press disk. Stars might be appropriate for one party, flowers for another, or you can make the initials of an honored guest. And it's fun to play with color occasionally—perhaps a bit of green for an Irish occasion or pink for a bride's shower.

MAKES ABOUT 100

2 sticks (½ pound) butter　　　　*1 teaspoon vanilla*
1 cup sugar　　　　　　　　　　*2½ cups flour*
1 egg or 2 egg yolks

Cream the butter and sugar well. Add in egg, vanilla and flour and mix all together well.

TO SHAPE AND BAKE　　PREHEAT OVEN TO 375°

Put dough through a cookie press onto an ungreased cookie sheet. This dough rises very little so the cookies can be closely spaced. Bake for 15 minutes or until lightly browned.

14
PICTURES AT THE EXHIBITION

A modest "Grand Opening" for 150

SESAME-CHEESE FINGERS

BLUE CHEESE BALL

SALMON MOUSSE

GINGER MEATBALLS

SPICY CODFISH BALLS

CLAMS BOROFSKY WITH MUSHROOMS

FRUITED CHICKEN WINGS

SPICY EARLY POTATO BALLS
OR
POTATO SKIN CHIPS OR BOATS

CAVIAR PIE STUFFED EGGS

ASSORTED COCKTAIL SANDWICHES

SEASONAL VEGETABLE PLATTER WITH
CURRIED AVOCADO DIP

ENGLISH TOFFEE BARS

MARINATED LICHEE NUTS AND KUMQUATS

STUFFED DATES PECAN TASJES

WINE PUNCH WINES FRUIT PUNCH

COFFEE

PICTURES AT THE EXHIBITION

The opening of a new art exhibit is a time to celebrate. Often a reception is planned to mark the occasion—to honor the artist or artists, if that is possible, and their friends, and of course the staff who worked so hard to get the exhibit installed. If this is a museum exhibit the members are invited and often the general public; in a gallery the number might well be smaller.

For a museum the event is usually planned by a continuing hospitality committee or by a special committee chosen especially for that one affair. It is designed to be gracious but not elegant—after all, the costs will have come from much laborious fund-raising. The committee will call heavily on volunteer help, drawing on the men and women who serve the museum, to contribute the wines, flowers and hors d'oeuvre and to help with the preliminary setting up and with the hosting. In a small museum or gallery this can mean clean-up work as well—both before and after. But many hands do make light work—and this work does help people feel a part of things, especially nice for the shy among us and for those new to town.

With this in mind, in making up the menu for this reception I've put together a selection that can be farmed out in parcels. In that way, no one gets too much of the work and the menu offers vitality and variety—as well as good food (one soon learns, of course, who makes the best what). Good planning will ensure a balance of items, and if the budget is particularly constrained the less expensive items can be doubled and the more expensive dishes limited. One or two fancy platters or special dishes will carry others not quite so grand as long as all are presented attractively (but please, not too much cream cheese). Remember: it only takes a little extra care and a few nice touches to give that "special" feel that every good party requires.

In the Brattleboro Museum & Art Center, where I spend a good amount of time, we open the season with a different show in each of our three galleries. At a recent opening, Victorian paintings and historical artifacts were displayed in the central gallery, while in the mid-sized gallery there was an exhibit of art from the People's Republic of China and the third gallery showed local photography. To highlight that opening, the reception committee had a Victorian table heavy with flowers and sweets in the Victorian gallery; for the China gallery, one of the members lent a magnificent old Chinese vase and a simple table was set with various Oriental tidbits (our town is lucky enough to have a lovely Korean national in residence who graciously shares her knowledge of oriental cooking every now and then when needed; several of her recipes lurk here and there in my book). Both tables offered chilled white wine and tea.

It's always fun to tie the exhibit to the reception in some way if possible. I still recall a medieval show in the great rotunda of New York's Metropolitan Museum where a members' reception committee had made appropriately simulated coins for people to use to purchase their refreshments—a delightful idea and something my daughter has never forgotten. The possibilities are almost limitless.

In preparing for any party that is not private, check the local bylaws. In some towns a permit for serving wine and alcoholic beverages is free for the asking; in others there is a small fee. Some places allow the sale of such beverages and others do not.

As with all parties, when planning this reception it is important to have a clear idea of just what you want your reception to be. If it is chiefly to honor the artists and staff and perhaps intrigue the community, there should be no charge (you can always have a donation basket in view). On the other hand, if it is a reception to preview an expensive exhibit for the members, a fee may well be appropriate. Whatever you plan, be sure the party is inviting and pleasant—one that will encourage people to come again the next time.

You'll find recipes for most of the dishes on this menu directly following; the index will point you to the rest. And remember: it's flexible. Potato Skin Chips or Boats could easily be substituted for the Spicy Early Potato Balls when early potatoes are not available. The High Tea segment has several recipes for cocktail-sized sandwiches; or, if you're feeling fancier the Cocktail Quiches might be nice instead. Try the Curried Avocado Dip here with a seasonal vegetable platter of your own choosing, or look into the Vegetarian and Southern "At Home" sections for some more ideas. No doubt the committee members will have their own favorite foods they'll want to suggest: just be sure someone is keeping track to be certain there will indeed be enough and that the balance is good.

BLUE CHEESE BALL

These cheese balls should be made up a day ahead as they taste better if they season a while.

MAKES 35 OR 40 PORTIONS

2 (8-ounce) packages cream cheese, softened
1 (8-ounce) package blue cheese, softened
4 tablespoons butter

1 tablespoon minced fresh chives (1 or 2 more if using for garnish)
½ cup chopped ripe olives
2 to 3 tablespoons chopped nuts (optional, for garnish)

Mix together cheeses and butter well. Add chives and olives and again mix well. Roll into ball and refrigerate, covered, until ready to use.

When ready to serve, roll ball in additional chopped chives or finely chopped nuts.

Note: This cheese roll, ungarnished, will keep very well, covered, in the fridge for several weeks. If kept after garnishing, chives will wilt a bit but can be refreshed when needed. If fresh chives are not avaible, try chopped red onion or parsley.

GINGER MEATBALLS

It seems to me that the hot meatballs are the first thing to disappear at almost every party. This delicious and different variation comes to me from Carol Eaton and Joan Mrlik.

MAKES APPROXIMATELY 24 TO 30 MEATBALLS

¾ pound each lean ground pork and beef
¼ pound veal
2 tablespoons minced onion
½ teaspoon butter
2 eggs

½ cup milk
½ cup breadcrumbs
1 teaspoon salt
½ teaspoon pepper
2 tablespoons chopped fresh ginger

With meat grinder or food processor grind the meat together twice into a chilled bowl. Sauté the onion in the butter until soft. Beat eggs and milk together and pour over the breadcrumbs. Add salt, pepper, ginger and the sautéed onion to the meat, and then combine both mixtures. Form into balls about the size of a walnut.

TO BAKE   **PREHEAT OVEN TO 350°**

Bake the meatballs on ungreased cookie sheets, preferably with a rim, for about 15 minutes, turning every five minutes or so to get them browned on all sides. If fat should accumulate, tip slightly to drain off the excess or blot the excess away with paper towels.

Serve with Ginger Sauce following.

Ginger Sauce

1 teaspoon cornstarch	*1 teaspoon soy sauce*
½ cup sugar	*2 to 3 tablespoons chopped fresh*
½ cup cider vinegar	*ginger*
¼ cup dry sherry (not cooking	
sherry)	

Soften the cornstarch in a small amount of water. In a small saucepan, mix the sugar, vinegar, sherry and soy sauce, and bring to a boil. Add the cornstarch mixture and stir until sauce is transparent. Add the ginger. Pour the sauce over the meatballs and serve hot, or keep warm until ready to serve.

Notes: These meatballs may be made without the veal, by increasing the amount of pork and beef accordingly. The key to meatballs that hold together properly is using meat that is truly lean. Without the sauce, they freeze well.

SPICY CODFISH BALLS

Salt codfish is usually sold in small wooden boxes approximately 2 cups in measure.

MAKES ABOUT 100

5 medium potatoes (about 2½ cups	*1 teaspoon dry English mustard*
when mashed)	*1 teaspoon Worcestershire sauce*
2 cups salt codfish, soaked overnight	*Dash cayenne*
in cold water	*Flour, for rolling*
3 egg yolks	*Oil, for frying*
3 tablespoons butter	

TO PREPARE CAKES

Cover unpeeled potatoes with cold water, bring to boil, and cook slowly for 30 minutes or until done. Drain and peel them at once, put through a ricer or food mill into top of a double boiler and set over hot water. Drain soaked codfish, cover with cold water, bring to boil and cook about 8 minutes. Drain very well and spread out on clean cloth, rubbing the fish with the cloth until it is dry and fluffy.

Combine potatoes and fish and mix well with a wooden spoon. Add egg yolks, one at a time, beating the mixture vigorously. Beat in the butter, mustard, Worcestershire and cayenne.

Shape mixture into bite-sized balls and roll them in flour. Then chill until ready to cook, 1 hour or more.

TO FRY AND SERVE   **HEAT FAT TO 375°**

Fry the balls, 12 or so at a time, in deep hot oil until golden brown. Drain on paper towels and serve very hot with toothpicks and Ritz Cocktail Sauce below.

Ritz Cocktail Sauce

MAKES 1 CUP

⅔ cup catsup
¼ cup chili sauce
1 tablespoon Worcestershire sauce
1 tablespoon freshly grated
  horseradish

4 dashes Tabasco sauce
Juice of ½ lemon

Mix all ingredients together well and chill until ready to serve.

Note: This sauce can be combined with mayonnaise and served warm with cooked fish or shellfish.

Adapted from *The Ritz-Carlton Cook Book and Guide to Home Entertaining* by Helen Ridley.

CLAMS BOROFSKY WITH MUSHROOMS

This hors d'oeuvre is another from Linda King, a young Vermont friend.

MAKES 50 SERVINGS

½ cup finely chopped scallions,
1 pound cream cheese, softened
2 tablespoons bottled clam juice
1 tablespoon gin
1 egg, well beaten
Freshly ground black pepper

2 (7½-ounce) cans minced clams,
  well drained
2 to 3 pounds medium mushroom
  caps, to make 50 or so,
  cleaned

Beat together well the chopped scallions, cream cheese, clam juice, gin, egg and pepper. This much can be done with either a hand or a regular beater or in a food processor (if you use processor, be careful not to overprocess). When well mixed, add the clams, mixing only enough to blend in (you don't want to break up the clams). It will be a thick mixture—more a filling than a dip.

TO BAKE   **PREHEAT OVEN TO 325°**

Place mixture in oiled 1½- or 2-quart casserole and bake 45 minutes to 1 hour.

TO SERVE

Serve kept warm in chafing dish, over a candle warmer or on a warming tray with the mushrooms in a basket nearby (and a reserve basket of nonsalty crackers for catching the last dabs of clams). For a large party you might start off with one tray of mushroom caps filled ahead; then just let the guests dip their own.

Note: If you can find it, use bulk cream cheese for this recipe. As it is less gelatinous, it beats up more easily. It is often available at health food stores and in specialty shops.

FRUITED CHICKEN WINGS

These chicken wings, from Marjorie Blanchard, are somewhat sweeter than the recipe I give for Cocktail Chicken Wings in the Intimate Winter Wedding chapter.

TO MAKE 20 OR SO

20 or so chicken wings　　　　*1 clove garlic, minced*
1 cup maple syrup　　　　　　*1 cup catsup*
½ cup each orange and apricot
　juice

First, prepare chicken wings by removing wing tips with a sharp knife or scissors.

Combine the other ingredients in saucepan and heat, stirring until well blended. Dip wings in sauce and spread on baking sheet.

TO BAKE   **PREHEAT OVEN TO 400°**

Bake sauced wings about 40 minutes, brushing occasionally with any remaining sauce. Then broil 5 minutes, or until golden and crusty.

Serve at room temperature or warm from a Crock-Pot.

SPICY EARLY POTATO BALLS

Here's something a little different to do with those first baby potatoes or the little ones left at the end of the season that you can't bear to toss. If you don't have these little potatoes available, you might try the potato skin ideas following.

TO MAKE 40 OR 50

40 to 50 baby potatoes (½-inch diameter)
1 cup olive oil, or ½ vegetable oil and ½ olive oil
1¼ cups red or white wine vinegar
5 grinds pepper
2 teaspoons salt

6 scallions or chives, finely minced
1 medium green bell pepper, or ½ red pepper and ½ green, thinly sliced
Tomato quarters, for garnish
½ cup minced parsley, basil or dill, for garnish

Wash and scrub the potatoes well. Prick each three or four times with a cake tester or fine skewer. Combine the oil, vinegar, pepper and salt in a good-sized kettle. Add the potatoes, making sure there is enough fluid to cover them (if not, add more in the same proportions). Bring to boil, then cover and lower heat to a gentle simmer. Cook 20 to 30 minutes or until potatoes are just tender. (Small *new* potatoes can take longer to cook than big old ones.) Remove from heat and transfer potatoes and liquid to bowl. Place in refrigerator to chill.

When ready to serve, drain, add scallions or chives and pepper slices. Surround with quarters of fresh tomatoes, sprinkled with minced parsley, basil or dill. Supply sturdy toothpicks and napkins or plates.

POTATO SKIN CHIPS OR BOATS

Baked potato skins can be used as either dipping chips or boats. This recipe eliminates the frying so many of us are loathe to do these days.

MAKES 48 CHIPS OR 8 BOATS

4 large baking potatoes
3 tablespoons oil
1 tablespoon Parmesan cheese
½ teaspoon salt

¼ teaspoon garlic powder
¼ teaspoon paprika
⅛ teaspoon pepper

TO PREPARE   **PREHEAT OVEN TO 425°**

Prick each potato and bake about 45 minutes, or until tender. Cool and cut in half lengthwise. Scoop out pulp, leaving a shell about ¼-inch thick.

Mix the remaining ingredients together in medium-sized bowl.

For chips, cut each shell into sixths; add cut-up chips to cheese mixture and toss. *For boats,* brush half shells with cheese mixture.

FOR FINAL BAKE   **RAISE OVEN TO 475°**

For chips, bake 8 to 10 minutes until crisp, turning once. *For boats,* bake, hollow side up, for about 7 minutes. Turn and continue baking until crisp.

To serve, when well-crisped, put chips in basket and serve with the Curried Avocado Dip following. Or try any of the others suggested in the dips section at the back of the book or listed in the index.

Note: *The Victory Garden Cookbook,* by Marian Morash, offers good variations for potato skins.

Curried Avocado Dip

MAKES 1½ TO 2 CUPS

2 medium avocados   *1 tablespoon mayonnaise*
4 tablespoons lemon juice   *1 teaspoon Worcestershire sauce*
2 slices bacon   *¼ teaspoon Tabasco sauce*
¾ teaspoon curry powder   *½ teaspoon chili powder*
1 clove garlic, minced or mashed   *Salt to taste*

Carefully cut the avocados in half lengthwise and remove the pits. With a spoon take out the pulp, being sure to leave two of the halves as firm shells. Sprinkle these shells with 1 tablespoon lemon juice.

Cook bacon until crisp and chop into fine bits.

Mash avocado pulp, add bacon and other ingredients, including remaining lemon juice. Beat with fork or beater until smooth and heap into 2 prepared shells. Then chill until ready to serve.

ENGLISH TOFFEE BARS

These bars combine toffee flavor with chocolate and nuts.

MAKES ABOUT 4 DOZEN BARS

2 sticks (½ pound) butter, softened   *2 cups flour*
1 cup brown sugar   *6 ounces chocolate chips*
1 teaspoon vanilla   *¾ cup chopped walnuts or*
1 egg yolk   *   almonds, more or less*

Cream butter, sugar and vanilla. Add egg yolk and flour, and mix until a smooth dough forms.

TO BAKE   **PREHEAT OVEN TO 350°**

Press dough evenly onto greased jelly-roll pan. Bake 15 to 20 minutes until lightly browned. While still hot, sprinkle with chocolate chips. When chocolate softens, spread evenly over crust, then sprinkle nuts over top. Cut while still warm.

Variations: Try replacing the brown sugar with ¾ cup maple syrup and increasing the flour to 2¼ cups. Another variation exchanges seven (5-ounce) Hersey bars for the chocolate chips; just melt the bars and pour oven baked dough while still warm.

PECAN TASJES

East Indies Southern cookies from the Dutch.

MAKES 2 DOZEN

> *1 stick plus 1 tablespoon (9 tablespoons) butter, at room temperature*
> *1 (3-ounce) package cream cheese, at room temperature*
> *1 cup sifted flour*
> *1 egg*
>
> *¾ cup brown sugar*
> *½ teaspoon ground cinnamon*
> *1 teaspoon grated orange rind*
> *2 teaspoons Dutch Curaco*
> *Dash salt*
> *⅔ cup coarsely broken pecans*

Cream 1 stick butter and cream cheese together, stir in flour and chill for 1 hour in mixer. Shape into 2 dozen 1-inch balls. Place in ungreased 1½-inch muffin cups. Press dough against bottom and sides of cups, pushing up firmly to make a cup.

Beat together egg, sugar, 1 tablespoon butter, cinnamon, rind, Dutch Curaco and salt until smooth.

Divide half the pecans among pastry-lined cups; add egg mixture and top with remaining pecans.

TO BAKE   **PREHEAT OVEN TO 325°**

Bake for 25 minutes or until filling is set. Cool and remove from pans.

Note: These cookies can be made 2 days ahead and will still be nice and fresh for the party, or they can be frozen well ahead.

MARINATED LICHEE NUTS AND KUMQUATS

This is a delightful sweet—both for this party and for after a heavy meal.

SERVES 14 OR 15

> *1 (16-ounce) can lichee nuts*
> *1 (20-ounce) can kumquats*
> *¼ cup rum, more as needed*
>
> *1 (20-ounce) can pineapple chunks, drained*

Wash nuts and kumquats carefully, trimming any questionable spots. Drain well and marinate nuts and kumquats separately in rum almost to cover. Refrigerate until ready to serve.

At last minute, combine nuts, kumquats and pineapple chunks and serve on a bowl of chopped ice, pouring any remaining rum into the bowl. Have sturdy cocktail picks nearby.

STUFFED DATES

There are a number of ways to stuff dates. Washed and dried dates can be pitted and slit and then stuffed with a mixture of crème fraiche or cottage cheese seasoned liberally with salt and cayenne. Or try this: soak dates in fruit juices or liquors or steam them for 10 minutes or so; then seed and stuff with broken nut pieces, candied ginger, coconut, peanut butter or fondant and roll in confectioners' or granulated sugar.

RHUBARB-GRAPE JUICE PUNCH

Here is another delicious rhubarb punch, and if one cans or freezes rhubarb juice when these abundant plants are bearing, one that can be used year-round. (For foolproof and crystal-clear instructions on freezing or canning rhubarb juice, see the excellent *Putting Food By* by our southern Vermont neighbor Janet Greene.)

MAKES 50 CUPS OR SO

1 quart rhubarb juice
1 (24-ounce) bottle Welch's white grape juice
1 (10-ounce) can frozen limeade, thawed

Sugar to taste
2 quarts ginger ale
1 pint strawberries or other fruit of choice

Mix fruit juices, limeade and any sugar together well. Pour over block ice in punch bowl. Add ginger ale and float fruit over all.

Note: There is a Strawberry Rhubarb Punch in the Country Wedding section as well as several other punches in the index if you want additional ideas for this exhibition reception.

15
AN
OLD-FASHIONED SALON

Culture and collation for 25 or so

MUSHROOM TARTLETS

WATERCRESS ROLLS

DEVILISH CUCUMBER SLICES

LEMON AND APRICOT-PECAN BREADS

CINNAMON TOAST

HAZELNUT MERINGUE COOKIES

MINIATURE CHEESE CAKES

RITZ SPONGE CAKE

COFFEE   TEA   WHITE WINE

LILLET SHERRY

AN OLD-FASHIONED SALON

A Boston lady, from the time when many Bostonians still felt their city was "the hub of the universe," is quoted as saying that her idea of perfect happiness was sitting by an open fire with an author eating sponge cake.

There must have been many such ladies in Boston and elsewhere, for the idea of sitting—before a fire or not—ingesting culture, as well as sponge cake, was one that spread across much of the country. These salons, some a rather tamer version of the French soirée, were a subject of many early American writers as well as some of the early painters. Philip Hale is a good example: his painting of just such an event on Boston's Beacon Hill is well known.

These groups, begun and nurtured by the ladies of that time when "ladies" did not go out to work, were generally formed around an uplifting or educational purpose and met at different members' houses. Some of the earliest were Shakespearean "reading" and other book clubs at which members would take turns reading from Shakespeare or reporting on another author of interest. Others turned to more practical pursuits: a series of classes on china painting, book binding or perhaps foreign affairs.

These salons often championed worthwhile projects. Some developed new libraries; others, morning musicales where rising young musicians were given an opportunity to play. Others took a more immediate turn, especially during the Civil War when ladies would gather to make bandages and secure badly needed medical supplies.

Many of these salons have survived, though in modern dress—some with their original purpose, others moving on to other things. Several of the Civil War sewing groups, for example, have evolved into groups gathering over needlepoint or crewel work, often while a member reads or the group listens to readings of classical works on Caedmon or other records, thus combining the groups' cultural interests with the practical.

At these salons the hostess served a light repast, and if there was a speaker, she usually led the discussion. For some meetings the refreshments would have been fairly elaborate, for others rather simple.

I've put together some ideas for things to serve at such an occasion. For a simpler meeting, you would want only a sampling of this menu, for a large meeting, more. Any group would certainly enjoy a light repast of tea or coffee, one or two of the little sandwiches and indeed—as our Boston lady of yore—sponge cake.

You'll find the recipes for the Mushroom Tartlets, Devilish Cucumber Slices, Cinnamon Toast, Hazelnut Meringue Cookies, Miniature Cheese Cakes and Ritz Sponge Cake here. The Watercress Rolls and the Lemon and Apricot-Pecan breads are in the High Tea section.

Of course in days gone by the service for these salons would have been rather elegant; today things would be much simpler. However, if you have the time and want to make such a meeting special, go ahead—get out your best china and glasses and even your silver teapot—and take yourself and your fellow members back to the time when there was time, if only for a while.

MUSHROOM TARTLETS

These little tartlets are delicious and quite elegant. And, since the shells can be made in advance and either refrigerated or frozen, not all the preparation time need fall on the day of the salon.

MAKES 2 DOZEN

1 recipe Pâte Brisée (see page 401)
2 tablespoon Dijon mustard
½ cup imported Swiss or creamy Dutch cheese, slivered, plus ½ cup, grated

1 recipe Mushroom Filling (see below)

TO MAKE SHELLS

Prepare the Pâte Brisée recipe recommended or one of your own choice, and refrigerate until firm. Roll the chilled dough out to a thickness of about ⅛ inch and line 24 tartlet molds or 2-inch muffin tins.

When lining the tartlet molds or tins remember that these French tarts are not served in their molds but free-standing. This means the side crusts must be thick enough not to collapse. To ensure this, cut dough circles just over a full inch larger than the mold or tin. Then lay the dough round in the mold or tin. If using molds, this will leave about an inch hanging over the edge. If using muffin tins, you will have to imagine that the tin is only about ½ inch deep. Gently press the dough against the sides and bottom of the molds and against the bottom and about ½ inch up the sides of the tins. Then take the excess pastry and gently tamp it down along the inside of the molded shell sides to make a double-thick pastry wall. Brush the shells evenly with the mustard and sprinkle well with the *slivered* cheese. Prick the bottom crusts in several spots and refrigerate shells 15 minutes to 1 hour to firm.

TO FINISH SHELLS   PREHEAT OVEN TO 375°

Partially bake the shells 10 to 12 minutes. Shells can then be filled and the recipe completed, or refrigerated or frozen for future use. These shells can be safely kept in the fridge two or three days and in the freezer several weeks or even longer.

TO FILL, BAKE AND SERVE TARTLETS

If prebaked shells have been frozen, thaw. Then fill shells about ¾ full with Mushroom Filling below. Sprinkle with the *grated* cheese and bake, still at 375°, about 15 minutes—just long enough to heat pastry and filling and melt the cheese, which will form a glazed crust lightly covering the mushroom mixture.

When done, unmold and serve warm.

Note: Any number of other fillings may be used interchangeably with the mushroom: try your own favorite.

Mushroom Filling

1 pound mushrooms	*2 tablespoons flour*
2 tablespoons butter	*Salt and pepper to taste*
1 tablespoon dry sherry	*¼ cup cream, more or less*
Several drops Tabasco sauce	

Wash and chop the mushrooms and sauté in the butter. Add sherry and Tabasco and keep over low heat until all liquid has evaporated. Sprinkle in flour and cook until well integrated. Season and add enough cream to make a simple filling. Let cool and fill pastry cups.

Variation: This switch will offer a delightfully different flavor. Using the above recipe as your base, add 2 tablespoons lemon juice when sautéing the mushrooms with the butter. Delete the sherry and Tabasco; and add a good-sized pinch of dried crushed rosemary with the flour.

DEVILISH CUCUMBER SLICES

MAKES ABOUT 40 TO 50 SLICES

2 medium fairly fat cucumbers, peeled
1 (3-ounce) can deviled ham spread

3 ounces whipped cream cheese
Several lavish dashes Worcestershire sauce

With a grapefruit spoon or small serrated knife scoop out the central core from the cucumbers, leaving as much flesh as possible but being sure to catch all the seeds.

Mix together the remaining ingredients, blending well. Use mixture to fill cored cucumbers. Chill until ready to serve and then slice into approximately 1/4-inch rounds.

A tomato or radish rose would be a pretty addition to the plate.

CINNAMON TOAST

This is the more traditional cinnamon toast, as opposed to the Cinnamon Sticks found in the High Tea section. There are two methods I like to use. *One method* spreads thin slices of bread with a creamed mixture of 2 tablespoons butter, 1/3 cup confectioners' sugar and 1 teaspoon cinnamon and then crisps it in a 350° oven, or under the broiler. The *second method* spreads buttered crustless bread with a mixture of sugar, nutmeg and cinnamon (1 teaspoon spices to every 3 tablespoons brown or white sugar) and toasts it quickly under the broiler.

HAZELNUT MERINGUE COOKIES

MAKES ABOUT 75 COOKIES

3/4 cup ground toasted hazelnuts, plus 1/4 cup coarsely chopped
1/4 cup Frangelica or hazelnut liqueur

2 large egg whites
1/4 teaspoon cream of tartar
1/2 cup sugar
1/2 teaspoon vanilla

TO PREPARE

In a small mixing bowl, blend the ground hazelnuts and the Frangelica. Allow the egg whites to come to room temperature, then beat with an electric mixer at moderate speed until they become foamy. Add the cream of tartar and continue to beat until they hold soft peaks. Add the sugar, a spoonful at a time, while beating. Beat in the vanilla. Continue to beat the mixture until it holds very stiff peaks. Carefully fold in the ground hazelnuts, a little at a time.

TO BAKE **PREHEAT OVEN TO 325°**

Cover two baking sheets with parchment paper to prevent meringues from sticking, securing the parchment in place by dabbing a small amount of meringue on each corner. Drop the mixture onto the parchment by teaspoon-fuls, 2 inches apart. Smooth the top of each cookie with a spoon and sprinkle with chopped hazelnuts. Place trays in preheated oven and bake for 15 to 20 minutes, or until they are dry to the touch. (If cookies begin to brown, reduce the heat to 300° and open oven door slightly.) Let rest for about 3 minutes before transfering them to racks to cool.

Note: These cookies may be stored in an airtight container for up to 2 weeks.

MINIATURE CHEESE CAKES

I was first introduced to these delicious little cheese cakes by Linda King.

MAKES SEVERAL HUNDRED

3 (8-ounce) packages cream cheese, softened

1 cup sugar

5 eggs

2 tablespoons vanilla, or 1 tablespoon vanilla and 1 teaspoon almond extract

1 recipe Cheese Cake Filling (see below)

1 (4-ounce) package slivered almonds

1 (8-ounce) jar rose geranium, currant or other jelly of choice

Blend cream cheese with sugar. Add eggs, one at a time, then the extract(s), blending all together well.

Make the Cheese Cake Filling below and set aside.

TO BAKE
AND FINISH CAKES **PREHEAT OVEN TO 300°**

Fill miniature cupcake tins about ¾ full with cream cheese mixture. Bake for 20 minutes. Remove from oven and allow to cool about 5 minutes. Centers will fall, leaving room for filling. Keep oven on.

Drop Cheese Cake Filling into each cupcake by the teaspoonful. Decorate with finely slivered almonds fanned around a small dollop of the jelly. Then bake cakes (still at 300°) another 5 minutes to set. Remove and let cool.

These cakes will keep several days in the refrigerator or, properly wrapped, can be frozen until needed.

Cheese Cake Filling

1 cup sour cream
½ cup sugar

1 tablespoon vanilla

Mix ingredients together well and set aside until needed to fill Miniature Cheese Cakes.

RITZ SPONGE CAKE

This lovely, lightly flavored sponge cake is served at the Boston Ritz-Carlton.

MAKES 1 (10-INCH) CAKE

4 whole eggs, plus 1 extra yolk
½ cup sugar
1 cup sifted cake flour

4 tablespoons butter, melted and
cooled
1 teaspoon vanilla

TO PREPARE BATTER

Combine eggs and sugar in large (3-quart) mixing bowl, preferably stainless steel. Set inside bowl partially filled with boiling water. Beat with wire whisk until mixture is warm but not hot. Remove bowl from hot water and continue beating, changing to an electric beater, until mixture is fluffy and stands in peaks (about 15 minutes). Fold in flour gradually and carefully, then fold in the butter and vanilla, lifting up mixture as you fold so no melted butter slipping to the bottom of the bowl remains unmixed.

TO BAKE   PREHEAT OVEN TO 325°

Pour batter into buttered and floured 10-inch baking pan and bake for 30 minutes.

Turn out and cool on cake rack.

Adapted from *The Ritz-Carlton Cook Book and Guide to Home Entertaining* by Helen Ridley.

16
BEFORE
THE FOOTLIGHTS GO UP

A springtime supper for 8

SEVICHE OR SHRIMP APPETIZER

MARINATED MUSHROOMS

FRESH ASPARAGUS
WITH FOOLPROOF HOLLANDAISE
ON TOAST POINTS

BROWNIES

Dinner for 8 on a summer weekend

BAKED POTATO SKINS

HERB-STUFFED BROILED MUSHROOMS

CHICAGO CUCUMBER SOUP

TURKEY, PAPAYA AND WALNUT SALAD

CORNSTICKS

MINTS

A wintertime menu

CHEESE ROLL AND CRACKERS

COUNTRY HAM AND VEAL PÂTÉ
EN CROÛTE

MIXED LETTUCE SALAD

HELENE'S HERMITS

BEFORE THE FOOTLIGHTS GO UP

With the high cost of theater tickets these days, it's not only fun but economical if one member of the party prepares a simple meal beforehand. In that way the additional worry of time is also lessened, as everyone is already assembled and can go off to the theater together in ample time to make the first curtain.

I met this idea head-on one time when I flew into Boston to see the exhibit of a Vermont artist-friend. After letting me in, the gallery guide quickly locked the door behind me, explaining that she was preparing supper for friends and needed to go downstairs to put the food together. It seemed that she and her friends were off to the ballet and couldn't afford the time or the price for a Boston in-town dinner so had gotten permission to prepare a light supper there in the gallery before going on.

Not all of us have the chance to wind down over supper and drinks while enjoying the ambiance of a lovely art gallery before going to a performance. However, we can try something similar, keeping in mind that the underlying principles for this pretheater supper are simplicity of preparation and lightness of food, the latter if for no other reason than that your share of the audience not fall asleep.

For the springtime version of this supper, I suggest my own favorite springtime main course, Asparagus with Foolproof Hollandaise Sauce on Toast Points, preceded by a refreshing Seviche or Shrimp appetizer and a plate of Marinated Mushrooms. All of this, except the asparagus, can be ready beforehand, making the supper party an especially attractive one for the working host or hostess. Recipes for the appetizers are listed in the index, an easy Hollandaise follows here and I leave the asparagus, hopefully fresh from your own or a neighbor's patch, to you. Cocktails and wines of choice will round out this supper party, while the plate of Chocolate or Butterscotch Brownies (also indexed) can be placed by the door for a quick sweet as you travel on.

For the summer weekend supper, a more ambitious bill-of-fare seems right, but again based on the same two premises—this one using seasonal vegetables and combining some hot dishes with some cold. Unless the weather is very hot and humid a warm appetizer will contrast nicely with the Chicago Cucumber Soup and Turkey, Papaya and Walnut Salad that follow, both dishes that, again, can be made ahead. Tasty warm Corn Sticks can complete the simple meal, while the dish of mints provides a handful of "in pocket" sweets to take along to the show. Recipes for the salad and Corn Sticks follow; the other dishes are listed in the index. Favorite summertime drinks will do their part to add to the pleasant anticipation.

When the winds blow and snow is in the air, the ballet opens and transports those of us lucky enough to go to the make-believe land of *Who Cares?* or *Jewels* or *Coppelia.* Why not spend some time the weekend before making the cheese roll and then, a day or two before, the Country Ham and Veal Pâté en Croûte? This is an elegant dish which actually improves from being put together and baked ahead (as the recipe tells you, it can then easily be reheated while you're tossing the salad). Remember: the presentation of such a dish is half the fun, so if you're going to do it, do it right and take the pains to decorate it properly. And a nice bonus: it really isn't *that* difficult. The hermits will add just the right spicy sweet, and if the night is really chilly you might want to offer a mulled wine along with the other liquid refreshment.

Recipes for the Pâté en Croûte and Helene's Hermits follow. The others are elsewhere. Enjoy the show!

FOOLPROOF HOLLANDAISE

There are many ways to make hollandaise: I guess everyone has their favorite. I especially like one from the wonderful *Joy of Cooking* but it is a little complicated. I found this one in the Boston Museum's *The Fine Arts Cookbook.* It has the great advantage for this party of being able to be made ahead without separating and then be reheated when needed.

MAKES APPROXIMATELY 2 CUPS

4 egg yolks
4 tablespoons lemon juice
4 tablespoons cream
1 teaspoon salt

8 tablespoons (1 stick), cut in 8
  pieces
dish of cold water

Combine all but butter and water in bowl over, but not touching, simmering water. Whisk constantly but slowly with wire whisk until mixture begins to thicken. Add butter, a piece at a time, waiting until one is melted and blended in before adding the next. After 7th piece is melted in, remove bowl from steam and put into dish of cold water to cool. Add additional butter, continuing to blend in. If sauce is not thick enough, it can be cooked more to thicken it further.

This sauce can stand for hours without separating. To use in this way, cover it until serving time. Then put bowl of sauce into warm water and stir until it warms up again.

TURKEY, PAPAYA AND WALNUT SALAD

This recipe is a variation of one I found in an issue of *Gourmet* magazine.

SERVES 8

6 cups cooked moist turkey meat
    (both white and dark), cooled
    and sliced
2 papayas, peeled and seeded
½ cup fresh lime juice
1 cup walnuts
½ teaspoon salt
½ teaspoon white pepper

4 tablespoons walnut oil
1 cup vegetable oil
1 large or 2 small heads Bibb
    lettuce
3 or 4 tablespoons snipped fresh
    chives
1 or 2 slices lime, for garnish

TO PREPARE SALAD

If the turkey you plan to use is not amply moist, marinate the slices, covered, for several hours, being sure to drain well when done. (You might like to use the Ginger-Soy Marinade on page 394 in the back of this book, but any marinade, even a simple slightly seasoned turkey or chicken broth, will do.)

Thinly slice the prepared papaya lengthwise and, using the lime juice, macerate the slices in a shallow ceramic or glass dish for about 30 minutes. Drain the slices, reserving about 6 tablespoons juice.

Toast the walnuts in a single layer on a jelly-roll pan or cookie sheet with sides in a preheated 350° oven for about 10 minutes, shaking the pan occasionally. Then coarsely chop the toasted nuts.

TO PREPARE DRESSING

In a small bowl combine the reserved lime juice with the salt and white pepper. Add the walnut and vegetable oils in a stream, whisking, and continue to whisk until the dressing is emulsified.

TO SERVE

Line a large platter with the lettuce. Arrange the sliced turkey on 1 side of the platter and the drained papaya on the other. Spoon the dressing lightly over the whole salad (or if you prefer, serve separately). Then sprinkle the papaya with the toasted walnuts and the turkey with the chives, and top with 1 or 2 paper-thin lime slices.

Note: If papaya is not available, seedless white grapes go very nicely with turkey.

Variations: Chicken and apple slices make a good alternative for this salad. The apples should be large and sliced thin. Another attractive and easy-to-make salad can be made from 6 cups cooked ham, 1 large well-ripened honeydew melon and 1 cup blanched hazelnuts in place of the turkey, papaya and walnuts used here. You can follow the same method except add a little Dijon mustard to the marinade or in the dressing. This is an excellent way to use up leftover ham.

CORNSTICKS

MAKES ABOUT 12 CORNSTICKS

1 cup flour	*½ teaspoon salt*
¾ cup cornmeal	*1 egg, well beaten*
5 tablespoons sugar	*1 cup milk*
3 teaspoons baking powder	*2 tablespoons bacon drippings*

In a large mixing bowl, combine the flour, cornmeal, sugar, baking powder and salt. Add the egg and mix well. Gradually blend in the milk. Add the bacon drippings and mix thoroughly. Cover and refrigerate for 1 hour.

TO BAKE **PREHEAT OVEN TO 425°**

Thoroughly grease a cast-iron cornstick mold. Place the empty cornstick mold in the hot oven until very hot. Remove and carefully pour the batter into the hot mold. Return to the oven and bake about 15 minutes, until golden. Serve hot.

COUNTRY HAM AND VEAL PÂTÉ EN CROÛTE

Friendly warning: Pâtés wrapped in pastry, as this one is, are time-consuming to make. But the ingredients need be no more extravagant than you want to make them. This is, except perhaps for the pistachio nuts, quite modest in cost. However, it can be quite expensive in time, depending on how elaborately you wish to decorate the pâté. If you are a seasoned pastry cook, you will, no doubt, have many ideas of your own. However, my plan is not to be too elaborate.

14 TO 16 SERVINGS

1 1-inch thick slice country ham (about ½ pound)
1 1-inch thick veal scallop (about ½ pound)
2 tablespoons finely chopped shallot
2 teaspoons chopped parsley
½ teaspoon ground allspice
Freshly ground black pepper
¼ cup each dry white wine, Cognac and port

Salt to taste
1¼ pounds ground pork
½ teaspoon thyme
¼ cup breadcrumbs
2 eggs
⅓ cup shelled pistachios
1½ pounds Short Crust for Pâté en Croûte (see page 403)

TO PREPARE FILLING

Cut the ham and veal into long, ½-inch-wide strips, removing any fat or membrane, and place in separate glass bowls. Divide the shallots and parsley between the ham and veal. Season ham with ¼ teaspoon of the allspice, pepper and a tablespoon each of white wine, Cognac and port. Season veal with salt and pepper, a tablespoon Cognac and remaining white wine. Mix meats with the hands to distribute seasonings well. (Meats should be just moistened, not covered; drain off any excess liquid.) Cover and refrigerate for at least 3 hours, turning occasionally.

Process the pork in a food processor fitted with a steel blade until smooth. (Or ask butcher to grind the meat 2 or 3 times when purchasing.) Transfer pork to a mixing bowl and season with remaining allspice, thyme, salt and pepper, and remaining Cognac and port. (Again, liquid should just moisten the meat.) Add the breadcrumbs and 1 beaten egg and mix thoroughly.

TO PREPARE PASTRY

On a well-floured board or marble slab, roll out the pastry to an 18-by-12-inch rectangle about ¼- to ⅓-inch thick. Trim the edges to make a neat rectangle, reserving trimmings.

TO FORM PÂTÉ

Place about ¼ of the ground pork mixture in the center of the dough rectangle and, working with wet fingers or spatula, spread into an 11-by-4-inch rectangle. Drain the marinated ham and veal; arrange half of each on top of the ground pork, alternating ham and veal strips and laying strips loosely in place. (The meat will shrink when cooked; if stretched tightly, gaps will form around it.) Tuck pistachios between the rows of veal and ham. Pat the meats in place as you work to keep edges neat and firm.

Spread ½ of remaining pork mixture over top of the ham and veal layer. Arrange remaining ham and veal strips on top, tucking remaining pistachio nuts between rows. Spread remaining pork mixture on top, and pat meat firmly in place.

TO FORM CRUST

Being careful not to cut in as far as pâté, cut away triangles of dough from the four corners of the extended pastry, reserving trimmings. Beat the remaining egg and brush some of it over the pastry. Without stretching the pastry, lift one of the long sides up and pull it carefully over the pâté. Brush the top of this strip with some of the egg. Lift up opposite side and pull up over pâté, gently pressing in place over first pastry flap. Brush with egg. Lift and fold end flaps of pastry in place in same manner, brushing with egg and pressing down gently to secure in place.

Butter a large baking sheet well. Gently slide a large spatula under the pâté to make sure no part of it sticks to the board; lift and invert pâté, placing it bottom side up onto baking sheet.

Roll a small amount of the reserved dough trimmings between your palms to form a ½-inch "rope." Paint the bottom edge of the pâté crust with egg, gently twist the pastry rope and press into place around bottom edge of pâté to form a decorative base. (If rope is made of several lengths, brush overlapping ends to secure.)

Roll out remaining dough trimmings and use to decorate crust, brushing decorative pieces with egg to secure in place. Brush remaining egg over entire surface of pastry, wiping away any excess egg from baking sheet. (See box page 246).

TO BAKE   PREHEAT OVEN TO 450°

Cut two round holes in the top of the crust and insert parchment paper chimneys (see box) to allow steam to escape. Place in the center of preheated oven and bake for about 15 minutes or until the crust starts to whiten a little. Reduce heat to 375° and bake for 1 to 1¼ hours, or until a meat thermometer inserted into the chimney reads 160°. If crust seems to be browning too quickly during baking, cover with a loose aluminum foil tent. Remove pâté from oven and let cool for 30 minutes before slicing. Remove parchment chimneys and tuck parsley sprigs into holes. Serve warm with light tomato or the Orbec sauce below.

Note: Pâté can be formed and refrigerated the day before baking. It can also be baked, cooled, wrapped in foil and refrigerated. To reheat, bring pâté to room temperature and bake in foil at 325° for about 30 minutes.

Orbec Sauce

MAKES 1⅔ CUPS

1 cup red wine
1 cup beef stock or broth
1 small tart apple (about 4 ounces)
½ teaspoon aromatic bitters

1 tablespoon cornstarch
1 tablespoon Madeira or port
4 tablespoons butter, cut into pieces

In a saucepan (preferably enamel or copper), boil the wine and stock together, uncovered, for 10 minutes. Meanwhile, quarter and core the apple but do not peel. Add the apple to the wine and cook another 15 minutes, or until it is soft.

Remove apple, and when cool enough to handle, pull off skin. Place apple and about ½ cup liquid in blender and blend briefly. Do not overblend or purée will become pale and too foamy, and will not blend well with remainder of sauce. Return purée to pot and add bitters. Make a paste of the cornstarch and Madeira and stir into the sauce. Cook for 2 to 3 minutes, remove from the heat and whisk in the butter pieces. Transfer to a warm sauce boat and serve.

Note: This may be made several days ahead, preparing through the addition of the bitters and then refrigerating. When ready to serve complete the sauce with the cornstarch paste and butter additions.

DECORATING PÂTÉ EN CROÛTE

These elegant pâtés can be decorated in many ways. Strips, ropes, cutouts and scallops are only some of them. Here are a few simple ideas, using the leftover dough from the recipe itself.

Strips may be cut with a knife or pastry wheel. The designs below are only two of many possibilities.

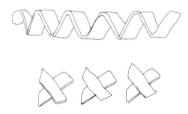

Ropes rolled between the palms can turn into any number of patterns. These wreaths are attractive but flower faces would do just as well. Let your imagination roam.

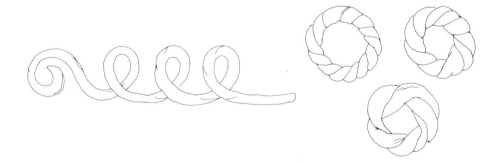

Cutouts can be made in the shape of circles, crescents, diamonds, leaves or perhaps some shape befitting the occasion (musical notes for a symphony opening). Small cookie cutters offer all sorts of ideas. In this picture leaves are being lightly scored with a knife to suggest veining.

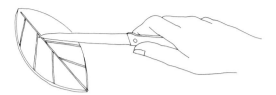

Scallops take a little more work. Circles are stamped with a 1½-to 2-inch cookie cutter. Then, using the floured back of a small chef's knife, working from left to right and holding one end firmly in place, score the pastry circle with radiating lines.

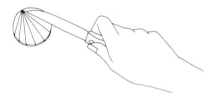

Here is a fully-decorated pâté en croûte. The flower-shaped cutouts cover the holes that were made to accomodate steam escape chimneys.

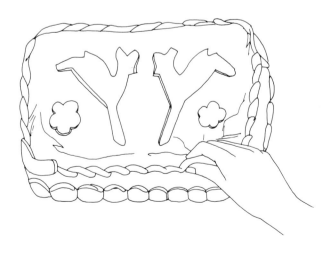

HELENE'S HERMITS

MAKES ABOUT 4 DOZEN

1½ sticks (12 tablespoons) butter	3 teaspoons cinnamon
1 cup light brown sugar	1 teaspoon ground cloves
½ cup white sugar	1 teaspoon nutmeg
2 eggs	1½ cups raisins
2 scant cups flour	1 cup coarsely chopped walnuts
3 teaspoons baking powder	

Cream butter and sugars. Add eggs one at a time and beat until smooth. Mix other dry ingredients together and gradually add to butter mixture. Then stir in raisins and nuts.

TO BAKE   **PREHEAT OVEN TO 350°**

Drop by large spoonfuls on well-greased cookie sheets and bake 8 to 10 minutes or until golden brown. Immediately remove cookies to racks to cool.

Note: These can be made ahead and frozen.

17

AFTER THE NIGHT MUSIC

A dessert party for 10 or more

Cool Weather

CHEESE AND FRUIT PLATTER

FRENCH-FRIED ALMONDS

QUEEN MOTHER CAKE OR
TRINIDAD TORTE

FLORENTINES

GIU MA BANG COOKIES

LIQUEURS   DRINKS OF CHOICE

CAFÉ BRÛLOT

COFFEE

Summer Alternative

GALA FRUIT BOWL

BLUEBERRY-PEACH TART

POPPYSEED CAKE

THUMBPRINT COOKIES

MAPLE FRUIT SHRUB OR
WATERMELON SHERBET

COOL DRINKS OF CHOICE

AFTER THE NIGHT MUSIC

T his party has a different feel from most, for it is at the end of the evening, when everyone enjoys a chance to unwind after one or another entertainment and share their feelings and critiques.

The menu is of course quite different too—and combines cheese, fruit and sweets, with warm and cool drinks of choice.

Try to have as much ready as possible before you leave for the performance. The glasses, bottles and openers can be set out on a tray, with the corks just waiting to be popped and the coffee to be brewed.

You might want to offer champagne; lovely and light, it blends well with all three food tastes. On some winter evenings, though, our old friend Richardson Wright's warmly touted Café Brûlot might be even more welcome.

For a cool-weather party, a lovely cheese and fruit platter would be a good place to start. I suggest a Montrachet (best when fresh), a Puligny or a very young Poivre—all goat cheeses; plus a slice of Roquefort and a Cheddar, perhaps a Welsh Caerphilly or a Black Diamond from Canada. Lastly a Brie or St. André to go well with the fruit.

Select fruit in season and then add the old standbys. In the fall, three kinds of grapes, little lady apples and pears make a colorful display. Later, in the winter, the ripening citrus fruits will take their place too. And the French-Fried Almonds will add a nice crunchy contrast.

Sweets for this party offer a choice between the rich chocolate Queen Mother Cake and the equally tempting nonchocolate Trinidad Torte, aided and abetted by tasty Florentines and Giu Ma Bang Cookies. Recipes for these are here.

Deep red cherries and strawberries with their hulls on for easy dipping into confectioners' sugar are my favorites for summer fruits. But you may want to expand this into the gay Gala Fruit Bowl suggested on the menu: you'll find other ideas for this in the teenage party (page 136). The sweets are simpler and lighter—perhaps the Blueberry-Apple Tart from the Visiting Fireman menu, substituting a ring of peaches for the ring of apples, and the always popular Poppyseed Cake from the harvest vegetarian party. A cool sherbet or shrub with cookies is another possibility, and I give you several of my druthers here.

Any of these will put a lovely cap on an evening of splendid ballet, opera or theater. So, whether raspberry fool or sugarplums, sweet dreams!

FRENCH-FRIED ALMONDS

For this party you can prepare the almonds a little earlier in the day, cover tightly and reheat just a bit before serving.

SERVES 10 TO 12

1 pound shelled almonds, blanched	*Salt, for sprinkling*
Olive or salad oil, for frying	*1 egg white (optional)*

To blanch the almonds, drop into boiling water and cook 1 or 2 minutes until skins loosen. Drain and cool in cold water. Drain again and remove skins (rubbing the nuts with a coarse towel helps loosen them). Dry them well.

To fry the almonds, heat about 1 inch olive or salad oil in a shallow saucepan. When hot, add a few spoonfuls of nuts at a time and cook until golden brown. Remove with a perforated spoon and dry well on paper toweling. Sprinkle with salt. Or, if desired, roll fried nuts in lightly beaten egg white and then sprinkle with salt. Continue until all are done.

Variation: Following the same procedure, raw shelled peanuts also make a tasty fried nut. Again, they should be served fresh.

Adapted from *The Ritz-Carlton Cook Book and Guide to Home Entertaining* by Helen Ridley.

QUEEN MOTHER CAKE

This delicious cake is served at La Tourelle Restaurant in Memphis.

14 ounces semi-sweet chocolate	*Pinch cream of tartar*
1½ sticks (12 tablespoons) sweet	*Pinch salt*
butter, softened	*Dry breadcrumbs, for pan*
6 large eggs, separated	*½ cup heavy cream*
⅔ cup sugar	*2 teaspoons instant coffee powder*
1¼ cups ground blanched almonds	

TO PREPARE

In the top half of a double boiler, slowly melt 6 ounces of the chocolate. Set aside to cool.

Meanwhile, in a large mixing bowl, work the softened butter with a fork until light and fluffy. Add the egg yolks, one at a time, beating thoroughly after each addition. Stir in the sugar and ground almonds and blend well. Beat in the melted chocolate.

In a separate mixing bowl, combine the egg whites, cream of tartar and salt and beat until soft peaks form. Fold the whites into the chocolate mixture.

TO BAKE   PREHEAT OVEN TO 350°

Dust a buttered 8-inch spring-form pan with the breadcrumbs and fill with the cake batter. Bake for 15 minutes; reduce heat to 325° and bake another 25 minutes or until a toothpick inserted in the center of the cake comes out clean. Let cool in the pan on a rack for about 45 minutes. Run a knife around the edge of pan to loosen cake and turn out onto serving plate to cool completely.

TO FROST

Chop the remaining chocolate into ¼ inch pieces. In a small saucepan, combine the cream and instant coffee and bring to a boil, stirring until coffee is dissolved. Remove from the heat and add the chocolate, stirring until it has completely melted. Spread the frosting over top and sides of the cake. Chill until frosting is set.

TRINIDAD TORTE

I first met this tantalizing torte, made by Susan Schulz, at one of Putney, Vermont's Yellow Barn Music Festival's Midsummer Fêtes.

SERVES 10 TO 12

1 teaspoon baking powder	*¾ cup sour cream*
1 teaspoon baking soda	*2 teaspoons grated orange rind*
2 cups sifted flour	*2 teaspoons grated lemon rind*
4 ounces walnuts, finely chopped	*⅛ teaspoon salt*
2 sticks (½ pound) butter, softened	*Fine dry cakecrumbs, to coat pan*
1¼ cups sugar	*2 tablespoons orange juice*
3 eggs, separated	*2 tablespoons lemon juice*

Sift together baking powder, baking soda and flour. Stir a few spoonfuls dry ingredients into nuts and set both mixtures aside.

Cream butter and 1 cup sugar. Beat in egg yolks one at a time. Add dry ingredients alternately with sour cream. Add nuts and grated rinds.

Beat egg whites with salt until they hold peaks, and fold into batter.

TO BAKE   **PREHEAT OVEN TO 350°**

Butter 9-inch spring-form pan and coat with cakecrumbs. Pour in batter and bake about 1 hour, or until done (tester will come out clean).

Shortly before baking time is up, in a small saucepan make a glaze by mixing the remaining ¼ cup sugar with the orange and lemon juices. Bring to boil, stirring to dissolve sugar.

After removing cake from oven, quickly prick the top generously with a small sharp knife and brush hot glaze over hot cake until all glaze is absorbed. Cool in pan.

Note: If using a food processor to chop nuts pulse several times. Then see how finely the nuts are chopped, and pulse slowly again to your satisfaction (they shouldn't be allowed to become buttery).

FLORENTINES

MAKES ABOUT 4 DOZEN

½ cup heavy cream
¼ cup sugar
¼ cup corn syrup
¼ cup finely chopped orange peel or
   1 teaspoon dried rind

⅓ cup almonds, finely chopped
¼ cup flour
6 ounces semi-sweet chocolate bits

In a small saucepan, combine cream, sugar and corn syrup and heat to boil. Cook to soft ball stage (238°). Then stir in orange peel or rind, almonds and flour.

TO BAKE   **PREHEAT OVEN TO 350°**

Drop the mixture by teaspoonfuls onto a buttered baking sheet, leaving several inches between each. Flatten each slightly with the bottom of a small glass dipped in water to prevent dough from sticking. Bake for 8 to 10 minutes, or until cookies are golden brown with crisp lacy edges. Let cool for a minute, then transfer to a wire cooling rack.

TO FINISH

In the top half of a double boiler, melt the chocolate bits. Brush a thin layer of the chocolate over the smooth underside of cookies and let dry. Invert cookies and brush top with a layer of chocolate. Let cool.

GIU MA BANG COOKIES

This simple but delicious Chinese sesame seed cookie recipe was given to me by Hi Kyung Brandt.

MAKES APPROXIMATELY 4 DOZEN

2½ sticks (1¼ cups) butter
1¼ cups sugar
1 egg, lightly beaten
4 cups flour

½ teaspoon baking powder
1 teaspoon salt
⅓ to ½ cup sesame seeds, for
rolling

Cream the butter and sugar and add the egg. Combine the dry ingredients and mix together with the creamed mixture, kneading well. Pinch off small pieces of the dough, about the size of a walnut, and form into balls, rolling each in the sesame seeds.

TO BAKE   PREHEAT OVEN TO 375°

Place on ungreased baking sheets about 1 inch apart and bake until golden brown, about 12 to 15 minutes.

Variations: Walnuts, almonds and raisins in ½-cup lots—either singly or in combination—make nice additions to this recipe.

CAFÉ BRÛLOT

This is a lovely beverage alternative suggested by Richardson Wright in *The Bed Book of Eating and Drinking.*

SERVES 10

Peel from ¾ orange, cut into pieces
3 longish sticks cinnamon
15 cloves

10 or 11 lumps sugar
9 ounces brandy, kept in carafe
2 quarts hot fresh coffee

Put dry ingredients into small punch bowl (a lovely silver one if you have it), pour in the brandy, which is then lit (a long fireplace match works nicely for this or a long taper if you're sure it's dripless). Immediately add the hot coffee to the brandy mixture and ladle into demitasse cups at once.

ELLEN'S THUMBPRINT COOKIES

This recipe first came from Ellen Thompson, then a young high school student, now a full-fledged M.D. and accomplished cellist.

MAKES ABOUT 4 DOZEN

1½ sticks (12 tablespoons) butter
½ cup sugar, plus extra for rolling
1 teaspoon baking powder
1 teaspoon vanilla
1 teaspoon grated lemon rind
2 cups flour
1 egg
Jelly or jam of choice, for filling

Mix all ingredients, except jelly or jam, by hand (or fork if you must). Wrap and refrigerate for at least 30 minutes (longer is fine). Shape into walnut-sized balls and roll in granulated sugar.

TO BAKE   PREHEAT OVEN TO 350°

Place sugared balls on ungreased cookie sheet, well spaced. With index finger or thumb, make indentation in center, taking care not to go through. Fill with jelly or jam of choice and bake for 15 minutes or so, until just brown.

Note: Apricot and raspberry jam seem especially good in these cookies, with good English-style orange marmalade a close third.

MAPLE FRUIT SHRUB

The Inn at Weathserfield, Vermont, serves this shrub as a first course.

SERVES 6

2 pineapples, peeled, cored and cut in 1-inch pieces
1 small apple, peeled, cored and chopped
½ navel orange, peeled and chopped
½ ripe banana, sliced
½ cup chopped honeydew melon or cantaloupe
¼ Anjou pear, peeled and chopped
1 thick slice lemon, with rind
½ cup unsweetened pineapple juice
½ cup freshly squeezed orange juice
1 tablespoon Amaretto
1 tablespoon Vermont maple syrup
1 to 2 drops teaberry flavoring or oil of wintergreen
1 quart rainbow sherbet (lime, raspberry and orange is nice)
Fresh mint

TO PREPARE

Purée the pineapple, apple, orange, banana, melon, pear, lemon slice, pineapple and orange juices in several batches in a blender or a food processor, transferring puréed batches into a large mixing bowl. Stir the mixture to blend thoroughly. Then return it to the blender or processor in batches, adding a few ice cubes to each batch and blending until liquified. (You will need about half a tray of ice cubes in all.) Return the iced purée to the mixing bowl and stir in the Amaretto, maple syrup and the teaberry or wintergreen. (This should make about 8 cups.)

TO SERVE

Spoon small scoops of sherbet into six 6-ounce wine glasses. Top with the fruit sauce and garnish with fresh mint.

Note: If your supermarket does not carry teaberry flavoring or oil of wintergreen, look for it in specialty food shops or in a pharmacy.

WATERMELON SHERBET

This recipe, from Norman Runnion, our local newspaper editor, is designed for use with a food processor, but should work well, in smaller quantities, in any good blender.

All you need is watermelon—about a 2-inch slice per guest—and sugar.

To make, simply pit and peel (this is a bit messy but goes quickly) however much watermelon you need. Cut the prepared melon into chunks and sprinkle lightly with sugar (this is a matter of taste, a sweet melon needs very little). Then freeze solidly, 3 or 4 hours.

When ready to serve—this can be just as your guests arrive from the evening's entertainment or at the end of a summer dinner party's main course —put the frozen melon in your food processor or blender. There will be a horrible noise as the machine begins its work, but take heart, soon you will have a lovely sherbet.

If you are serving this sherbet as part of a dessert buffet, you might want to put it in a glass bowl placed in another somewhat larger bowl filled with ice—this to help keep the sherbet firm and fluffy while your guests serve themselves. Try to have individual glass cups for the individual portions so the lovely color can show through. Whether served directly from a serving bowl or in individual cups, decorate the sherbet with bits of fresh mint: it adds just the right touch!

18
AN INTIMATE
WINTER WEDDING

A private celebration for 25 to 30

PROSCIUTTO AND MELON

SMOKED SALMON
WITH CAPERS AND LEMON

COCKTAIL CHICKEN WINGS

STEAK TARTARE

LOBSTER SALAD BASKETS

MUSHROOMS NONPAREIL

STUFFED CHINESE PEAPODS
AND BELGIAN ENDIVE

AN ELEGANT CHEESE PLATTER
WITH
WATER BISCUITS

GRAMERCY PARK WEDDING CAKE

PUITS D'AMOUR

KIRSCH SORBET

CHAMPAGNE   WHITE WINE

RHUBARB PUNCH

COFFEE

AN INTIMATE WINTER WEDDING

An intimate wedding like this one is often a second wedding for one or both partners, which means the couple will want to include any children as well as a few close friends. Sometimes another couple with no family where they live and work will want an equally simple affair. Winter does limit the options, but a lovely personal wedding can be performed and enjoyed in any convenient apartment or home—either the bridal couple's or that of a friend.

An attractive spot for the service can be made in front of a fireplace or picture window, making sure the guests are allowed a clear view. A bank of plants—cyclamens, poinsettias or various greens—can be a most effective backdrop. Music can be provided by a guitar, string trio or piano. And as the service and reception will be in the same place, careful planning and stage direction are essential, with perhaps the best man assigned the task of preparing several special toasts or a few personal, even humorous, words.

When deciding upon the menu, let the composition of the guest list give you direction. I have chosen a rather glamorous menu for the grownups, but of course if children are to be present, ample simple sandwiches and cookies should be added. The cake—an elegant vanilla *génoise* with Apricot Glaze Filling and Mocha Butter Cream Frosting—should be popular with both groups.

Recipes follow for the Prosciutto with Melon, Smoked Salmon, Cocktail Chicken Wings, Steak Tartare, the wedding cake, other sweets and the Rhubarb Punch. Recipes for the Lobster Salad Baskets and Stuffed Chinese Peapods and Belgian Endive are both with the Southern "At Home" party menu and that for the Mushrooms Nonpareil in the summer Portable Feasts party. Cheeses might include a Brillat-Savarin, a Double Crème and a Morbier.

The table flowers could match the bride's bouquet—perhaps the little chrysanthemums or little sweetheart roses—and if possible, extend these to the cake. If this is not easy, chocolate curls made with a cheese slicer and whole hazelnuts will lend the festive touch you want. And don't forget the lovely silk flowers available at various boutiques and fairs: those combined with gold leaves make an elegant topping for any wedding cake.

As the reception is small, champagne can be served throughout, or you can supplement it with another fine white wine. While the very finest French champagne is expensive, Korbel and Domaine Chandon are excellent American champagnes and we are now importing delightful dry Spanish champagnes as well as the excellent French sparkling wines not grown in the Champagne district. If in doubt, by all means consult a reputable wine merchant.

One of the joys of working on this book is the many recollections it has called to mind. In putting together this chapter I thought again of the very first small wedding I helped plan—one which happened in 1941 while I was still at university in Montreal. One of the foreign students there—a girl from the Dominican Republic—was engaged to an air force officer, and when, suddenly, he was given leave before going overseas, there was no way to plan a family wedding. I lived at home so the natural thing was to have it there. A friend and I, with the warm enthusiasm of my mother, planned a simple affair at our house (which incidentally was already a semiofficial annex to the girls' dorm).

The procedural necessities—the bans, license, etc.—were attended to by my father, while the rest of us took care of the invitations, the flowers, the clothes and of course the menu. I learned a lot about the proper sharing of expenses, who bought the flowers and the rings and how to adapt a well-worn suit to a bridal outfit, as well as the particulars of wedding cakes and such.

Fortunately the bride's father arrived in time to give the bride away and it was a lovely occasion all around. A hectic but wonderful wedding, with many to follow.

But whatever the circumstances and the details, the central idea for any intimate wedding party is to have a very special and serious event celebrated with personal flair and gracious warmth.

PROSCIUTTO WITH MELON

Using thin slices of good-quality prosciutto, wrap around finger-sized slices of honeydew melon—and enjoy!

SMOKED SALMON WITH LEMON AND CAPERS

True Atlantic Ocean salmon is so expensive you'll obviously want to reserve it for a very special occasion. A small personal wedding such as this is just right!

You'll need about 1 pound to serve the 25 to 30 guests we are accommodating for this party. Be sure you are getting genuine Scotch or Irish salmon and treat it with great respect for it has a most delicate flavor, color and texture. Ask that it be sliced paper thin wherever you purchase it, but avoid any that has been presliced: it may not be fresh.

To serve, butter thin slices of brown bread and place the sliced salmon on top. Sprinkle lightly with fresh lemon juice and garnish with capers.

COCKTAIL CHICKEN WINGS

These delicately flavored chicken wings are less sweet than the fruited variation in the Pictures at the Exhibition party.

SERVES 20 TO 30 NICELY

32 to 40 chicken wings
8 scallion stalks
1 cup soy sauce
1 cup dry sherry

2 cups water
4 to 8 tablespoons maple syrup, to
taste

Chop off and discard the bony tips of the chicken wings and cut each wing in half. Cut the scallions into 1-inch sections. Place the halved wings and scallions in a large pan with the soy sauce, sherry, water and maple syrup. Bring to a boil and simmer, covered, 30 minutes. Uncover and simmer an additional 15 minutes, stirring and basting frequently for a uniform color. Drain and refrigerate. Serve at room temperature in a pretty serving dish.

Variation: The following ingredients make an equally tasty end result. Just substitute these for the sauce ingredients above and follow the same procedure: 1 cup soy sauce, 1⅓ cups water, 6 tablespoons maple syrup, 6 ounces oyster sauce, 8 slices fresh ginger, 8 cloves star anise.

STEAK TARTARE

This recipe comes from Barclay McFadden and will always be a favorite of mine—partly because it's so good and partly because of the occasion at which I first enjoyed it. Good steak tartare must be cold—and light.

20 OR SO PORTIONS

1 pound beef tenderloin or fillet or
ribeye of beef (depending on your
budget)
⅓ cup finely chopped onion or
scallions (if scallions, use only
the white part; save the green
for garnish)

1 teaspoon Worcestershire sauce
(instead of salt)
Freshly ground pepper
1 egg white

Ask your butcher to grind the meat, but only once (if ground too much the meat gets mushy). If this is not possible, grind at home in a food processor or grinder but watch carefully.

Mix all together quickly, and chill. The less this is handled the better.

When ready, serve on a bed of lettuce or spinach leaves, sprinkled with lots of chopped parsley, capers and perhaps with chopped hard-cooked eggs sprinkled over all for color, and with some melba rounds or cocktail-sized rye bread slices nearby.

GRAMERCY PARK WEDDING CAKE

Of course the bridal couple's wishes come first in choosing any wedding cake, but this combination of vanilla *génoise* cake with apricot filling and mocha butter cream frosting is elegant, light and delicious, and relatively foolproof given any not-too-hot day. I recommend it heartily! For this wedding cake, I would double the standard two-layer cake recipe given here, make the same amount as the filling recipe below and make at least half again the frosting recipe. Dividing the batter into two standard-depth 9-inch layers, two 6-inch layers and two 3-inch layers, you will have a pretty cake standing about twice as high as the usual dessert cake. When decorated it will be lovely! (See the Wedding Cake Guidelines in the Country Wedding chapter for instructions on assembling and ideas for decorating.)

Vanilla Génoise Batter

It is easier just to make this twice rather than trying to double. This particular method is designed for an electric mixer. It can be done by hand but it will take *much* longer and the cake will not be as light. You'll need to prepare two standard 9-inch, two 6-inch and two 3-inch pans ("standard" means not the commercial 3-inch deep pans).

MAKES 2 (9-INCH) LAYERS

6 large eggs
1 cup sugar
1 cup sifted flour

1 stick (8 tablespoons) sweet butter,
*   melted and clarified*
1 teaspoon vanilla

TO PREPARE BATTER

In large bowl combine eggs and sugar. Stir for a minute, or until just combined. Set bowl over saucepan filled with 1 to 2 inches hot water. Water in pan should *not* touch bowl nor be allowed to boil. Place saucepan over low heat for 5 to 10 minutes or until eggs are lukewarm (this heating increases their whipping volume). It is not necessary to beat eggs constantly while heating; however, stir occasionally to keep bottom from cooking.

When eggs are warm and a rich yellow syrup, remove from heat and beat at high speed with electric mixer for 10 to 15 minutes, scraping sides of bowl with rubber spatula as necessary, until syrup becomes light, fluffy and cool. The syrup will almost triple in bulk and look similar to whipped cream. (Hand beating takes about 25 minutes.)

Sprinkle flour, a little at a time, on top of whipped eggs. Fold in gently, adding slightly cooled butter and vanilla. (Folding can be done with mixer at lowest speed or by hand: be careful not to overmix.)

TO BAKE   **PREHEAT OVEN TO 350°**

Pour batter into greased and lightly floured pans. Unless you have a commercial oven, I would bake the two 9-inch layers together and the 4 smaller layers together. The 9-inch layers will take about 25 to 30 minutes; the smaller layers 10 to 15 minutes less. But watch carefully. The cakes are done when they pull away from sides of pan and are golden brown and springy when touched lightly on top.

Remove from pans immediately and cool on cake racks.

Apricot Glaze Filling

This recipe is double that needed for the standard dessert cake recipe. It should be enough for this wedding cake. If you need more, you can easily make more just keeping the same proportions.

Heat 2 cups sieved (a Mouli grater works well) apricot jam until it is boiling. Add 4 to 8 tablespoons Cognac, kirsch or applejack and stir until blended and hot through. Spread glaze while still hot.

If you prefer a custard filling, see the Apricot Custard Filling in the Country Wedding section, reducing the quantities to about ⅓.

Mocha Butter Cream Frosting

Depending on how thick you like your frosting, for this wedding cake you'll need either half again or double this amount.

MAKES ABOUT 1¾ CUPS

*1 stick (8 tablespoons) butter,
  softened*
*6 ounces semi-sweet chocolate,
  melted and cooled*

1 egg yolk
½ teaspoon vanilla
2 teaspoons Cognac
1 teaspoon powdered instant coffee

Cream butter until fluffy. Beat in cooled melted chocolate, egg yolk, vanilla and Cognac; add coffee powder. This frosting can be used immediately or stored in the refrigerator until needed. It will harden in refrigerator; bring to room temperature before using (and remember to chill cake so it won't crumb into frosting). (See Wedding Cake Guidelines in Country Wedding chapter for frosting and decorating help.)

PUITS D'AMOUR
(WELLS OF LOVE)

MAKES ABOUT 2 DOZEN

1 recipe Puff Pastry (see page 400)
1 recipe Dorure (see page 406)

1 cup red currant jelly
Confectioners' sugar, for dusting

TO FORM

On a lightly floured board roll out the already prepared Puff Pastry to a thickness of ¼ inch. Then, with a fluted cutter, cut out 1½-inch rounds. Cut the centers from half these rounds to make rings. Brush the edges of the remaining rounds with water and press a ring on top of each. Lay these shells on a baking sheet moistened with cold water and brush them lightly with the Dorure. Then chill for 20 minutes.

TO BAKE   PREHEAT OVEN TO 450°

Bake in the 450° oven for 15 minutes, or until they are well puffed. Then reduce the temperature to a moderate 350° and bake until shells are golden.

TO SERVE

Fill the cooled Puits d'Amour with the jelly and sprinkle with the confectioners' sugar.

KIRSCH SORBET

The flavor of this sorbet will change subtly with the ingredients. A less expensive kirsch may well be a little sweeter and of course lemons vary in both tartness and amount of juice. You may want to vary this slightly to your own taste.

SERVES 20 TO 24

5 ¼ cups sugar
3 cups water
Juice of 6 lemons

1 ½ cups kirsch
6 egg whites, stiffly beaten

Heat the sugar and water in a large saucepan to make a syrup and boil for 5 minutes. Stir in the lemon juice and cool completely. Then stir in the kirsch and fold in the egg whites. Pour into shallow and well-scoured baking pans, roughly equivalent to 3 quarts, and put in freezer. Freeze until the edges are firm. Then remove from the freezer, beat very well for 1 minute and return mixture to freezer until firm.

Note: Of course if you have an electric ice cream machine, by all means use it, following the manufacturer's directions. If you are working from scratch you might prefer, after the first beating, to transfer the mixture to a bowl for its final freeze, thereby eliminating an excess of pots and pans in the freezer.

RHUBARB PUNCH

Here is still another refreshing rhubarb punch. If you do not have the frozen juice "put by," see the index for other ideas.

SERVES 20 TO 30 GENEROUSLY

1 quart frozen rhubarb juice (see Notes)
1 (10-ounce) can frozen limeade
Sugar to taste, about ¼ cup

1 quart ginger ale
1 quart sparkling water
1 pint fresh berries if available, for garnish

Combine the rhubarb juice, limeade and sugar, blending thoroughly. Shortly before serving, pour over ice in punch bowl. Add ginger ale and sparkling water, mix lightly, then add fruit. (Frozen *whole* strawberries or blueberries can be used for garnish if fresh are not available.)

Notes: Ice blocks always work better for punch bowls than ice cubes; cubes melt too quickly. A block shaped in a heart-shaped mold, perhaps even colored red with food coloring, would be especially nice for a wedding party.

If you should want to make this punch in the summer, a food processor or blender will soon make you ample rhubarb juice, though the liquid derived from cooking up rhubarb will serve just as well; any rhubarb shreds just add to the flavor.

19
TWO EXTRA-SPECIAL WEDDINGS

An Elegant Afternoon Wedding
Reception for 125 to 150

CHILLED SHRIMP   SEA SCALLOP SEVICHE

MARINATED CHICKEN FINGERS

TENDERLOIN OF BEEF WITH
BÉARNAISE SAUCE AND BROWN BREAD

CUCUMBER SANDWICHES

STUFFED MUSHROOMS

LOBSTER MOUSSE BOUCHÉES

VEGETABLE PLATTER IN SEASON

CHEESE AND FRUIT PLATTER

RAISIN DELIGHTS

HAZELNUT MERINGUES

JONATHAN'S DREAM WEDDING CAKE

CHAMPAGNE   WHITE WINE FRUIT PUNCH

COFFEE

Candlelight Wedding Supper

for 75 to 100

PÂTÉ DE FOIE GRAS
ON FRENCH BREAD

ASSORTED OPEN-FACED TEA SANDWICHES

SMOKED BLUEFISH WITH
SOUR CREAM AND CAPERS
OR
BLUEFISH MOUSSE

CHINESE PEA PODS AND ENDIVE
WITH
ORANGE-ALMOND DIP

COCKTAIL QUICHES

PAPRIKA MEATBALLS

COLD WHOLE SALMON
WITH SORREL SAUCE

CHICKEN IN CHAMPAGNE

LEMON RICE   ASPARAGUS IN SEASON

OLD-FASHIONED DAISY WEDDING CAKE

LEMON AND CASSIS SHERBETS

OPEN BAR   TOASTING CHAMPAGNE

COFFEE

AN ELEGANT AFTERNOON WEDDING

This is for the wedding for which the pocketbook is open, the champagne is flowing and the imagination takes flight.

The bride will choose a very special dress and the reception will be at her home or a club. The home allows use of the family silver, crystal and china; the club offers space and a willing staff. Whichever the locale, the whole affair is understated but perfect.

As with other parties of this size, there will have to be well-briefed help; bartenders, people in the kitchen and others to be sure things are passed and kept tidy. As I've said before, one in help to every 20 or 25 guests is the rule. At a club, this is of course no problem; at home, with a little care ahead, it need not be.

Flowers and music will play their part as well. As for the Intimate Winter Wedding planned in the last chapter, try to coordinate the buffet table flowers and wedding cake flowers with those of the wedding party. Big and little bouquets placed wherever possible will add to the elegance and are a must for any little tables set about. If space permits, music for dancing is a lovely addition; if not, a trio or even a solo piano will add to the festive air.

If the family linen and china closets are not full enough to supply this many guests, rentals of linens, glasses and china can be arranged. This is not the party for paper goods, except perhaps for the specially printed wedding napkins into which homeward-bound wedding cake pieces can be tucked.

The menu includes many of the world's most prized foods—choice shrimp, tenderloin of beef, lobster, cheeses and fruits, concluded by lovely pastries and a magnificent cake. And all the while, champagne, wine, and a delicious punch.

Recipes for the shrimp and beef tenderloin for this wedding are here, as are those for the Lobster Mousse Bouchées. The Raisin Delights and the wedding cake follow too—the cake, by the way, gets its name from my son-in-law who chose this combination for his wedding to one of my daughters. For the vegetable platter, I prefer snow peas, asparagus or endive, in season, and of course the little cherry tomatoes, but you should include your own family's favorites. A nice touch is to add a few chopped calendula petals or other unusual garnish to whichever dip you choose. The cheeses of course should be the best—perhaps a Brie, a St. André, a Roquefort and your favorite Cheddar. And settle for only the very best fruits in season. When possible, strawberries with confectioners' sugar nearby remain my favorite, but the little lady apples, fresh pineapple sticks and grapes of all shades are nice too. The rest of the menu, including the White Wine Fruit Punch, has been used elsewhere for other parties and can be found through the index. Consult your local wine merchant regarding the champagne and wines for this reception.

The attainment of the perfection we seek for this Elegant Afternoon Wedding party requires scrupulous attention to detail and a sensitive understanding of presentation. With these, and a full appreciation of the needs of your guests and the wishes of the wedding party, your "elegant afternoon" wedding will be a lovely affair long remembered.

CHILLED SHRIMP

Cooked and chilled shrimp, served with a mild sauce for those who like that and a stronger horseradish sauce for those who prefer it, are a delight for any party. These days most shrimp reach the markets frozen, and for the most part, in three sizes—6 to 8 per pound, 12 to 16 per pound and 18 to 25 per pound, plus broken pieces for salads and such. The tiny ones from Maine and the Pacific are very pleasant and can be used for hors d'oeuvre, but they are not always available.

For this special party I would choose the middle size (your guests can go back for more without feeling guilty). With 12 to 16 to the pound, you'll need at least 12 pounds.

Shrimp that are shelled and deveined need very little cooking, 3 to 5 minutes for the size we're planning here. (If they are not yet shelled and deveined, it will take longer, about 10 minutes.) If the shrimp are indeed frozen, do not defrost; simply make a Court Bouillon (see page 398), bring to a boil and drop in the shrimp, making sure they are completely separated (with this many, you'll either need a very large pot, or to do them in several batches). Cook until shrimp turn pink. This shouldn't take much more than 3 minutes. If in doubt, test one: overdone shrimp is a travesty. When done, remove from heat immediately and cool under cold water. Then shake and dry.

Chill the shrimp and serve on a bed of lettuce garnished with watercress sprigs. Nearby set a bowl of mayonnaise thinned with ⅓ as much sour cream and dusted with chopped watercress. This is for your guests who prefer a mild sauce. For those who like a bit more bite, offer James Beard's Shrimp Sauce (below) in a second bowl.

Note: See the index for an even wider selection of shrimp sauces.

James Beard's Shrimp Sauce

You'll need to make this recipe several times over for a party this size.

MAKES ABOUT 1 CUP

½ cup chili sauce
1 tablespoon Worcestershire sauce
½ cup catsup
½ teaspoon dry mustard

½ teaspoon salt
1 tablespoon horseradish
1 teaspoon freshly ground pepper

Blend all ingredients together and chill before serving.

TENDERLOIN OF BEEF

As soon as you hear the sound of wedding bells distant on the wind and begin your plans for this special wedding party, start watching the markets for sales of whole beef tenderloins. Since these roasts usually run from about 3½ to 4 pounds and serve perhaps 20, or at the most 25, as an hors d'oeuvre, you'll need several and quite a savings can be made if you buy ahead when they are a bargain. One especially happy attribute of this beef cut is that it is not all of equal width, which allows the middle of the tenderloin to be served rare while the thinner ends are served better done.

First be sure that the tenderloin has been well trimmed by your butcher (ask if the "chain," or gristle, has been removed; if not, cooking time will be a little longer). Then rub the tenderloin, which should be at room temperature, with garlic and season with freshly ground black pepper. Preheat oven to 350° and roast for approximately 45 minutes, which will yield rare beef in the center and medium at the ends. Remove from oven and allow to rest.

When ready to serve, slice thinly and arrange on a platter decorated with baby tomatoes and watercress or parsley sprigs. Serve with thinly sliced brown bread and a bowl of Béarnaise Sauce (below). Just before the party some of the beef slices can be put on the bread slices to be offered as canapés, but be careful not to prepare too many ahead: they tend to get soggy. This is a very popular hors d'oeuvre and will most likely disappear before the guests do.

Notes: Some prefer to cook this roast for a much shorter time at much higher heat (10 minutes on a side at 475° or 500°—rubbing the meat with oil and seasonings first). If buying tenderloin for a smaller party, you may want to use only the center section for your party and save the ends for use as small individual steaks or for barbecuing cubes.

BÉARNAISE SAUCE

Blender or food processor method. For this party, you will need at least 2 batches. Do not double recipe: make each batch separately.

MAKES 1–1½ CUPS

¼ cup white wine	1 tablespoon finely chopped shallots
2 tablespoons lemon juice	3 egg yolks
⅛ teaspoon white pepper	⅓ cup (5⅓ tablespoons) butter
1 tablespoon dried tarragon	½ teaspoon salt

Reduce first 5 ingredients by half in a small pot boiling gently. Scrape into blender with egg yolks. Melt butter until warm and with blender or food processor on, add butter and salt slowly. Continue for 30 seconds. If using immediately, place in a bowl or enamel pot perched over—but not in—warm water to keep warm. This sauce freezes well and can be reheated over warm water. If it curdles, add 2 tablespoons heavy cream or boiling water and beat well.

LOBSTER MOUSSE BOUCHÉES

Combining this delicious, though rich, mousse with puff pastry makes a lovely hors d'oeuvre for this fancy party and also stretches precious lobster about as far as it can go. As I have said, I usually use frozen lobster meat.

MAKES 4 TO 5 DOZEN

2 recipes Puff Pastry (see page 400)	⅔ cup peeled minced apple
1 envelope (1 tablespoon)	(optional)
unflavored gelatin	Salt and paprika to taste
¼ cup water	¾ cup mayonnaise
½ cup minced celery	3 tablespoons lemon juice
1½ cups cooked frozen or fresh	⅓ cup heavy cream
lobster meat	1 recipe Dorure (see page 406)

TO PREPARE

First make up the pastry and put in refrigerator to firm.

Then soak gelatin in water, dissolve over boiling water and set aside. Combine celery, lobster meat and, if desired, apples, and season. Blend mayonnaise and lemon juice, stirring in the dissolved gelatin. Then combine these 2 mixtures. Whip the cream until stiff and fold into the lobster mixture.

Pour mousse into wet 8- or 9-inch mold and chill thoroughly.

TO ASSEMBLE AND BAKE   **PREHEAT OVEN TO 400°**

Prepare the Dorure.

Roll the chilled dough out to a thickness of ⅛ inch. Cut into 4-inch rounds (two recipes of pastry should make close to 60 rounds). Place rounds on baking sheets, separating any layers with wax paper, and refrigerate to firm again.

Put about 1 teaspoon mousse in center of each pastry round, moisten edges with cold water and fold over to make half-moons. Press edges firmly with fork to seal and glaze bouchées with Dorure. (See art illustrating this technique on page 193 in the Southern "At Home" party.) Then refrigerate again for a few minutes before baking.

Bake for 12 to 15 minutes, until a deep golden brown, and serve hot.

Notes: Remember that there is whipped cream in this recipe: it should not be left standing idly for long in hot weather. Also, this mousse can be served by itself either as a light main dish (serving perhaps 18) or as hors d'oeuvre in bite-sized pieces on crackers or thinly sliced bread.

RAISIN DELIGHTS

MAKES ABOUT 5 DOZEN

½ cup raisins	*Grated rind of 1 lemon*
2 to 3 tablespoons whiskey	*1 tablespoon lemon juice*
½ cup butter, softened	*1¼ cups flour, sifted*
¾ cup sugar	*¼ teaspoon salt*
1 egg, lightly beaten	*½ teaspoon baking powder*

First put the raisins to soak in the whiskey (I keep a jar of these ready in my fridge, but not everyone does).

Then, in a mixer (or by hand), cream the butter and sugar, add egg, lemon rind and juice. Then sift together the flour, salt and baking powder and add, mixing slowly.

TO BAKE   **PREHEAT OVEN TO 375°**

Drop by the teaspoonful on greased cookie sheets about 2 inches apart, and press flat. Drain and press 3 raisins into center of each cookie. Bake until brown at the edges, 5 to 10 minutes (watch carefully!). Remove to rack to cool.

Note: If dough spreading too far is a worry, use ½ margarine and ½ butter.

Variation: If a fancier sweet is wanted, these cookies may be rolled around a wooden spoon handle while still warm into a cornet shape and then filled with a butter cream (see index for butter cream recipes).

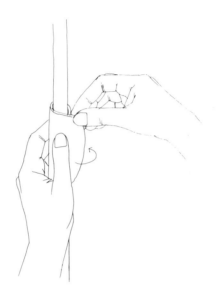

JONATHAN'S DREAM WEDDING CAKE

This is an especially lovely wedding cake combining a chocolate *génoise* and filling and a vanilla frosting with a hazelnut *broyage.* Linda King, who was helping us with the wedding, made it and it was delicious! However, it is a tricky cake to make, especially in hot weather. If you have help or are an accomplished baker, by all means go ahead; if not, perhaps the simpler Applesauce Wedding Cake in the Country Wedding section or the Old-Fashioned Daisy Wedding Cake coming up in the next party segment will suit you better. This is an ample recipe for 125 to 150 people, even up to 180; so in all likelihood, your guests will have some to take home as well as to eat at the wedding. Plan to start the cake a good week ahead to allow ample time

© Robert Grant

An Intimate Winter Wedding

GRAMERCY PARK WEDDING CAKE
PROSCIUTTO AND MELON
LOBSTER SALAD BASKETS

Basket Lunch

SESAME CHICKEN PASTA SALAD
CORNISH PASTIES
CHEESE AND FRUIT

for all the steps, and unless you are experienced, look over the Wedding Cake Guidelines on page 153 before you begin: it should help.

Chocolate Génoise

To complete this cake you will need two 12-inch cake layers, two 10-inch layers, two 8-inch layers and two 6-inch layers. Since 1 recipe makes one 12-inch or one 10-inch or one 8-inch *and* one 6-inch layer, you will need to make the recipe 6 times over. You can divide this any way you like, depending on the number of the various-sized cake pans available. I like to make it in 3 batches, baking 2 of the larger layers together twice and, if I have the pans, the 4 smaller layers together at once.

FOR THIS 4-TIER CAKE, MAKE 6 TIMES

> *6 large eggs, at room temperature*   *½ cup flour, sifted*
> *1 cup sugar*   *½ cup cocoa, sifted*

Beat eggs and sugar over a saucepan of hot water until lukewarm (if making double or triple batches, you will need large mixing bowl over wide-mouthed kettle of water). Continue beating until mixture triples in bulk. Sift together flour and cocoa and gently fold into egg mixture with fingers, or with mixer at lowest speed.

TO BAKE   **PREHEAT OVEN TO 350°**

Prepare pans by greasing and lightly flouring. Then fit pans with parchment paper circles to line pan bottoms. Pour in batter and bake about 20 minutes (larger layers may take a little more, smaller layers a little less) until layers pull away from sides and are golden brown and springy to the touch. Remove from pan immediately and cool upside down on cake rack; when cool, remove parchment liners.

When layers are cool, brush Raspberry Jam Glaze (see below) on all layers. Freeze each glazed layer separately until frozen; then wrap in plastic wrap and keep in freezer until needed. (Layers may be stacked when frozen.)

PREPARING THE BROYAGE

The next step is to make the Hazelnut Broyage (see below). This works best on a cool, dry day. Hopefully you will have one of these a few days before the wedding (another reason for allowing ample time to complete this cake). Anyhow, try to wait for one; it's dangerous otherwise and these meringue layers will keep for a few days until you want to use them if kept tightly sealed.

ASSEMBLING THE CAKE

Shortly before assembling the cake, make Chocolate Butter Cream Filling and Vanilla Butter Cream Frosting (both below). Then assemble the cake board, or plate you plan to use, along with pastry tube and a supply of clean bags (frosting works best if done in small amounts with clean bags to prevent melting from too much hand contact). If you are using a doily under the cake, it should be attached to the board, plate or tray with dabs of frosting. If you are using cardboards between the layers they should be cut to size and close at hand.

Working with the cake layers still frozen (so the large ones don't break or tear and they don't crumb on the frosting), place one 12-inch layer on cake board (remember: the doily goes first). Ice with generous amount Chocolate Butter Cream Filling. Place largest *broyage* layer on top and frost again. Place second 12-inch layer on top. Frost with Vanilla Butter Cream Frosting and dust sides with additional ground hazelnuts, if desired. With pastry tube, pipe borders of Vanilla Butter Cream around base of bottom layer, working in small amounts as above.

Next (10-inch) tier may be assembled on top of bottom tier or may be done on separate plate and refrigerated until very cold, when it can be moved over to bottom with spatulas. If you are using cardboards between the layers, do each tier separately and put in freezer to get hard. In this way, frosting will remain on cake layer it belongs on during serving. The 10-inch tier is topped with the 8-inch cardboard with icing piped around the edges, the 8-inch tier then placed on top of that when ready. And so on.

It's wise to anchor these tiers with skewers or chopsticks cut to fit tiers (see Wedding Cake Guidelines on page 153 of the Country Wedding section). Spin these "pillars" through the *broyage* and snip off with kitchen shears as needed, frosting over to disguise holes.

When cake is assembled, decorate according to your taste and the season (again see Wedding Cake Guidelines for ideas). If using real flowers, have enough to decorate all 4 tiers and top. If ordering from bridal florist, cake flowers may be ordered in flat arrangements to fit the various tier diameters. Chocolate curls make an attractive alternate decoration for this chocolate cake, if you opt against flowers.

Raspberry Jam Glaze

This recipe makes enough glaze for this 4-tiered cake. Boil together 1 cup seedless (sieved) raspberry jam and 1 cup cassis or other fruit liqueur. Use to brush all layers.

Hazelnut Broyage (Meringue)

This recipe makes ample for 1 meringue layer each for this 4-tiered cake, with a little left over for cookies

3 egg whites, at room temperature
2 tablespoons hazelnut liqueur
Pinch cream of tartar
Pinch salt
¾ cup sugar

⅓ cup cornstarch
½ cup ground toasted hazelnuts, with skins rubbed off (see Note below)

Beat egg whites and liqueur with cream of tartar and salt until foamy. Drizzle in ½ cup sugar. Continue to beat until mixture forms stiff peaks and fold in remaining sugar mixed with cornstarch and ground nuts.

TO BAKE   **PREHEAT OVEN TO 300°**

Butter and flour cookie sheets. Then draw appropriate-sized circles (1 for the 12-inch tier, 1 for the 10-inch, 1 for the 8-inch and 1 for the 6-inch). Pour batter onto sheets, keeping just inside the circles. Bake 10 minutes, then turn oven down to 200° and bake until dry. Depending on weather this can take from 2 to 4 hours. Don't let brown. Remove from pans and cool on cake racks.

Note: To prepare hazelnuts, toast in 350° oven until skins crack, 15 minutes plus or minus. When cool enough to handle, rub between palms to rub off skins. When skinned, grind fine. If you plan to dust sides of cake with ground hazelnuts as well as use them in the *broyage,* you'll want to double number for *broyage.*

Chocolate Butter Cream Filling (or Frosting)

This recipe makes enough for this 4-tiered cake.

9 egg yolks, at room temperature
¾ cup confectioners' sugar
¼ cup hazelnut liqueur

3 squares unsweetened chocolate, melted but not hot
3 pounds sweet butter, softened

Beat egg yolks, sugar, liqueur and chocolate until texture of whipped cream. Beat butter in a stick at a time and continue beating until butter is completely incorporated.

Vanilla Butter Cream Frosting (or Filling)

To make enough vanilla frosting for this 4-tiered cake, simply replace the 3 squares chocolate in the Chocolate Butter Cream Filling recipe above with 1 tablespoon vanilla and mix as in the Chocolate Butter Cream recipe.

Variation: Linda has a lovely variation of Jonathan's Dream Wedding Cake called Heide's Victorian. It is made exactly the same way but is based on a vanilla *génoise* rather than a chocolate. To make this add 1 tablespoon vanilla to the chocolate *génoise* recipe, replace the ½ cup cocoa with another ½ cup flour and add a dash Grand Marnier. It is mixed the same way. She uses the Hazelnut Broyage given and makes an orange butter cream frosting (see index for Orange Butter Cream frosting proportions and enlarge) instead of the Chocolate and plain Vanilla Butter Cream and replaces the Raspberry Jam Glaze with a marmalade glaze.

A CANDLELIGHT WEDDING SUPPER

Now we come to a lovely candlelight wedding followed by a simple but formal wedding supper.

The occasion should be a warm mixture of formality and ease. An hors d'oeuvre table should be set up near the bar beforehand for use during the receiving line and picture taking. There, the guests can serve themselves, or be served, while mixing with the bridal family and friends before going on into supper. The variety of appetizers can be changed to fit the season but the blending of soft, crunchy, hot, bland and smoked should be a constant no matter the particulars.

For this elegant party, I have started with perhaps the most elegant pâté of all—a store-bought Pâté de Foie Gras. If you prefer to make a simpler version yourself, the Pâté Maison in the Gala party or one from the index will do nicely. (The Reverend Sydney Smith defined Heaven as "eating pâté to the sound of trumpets." Even if there are no trumpets, let's hope there will be music.) Pâté of whichever kind you choose should be served on thinly sliced bland bread or unsalted biscuits, with cornichons, or little cucumber pickles, as accompaniment. A tray of tea sandwiches from the High Tea party will intrigue the eye as well as the tongue. Smoked bluefish is a new appetizer to me. It is less oily than mackerel and less expensive than salmon. A highly colored fish, sea-green above and silvery below, bluefish are found from Cape Cod to the Chesapeake Bay. This fish must be cooked right away as its flesh deteriorates quickly and the oil takes on a musty taste. After being smoked, bluefish can be kept up to a week or more, and can be frozen. Perhaps you would prefer the Bluefish Mousse, for which a recipe follows, to the plain. The plate of endive and briefly blanched pea pods adds freshness and crunch. And for a hot hors d'oeuvre I suggest the little spinach and ham or crabmeat Cocktail Quiches, the recipe for which appears in the Special Person party. These fillings could also be used to fill half-moon-shaped puff pastry with a dough initial drawn onto each one to indicate its flavor.

The main dishes for the buffet supper following are bracketed around a magnificent ice sculpture: most large restaurants and many clubs have a chef who can prepare these. Doves and swans are fairly common but graceful and lovely: perhaps you can arrange an even more spectacular one. At a Christmas wedding I catered several years ago a spectacular carved snow angel suddenly appeared. We quickly found a heavy stand to move it on and a way to get it properly displayed on the buffet table. It made a lovely centerpiece and, with greens circling it, was quite a Christmastime conversation piece. (This came about because the bride had worked for a prominent chef for several summers and he wanted to add his own special touch to her wedding celebration.)

The supper is a combination of hot meatballs, cold salmon and hot chicken, with simple but carefully seasoned side dishes, and baskets of bread sticks and butter pots on each of the individual dining tables set for 8 guests. The pièce de résistance is an old-fashioned wedding cake tastefully decorated with fresh, edible flowers. A table with coffee, coffee cups, cream and sugar can be close by the cake so the guests can serve themselves throughout the supper.

The recipe for the Paprika Meatballs is in the Country Wedding party section, though for this reception they will be in a lovely silver chafing dish. The Cold Whole Salmon may be purchased and decorated with cherry tomatoes and strips of green pepper. Included is a recipe for the Sorrel Sauce I like to serve with the salmon. The Chicken in Champagne is a favorite party dish of mine and very elegant; the recipe follows, as does that for the Lemon Rice. I leave the asparagus or other green vegetable in season to you. Recipes for the cake and sherbets follow as well.

During the evening the open bar provides an assortment of liquid refreshment and perhaps each table could have its own bottle or two of chilled white wine. Champagne, of course, will be served just before the bride and groom cut the cake so the toasts can be made.

Even though this supper is buffet, there will need to be several in help— at least one bartender, one helper in the kitchen, one at the buffet table to oversee the serving and one or two others to clear tables, bring out the cake and refresh platters and dishes as needed.

And although this party calls for china and glassware, do have a pile of pretty paper cake plates matching the wedding colors. Many guests like to take their wedding cake along home, and with a napkin as cover these little plates make good cake carriers.

The planning and timing of a formal reception like this candlelight supper are very important and it is essential to work in concert with your catering staff. Also important is that everyone agree what is to happen when. The party should flow but not drag on. Remember that many people do not like to leave a wedding party until after the bride and groom have gone, so even if they plan to change and return to the party again, be sure the bridal couple leave, at least for a while, shortly after the supper is over so the guests who want to may depart with a clear conscience.

BLUEFISH MOUSSE

This will stretch smoked bluefish a little further.

MAKES 40 OR SO SERVINGS

2 tablespoons unflavored gelatin
½ cup warm water
1 pound smoked bluefish, well
   broken up
4 tablespoons finely chopped shallots
4 to 6 tablespoons butter
⅔ cup softened cream cheese

6 tablespoons minced parsley
2 tablespoons lemon juice
2 tablespoons vermouth or gin
Salt and pepper to taste
⅓ to ½ cup Mock Crème Fraîche
   (see page 398)

Soften gelatin in water and then combine all ingredients well. Pour into oiled 1-quart ring or fish mold and let set.

Serve with thinly sliced French bread or unsalted crackers.

ORANGE-ALMOND DIP

This refreshing dip is a bit different and goes well with both fruits and vegetables. I usually serve it to accompany a vegetable platter with pea pods and endive or thin strips of lightly blanched carrots, beans, and early asparagus.

MAKES ABOUT 2 ½ CUPS

1 cup blanched almonds, chopped
   (see Note)
1 tablespoon butter
⅓ cup orange juice, freshly
   squeezed
1 cup firm yogurt
Pinch ground ginger, or more to
taste

¼ teaspoon tamari sauce
2 tablespoons freshly minced parsley
2 tablespoons finely minced fresh
   chives
¼ well rounded teaspoon grated
   orange rind
Salt and black pepper to taste
Cayenne to taste

Sauté almonds in the butter, stirring over low heat for about 5 minutes, or until nuts are lightly toasted. Remove from heat and transfer almonds to blender or processor container. Add the orange juice and purée. Move to bowl, add remaining ingredients, and mix well with a whisk. Season to taste, cover tightly and refrigerate. Serve cold.

Notes: If you prefer a hotter dip, add a little more tamari sauce. For instructions on blanching almonds, see recipe for French-Fried Almonds on page 252.

SORREL SAUCE

Somehow this lovely sauce is just right with cold salmon. For this wedding supper you'll need several batches.

MAKES 4 CUPS OR SO

½ pound sorrel
1½ sticks (12 tablespoons) sweet
*   butter*

3 cups heavy cream
2 teaspoons salt
Freshly ground black pepper

First, be sure sorrel is thoroughly washed and rinsed. Fold leaves over and tear stems off clear up into the leaves. Chop leaves coarsely.

In a 9-inch cast-iron skillet over medium heat melt 4 tablespoons butter. Add sorrel and stir about 5 minutes until sorrel blends into a purée. Add 2 cups heavy cream and bring to boil. Season with salt, pepper to taste, and cook, stirring once in a while over medium-low heat, for about 10 minutes.

When ready to serve, reheat the sauce with 1 cup heavy cream. Bring to boil, stirring continuously. Turn off heat and whisk in remaining 8 tablespoons butter. Taste and correct seasonings if necessary.

Sauce can be kept warm over a pan of warm water for a short while if necessary.

CHICKEN IN CHAMPAGNE

This elegant French recipe makes a delightful wedding supper main dish. It is richly flavored, yet light on the stomach and, almost as important, easy to manage. Also, it can be made ahead (see Notes). Required equipment: a kettle large enough to hold the chicken yet small enough to slide into your oven

MAKES 40 TO 60 SERVINGS

9 (approximately 3½-pound)
*   chickens, cut into serving pieces*
1½ sticks (12 tablespoons) butter
Salt and freshly ground pepper to
taste
2 cups finely chopped onions
½ teaspoon nutmeg
2 cups flour
½ cup Cognac
2 bay leaves

12 cups chicken broth, preferably
*   made fresh from the giblets and*
*   unusable parts*
1 bottle dry champagne, or, if you
*   prefer, other dry white wine*
6 sprigs fresh thyme, or 1 teaspoon
*   dried*
1 quart quartered mushrooms
5 cups heavy cream
Chopped or sliced truffles (optional)

TO PREPARE AND BAKE
THE CHICKEN   PREHEAT OVEN TO 475°

In a kettle large enough to hold them, over medium heat toss the chicken pieces in 4 tablespoons butter. Stir with a wooden spoon until the pieces are well coated, but not browned. Sprinkle with the salt and pepper to taste and stir in the onions and nutmeg. Continue cooking, stirring lightly, about another 5 minutes.

Place the kettle in the oven and bake, uncovered, about twenty minutes, stirring occasionally. Sprinkle with the flour and stir to coat the pieces. Bake another 20 minutes, stirring once in a while.

Then with the kettle on top of the stove again, add the Cognac, bay leaves, chicken broth, champagne, additional salt and pepper if wanted, and thyme. Bring to a boil, then reduce heat, cover and leave to gently simmer.

In a large skillet, combine the mushrooms and 1 cup cream. Bring to a boil, then simmer about two minutes, season with salt and add to the chicken. Cover the kettle and bake another 45 minutes. When through baking, carefully remove the chicken pieces and keep warm while making the sauce. At this point I like to cool the chicken slightly and gently debone it for easier serving and eating.

TO PREPARE THE SAUCE

After removing the chicken pieces, boil down the sauce in the kettle by about ⅓. Add the remaining 4 cups cream and continue cooking, stirring frequently, about an hour. Strain the sauce and return it to a boil, then remove from the heat and swirl in the remaining 8 tablespoons butter.

TO SERVE

Arrange the chicken on several large serving platters, pouring a modest amount of the sauce over the chicken but holding the remaining sauce aside to serve in an adjoining sauceboat: too much sauce will escape on the plate and blur the flavor of the other dishes. If you are feeling very special, garnish the chicken with the truffles just before serving.

Notes: To make a day ahead, keep the prepared chicken and sauce separate until shortly before serving time. Then heat the sauce through well, adding the chicken at least 15 to 20 minutes ahead of serving time (if the chicken has been deboned this will have to be done carefully). Once warmed through, the chicken can be served as above or kept warm in a low, 140° oven for an hour or so.

A special word: This recipe sounds complicated and time-consuming but it isn't nearly as demanding as it seems and other things can always be tended to while it is cooking. Besides, it's worth it!

CRAFTSBURY INN LEMON RICE

This particular rice dish was found at the Craftsbury Inn on a gourmet tour of Vermont inns and offers a pleasantly tangy variation of this timeless staple. For a wedding party this large, considerable multiplication of the recipe would be necessary.

SERVES 6 TO 8 GENEROUSLY

3 ½ cups water	Grated rind of 1 lemon
1 ½ cups uncooked rice	Juice of 1 lemon
1 ½ teaspoons salt	Freshly ground black pepper
¾ stick (6 tablespoons) sweet	Lemon slices, for garnish
butter, melted	Mint sprigs, for garnish

In a large saucepan, bring the water to a boil. Stir in the rice, salt and 1 tablespoon of the butter, cover tightly and simmer 20 minutes. Remove from the heat and let stand covered until all water is absorbed into the rice, about 5 minutes. Add the remaining butter, lemon rind and juice, season with pepper and toss thoroughly. To serve, surround rice with paper–thin lemon slices sprinkled with mint sprigs.

Note: When preparing rice for large numbers, be sure to plan ahead just how you will keep it warm. Setting several panfuls over warm water is one way, though if you have or can borrow a rice basket, so much the better.

OLD-FASHIONED DAISY WEDDING CAKE

This is a remarkably simple wedding cake—as wedding cakes go. It is another from Linda King who also cuts the recipe in half to make an equally successful cake for a more intimate wedding. In fact, unless you have commercial equipment available, I suggest you mix it just that way, by halves, setting the first batch aside until you are ready to bake the three layers you will need.

TO SERVE 100 TO 120

1 pound sweet butter	3 cups milk
4 cups sugar	1 recipe Apricot Custard Filling
4 teaspoons vanilla, almond, orange	(see page 152 in Country
or lemon extract, as you choose	Wedding)
16 egg yolks	1 recipe Fluffy Butter Cream
12 cups cake flour	Frosting (see page 152 in
½ teaspoon salt	Country Wedding)
¼ cup baking powder	

TO PREPARE BATTER

Beat butter until creamy. Add sugar, creaming well. Then beat in flavoring of choice and egg yolks, one at a time. Mix together flour with salt and baking powder. Then stir in dry ingredients and milk in alternate batches, mixing gently but well.

TO BAKE   **PREHEAT OVEN TO 350°**

Fill well-greased and floured 6-, 9- and 12-inch commercial cake baking pans about ⅔ full, spreading batter a little higher on sides. Bake, reducing the heat to 325° after about 20 minutes, until done. (See the Wedding Cake Guidelines checklist on page 153 in the Country Wedding chapter for more detailed instructions; I usually bake the 6- and 9-inch layers together and the 12-inch layer by itself).

TO ASSEMBLE, FROST AND DECORATE

Using the Apricot Custard Filling and Fluffy Butter Cream Frosting in the Country Wedding party, follow the Wedding Cake Guidelines there to assemble, frost and decorate cake. Mix or match the frosting flavor with the one you have chosen for the cake, according to your taste.

LEMON SHERBET

This is a lovely, light sherbet. For a party this size arrange to borrow an electric freezer if you don't have one. Four times this recipe will make 6 quarts, which, when combined with an equal amount of the Cassis Sherbet, should be more than ample for this supper. It can be made a day or two ahead.

MAKES 1½ QUARTS

2 teaspoons grated lemon rind	*⅜ teaspoon salt*
2 cups sugar	*¾ cup lemon juice*
2 cups water	*2 egg whites*

Combine lemon rind and sugar, then add water and ¼ teaspoon salt. Heat until sugar is dissolved, then boil 5 minutes. Chill this syrup and add lemon juice.

   Freeze sherbet according to freezer instructions. When the consistency of mush, beat the egg whites with ⅛ teaspoon salt until stiff and fold lightly into sherbet. Then freeze again until firm.

   Allow sherbet to "season" by packing well in ice and salt at least an hour before serving.

CASSIS SHERBET

Again, four times this recipe will make 6 quarts. Since this sherbet improves with aging, plan to make it at least the day before.

MAKES 1½ QUARTS

3 cups raspberry purée (2 to 3 [10-ounce] packages unsweetened frozen raspberries)
1½ cups sugar

1½ cups water
2 egg whites, stiffly beaten
⅛ teaspoon salt
2 tablespoons cassis, or more to taste

Prepare the purée by running the frozen raspberries through the blender or food processor and then through a sieve to be sure the seeds are all removed.

Dissolve sugar in water (if you were unable to find unsweetened berries you will want to cut the sugar down by about half), boil for 5 minutes and combine with raspberry purée. Cool completely; beat egg whites with salt until stiff and fold into purée with the cassis. Then freeze according to freezer instructions.

III

FOR PLEASURE... AND PROFIT

FOR PLEASURE . . . AND PROFIT

AN INTRODUCTION

Like cats and Christmas, fund-raising is always with us. Direct-mail appeals and corner Santa Clauses are all very well, but I prefer parties—parties combined with a special attraction. For one thing, they work; for another, they're fun.

For successful fund-raising, perhaps the hardest thing of all is to pick the right event and the right people to run it. Beyond that, there are three major targets to be met: publicity for your cause, enjoyment for all, and a solid cash balance at the end. This takes a good deal of planning and hard work but is much easier if an appealing event has been chosen in the first place and good people are in charge.

Some agencies lend themselves readily to ideas for events. For others it is more difficult. It helps if the event chosen, especially if it is to become an annual one, is something both fitting and original—something not already done to death in your community. For a town already strong in music, one would not choose a musical event, and so on.

Many things go into these decisions, and the challenge varies considerably from town to town and organization to organization. Some groups have a large membership and volunteer corps and wide community support; others are just beginning and don't yet have a strong support system. Certainly it is wiser to have a small, well-run and enjoyable event than a large disaster.

How much money do you need to raise? What facilities are available? How many people do you have to help? What does the community enjoy? When is the best time—and do you have enough? What are others doing? (Be sure to check for conflicts!) Do you want a single large event or a series of smaller ones—perhaps tied to a central theme? What will it cost? What is a reasonable profit projection? Do you have the necessary upfront money? Are there any chances of getting community business support? (In the case of the local museum with which I am involved, one of our local banks underwrites a good share of the cost of bringing a small ballet troupe to town for a once-a-year benefit. Their support helps us tremendously: certainly our cash balance at the end is a lot blacker, and meanwhile the bank gains excellent publicity and good will, and, we trust, a sense of satisfaction.)

These are only some of the questions involved in making a wise fund-raising decision. You may well need a small exploratory committee to help answer some of them before you can reach a decision or present a particular project to your board of trustees for theirs. And don't forget the most important ingredient of all: *enthusiasm.* If your board or committee and most of the membership aren't enthusiastic, you would do well to search for another idea —or a better salesperson.

Once the decision is made, the work begins.

You'll need the best committee you can find and a strong chairperson. (Actually I have found that a co-chair system works best. Not only does it lighten the load for each, it allows—at least for annual events—a chance for the senior chair to train the junior chair to take over, in turn, the following year.)

Each event will require its own special committee members, but there are bound to be some common to all: 1) someone to oversee the details of the event itself whether it is a concert, auction, ballet troupe, jazz party, special sale, fair or whatever; 2) publicity (few will come if they don't know about the event and expect it to be worthwhile—and fun); 3) ticket sales; 4) business liaison, if sponsorship or other donations are being sought; 5) patron arrangements, if that's appropriate; 6) program ad sales, if there's to be a program (an excellent way to add to that cash balance if you can make it work!); 7) program editor, again if there's to be a program (to oversee layout, written material, advertising copy, liaison with printer); 8) liaison with outside facilities, if that's necessary; 9) liaison with schools and other special organizations for group sales, etc.; 10) hospitality, if people need to be put up; 11) flowers and decoration; 12) party or refreshments (a big job if the event is to include a large celebratory party after a performance—but essential no matter how big or small: I'm convinced there's little money to be made at anything without good food and drink and a chance to enjoy it), and 13) someone, the treasurer most likely, to oversee the monies involved—the ins and the outs—and to be sure records are kept and any bills paid as promptly as possible.

One last thing about committees: do be sure that the different committee jobs are clearly defined. This ensures that no important chores slip between the cracks and helps eliminate confusion about who does what and when— and certainly makes the chairpersons' job easier. A good organizational chart is also very helpful, and accurate records are a must—both for the present and for the committees of the future. Make the meetings as few as possible—and as short! And perhaps most important: again, don't forget the enthusiasm. Many businesses, even some charitable organizations, spend big bucks to keep up their workers' morale. If your organization is committed to its cause, this shouldn't be necessary, but consideration of their time, talents and feelings is.

Now to our three main goals.

Publicity. Obviously you must get the basic information out: the what, where, when and how much. But be sure to include the why. It is important that the public understand the purpose of your event—whether it is to raise money for your local museum, for the public television station, for new instruments for the high school band, or to provide special care for special children—whatever it is, it is important that the community know and that they understand the need, and just what the money you raise will do for the community and for each of them as individuals. So, along with the basic nitty-gritty, be sure your publicity informs the community about your cause and brings them up-to-date on your organization.

This publicity can take many forms: mailings; steady newspaper coverage (remember that newspapers can't keep running the same story: they need new information each time, and in towns where there is competition, often completely different stories; also remember that much of the media will not allow "free" publicity if you are advertising for "pay" elsewhere); occasional feature articles (here especially, newspapers will not run the same material as their competition); radio (interviews and spots); TV, posters, special windows, street banners—and no doubt others (even spot ads on occasion if ticket sales become a worry). And of course it must all be well-written, tasteful, attractive, and as compelling as possible. This is no easy task, but it is worth every effort—not only in helping to ensure a successful event but also in building support for the future.

Enjoyment for all. Much of this has already been said. First, the event must be something that people want to be a part of. It must be run well and attractively. Any special permits (liquor, parking or whatever) and safety precautions (police, fire) must be arranged well in advance. It should give people an opportunity to participate (perhaps even earn free admission if especially tight budgets are a problem). The cost should be within reason even for those with not-so-tight budgets (keeping things within reason not only leaves good feeling, it builds enthusiasm for the next time around; if your organization has any outstanding IOU's, this might be a good time to honor them with a free invite).

Feelings must be considered and work appreciated—by word, by note and by attitude. If outside talent is involved, it must be treated thoughtfully and made to feel welcome (out of a sense of fair play and gratitude of course, but also—word gets around!). All monies must be handled carefully and bills paid promptly. Any refreshments offered must be of good quality and imaginative—and, if for sale, not too dear (with volunteers to do most of the making, this shouldn't be difficult). And of course, if there is to be a celebratory party, it must be as special as your budget will allow (more about this in the Gala chapter to follow).

Solid cash balance. There are a number of ways to enhance your profit margin, some of which I've already touched on. First, if you can find a local business to pick up some or all of the initial cost, you are already ahead of the game (this could pay for outside talent, for rental of a hall, the printing of tickets, underwriting advertising costs—or any number of other expenses). No matter how big or small the amount, it will be a great help. If at the same time you can involve the businessmen in the event personally, so much the better: it will help build attendance and community enthusiasm.

Selling program ad space is another excellent tool. But be sure to treat these advertisers in a businesslike fashion. A simple contract sheet is a good idea —to set down costs for the different amounts of space available, to indicate when payment will be made (the sooner the better, of course) and what copy requirements are involved—with a place for signatures. Unless the ad committee also follows up, someone from the program committee must be responsible for getting together any special copy or artwork needed: this sometimes requires trips to various ad agencies, publications and even other organizations which might have used it. Then someone must be sure the advertisers are properly thanked and get a copy of the program. This work is demanding but worthwhile. Not only does it make money, it offers another excellent opportunity to build enthusiasm and to solicit membership and/or suggestions for the future.

Obviously, whatever can be obtained free or at low cost will help build profit. Free or sponsored talent, a free hall, free refreshments—they all help; but unless yours is a very low budget operation, be careful not to throw the baby out with the bathwater. You do not want to jeopardize quality—and enjoyment—to save a modest extra expense.

Using volunteers to do as much of the work as possible is certainly one of the best cost-cutters. Many members—and friends—are glad to help, and of course a good board of trustees will expect to. These volunteers can send out mailings, make phone calls, man ticket offices or sales booths, serve as ushers, write publicity, make posters, put the program together, clean up (before and after), decorate, provide hospitality, organize dinner parties before the event, make refreshments and bartend—the list is long—and of course buy tickets and attend. But here again, be careful. Take care not to assign people tasks that do not match their talents or may be a bit beyond their spirit and their flesh. And do get paid help where it is really needed; depending on the event, proper sound and lighting people if that's important, and/or a professional to handle the food if you're planning a party with anything but the simplest of menus. Someone to tend to the kitchen and the bar, if needed, will guarantee that the food and drink is set out properly, kept hot or warm as required, and served attractively and in an orderly fashion. This help will free your committee to keep other things running smoothly, to make the public, and any special guests, feel welcome, and to enjoy themselves—and watch the cash balance grow!

As I said at the beginning, I like to combine parties with my fund-raising. With this in mind, there are a number of ways to go to make your own fund-raising both pleasurable and profitable: balls, theater parties, trips to sporting events, movie previews, progressive dinner parties, house tours—and this only scratches the surface. I can touch on only a few ideas here—all things I have been part of (in most cases as a worker, in one or two as a guest), chiefly with success but always with pleasure. And since this is primarily a cookbook they all include food as an important ingredient.

The first makes creative use of box lunches; the second combines simple food and drink for a political reception; the third, an antique sale preview party, does double duty, allowing the sale to make money before the main event as well as during; the fourth, a wine-tasting party, offers the opportunity for both education (about wines) and enjoyment (of wines); the fifth, a jazz bash, throws caution to the winds and combines special food with special music for a very special time (and $$). And lastly, a gala champagne reception celebrates an outstanding event and the end of weeks and weeks of hard work.

As I say, there are many ways to go. Just choose what seems best for your organization and your community. Then, with careful planning and creative attention to detail and to the enjoyment of those attending the event—and, I hope, using some of the menus and recipes from this book—your well-earned reward will be both pleasure . . . and profit!

Good luck!

20
BROWN BAGS
WERE NEVER LIKE THIS

Box Lunch Suggestions

HOT AND COLD SOUPS

CORNISH PASTIES

STUFFED PITA POCKETS

SESAME CHICKEN PASTA SALAD

HAM AND CHEESE BISCUITS

POOR BOY SANDWICHES

PÂTÉ AND MEATLOAF SLICES

SPRING ROLLS

CHINESE GINGERED VEGETABLES

BUTTERSCOTCH BROWNIES

PHYLLO FRUIT TARTS

OATMEAL CHOCOLATE CHIP COOKIES

KITTY'S FRUITCAKE

CHINESE SWEET NUTS   APPLE CAKE

FRUITS IN SEASON   CIDER   TEA   COFFEE

Box Breakfast Eye-Openers

STUFFED TOMATOES Á LA AMY

COLD SCRAMBLED EGGS

MARINATED SAUSAGES AND PEPPERS

CROISSANTS BAGELS MUFFINS

FRUIT JUICE TEA COFFEE

BROWN BAGS
WERE NEVER LIKE THIS

M ention box lunches and there immediately springs to mind the old-fashioned fourth of July picnic and its Gay Lothario in his straw boater bidding for the beribboned box lunch of the current apple of his eye. Surely the box lunch is an idea whose time has come again. It works wonderfully well for all those required lunch meetings—and, these days, breakfast ones as well.

Box lunches or breakfasts brought into an all-day seminar or even a hastily called conference before the workday begins are like a breath of fresh air—conjuring up the gustatory and psychic pleasures of the unexpected. Combining good food, served attractively, with work (or duty) encourages creative thinking and discussion—and bolsters morale.

Many places that have adequate facilities for such meetings—meeting rooms, restrooms, ample parking and the like—may not have a proper kitchen, or any kitchen; but a good box lunch requires only an electric outlet to brew coffee and tea, or perhaps heat some soup. And why shouldn't your organization make any profit—however small—rather than send it to a local delicatessen or lunchroom.

When I consider this, I think immediately of one such occasion. Not too long ago we were having an all-day meeting at our local museum with three speakers scheduled to talk about the preservation of various artifacts and how to make use of what a museum might have on hand to take proper care of costumes, prints and so forth. People came from almost every corner of southern Vermont, and even though Vermont is small, this meant early-to-rise and a long drive for most. So their day had begun well before the meeting.

As it happened, one of our museum's board members, who runs a local bakery, graciously greeted the participants as they arrived with a fluffy hot croissant and a cup of piping hot coffee. Then at lunchtime a friend of the museum arrived bearing a great pile of decorated bakery boxes. Inside she had devised a lovely luncheon treat: a toasty warm Cornish pastie, wrapped in a gay napkin, a little stack of fresh julienned vegetables, a piece of fruit and, tucked under the fruit, a surprise, a little sweet—a butterscotch brownie square. This, with pitchers of cider and coffee and tea made at the museum, was the perfect lunch for the occasion. And the boxes were delightfully decorated. Our lunchbox bearer had only white boxes to work with so asked her daughter's first-grade classmates to decorate the lids of the boxes with renderings of the museum and the Connecticut River running nearby. They may not have looked too realistic but were delightful and amusing, and when the time came many people took them home.

The original pasties were carried to work in the fields by Cornishmen whose wives wrapped them in a cloth to keep them warm. The ladies at our meeting were only working in the fields of the intellect, but the pasties were welcome nonetheless, and as the weather allowed us to move lunch outside to enjoy the good food and drink in the sun, it was a wonderful break in the day.

The pasties were not expensive and not difficult to make (there is a recipe following if you'd like to try). The charge was moderate: $3.00. So, the profit was small—but still again, pleasure and profit.

Other ideas for this type luncheon include pita bread "pockets" filled with guacamole, sprouts, lettuce and tomatoes, or other combinations of your own invention. On winter days, a hot cup of soup would be a good addition; in summer, perhaps a cold one (there are recipes for both here). Styrofoam cups will keep them either hot or cold as you like. The Sesame Chicken Pasta Salad, served with a piece of fruit and a bit of sweet, is another good idea—and there are many more. The Ham and Cheese Biscuits or Poor Boy Sandwiches filled with Pork Teriyaki or leftover meatballs from a recent party and slices of pâté and meatloaf all make tasty lunchtime treats. And don't forget that breadsticks make a pleasant change from the more usual breads and crackers if you don't need them to hold things together. The Gingered Vegetables from the Super-bowl Sunday party, make a good vegetable variation.

The range of sweets is equally limitless: I especially like the fruit-filled phyllo tarts given here. And the very light Kitty's Fruitcake is nice too—it combines fruit and sweet without the heaviness we usually associate with fruitcake. The Apple Cake is another lovely blend of sweet and fruit. Choose your own favorite here or in the index.

If, for one reason or another, a homemade box lunch is hard for your organization, it is still possible to arrange a very special box lunch without having to revert to a tired sandwich and tepid tea. Perhaps you could ask your local Chinese restaurant (most towns have at least one) to put together a box of hot and sour soup, a few fried noodles, a piece of parchment chicken or several of the tiny individual spareribs, and a spring roll, with maybe a few Chinese sweet nuts tucked in to one side. The beverage could again be cider, or maybe beer, and of course tea. (If you want to try this without the restaurant, you'll find the recipes for Hot-Sour Soup, spring rolls and accompanying sauces in this chapter and the Chinese Sweet Nuts elsewhere in the book.) Again, it should be possible to offer this at a reasonable price and still be able to make a small profit.

And don't forget the breakfast meeting. In every town there are people who meet to lay plans to raise money for one cause or another. Many of these people are hard to pin down. They work in the daytime; their evenings are precious and often already full of meetings—and many times their lunch hours are full as well. What better time to catch them than at the beginning of the day when everyone is fresh and life is still somewhat in order? Everyone has to eat at least a little breakfast and what better morale booster than a good hot muffin or a flaky croissant elegantly sweetened with marmalade butter (made by mixing half and half)?

Many banks and law and other offices have a room they are happy to loan for such meetings—especially before their workday begins—and many even have a small kitchen, some with a microwave oven and small refrigerator. But with only electric outlets you can still be creative: a toaster oven and electric coffeepot allow a lot of room to create.

With a little time and considerable thought, the breakfast box can also be a gourmet treat. Small hollowed-out tomatoes filled with egg salad, dotted with capers and served with an English or blueberry muffin is one way to go —or you could try the Stuffed Tomatoes à la Amy following here. Somehow tomato breakfasts appeal to me; I remember one with special pleasure. It was served on Canadian Pacific Airlines and combined a broiled tomato hollowed out to hold a freshly poached egg, along with two sausages and a croissant, juice and coffee. Sadly, my husband and I, so used to terrible plane meals, had eaten lightly beforehand so were unable to enjoy fully this unexpected breakfast treat.

Another possible breakfast meeting menu combines gourmet and surprise as well as any: Cold Scrambled Eggs. Peter Zilliacus, long a restaurateur of note—first in Sweden and then here in Vermont—makes this delicious dish. I share it with you here: together with a toasty warm bagel, coffee and a little fruit, you couldn't do better. And for an exotic dish you could try Marinated Sausages and Peppers, served warm, again with a muffin—perhaps apple this time.

So you see even the breakfast meeting menus can be different—and fun. And again, a reasonable charge should allow you at least a little profit. And don't forget the tea drinkers: all it takes is a pot of boiling water and some tea.

There is one more way to use these box meals: for the bus trips that so many organizations are sponsoring these days—to an in-town art show or concert, to a faraway tennis match or garden tour, or perhaps for a country leaf-peeping tour. These trips usually include a restaurant luncheon but start early and often end late: nothing is pleasanter than breaking the trip with a light box breakfast on the way out and maybe a late tea or happy hour on the way back home. Planning for this requires imagination and ingenuity —things are easily kept cold on buses, hot is more of a challenge—but it can be done. (Ask your local high school athletic department—you may be surprised; they often have such equipment to use when the football and other teams travel.)

Top honors for bus meal ingenuity go to Linda King. She once undertook to provide both a bus lunch and a bus dinner to a group going into a Boston Symphony Orchestra concert. Due to a mixup at the Boston end Linda found herself with no way to heat the dinner casserole. She finally convinced someone at the symphony to let her heat it in a back room—all very well, until about halfway through the concert she could clearly detect the aroma of her stew gently wafting through the concert hall. But all ended well, the aroma didn't get too strong, not too many in the audience were aware of it—and the stew was delicious.

I don't recommend anything quite so ambitious for a bus box lunch menu. Many of the items for the other box meals I've given here should work well, and party menus throughout the book will give you other ideas.

Do give it a try! In addition to making these trips much more enjoyable for everyone, bus meals allow still another chance to combine pleasure with profit.

BOX LUNCH SUGGESTIONS

HOT-SOUR SOUP

This Chinese soup is less complicated than some but still distinctive.

MAKES 5 TO 6 SERVINGS

3 or 4 dried black mushrooms	2 tablespoons white vinegar
¼ pound lean pork	¾ to 1 teaspoon salt
2 bean curd cakes	1 teaspoon soy sauce
2 tablespoons cornstarch	¼ teaspoon pepper
¼ cup water	1 egg, lightly beaten
5 cups stock or chicken bouillon	Few drops sesame oil
1 tablespoon sherry	1 scallion, minced

First set mushrooms in hot water to soak until soft. Remove and pat dry, reserving soaking liquid. Sliver mushrooms along with pork and bean curd. Blend cornstarch and water together to make paste.

Bring stock or bouillon and 1 cup mushroom liquid to boil. Add pork and mushrooms and simmer, covered, 10 minutes. Add bean curd and simmer, still covered, another 3 minutes. Stir in sherry, vinegar, salt, soy sauce and pepper. Thicken with cornstarch paste. Slowly add beaten egg, stirring gently once or twice, and remove from heat. Sprinkle with sesame oil and minced scallion.

Variations: Half pork, half white-meat chicken may be substituted for the pork; wine, cider vinegar or lemon juice may be used for the white vinegar and Tabasco sauce may be used for the sesame oil. For a more elaborate soup, ½ cup bamboo shoots (slivered) may be added with the pork and mushrooms —as may 4 cloud ear mushrooms and/or ¼ cup lily buds (both soaked and cut in half).

Note: The large thick dried black mushrooms with light skins and curled edges are the best.

GREEN SOUP

This soup is often made by my daughter Fiona. It is delicious served hot or chilled.

MAKES 6 TO 8 CUPS

3 large onions, sliced
5 to 6 tablespoons butter
2 large potatoes, peeled and sliced
1 (10-ounce) can chicken broth
2½ cups milk
Salt to taste
Bay leaf
3 sprigs fresh tarragon, or ½ teaspoon dried

1 (10-ounce) package frozen chopped spinach
2 teaspoons soy sauce
¼ teaspoon curry powder
1 cup heavy cream
Fresh mint or scallions, chopped, for garnish

Sauté onions together with butter in Dutch oven until wilted. Add potatoes, broth, milk, salt, bay leaf and tarragon. Simmer, covered, until potatoes are tender. Add spinach until cooked. Whirl all together in blender. Return to pot; add soy sauce, curry powder and cream.
     Garnish and serve, or refrigerate if serving cold.

COLD ZUCCHINI SOUP

This is a delicious zucchini-season soup.

MAKES 6 TO 8 SERVINGS

5 to 6 small to medium zucchini, well-scrubbed
1 large onion, thinly sliced
1½ teaspoons curry powder
3 cups chicken broth

1 cup heavy cream
½ cup milk
Several drops of soy sauce
Salt and pepper to taste
Chopped chives for garnish

Cut 1 zucchini in half crosswise; then, thinly slice 1 of the halves. Stack these slices and cut into very thin, match like strips (or use julienne disk of food processor). There should be about 1 cup. Place strips in saucepan and add cold water to cover. Boil 1 to 2 minutes, drain and set aside.

Cut remaining zucchini into 1-inch-wide lengths, cutting each length into quarters. Place zucchini pieces in soup kettle and add onion slices. Sprinkle with curry powder and stir to coat zucchini and onion. Add chicken broth and bring to boil. Cover and simmer about 45 minutes. Then place in blender and purée. Add cream, milk, soy sauce, salt and pepper, and the reserved zucchini strips. Mix well and chill.

When ready to serve, sprinkle lightly with chopped chives.

CHILLED TOMATO AND YOGURT SOUP

Another excellent summer soup.

MAKES 6 SERVINGS

2 tablespoons butter	3 fresh basil leaves, or 1 teaspoon
2 cups chopped onion	dried
2 cups peeled, seeded and cubed	2 cups chicken broth
cucumbers	2 cups yogurt
3 cups peeled, seeded and cubed	Salt to taste
tomatoes	Chopped fresh mint, for garnish

Melt butter in a large saucepan or soup kettle and add onion. Cook, stirring frequently, about 10 minutes. Do not brown.

Add the cucumbers, tomatoes, basil and chicken broth, and cook, again stirring frequently, about 30 minutes. Put soup through food mill; add yogurt, salt to taste and chill.

When ready to serve, sprinkle lightly with the fresh mint.

CORNISH PASTIES

These pies, also known as Forfar Bridies, are one of several Cornish pastie cousins, this one with less emphasis on vegetables. The recipe is sometimes made up in large pies but more often in these little individual ones.

MAKES 8 TO 10 SMALL PIES

1½ pounds lean round or flank   *1 onion, finely minced*
steak   *1 recipe Pastie Pastry (see below)*
4 teaspoons minced suet   *Salt and pepper to taste*

Slice meat into very thin slices, slightly on the diagonal. Cut strips into pieces an inch or so long. Mix the suet and onion.

Make and roll out pastry, cutting into 6 or 7-inch circles. Arrange meat on all the circles; sprinkle with suet and onion. Season with salt and pepper. Wet edges of pastry, fold one edge over, making into half-moon shape, and crimp edges together. Slit hole in each pie.

TO BAKE   **PREHEAT OVEN TO 400°**

Bake on lightly greased baking sheets about ½ hour.

Pastie Pastry

2 cups sifted flour   *⅓ cup cold lard*
1 teaspoon salt   *5 or 6 tablespoons ice water*
5⅓ tablespoons (⅓ cup) cold butter

Sift flour with salt into a bowl. Cut in butter and lard with pastry blender or 2 knives. Sprinkle water over all. Mix well with fork until mixture sticks together. Press into ball with your hands. (If pastry is not to be used right away, keep chilled until needed.)

When ready, roll out, half at a time, on lightly floured board.

SESAME CHICKEN PASTA SALAD

On a hot day this salad with a breadstick, perhaps, a piece of fruit and a sweet of some sort will make the perfect box lunch.

I like to use the spinach or plain fusilli pasta, broken into 1-inch lengths and cooked just *al dente.* The quantities will of course depend on the number of people you are serving, but to make the salad, simply combine in proportions of about ½ cooked pasta, to ¼ poached chicken, cut in large bite-sized pieces, with the last ¼ a mixture of blanched broccoli flowerets, green and red pepper chunks and carrot strips, all cut small. (Actually you can mix/match these proportions almost any way you like.) Then season and toss well with your favorite French or oil and vinegar dressing livened with a few drops of hot sesame oil. If you like, toss in a small handful of sesame seeds.

HAM AND CHEESE BISCUITS

These delicately flavored ham and cheese biscuits make a lovely light lunch-time treat.

MAKES 24 OR SO 2-INCH BISCUITS

1¾ cups flour
2½ teaspoons baking powder
¾ cup grated cheese (Cheddar
  preferred)
1 teaspoon salt

4 tablespoons butter, plus extra
  melted for brushing tops
⅔ to ¾ cup half-milk, half-water
1 egg, lightly beaten
1 (4½-ounce) can deviled ham

Mix together flour, baking powder, cheese and salt; cut in butter and add enough milk-water combination to make stiff dough. On lightly floured surface, roll very thin and cut with a 2-inch round lightly floured cutter. Moisten edges of rounds with beaten egg. Spread half the rounds with ham; cover with remaining rounds, pressing edges together.

TO BAKE   PREHEAT OVEN TO 400°

Place biscuits on lightly greased baking sheets; brush tops with melted butter and bake 12 to 15 minutes.

Serve fresh with small stack of julienned vegetables, a bit of fruit and a touch of sweet.

Notes: If you can't make these biscuits just before serving, they can be made ahead and kept in freezer, then reheated when ready to serve. Or you can reheat a bit ahead and wrap to keep as warm as possible. They also, if you use the little 1- or 1½-inch cutters, make lovely cocktail biscuits.

SPRING ROLLS WITH SHRIMP AND CHICKEN FILLING

Spring rolls are similar to egg rolls except that spring rolls are purely Chinese. Their skins are paper thin, like translucent crepes. They are crisp, smooth and delicate while egg roll skins are not so smooth nor so delicate. They can be made—or bought, as most do, in Chinese stores. As for all Chinese cooking, all ingredients should be wok-ready.

MAKES 20

3 tablespoons oil for stir-frying, plus 4 cups for deep frying

2 slices fresh ginger, each cut to size of a quarter

1 clove garlic, crushed and peeled

6 ounces fresh shrimp, shelled, deveined, rinsed in cold water, patted dry and cut into peanut-sized pieces

1 egg white (save yolk if using spring roll skins)

1 teaspoon pale dry sherry

1¼ teaspoons salt

8 Chinese dried mushrooms, soaked in hot water until soft

6 water chestnuts, cut into thin strips

3 cups fresh bean sprouts or shredded Chinese celery cabbage

1 cup shredded bamboo shoots

2 scallions, cut into 1½-inch lengths and shredded

8 ounces boned, skinless chicken breast, shredded into matchstick strips (to make 1 cup)

2 teaspoons cornstarch

⅛ teaspoon sugar

1 tablespoon black soy sauce

2 tablespoons thin soy sauce

1 tablespoon sesame oil

1 tablespoon water

20 spring roll or egg roll skins

TO PREPARE FILLING

Heat wok over high heat. Swirl in 3 tablespoons oil. When oil is hot, slightly brown ginger and garlic and then discard them. Combine prepared shrimp, ½ egg white, sherry and ¼ teaspoon salt and stir-fry briefly in wok until shrimp turns whitish (less than 20 seconds); remove, pressing shrimp with back of spoon to drain oil back into wok. Put shrimp in bowl.

Discard stems from soaked and drained mushrooms and cut caps into thin strips. Reheat oil in wok over medium heat. Add mushrooms to wok, and stir-fry about 15 seconds to draw out flavor. Add water chestnuts, bean sprouts or celery cabbage, bamboo shoots and scallions; stir-fry about 20 seconds. Remove to bowl.

Combine chicken, 1 teaspoon cornstarch, ¼ teaspoon salt, sugar and ½ egg white; add to wok and mix well. Combine black soy sauce, thin soy sauce, sesame oil, remaining cornstarch, 1 tablespoon water and ¾ teaspoon salt; mix well and add to wok. Stir in well and return shrimp and vegetables to wok. Stir-fry for another 15 seconds or until chicken is thoroughly hot. Put on plate to cool in refrigerator before wrapping.

TO WRAP AND FRY

Put 2 to 3 tablespoons filling on each spring roll or egg roll skin. Moisten edges with egg yolk, if using spring roll skins; with water, for egg roll skins. Wrap filling envelope-style, fastening down final fold with egg or water.

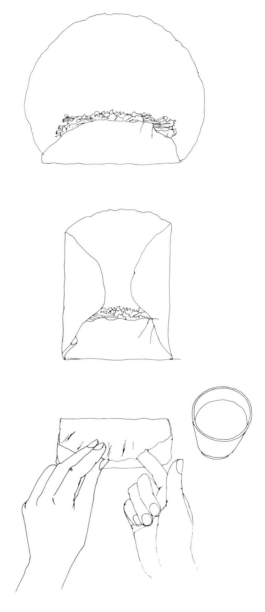

Heat 4 cups oil in wok to deep-fry temperature (375°) and fry rolls until golden brown. Drain well on paper towels and serve hot or at room temperature with Plum Sauce and Mustard-Oil Dip (recipes below).

Plum Sauce

MAKES 3 ½ TO 4 CUPS

1 cup pitted plums or plum jam
1 cup apricots or apricot jam
½ cup applesauce
½ cup pimiento strips
½ cup honey, more or less to taste
(less if using plum jam)

½ cup vinegar
Medium piece fresh ginger, peeled
and chopped
1 clove garlic, peeled and chopped

Process all together in processor or blender. Pour into clean glass jars. (Sauce will keep for months refrigerated in covered jar; for longer storage, use sterilized jars and seal.)

If a thinner dip is wanted, dilute with a little apricot or apple juice.

Variation: For a Simple Plum Sauce, combine ½ cup chutney, finely chopped, in saucepan with 1 cup plum jelly. Add 1 tablespoon sugar and 1 teaspoon vinegar; blend well and heat thoroughly, stirring. (If too thick, add a little juice.) Pour into clean jars, cap tightly and store in cool place.

Mustard-Oil Dip

This is very hot so you won't need much.

MAKES ABOUT ½ TO ⅔ CUP

6 tablespoons dry mustard

3 teaspoons sesame oil

Blend mustard with enough water to make thin paste; put in small serving bowl (or in individual serving cups for this lunch menu) and top with sesame oil.

PHYLLO FRUIT TARTS

This recipe uses the packaged phyllo pastry sheets, following the technique discussed and illustrated on page 169 for the Tiropitas, but substituting the Apple, Cherry, or Apricot given here for the spinach and cheese filling. A half pound (about 10 sheets) of the phyllo pastry—when tripled by cutting lengthwise into thirds—should be ample. If you want even smaller triangles the phyllo sheets can be cut into thirds lengthwise and then in half horizontally to make 60 little bites in all.

Apple Filling

TO FILL 30 MEDIUM OR 60 BITE-SIZED TRIANGLES

6 small tart apples, peeled and
    cored
1 cup raisins

1 cup chopped walnuts or almonds
1 cup sugar
1 teaspoon cinnamon

Combine all ingredients together well and use as filling.

Cherry Filling

TO FILL 30 MEDIUM OR 60 BITE-SIZED TRIANGLES

1½ to 2 pounds sweet black
    cherries, pitted

1 cup chopped walnuts or almonds
½ cup sugar

Combine ingredients and use as filling.

Apricot Filling

TO FILL 30 MEDIUM OR 60 BITE-SIZED TRIANGLES

2 cups dried apricots
1 cup walnuts or almonds

½ cup sugar
1 cup water

Chop apricots and nuts together. Put all ingredients in saucepan and simmer until water is absorbed. Cool before using.

OATMEAL CHOCOLATE CHIP COOKIES

MAKES ABOUT 50 COOKIES

1 stick (8 tablespoons) butter or
    margarine
6 tablespoons brown sugar
6 tablespoons granulated sugar
¾ teaspoon vanilla
1 egg
¾ cup flour

½ teaspoon baking soda
½ teaspoon salt
1 cup uncooked old fashioned
    Quaker Oats
1 (6-ounce) package real chocolate
    chips

Beat butter or margarine with the sugars and vanilla until creamy. Beat egg in well. Sift together flour, soda and salt, and add to the creamed mixture; mix well. Stir in the oats and chocolate chips.

TO BAKE   **PREHEAT OVEN TO 375°**

Drop dough by teaspoonfuls onto a lightly greased cookie sheet and bake for 8 to 10 minutes, or until nicely browned.

Note: This recipe works well doubled.

KITTY'S FRUITCAKE

I first encountered this lovely light English fruitcake through my friend Kitty, whose father was headmaster of the Canterbury Choir School. It was a great favorite at parent teas there and with Kitty's aunts when they came to call, but shouldn't be confused with the more highly spiced and liquored fruitcake so often seen at holiday time.

SERVES 10 TO 12

¾ pound light brown sugar	*½ cup milk*
1½ sticks (12 tablespoons) butter	*¾ pound currants or sultana*
3 eggs, well-beaten	*raisins*
2 cups flour	*4 ounces mixed fruit peel*
1 teaspoon baking powder	*Candied cherries, for garnish*

Cream the sugar and butter and mix in the well-beaten eggs. Mix together the flour and baking powder and add, following with the milk. Combine the currants or raisins and mixed fruit peel and add, mixing well.

TO BAKE   **PREHEAT OVEN TO 350°**

Butter an 8-inch loaf pan, or your favorite fruitcake pan, line bottom with wax paper and butter again. Then coat all with flour, knocking out the excess.

Pour batter into pan and bake for approximately 2 hours or perhaps a little longer; when done cake should shrink slightly from the pan sides and a tester poked into the cake through one of the small cracks that develop in the top should come out clean.

Cool the cake on a rack for about 25 minutes before turning over to unmold. Remove the wax paper and turn again. Then garnish with the candied cherries or other fruits of your choice.

Note: Sultana raisins are one of the 4 varieties of this fine fruit. They have a distinctive flavor and are much used in English recipes but are not always easy to locate in U.S. shops. Regular seedless raisins soaked in whiskey work well.

APPLE CAKE

This is a delicious, not too rich cake.

MAKES 8 TO 10 SMALL PIECES

¾ cup cooking oil
1⅓ cups sugar
3 eggs
2 cups flour
1 teaspoon baking soda
1 teaspoon cinnamon

½ teaspoon salt
3 large apples, peeled, cored and sliced
6 tablespoons brandy
½ cup chopped nuts

Cream oil and sugar together; add eggs and mix well. Sift together flour, baking soda, cinnamon and salt, and blend well with creamed mixture. Add apples and sprinkle all with brandy, again mixing well. Then add nuts.

TO BAKE   **PREHEAT OVEN TO 350°**

Using a greased and lightly floured 8-inch ring baking pan, bake about 45 minutes or until done. Cool on rack and serve.

BOX BREAKFAST EYE-OPENERS

STUFFED TOMATOES À LA AMY

You'll need a plate and fork for these.

SERVES 12

6 ripe but still firm tomatoes, cut in half
1 or 2 cloves garlic, minced

4 tablespoons minced fresh parsley, plus a few sprigs, chopped, for garnish

2 tablespoons minced shallots or
   scallions
⅛ teaspoon powdered thyme
¼ teaspoon salt

Large pinch black pepper
¼ cup olive oil
½ cup breadcrumbs

Drain the tomatoes as well as possible: a good way to do this is to place them upside down in a dish drainer for a few minutes after cutting in half.

Mix the other ingredients together well and lightly stuff the tomato halves.

TO BAKE   **PREHEAT OVEN TO 400°**

Bake stuffed tomatoes in a large baking pan for 10 to 15 minutes or until brown. Garnish with chopped parsley and serve warm.

Note: For an easy-to-eat finger food, stuff well-drained cherry tomatoes with this same stuffing.

COLD SCRAMBLED EGGS

This sounds improbable but is delicious. The recipe can easily be adjusted up or down for the number being served.

TO SERVE 10

10 large eggs
3 ½ tablespoons cream
Salt and white pepper to taste

10 strips bacon, cut into small
   pieces

Mix eggs with cream, salt and pepper. Then scramble slowly over simmering water in double boiler, keeping lumps fairly large and soft. Cool.

Cook the bacon well and add small pieces to cooled eggs, including a little bacon fat to meld the mixture.

Serve cold.

Variation: Mixed with bite-sized pieces of drained and sliced smoked eel, these cold eggs make a lovely hors d'oeuvre served on toast points, bread or crackers. Save a little of the eel juice to stir into the eggs

MARINATED SAUSAGES AND PEPPERS

Although baked, this spicy mix can be served at room temperature.

AMPLE FOR 10 TO 12

*2 pounds local or Park roll
sausage, sliced into bite-sized
pieces*
½ cup olive oil
3 cloves garlic, chopped
1 cup sliced onions

3 green peppers, cut in 1-inch cubes
3 red peppers, cut in 1-inch cubes
*1 (16-ounce) can Prego tomato
sauce*
Salt and pepper to taste
Pinch basil or thyme (optional)

Cook sliced sausage slowly until brown. Drain off fat and remove sausage to a covered baking dish. Heat olive oil; sauté garlic and onions and add peppers. When soft, add tomato sauce and taste for seasoning. Pour over sausage and mix well.

TO BAKE AND SERVE   PREHEAT OVEN TO 375°

Bake, covered, for about 1½ hours.

To serve as part of box breakfast, tuck in corner of plastic container; a fork will be needed. This dish can also be drained and offered with crackers as hors d'oeuvre.

Note: I use the Prego tomato sauce here because it comes without the sometimes heavy Italian seasoning: this way you can season to your own taste.

21
CHEERING THE
CANDIDATE

"Potluck" hors D'oeuvre Party for 50 to 100

WESTPHALIAN SQUARES

KIELBASA SLICES CODFISH BALLS

RED CABBAGE PORCUPINES
WITH
SHRIMP, OLIVE, PEARL ONION, RADISH
AND CHEESE CUBE QUILLS

PICKLED SALT HERRING

MEATBALLS CHINOISE

SWEDISH RYE ROUND WITH SPINACH DIP

SWEET AND HOT SAUSAGES
WITH PEPPERS

HOT CLAM RITZ DIP

STUFFED EDAM CHEESE

DRY ROASTED NUTS POPCORN MACHINE

BEER COFFEE CASH BAR

CHEERING THE CANDIDATE

"Or to some coffee house I stray
For news, the manna of the day.
And from the hipp'd discourses gather
That politics go by the weather."
—MATTHEW GREEN,
The Spleen

Whatever the overriding issues, the candidates come and go, and every four years the country is thrown into a frenzy of discourse and money-raising. Every second year the smaller issues gain the limelight, and the local contests somehow fit between. All in all, a lot of talk and much eating and drinking!

At some time in each one's life there is an issue or cause that stirs us deeply. How can we take part? We attend lectures, listen to speeches, read the papers and sometimes finally offer to work for a particular candidate.

In modern times, there are expensive TV debates, paid ads and the large $1000-a-plate dinners, but it is still at the grass roots that the vote is won and the work must be done. Often the national and state candidates will come to small communities (and big ones too) to stay with one or another fellow Republican or Democrat and needing a meeting arranged where they can discuss the issues and collect votes. I have helped with more of these than I can remember: simple cooking usually, to gather people, thank workers, gain support—and funds, if possible. Whether it's a small party to meet a local candidate or a large one to listen to this year's leading presidential hopeful or perhaps to celebrate a winner, food is always present. Cheese and crackers are universal (with luck, both donated) for the smallest of gatherings, cold cuts and hard rolls are added when a little more sustenance is in order—but for the final celebration and thank-you there will be a buffet and plenty to drink. Always a lot of food for little money: slices of six-foot hero sandwiches, lasagna, sausages and peppers, hot dogs and beans or spaghetti and meatballs are the usual fare—all washed down with beer and hot coffee, and many times drinks from a cash bar.

Should you be fortunate enough to have the winning candidate next time around, perhaps it will fall to you to help organize the victory party. Maybe you'll want to try something a little different. I suggest a "potluck" hors d'oeuvre table: it will guarantee a wide variety of foods (often mixing various ethnic dishes, always fun), it will share the work, and if it is politic in your circles to charge for this party, you might—once again—gain some profit with your pleasure.

The menu I've suggested does just that. The fun of a "potluck" party is the surprises it brings: no doubt yours will bring its own twists and turns.

Kielbasa is such a favorite at these political parties, I'm suggesting it again even though it's already been a part of several parties. If you'd like a change, serve it in dry slices with a favorite dip nearby. The Red Cabbage Porcupines are colorful and inexpensive: why not make several? You can decorate one cabbage with the not-too-expensive baby shrimp and cheese (maybe Cheddar, Swiss and Havarti) cubes on toothpicks and someone else can do another with pickled pearl onions, radishes and olives.

Page 209 in the When Congratulations Are in Order party tells how to prepare a Swedish rye round with chipped beef. For this party I suggest substituting an excellent spinach dip, the recipe for which follows, as do the recipes for the Westphalian Squares, Pickled Salt Herring (work but delicious), Codfish Balls, Meatballs Chinoise, Sweet and Hot Sausages with Peppers, and Hot Clam Ritz Dip (one of my favorite easy-to-dos). The Stuffed Edam Cheese is here also. And I do hope that someone will have a popcorn machine you can use: popcorn is always fun at a party. Or you might even try to find one of the snappy large professional machines: that way you could charge by the container—and perhaps add a little more to the evening's take.

WESTPHALIAN SQUARES

An impressive-looking but easy and inexpensive sandwich addition to this party.

MAKES UP TO 160 SLICES, DEPENDING ON THICKNESS

1 package thin-sliced Westphalian rye or pumpernickel bread, 12 to 16 slices
3 sticks (1½ cups) unsalted butter, at room temperature
2 heaping tablespoons coarse mustard or horseradish mustard
1 pound grated sharp Cheddar cheese
1 tablespoon Worcestershire sauce

Beat butter well; add mustard and Worchestshire; add cheese and beat until fluffy.

On first slice of bread spread enough cheese mixture to make a ⅛-inch layer (leave more in middle; it will spread to edges during cutting). Top with second slice of bread. Repeat process until there are 4 bread and 3 cheese layers. Press firmly together, wrap tightly and chill until firm.

Repeat this sequence until entire package of bread is used. This should give 3 or 4 layered "tortes."

At this point sandwiches may be frozen for up to 1 month before using or may be carried to the party for slicing there, being sure to keep cold until served.

TO SERVE

Unwrap each sandwich "torte" separately and, with a serrated knife, slice each rectangle into thin slices. When all are cut, arrange in checkerboard pattern on plate or sandwich board (for a picture of this, see the front book cover).

CODFISH BALLS

These are an easy and inexpensive party dish. But remember to allow enough time to soak the codfish before making up the recipe. For this party you may want to double the recipe.

MAKES 60 BALLS

1 pound salt codfish	*4 tablespoons butter or margarine*
6 cups diced raw potatoes	*½ teaspoon pepper*
2 eggs, beaten	*Oil for frying*

Freshen codfish by soaking in water overnight, then drain and dice. Cook potatoes and codfish in boiling water until potatoes are tender; drain. Mash and add remaining ingredients, beating together thoroughly.

TO FRY   **PREHEAT OIL TO 375°**

Form into walnut-sized balls, not too tightly packed. Then fry in deep fat until golden brown, turning over once (this takes 3 to 4 minutes). Drain well and serve warm in a chafing dish or Crock-Pot.

Note: In New England, one common brand of salt codfish is Stoney Island —from Nova Scotia.

PICKLED SALT HERRING

If you don't have time to prepare this tasty fish dish, by all means substitute a good-quality canned version.

MAKES 40 OR 50 THIN SLICES

1 large salt herring	*5 peppercorns, crushed*
½ cup vinegar	*10 whole allspice, crushed*
2 tablespoons water	*2 or 3 fresh dill sprigs, plus extra*
⅓ cup sugar	*for garnish*
2 tablespoons chopped onion	*Onion rings, for garnish*

Clean herring, removing head. Rinse under cold running water. Soak in cold water 10 to 12 hours, changing water several times to cut down saltiness (this can be started early evening with water changed several times and then left to soak overnight).

Cut herring along backbone. Remove big backbone and as many small bones as possible; pull off skin. (Bones come out easily after soaking.) Drain resulting fillets on absorbent paper, then place fillets together, one next to the other, to look like a whole fish again. Cut into thin slices with very sharp knife. With spatula slide herring onto long narrow, but fairly deep platter and set aside.

Combine remaining ingredients, including 2 or 3 sprigs dill, but excluding onion rings, in saucepan. Bring to boiling point and simmer a few minutes. Cool and strain. Pour over herring. Garnish with remaining dill and onion slices. Cover with aluminum foil and refrigerate for several hours before serving.

When ready to serve, drain well. Then set out with rye crackers or thin slices of dark rye bread.

Note: Salt herring is available in local fish stores and in many general markets.

MEATBALLS CHINOISE

This meatball is a very light one.

MAKES ABOUT 30

2 pounds ground pork (use pork
with some fat so it will be crisp
and juicy)
2 tablespoons minced scallions
2 tablespoons black soy sauce
2 teaspoons pale dry sherry

½ teaspoon sugar
½ teaspoon MSG (optional)
½ teaspoon salt
2 eggs, beaten
½ cup plus 2 tablespoons cornstarch
3 cups oil for frying

Mix all ingredients except ½ cup cornstarch and oil together in bowl: do not overmix or meatballs will be tough. Form meat mixture into walnut-sized balls and roll lightly in remaining ½ cup cornstarch.

TO FRY   **HEAT OIL TO 375°**

Deep fry meatballs in wok or electric fryer until golden brown. Drain well on paper toweling and keep warm in oven until ready to serve.

Serve with the mildly spicy Ginger-Scallion Dip below or a favorite of your own choice.

Ginger-Scallion Dip

YIELDS ABOUT 1½ CUPS

3 tablespoons peanut or corn oil
2 tablespoons sesame seed oil (not
the concentrated hot sesame oil)
3 tablespoons finely minced fresh
ginger

1 cup finely shredded scallions
1 teaspoon salt

Heat peanut or corn oil. Add sesame seed oil, cool, then pour over ginger, scallions and salt in a serving bowl. Mix together well and serve.

SWEDISH RYE ROUND WITH SPINACH DIP

Make Spinach Dip (below) and set aside before preparing the bread so the flavors will have a chance to blend.

To prepare bread, cut top off the loaf horizontally to use as lid. Scoop the insides out, leaving a solid wall attached to the crust to make a proper "bowl" for the dip. Shortly before using, cut bread into bite-sized pieces to use as "dippers." Keep "bowl," bread pieces and lid wrapped so they will stay moist until needed.

When ready to serve, fill bread "bowl" with dip and put out on platter surrounded by bread "dippers."

Spinach Dip

AMPLE FOR 25 TO 30

*1 (10-ounce) package frozen
  chopped spinach*
1 cup mayonnaise, more or less
½ cup sour cream

½ cup chopped onions
¼ cup minced parsley
1 teaspoon lemon juice
½ teaspoon freshly grated nutmeg

Defrost and squeeze out spinach. Mix all ingredients together well and refrigerate at least several hours before serving; overnight is even better.

SWEET AND HOT SAUSAGES WITH PEPPERS

Another relatively easy and inexpensive dish—just right for this type of party.

MAKES 30 SERVINGS

*2 pounds Italian sweet sausage, cut
  in bite-sized pieces*
*2 pounds Italian hot sausage, cut
  in bite-sized pieces*

*1½ pounds mixed red and green
  peppers, seeded and deveined
  and cut in small chunks*

Sauté sausage pieces until just about done; add pepper pieces and continue sautéeing until peppers are just tender.

Drain and serve warm with toothpicks handy and squares of Italian bread.

HOT CLAM RITZ SPREAD

This recipe may be made up ahead and then baked shortly before party time. The spread will then be hot when served and will keep warm for several hours.

SERVES ABOUT 30

3 cups finely crushed Ritz crackers,
*   or other cracker of choice*
4 tablespoons butter, melted
1½ medium onions, grated

¼ teaspoon lemon juice
2 cans minced clams, with juice
1 teaspoon gin (optional)

Mix the crushed crackers and butter together. Then add other ingredients and mix well. The gin will kill any possible tinny taste from the canned clams. If you use crackers other than Ritz, taste for salt and pepper.

TO BAKE   **PREHEAT OVEN TO 350°**

Turn clam and cracker mixture into 1½-quart baking dish and bake uncovered for 30 minutes.

Serve in the baking dish surrounded by crackers for spreading or dipping.

STUFFED EDAM CHEESE

For best results prepare this two days ahead.

SERVES 10 TO 12

1 (1-pound) whole Edam cheese
1½ sticks (12 tablespoons) sweet
*   butter*

2 tablespoons brandy
2 drops Tabasco sauce
1 teaspoon Worcestershire sauce

Cut off top of cheese horizontally and hollow out, leaving a ½-inch shell.

Cut butter into small pieces. Combine pieces of hollowed-out cheese with the butter and other ingredients, and process in food processor or blender until mixture is smooth and creamy.

When ready, pipe cheese mixture back into Edam shell with pastry bag using the star tube. Then chill until almost time to serve.

Serve at room temperature with a selection of crackers.

THE EARLY BIRD ...

A Preview Party for 200

CRUDITÉS AND CHIPS WITH
EGG CAVIAR DIP

SWEDISH ANCHOVIES

GOURMET HERRING

HAM AND ASPARAGUS ROLLS

TOMATOES STUFFED WITH CREAM CHEESE
AND CONSOMMÉ

SAGA, DILLED HAVARTI AND
BLUE CHEESE TRAY

SWEDISH MEATBALLS

STUFFED ONION SHELLS

LORENE'S SWEDISH COFFEE BREAD

RED AND WHITE WINE   GINGER ALE

THE EARLY BIRD . . .

Today's great interest in antique furniture, glass, china and other things of days gone by has led to still another means of combining fund-raising with pleasure. There have long been auctions and sales of these fascinating items of yesteryear, but only recently has a new wrinkle crept into the process.

The larger dealers of course have their own shops, and can, if they like, collect for an auction or special sale several times a year (the largest houses do this even more frequently, but more about that later). However, dealers with smaller collections—and whose shops, if anything, are usually just appendages of their sometimes out-of-the-way homes—often need a promising place to offer their wares. This, and the constant need for organizations to come up with new ways to raise funds, has led to a creative new special event, whereby one or another organization arranges—with professional help—to sponsor just such a sale. Then, to enhance the event and the profit margin, plans are also made for a special preview party to give an invited list a chance —for a price—to look over the wares and make early purchases or bids.

Adding the preview party allows one event to do double duty as a fund-raiser—once for the tickets to the preview and again for admission and refreshments sold at the following day's general sale (in fact, at a preview I recently attended the sponsors arranged a booth of their own as well—making even another way to add a little more profit). And the new scheme seems to work. This preview sale raised several thousand dollars. At the same time, the caliber of the antiques offered was excellent and it was a fun party besides.

There are many considerations that go into a successful preview party and sale, but perhaps the three most important—for both the sponsor and the dealers—are the quality of the articles to be offered for sale, good exhibit space (ample room, comfortable traffic flow, parking facilities, etc.) and sufficient exposure for the sale items (both in numbers and in purchase potential).

To do this well, there must—beyond the usual committee people involved in any good fund-raising project—be someone in the sponsoring organization with some knowledge of how these sales and previews are run or where to get the professional help and information needed.

In the case of the preview and sale I'm sharing here, the dealers were represented by two managers who—for a percentage (from the dealers) of the sales from both the preview and the following day—undertook to get reliable dealers, guarantee the quality of the sale items, keep the necessary sales records, advertise the sale in the professional journals (much of the attendance at such sales is from these professionals) and work with the sponsoring organization to make sure everything went smoothly.

The sponsor, in this case a facility for special children, undertook to secure the space (charging the dealers for their own individual booth areas), arrange (and sell tickets for) the preview party and publicly advertise the following day's sale. In addition it oversaw the final arrangement of the exhibit area to ensure it was attractively and carefully attended to and set up its own booth displaying the plants, dried arrangements and handicrafts to be on sale at both the preview party and the public sale. Beyond that the sponsor prepared the refreshments for the preview party and for the luncheon to be sold at the public sale.

For this type of sale to be a success it is crucial that it draw a large and relatively prosperous attendance. The preview party helps with this in two ways: first, by a lively attendance at the party itself, and second, by the word-of-mouth attendance for the following day a good preview party engenders. To be sure your party fulfills this double role it is essential that it be a bang-up party. This requires—in addition to careful planning and an attractive setting—good food and drink.

I'm basing my suggestions for this preview party on a Scandinavian smorgasbord. It'll give the party a special feeling and provide your fellow cooks with some different dishes to work on. The Egg Caviar Dip is easy to make and uses only a modest amount of caviar. The Swedish Anchovies and Gourmet Herring offer fishy delights in two very different ways. The Ham and Asparagus Rolls and Tomatoes Stuffed with Cream Cheese and Consommé are familiar on American party buffet tables but are part of the Swedish buffet as well. The Swedish Meatballs and Stuffed Onion Shells will add some welcome hot hors d'oeuvre and the Swedish Coffee Bread a welcome bit of sweet. Recipes for all these follow.

Of course it takes even more than good food and drink to give a party that extra special feel. Decorative plants and flowers will help, as would some music. The preview party I attended had invited a barbershop quartet to entertain at random around the hall. I don't know how Swedish that would seem—but it was great fun. If you'd like to consider the same and have a good group available to invite, perhaps they can learn a Swedish number.

The preview party we have planned here is only one of several approaches to the same idea. One of the delights I've had in writing this book has been some of the research I've done—in some cases by chance and in some by intention. For this preview party chapter I did both: the chance research was the invitation to the preview party I've told you about; the intentional research was to seek out a friend who works for Christie's, the big New York auction house, to find out how they run their preview parties. This gave me a chance to visit their gallery and, as a special treat, their kitchen—where they manage miracles in very crowded quarters. The exhibition rooms are large enough to offer good viewing space for the sale items, but the kitchen is minute. It had been modernized to make use of every inch but chiefly up and down: a basketball player, it seemed to me, would be more at home in that kitchen than the stunning young lady who is in charge.

However, it's from this kitchen that they engineer both the intimate luncheons they serve prospective buyers in a small adjacent dining room and the larger parties for the press and public. Working in their dining room must be rather like working in a house of mirrors, since all but the main dining table changes as the various furniture pieces are bought and sold. And in fact, even the modest-sized dining table is chameleonlike: it changes in size as needed with the addition of shorter or longer plywood slabs. The meals, they told me, are planned to be simple but elegant, with many of the fruits and vegetables brought in from the chef's own garden: a recent example was baby lamb chops served with asparagus and a potato, followed by fresh strawberries and cream (sounds good!). For the large parties they fill endless hors d'oeuvre platters, decorating them with delicately shaped vegetables. Meantime, hot appetizers are whisked from the kitchen ovens and served to the Christie customers with appropriate speed.

It was refreshing to see the obvious concern the small staff had for doing things correctly and yet without ostentation—and I was delighted to see, amidst so much elegance, that their party table was also at times put to use for their working papers and brown bag lunches.

In this section we've seen how two very different organizations might put on a pre-auction party—both quite different and yet quite successful in their own way, and both excellent examples of combining profit and pleasure.

CRUDITÉS AND CHIPS WITH EGG CAVIAR DIP

The combination of crunchy fresh vegetables in season and chips with the lovely piquant Egg Caviar Dip (below) should both please and fill your guests.

Egg Caviar Dip

MAKES ABOUT 1 CUP

½ cup heavy cream
2 to 3 tablespoons Swedish caviar,
  or to taste

1 to 2 tablespoons finely chopped
  onion, or to taste
2 hard-cooked eggs, sliced

Whip cream. Fold in caviar and onion to taste. Pile in mound in center of serving plate. Arrange egg slices around mound and border with small rye and other crackers.

SWEDISH ANCHOVIES

These are wonderfully tangy morsels.

MAKES ABOUT 36

2 (2-ounce) cans Swedish anchovy
   fillets (about 36 fillets)
6 *tablespoons salad oil*

6 *tablespoons chopped parsley*
6 *finely chopped shallots or scallions*
2 *tablespoons tarragon vinegar*

Drain anchovy fillets; arrange attractively on small serving dish.

Mix remaining ingredients until they make a thick paste (if paste is not thick enough add more onions or parsley).

Pour sauce over anchovies and marinate for at least 1 hour before serving.

Serve with whole wheat crackers or small thin slices of whole wheat French bread.

GOURMET HERRING

This is both tasty and attractive.

SERVES 40 OR 50

2 *large salt herring*
1 *cup sour cream*
2 *hard-cooked eggs*

¼ *cup pickled red beets, chopped*
2 *tablespoons chopped chives or*
   cucumber

Prepare herring as in Pickled Salt Herring (see page 320), place on rectangular platter and spread with sour cream.

Separate egg yolks from egg whites, and chop finely.

Spoon egg yolks, egg whites, beets and chives or cucumbers in rows on top of herring to achieve a striped effect.

Chill several hours before serving.

When ready, serve with Swedish rye bread and crackers.

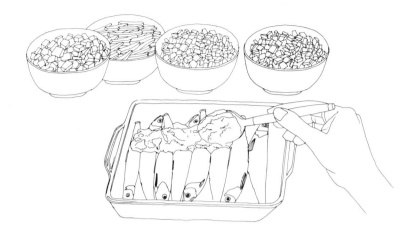

HAM AND ASPARAGUS ROLLS

This combination is an especially refreshing one—and is attractive as well.

To make, simply roll thin slices of ham, spread with Béarnaise Sauce (see page 274) or the Classic Mayonnaise on page 384 around an asparagus spear and hold together with a sturdy pick.

Note: If asparagus is very fresh and thin, it may be used raw; otherwise, steam until tender—or used canned.

TOMATOES STUFFED WITH CREAM CHEESE AND CONSOMMÉ

MAKES 30 OR SO SERVINGS

1 box cherry tomatoes
1 recipe Mrs. Hyslop's Hors d'Oeuvre Filling (below)

Chopped parsley or chives, for garnish

Slice the tops off the tomatoes; turn upside down on paper toweling or in a strainer to drain. Scoop out a little of the tomato meat and fill shells with the hors d'oeuvre filling below. When stuffed, sprinkle each tomato with bits of chopped parsley or chive.

Note: For best results, stuff tomatoes not too far before needing them.

Mrs. Hyslop's Hors d'Oeuvre Filling

This recipe comes from an old friend, Mary Zehnder. It is usually served in demitasse cups or small ramekins and eaten with a demitasse spoon, but works nicely as a filling.

MAKES ENOUGH FOR 30 OR SO CHERRY TOMATOES

1 (10-ounce) can consommé
1 small clove garlic, put through garlic press, or crushed and peeled

6 ounces cream cheese

Mix well and refrigerate until ready to fill tomatoes.

SWEDISH MEATBALLS

MAKES ABOUT 70 SMALL MEATBALLS

¾ pound ground beef (round steak)
¼ pound ground lean pork
¼ cup finely chopped onion
1 tablespoon shortening
¼ cup fine dry breadcrumbs
⅓ cup water
⅓ cup cream

2 teaspoons salt
¼ teaspoon pepper
Dash ground cloves
5⅓ tablespoons (⅔ stick) butter or margarine
¼ cup boiling water

Use only very fresh meat and have it freshly ground just before making meatballs.

Sauté onion in shortening until golden brown. Soak crumbs in water-cream mixture. Combine onion, crumb mixture, meats and seasonings. Mix thoroughly until smooth and shape into small balls (wet hands so meat won't stick to them), handling as little as possible.

Fry in butter or margarine until evenly brown, shaking pan continuously to keep balls round. Add boiling water, cover and simmer 5 to 10 minutes or until tender. Drain and serve hot in chafing dish or Crock-Pot, with a container of toothpicks nearby.

Note: For a lighter main-dish meatball, the Swedes substitute cold, mashed potatoes for the breadcrumbs.

STUFFED ONION SHELLS

Once you learn the knack of keeping these onions together, they make a wonderful addition to a buffet party table.

MAKES 30 OR 40

 30 or 40 small onions
 1 recipe Veal Meatball Stuffing (see below)

 2 tablespoons butter or margarine
 ¾ cup onion liquid, reserved from cooking

Peel onions and boil in lightly salted water 10 minutes. Drain, reserving ¾ cup liquid. When cool, make slit down side of onion just to center. Gently remove inner onion layers to leave hollow onion "shells."

Make Veal Meatball stuffing, or other of choice, and fill each shell with teaspoon of meat stuffing, wrapping the onion shell in around the meat. The onion shells will shape themselves around the meat and stay without tying.

Melt butter or margarine in skillet; cook stuffed onion shells in butter 10 to 15 minutes, until nicely browned. Add onion stock, cover and simmer gently for another 10 to 15 minutes. When done, drain shells on absorbent paper.

When ready, serve as is; warm, if possible.

Note: Onion innards can be used for filling or other recipes.

Veal Meatball Stuffing

MAKES AMPLE TO FILL THE 30 TO 40 ONIONS

 ¼ pound ground veal
 ¼ pound ground pork
 2 tablespoons fine dry breadcrumbs
 1 tablespoon minced onion

 1 teaspoon salt
 Dash pepper
 ¼ cup cream

Combine meats, breadcrumbs, onion, salt and pepper. Gradually mix in the cream.

Refrigerate veal mixture until ready to use.

LORENE'S SWEDISH COFFEE BREAD

The recipe for this delicious Swedish coffee bread is from my friend Lorene O'Bryan.

MAKES 3 (10- TO 12-INCH) LOAVES

2 cups milk, scalded, plus extra
   cold for brushing crusts
1 stick (8 tablespoons) good-quality
   butter, melted
8 to 9 cardamom seeds, ground
1 cup sugar, plus extra for
   sprinkling

1 teaspoon salt
1 egg
1 yeast cake, dissolved in ¼ cup
   lukewarm water
6 to 7 cups flour

In a bowl, mix scalded milk and butter. Cool and add other ingredients, adding enough flour to hold spoon upright in dough. Let rise until doubled. Cut dough back, knead, and let rise again. Divide dough into 3 parts. Divide each part into 3 long, narrow (about 1½-inch wide) ropes. Braid 3 ropes into 10- to 12-inch loaf, pinching ends together and folding under slightly to hold. Repeat for other dough, making 3 loaves in all. Let loaves rise again (will not quite double). Set dough on lightly greased baking sheets, brush tops lightly with milk and sprinkle with sugar.

TO BAKE   **PREHEAT OVEN TO 350°**

Bake loaves about 20 minutes until only light golden brown. Do *not* over-bake.

Note: Some like to decorate this bread with candied fruits but I like it just as it is.

23
SPARKLING WINES AND SUGARPLUMS

A Wine Tasting for 100 or more

THREE SPARKLING WINES
FOR SAMPLING

Assorted Sugarplums
SAND TARTS

RASPBERRY RINGS

PIROUETTES

VIENNESE BALLS   CHOCOLATE DIAMONDS

MINIATURE ECLAIRS

PUITS D'AMOUR

PHYLLO FRUIT BASKETS

OPEN BAR   COFFEE

A WINE TASTING

We have only to look around to see that the interest in wines has grown appreciably in recent years. Combining this growing interest with a money-raising event seems a natural, but how best to go about it?

There is certainly much to learn about wines. Different grapes produce very different results, as do different regions—for reason of both climate and soil. Some wines improve with age and careful storing; others are better enjoyed as is—and right away. Certain foods—for many reasons, including their chemical makeup—go better with certain wines and vice versa. Of course, the proper study of wines is a lifetime pursuit. But even if we don't want to take the high dive, many of us would like at least to dabble a bit and learn a little more about many of the wines around us today.

There are many excellent books on the subject—and I urge you to turn to them. I have found Hugh Johnson's *Pocket Encyclopedia of Wine* and *The Connoisseurs' Handbook of California Wines,* by Olken, Singer and Roby, especially useful. Both of these are easy to read and fit in your pocket to be handy when tasting or shopping. And, as I say, there are many more.

Another excellent source of information is your wine merchant. He can show you his varieties and give you suggestions for the menus you are planning. We should all remember that wine is not meant to be an end in itself, but rather a pleasant and enhancing accompaniment to the food we eat. In fact, one way your own wine-tasting program might begin is to buy two or three bottles—each from a different vineyard—of the two or three leading wine categories. That way—without too much expense—you could begin to narrow in on what you and your family prefer. Then, as time and your pocketbook allow, you can expand this tasting program more and more.

However, most of us are impatient, and lazy, and really do better with professional guidance. In wondering how best to combine this interest in wine with the proper structure for a money-raising event, I became intrigued with the idea of a short series of lectures on wine and its uses—with the thought that the course could lead to two different types of parties: the first, an intimate one, for the small study group itself; and the other, perhaps put on by the group, a money-raiser for the public.

Such a course would require a knowledgeable instructor. Unless your organization is lucky enough to have a real expert in its midst, you will need a recognized oenologist to give the lectures and help the group plan the resulting wine-tasting parties. (A local gourmet society, a branch of the international Les Amis du Vin or even your local wine merchant should be able to help you find a qualified person.) In consultation with the instructor the number of lectures to be given would be set (and an outline of what's to be covered devised), a maximum and minimum student number decided and of course a fee agreed to.

Then, as a way to culminate your wine-tasting course, I suggest a wine-tasting party to meld your new knowledge of wine with various simple hors d'oeuvre. I do not want to get into the precise details of this party: they should be worked out between the instructor and the class members. One way might be to set up three tables—well separated—each with a pleasant sampling of a distinct category of wine and of the foods best complementing it. Cards could be supplied for each student's use to note the appearance, bouquet, taste and overall preference for each wine tasted, and perhaps space left for a comment on the appropriateness of the various foods. Each guest could carry along his or her own glass, with pitchers of water and a catch basin available to allow rinsing the glasses between tastes. At the same time, cubes of bread should be available to clear the palate. Surely no more than two or three wines should be at any one table, and time as well as space should be allowed between the tables.

One table could offer an assortment of white wines—perhaps a bone-dry Chablis from France, a California Muscadet and a Pinot Grigio from Italy. The hors d'oeuvre could be simply prepared seafood—oysters or clams on the half shell, crabmeat puffs or a scallop terrine.

The second table could offer another category of white wine to include a Vouvray from France, a California Gewurztraminer and an Italian Verdicchio. Here we could broaden the selection of hors d'oeuvre to include a smoked salmon or bluefish with brown bread, Caviar Pie and perhaps Curried Shrimp and Crabmeat Balls or Benne Chicken Fingers (all with recipes elsewhere in this book).

The third table, again after some time, might offer three of the reds—a young French Beaujolais, a Gamay Beaujolais from California and perhaps a Valpolicella from Italy. These are all light purple wines eager to be enjoyed young. At this table the food might include Cocktail Quiches, Stuffed Mushrooms, lamb Keftedes and pork tenderloin slices (recipes, again, elsewhere), with a platter of stuffed vegetables and a well-stocked cheese tray (Jarlsberg, Port Salut and perhaps a St. André or Brillat-Savarin would be good). Italian bread and bunches of grapes—with mints at the door—would wind up this party.

These are just ideas that appeal to me. The particulars should be tied to your course and to what the class leader feels appropriate and the class members enthusiastic about.

Such a party would be costly, depending in part on how expensive the wines chosen (a $6 to $20 range should be adequate), and whether the food would be bought or supplied by the class members. Perhaps one way to make up a little of this cost would be to encourage each class member to invite a paying guest.

Now to our public fête.

A good wine course would include a study of the various sparkling wines. And here is where I thought we might work in a good money-raising event. Trying to arrange a really comprehensive wine-tasting party for a large number of people seems very awkward indeed—if not impossible. But a party revolving around a few Sparkling Wines and appropriate Sugarplums should work very nicely. It could be organized by the wine-tasting class and focused around an evening of dancing or perhaps a variety show or other entertainment, and could be complemented by a series of dinner parties culminating at the fête for sparkling wines and dessert.

Recently, a chamber music group in our town planned a "Riverboat" ball combining an appropriate location on our native Connecticut River with dancing and a series of entertainments. It was a lovely evening and a successful one—partly due to the string of dinner parties held by trustees and friends prior to the dance. This idea not only encourages attendance but helps guarantee a joyful spirit of camaraderie on arrival.

Again you should consult your expert, but perhaps three sparkling wines could be offered to give the partygoers a chance to sample at least a not-too-expensive French, an American (maybe a Napa Valley Schramsberg or a Piper Sonoma) and the Italian Asti Spumante. To accompany these would be great trays of confections, fairly simple ones to allow the taste of the wine to come through: Sand Tarts, Raspberry Rings and Pirouettes are only a few ideas. For chocolate lovers there could be Viennese Balls, Chocolate Diamonds and Miniature Eclairs filled with vanilla, chocolate and mocha custard and topped with a dollop of chocolate, and to vary the taste a bit, the Phyllo Fruit Baskets (see page 214) would be nice. And you might want to add a plate of Broccoli Mousse-filled puffs or another savory for the non-sweet-eaters. Also, of course, pots of good hot coffee for anyone wanting it.

Your plans could include an open cash bar for those who would prefer it as the evening runs on, but the emphasis should be on the wines and the ticket price should be high enough to assure an ample supply so that no one leaves feeling he or she didn't have a good sampling opportunity.

It is the assortment of wines chosen that will challenge the partygoers and make the evening memorable. The good American and Spanish sparkling wines are new and offer real competition to the better-known French wines, and of course the very presence of so much "bubbly" suggests gaiety and good fellowship. With lovely wines, delightful sugarplums, good entertainment and good company, the party is bound to be a success—proving that, although a little learning may indeed be a dangerous thing, it can also be a lot of fun . . . and profit!

CARE AND HANDLING OF WINES

Optimum storage. All wine improves by resting in a cool, dry place away from noise and clatter and sudden swings in temperature. (Strangely enough, I've found that even minor jug wines improve in a proper wine cellar.) In today's modern housing, finding such a place may be difficult. The temperature should range between 45° and 65° Fahrenheit; a somewhat lower temperature simply slows up the aging process but heat can be disastrous. A minimum-maximum thermometer is a useful tool to help you find the best spot even though it does take a little time and effort to record the temperatures.

The storage bin. You can, of course, buy an already-made wine storage rack (or racks). Or you can start from scratch or use a wooden wine case, putting in your own shelves. The bottles should lie on their sides with the front label faced up for easy reading and with the wine touching the cork to keep it moist.

Make a place to keep a notebook handy. You should keep a record of your various wine purchases, noting the name, date and place of purchase (and cost if you like), with space left for comment on how each wine aged. This record will prove invaluable as your wine tasting and serving develop.

Proper serving. Do not chill white wines too long (a mistake many people make). They should be comfortably cold, not frigid; 46° to 48° for many, as warm as 55° for some. The same applies for the rosé wines. The red wines for the most part should be served at cellar temperature (Beaujolais Nouveau, for one, is chilled); ideally the lighter reds at 55° and the heavier at about 65°. The sparkling wines should be treated as the whites.

If you have questions about a particular wine, the wine books mentioned in this chapter—and others—have detailed listings, or, again, ask your wine merchant.

© *Robert Grant*

Sugarplums Wine Tasting

SUGARED FRUIT
ASSORTMENT OF: FLORENTINES, PUITS D'AMOUR, RASPBERRY
RINGS, PETIT FOURS, FRUIT TRICORNES, PECAN TASJES AND
WHIPPED CREAM TARTLETS
BROCCOLI MOUSSE PUFFS

Gala Champagne Evening

COUNTRY PATÉ EN CRÔUTE
ROLLED MEATS AND ARTICHOKE SQUARES
WATER CHESTNUT MEATBALLS
SANDWICH TOWER WITH DEVILED EGGS

SAND TARTS

These *petits fours sec* are also called *sablés*.

MAKES ABOUT 36

4 cups flour

2 sticks (½ pound) sweet butter, at
  room temperature

1 cup sugar

8 hard-cooked egg yolks, rubbed
  through a fine sieve

8 raw egg yolks

Pinch salt

Grated rind of 4 lemons

Put flour in large bowl and cut in the butter, rubbing with fingertips until mixture resembles coarse cornmeal in texture. Mix in sugar and hard-cooked egg yolks. Beat raw egg yolks until light and fluffy. Add to the flour mixture with salt and lemon rind and work up quickly into firm dough. On lightly floured board roll dough out to ½-inch thickness and cut into 1-inch rounds with cookie cutter.

TO BAKE   **PREHEAT OVEN TO 350°**

Place dough rounds on unbuttered cookie sheets, crisscross the tops with the back of a knife, and bake about 25 minutes, until nicely browned.

If not used right away, these Sand Tarts can be chilled and stored in an airtight container.

Note: I use an electric mixer for these petits fours. You can use a food processor if you like but be careful not to overprocess.

RASPBERRY RINGS

Raspberry jam is recommended for the filling, but other not-too-thin jams and preserves are also good.

MAKES ABOUT 35

1 cup flour

⅓ cup sugar

½ cup (8 tablespoons) sweet butter,
  cold

1 egg

½ cup raspberry jam

TO PREPARE DOUGH

Sift the flour into a large mixing bowl, add the sugar and cut in the butter until mixture resembles coarse meal. Add egg and blend to a firm dough. Form into a ball, wrap in wax paper or plastic and chill for at least an hour. Roll dough out between two sheets of wax paper to ¼-inch thickness. Using a 1½-inch round cookie cutter dipped in flour, cut out as many rounds as possible; reserve dough scraps. Remove the centers from half the rounds using a 1-inch round cutter dipped in flour. Repeat the rolling and cutting with the dough scraps and the centers until all dough is used. Arrange the rounds and rings about 1 inch apart on buttered cookie sheets.

TO BAKE   PREHEAT OVEN TO 325°

Bake in the center of a preheated oven for about 15 minutes, or until pale golden in color. Transfer with a spatula to cooling racks. While still warm, spread the top of each round with a thin layer of the jam and top each with a ring. Fill centers with an additional ¼ teaspoon of the jam.

PIROUETTES

This delicate pencil-slim sweet can be served with or without its ends dipped in chocolate.

MAKES 36 OR SO

4 egg whites
½ cup sugar
Pinch salt
1 cup sifted flour
1 stick (8 tablespoons) clarified
*   sweet butter, cooled*

4 ounces dark sweet chocolate,
*   melted (optional)*
½ cup chopped pistachio nuts
*   (optional)*

Beat egg whites and sugar together with a whisk until mixture is literally white. Add salt, then mix in flour and butter.

TO BAKE   PREHEAT OVEN TO 350°

Butter a jelly-roll pan or baking sheet (do not dust with flour).

Make little mounds of dough (about 1 teaspoon) on the baking sheet. Allow ample room between; they spread a good bit. With back of spoon, spread dough out into thin rectangles. Then bake until delicately brown, about 10 minutes.

TO FORM AND DIP

As soon as cookies are browned, remove immediately from oven and loosen from pan. Roll each flat cookie around a pencil while still warm to achieve a cigarette shape. If you like, when shaped dip both ends of each cookie in partially cooled chocolate; then, when chocolate is almost set, dip ends in chopped nuts. Put on wax paper to set and store in airtight container until needed.

Note: It's important to let the chocolate almost set, otherwise the nuts get "muddy" and will not adhere.

VIENNESE BALLS

The original recipe calls for the entire ball to be glazed with chocolate, but for this party—where finger foods are the rule—I have modified it.

MAKES ABOUT 25

1 recipe Sponge Sheet Batter (see below)

½ cup Cognac, plus ⅓ cup Cognac (to be folded into cream after whipping)

3 cups unsweetened heavy cream, whipped

1½ cups apricot jam

1 recipe Creamy Chocolate Glaze (see below)

First make sponge batter.

TO FORM AND BAKE   PREHEAT OVEN TO 400°

Fit large pastry bag with large, round No. 7 tube. Fill bag with batter and onto well-greased baking sheet press out high rounds of batter 1¼ inches in diameter. (If you don't have pastry tube, rounds may also be formed working with 2 teaspoons; keep mounds high.) Bake about 12 minutes or until cakes are lightly browned. Let cool.

TO FILL BALLS

Add ⅓ cup Cognac to whipped cream.
    When cakes are cool, cut out some of soft center from the bottom of each ball, leaving a ¼-inch shell. Brush inside of shells with Cognac, then with jam.

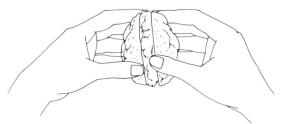

Fill shells with whipped cream and place two shells together to make balls. Chill, or even freeze, balls at least an hour before serving.

While balls are chilling, prepare and cool Creamy Chocolate Glaze. When both are ready, glaze tops of balls. Then keep glazed balls chilled until ready to serve.

Sponge Sheet Batter

This is an excellent batter for jelly rolls, petits-fours and sponge layers as well.

MAKES AMPLE BATTER FOR 25 OR SO VIENNESE BALLS

8 eggs, separated　　　　　　*1 teaspoon vanilla*
Large pinch salt　　　　　　*½ cup sifted cornstarch*
½ cup sugar　　　　　　　　*½ cup sifted flour*

Beat egg whites with salt until they hold soft peaks. Gradually beat in sugar, sprinkling in a tablespoon at a time. Continue beating until whites are very firm, about 5 minutes in all.

Break up egg yolks with fork; add vanilla. Fold ¼ egg whites into yolks thoroughly. Pour egg yolk-white mixture on top of remaining beaten whites. Sprinkle cornstarch and flour over mixture. Fold in very gently, by hand or with mixer at low speed. Fold until no pieces of egg whites show but be careful not to overmix.

Creamy Chocolate Glaze

This glaze can also be used as a cake filling.

MAKES AMPLE TO GLAZE 25 OR SO VIENNESE BALLS

3 ounces unsweetened chocolate　　*1 tablespoon light corn syrup*
¾ cup heavy cream　　　　　　　*1 egg, lightly beaten*
1 cup sugar　　　　　　　　　　*1 tablespoon vanilla*
¼ cup water

In saucepan, combine chocolate, cream, sugar, water and corn syrup. Stir over low heat until chocolate is melted and sugar is dissolved. Raise heat slightly and cook without stirring about 5 minutes, or until mixture forms a soft ball when small bit is dropped into glass of cold water (234°).

Stir 2 to 3 tablespoons hot chocolate into beaten egg. Then pour egg mixture back into remaining chocolate, stirring briskly. Return to low heat and, stirring constantly, cook several more minutes until chocolate is thick enough to make a nonrunny glaze.

Remove from heat; add vanilla. Cool slightly before using to glaze. (To use as filling, cool completely.)

Note: This glaze stays shiny and pliable for several days.

CHOCOLATE DIAMONDS

I like to combine the sponge batter and choclate glaze from the Viennese Balls recipe with one of the fillings from the Miniature Eclairs recipe to make various petit fours. One of my favorites—adding almond flavoring for a new taste—is this Chocolate Diamond variation. In hot weather a more conventional filling would be safer than these requiring eggs and milk.

MAKES ABOUT 2 DOZEN

> *1 recipe Sponge Sheet Batter (see page 344)*
> *1 recipe Vanilla or Coffee Eclair Filling (see page 346), plus 1*

> *teaspoon almond flavoring, or more to taste*
> *1 recipe Creamy Chocolate Glaze (see page 344)*

TO BAKE   **PREHEAT OVEN TO 375°**

Prepare Sponge Sheet Batter. Line 9-by-13-inch baking pan with parchment or wax paper, grease and fill with batter, smoothing it out evenly. Bake 10 to 12 minutes, or until cake tests done.

While still hot, turn cake out onto unglazed brown paper and let cool. When cool, slit into two layers and set aside.

TO FILL AND GLAZE

Prepare the Vanilla or Coffee Eclair Filling, adding the almond flavoring. Spread generously between the sponge layers; then with cutter or knife carefully cut into diamond shaped petit fours. Prepare the Creamy Chocolate Glaze, and while still warm, glaze each diamond and then set aside to cool.

MINIATURE ECLAIRS

Despite rumors to the contrary, these little eclairs aren't difficult; just be sure to have the ingredients at room temperature.

M A K E S   A B O U T   6 0

1 recipe Pâte à Chou (see page 399)

1 receipe Vanilla, Coffee or Chocolate Eclair Filling (see below)

1 receipe Chocolate or French Coffee Eclair Icing (see below)

T O   B A K E   A N D   F I L L   P R E H E A T   O V E N   T O   4 0 0°

Shape dough into 1½-inch oblongs on lightly greased baking sheets, using a spoon or pastry tube, heaping it higher in the centers. Bake for about 30 minutes, then reduce heat to 350° and bake another 5 minutes. Test by removing a single puff from the oven; if it doesn't fall, they are done. Remove from oven and let cool.

When cool, make slit in top of puff. Fill with filling of choice and frost lightly with Chocolate or French Coffee Eclair Icing. Keep finished eclairs well-cooled until ready to serve.

Vanilla Eclair Filling

1½ tablespoons cornstarch
¼ teaspoon salt
5 tablespoons sugar

1½ cups milk, scalded
2 egg yolks, lightly beaten
1 teaspoon vanilla

In a bowl combine cornstarch, salt and sugar, add scalded milk and blend well. Place eggs in top of double boiler and add milk mixture. Stir and cook custard over low heat until thick. When cool, add vanilla.

Coffee Eclair Filling

Following the recipe for Vanilla Eclair Filling, substitute ½ cup strong hot coffee and 1 cup scalded cream for the milk, and frost with the coffee icing below, instead of the chocolate.

Chocolate Eclair Filling

Following the Vanilla Eclair Filling recipe, add 1 ounce melted chocolate and 3 extra tablespoons sugar to the hot milk.

Chocolate Eclair Icing

1 ounce dark unsweetened chocolate
1 tablespoon butter, or a little more
2 tablespoons hot water or cream
Scant ⅛ teaspoon salt

½ teaspoon vanilla
1 cup sifted confectioners' sugar, or
  a little less to taste

Melt chocolate in top of double boiler over low flame. Add butter, allowing it to melt. Add hot water or cream and salt. Remove from heat. When cool, add vanilla and gradually add sugar, stirring in until icing is of good spreading consistency.

French Coffee Eclair Icing

4 tablespoons butter, softened
1 cup sifted confectioners' sugar
Scant ⅛ teaspoon salt

1 ½ tablespoons strong hot coffee
1 teaspoon rum or vanilla

Beat butter until soft. Add sugar gradually. Blend until creamy and add salt and hot coffee. Beat for about 2 minutes and let cool. When cool add vanilla or rum. Permit icing to stand 5 minutes before spreading, beating well again just before applying.

24
"RIFFING"
ON RAMPART STREET

Jazz Party for 200 to 300

OPEN BAR   WINE BAR   SOFT DRINKS

COURTESY NIBBLES BASKET

OYSTER AND CLAM RAW BAR

CREOLE CRAWFISH BOIL

BEEF TENDERLOIN AND
FRENCH BREAD DIP

COURTESY SWEETS BASKET
OF
FRENCH BEIGNETS, CREOLE PRALINES,
BOURBON BALLS AND DATE SQUARES

COFFEE   LIQUEURS

"RIFFING" ON RAMPART STREET

Oscar Hammerstein may have believed it when he wrote "Money Isn't Everything!" but if you're trying to make your favorite arts or charitable organization's budget balance, it certainly helps. We've already explored several ways to help make this budget balancing both easier and more fun: this time let's concentrate on the fun. Let's have a jazz bash.

To accomplish this, I suggest we swing down to New Orleans—or pretend to—where we can plan an all-out party to raise money for the local public TV station, symphony orchestra or the worthy cause needing it most. Using that picturesque setting as our real—or fancied—background, we can combine some classic New Orleans food with some classic New Orleans music for a memorable evening.

New Orleans, well known as the cradle of American jazz, is also well known as the cradle of creole cooking. It's these elements we'll put together for our very special evening. Interestingly, both are a mélange: the creole cooking, of French, Spanish, American Indian and black cuisines; the American jazz of, among other things, the European quadrille, black music from Africa and the "blues" of the black cotton fields.

Today, although the Waif's Home Band, in which Louis Armstrong—in all likelihood the most innovative of all American jazzmen—got his start, no longer strolls the streets of the French Quarter, other street bands still do, and there's always Preservation Hall, where Al Hirt oversees the comings and goings of many of America's jazzmen of the 1980's.

Of course, in New Orleans it might be possible to rent Preservation Hall itself for our projected jazz bash, but surely your town has a hall that would work. It should be big enough to hold several hundred comfortably, with the seating, if possible, fashioned in the style of the Boston Pops or the old Lewisohn Stadium in New York, with the center area reserved for more expensive seats grouped around individual tables (for this party, perhaps even as much as $50 a head), and with less expensive seating available either in a balcony or ringing the more expensive center seats. If possible, there should be a well-lit spot for the band in the middle, much as the hub of a wheel, or at least surrounded by tables on three sides; this to allow more people to be close to the music and the players.

The tables should be gaily bedecked with cloths and set with a basket or bowl of nibbles already in place: for the nibbles, why not try the Bridge Nibbles here or the Nuts and Bolts from the "For Parents at a Children's Party" chapter—though chips, nachos or other crunchies would do as well.

The rest of the food and the cash bars—along with great stacks of sturdy plastic plates and napkins—could be set out either in a closely adjoining room or at the back of the hall so as not to interfere with the music. The seafood from the Raw Bar and the bowls of the steaming Creole Crawfish Boil could be available even as the revelers arrive and on into the mid-part of the evening; the idea being that the audience fetch their own food as they please (eating it either right there at the serving bars or carrying it back to their tables)—each item having its own price and being paid for by the portion. (You'll need at least one large menu board clearly listing the prices. Money could be exchanged for chips at a central "bank," thereby eliminating much of the money handling and the worries that go with that.)

Then, perhaps halfway through the evening, the seafood would be replaced or amplified by the Beef Tenderloin and French Bread Dip, again to be purchased by the audience for a set price. And, finally, to cap off the evening's menu the committee could deliver a basket of mixed sweets to each table, with pots of hot coffee and liqueurs ready in the service area for those wanting them.

Recipes for the the Bridge Nibbles, Creole Crawfish Boil, Beef Tenderloin and French Bread Dip, French Beignets, Creole Pralines and Date Squares follow here, along with those for the Raw Bar and Crawfish Boil sauces. (The Bourbon Balls are in the Southern "At Home" party on page 196.)

The open bars would be well stocked with a wide variety of liquors and wines, especially those popular in the area, and of course with soft drinks and beer available for those who want them. (If your bash is to be a mixed-age affair, your committee will need to decide how this will be handled to be sure that minors are served only what's allowed; states and towns vary in this regard—and this is a good place to mention that any necessary liquor permits should be well in hand.)

There will be plenty for your volunteers to do at this party. The Raw Bar will need to be kept well supplied. Shells will need to be cleared away, both from the Raw Bar and from the tables, and the coffee pot and soft drinks watched over. Be sure to have enough volunteers so there can be shifts: it would be a shame for anyone to miss all the music and fun.

However, professionals will be needed too, both at the cash bars and at the Raw Bar: opening oysters and clams properly and quickly is a considerable skill. Beyond that you will need a food manager to make sure the basic foods are in adequate supply, properly cooked and properly served, and that all moves along on schedule.

No party of this size is simple; there is always a lot of work. However, as large parties go—with careful planning, adequate publicity, well-trained help, a proper food manager, and wonderful music—it should come off fairly easily and be a great success.

By all means try to reflect the New Orleans theme in the decor as much as possible. And allow some space to promote your cause visually and some time to promote it verbally with a few well chosen words. One way to accomplish this unobtrusively might be to combine the talk with the awarding of raffle or door prizes. The prize drawing allows time for a few painless words, as well as adding extra excitement—and raffles, of course, are always a good way to add a little more to the evening's take.

The very special cuisine and New Orleans' love for a good time over the years make a New Orleans theme a natural for this kind of party. But of course a successful jazz bash must have good jazz. I leave that to you. It won't matter if it's from Rampart Street or 125th Street, from Preservation Hall or from the Savoy—as long as it's good!

Take the plunge, "Take the A Train," take the money to the bank—and have a boffo time!

BRIDGE NIBBLES

This nibble recipe was given to me by Jeanette Kennedy.

MAKES 5 CUPS OR SO

1 cup roasted peanuts
1 cup chopped Brazil nuts or cashews
1 cup golden raisins

1 cup chopped mixed dried fruit
½ cup pumpkin seeds or sunflower kernels
½ cup dried coconut chips

Toss ingredients together in large bowl. Serve when ready.

Mixture stores nicely for several months in tightly covered jar.

OYSTER AND CLAM RAW BAR

For the Raw Bar for this party, we will serve oysters and clams.

Oysters. Raw oysters should be served ice cold on the half shell on a bed of ice. Oysters have a shallow shell on one side and a deep shell on the other: they are served in the deep shell. Oysters can be bought in their shells or by the pint and quart already shucked in their own liquor. For this party they should be bought in the shell and opened at the party. (If oysters are opened off the premises they must be used immediately.) The quantity needed will depend on the number of tickets; six per person is a good general rule of thumb. Discard any with broken or gaping shells. Types of oysters differ around the country: ask your fish merchant for the best variety available to you for this party. The old wives' tale that oysters may be eaten only in months ending in R is strictly that: oysters may be less plump and tasty during the non-R months, but they may be eaten any time as long as they are properly refrigerated.

Opening oysters is difficult and time-consuming; I strongly recommend you hire a professional for this task. If you have volunteers who insist they want to tackle this job, there are excellent instructions in the shellfish section of the *Grand Central Oyster Bar & Restaurant Seafood Cookbook* and in *The Joy of Cooking*. All oysters should be kept chilled and eaten soon after opening.

To serve the oysters, arrange the bar so that salt and pepper and lemon slices as well as several sauces are available. Many people prefer oysters without sauce, but for sauce lovers I am suggesting a fairly traditional Raw Bar Cocktail Sauce here (other sauces can be found in the index or use your own favorite). Remember that many will also want to sip the oyster liquor from the shell.

Clams. On the East Coast, it is the Littleneck and Cherrystone clams that are eaten raw on the half shell (actually they are the same clam in different stages of development). On the West Coast, there are two I know—the Pismo and the Razor. Again, ask your fishmonger for the best clam available in your area. Clams can be bought in the shell or preshucked by the pint or quart. For this party, you will want to buy them in the shell (again, 6 per person seems the rule). However, there is a difference in serving clams: clams are very sandy and must be cleaned before serving, cooked or raw. Proper cleaning will also cause them to excrete the undesirable black material in their stomachs.

To clean clams properly, first discard any with open or broken shells or shells that don't close tightly when clams are touched. Clams must then be washed several times in clean water, then left to soak in cold water mixed with ¼ cup cornmeal to each quart of clams for at least 3 hours.

To open clams, again, I recommend a professional. The muscle has to be severed and the meat cut away. It takes time and can be tricky.

To serve the clams, more lemon, salt and pepper are all that's needed; however, with sauce(s) available. Again, be sure to retain the juice.

Raw Bar Cocktail Sauce

This sauce, from the *Grand Central Oyster Bar & Restaurant Seafood Cookbook*, is similar to the James Beard's Shrimp Sauce on page 293; you can use either one, both, the Burgundy Sauce below, or others. You'll need several lots.

MAKES ABOUT 2 CUPS

1½ cups chili sauce
Prepared horseradish to taste
2 teaspoons Worcestershire sauce
Juice of 2 small lemons
Several dashes Tabasco sauce

2 cloves garlic, minced or mashed
Salt to taste
Freshly ground pepper to taste
2 teaspoons minced fresh celery
  (optional)

Combine all ingredients and mix well. Refrigerate in tightly covered container until ready to serve.

Burgundy Sauce

This somewhat milder sauce makes a nice alternative for this Creole-oriented menu.

MAKES ABOUT 4 CUPS

¼ cup olive oil
¼ cup light vegetable oil
3 cups finely sliced onions
3 cups finely sliced green, red
  and/or yellow peppers
3 tablespoons sugar
1 bay leaf

½ teaspoon cinnamon
1 pinch powdered cloves
¼ cup wine vinegar
4 cups peeled, seeded and chopped
  ripe tomatoes, or 1 (32-ounce)
  can plum tomatoes

Heat the oils in a saucepan and cook the onions and peppers until wilted but not brown. Add the remaining ingredients and simmer for 2 hours or so, stirring occasionally.

Serve with the seafood either hot or cool.

Note: The Shallot Seafood Sauce in the dips and sauces section is another nice sauce, especially for oysters.

CREOLE CRAWFISH BOIL

This recipe for a combined shrimp and crawfish boil comes originally from the New Orleans French Market. The crab, shrimp and crawfish "boil" called for in the recipe is available at many good seafood and specialty shops. Crawfish, for those not familiar with them, look much like tiny lobsters. Crawfish are hard to come by in the East but are readily available in the Gulf area, the Northwest and in the Wisconsin-Minnesota region.

SERVES 40 TO 45

5 gallons water	2 ounces cayenne or ground red
6 lemons, quartered	pepper (about ⅔ cup)
2 (26-ounce) boxes salt	25 pounds live crawfish
2 (3-ounce) bags crab, shrimp and	5 pounds fresh shrimp in the shell
crawfish "boil"	

In very large kettle bring water to boil over very high heat. Add lemons, 1½ boxes (3¾ cups) salt, the crab, shrimp and crawfish "boil" and cayenne; boil 25 minutes.

Next purge crawfish: place crawfish in large washtub, cover with water and sprinkle with remaining ½ box (1¼ cups) salt. Let stand 10 to 15 minutes and drain, rinsing well. (This process cleans out crawfish entrails.) Pour purged crawfish into boiling water and bring to boil again; boil another 15 minutes.

When almost done, add shrimp; they should cook only 3 to 5 minutes. To serve, drain well and offer with or without sauces.

BEEF TENDERLOIN AND FRENCH BREAD DIP

This is a traditional favorite in the deep South and is just right for our New Orleans theme.

MAKES 50 TO 60 SERVINGS

½ pound bacon	2 sticks (½ pound) butter
1 whole beef tenderloin (5 to 7	2 (5-ounce) bottles top-quality steak
pounds untrimmed)	sauce
1 pound fresh mushrooms, cleaned	½ cup red wine
and sliced	3 loaves French bread

TO ROAST BEEF   PREHEAT OVEN TO 400°

Lay bacon strips over the tenderloin, place on rack in roasting pan and roast uncovered for 15 to 25 minutes (15 minutes for rare; 25 for well done).

TO PREPARE DIP AND SERVE

While meat is cooking, sauté mushrooms in 4 tablespoons (or more) butter; then add steak sauce and remaining butter and bring to boil. Cut bread into bite-sized slices.

While still hot, put meat on serving platter with the bread on a separate tray and with a chafing dish holding the dipping sauce nearby. When the meat has rested; slice into thin, bite-sized pieces. Dip meat slices in sauce, place on bread and eat as small open-faced sandwiches.

FRENCH BEIGNETS

These are very light rectangularly shaped doughnut-like cakes.

MAKES 36

2¾ to 3¼ cups flour	¼ cup sugar
1 tablespoon (1 envelope) dry yeast	¾ teaspoon salt
½ teaspoon nutmeg	1 egg
¼ cup cooking oil	Fat for deep frying
1 cup milk	Sifted confectioners' sugar

In mixer bowl stir together 1½ cups flour, yeast and nutmeg. Heat oil, milk, sugar and salt just until warm (115° to 120°), and add to flour mixture. Add egg and beat with electric mixer at low speed for ½ minute, scraping bowl constantly. Then beat 3 minutes at high speed. By hand, stir in enough remaining flour to make a soft dough. Place in greased bowl, and turn once to coat all sides with shortening. Cover; chill. Turn out dough on floured surface, cover and let rest 10 minutes. Then roll dough into an 18-by-12-inch rectangle. Cut into 36 rectangles 3 by 2 inches. Cover again and let rise for 30 minutes (dough will not double).

TO FRY AND SERVE　　　　　**HEAT FAT TO 375°**

Fry in deep hot fat until golden, about 1 minute, turning once. Drain well on paper toweling and sprinkle with confectioners' sugar.

Serve as fresh as possible.

CREOLE PRALINES

Among several recipes our Senator Patrick Leahy sent me for this cookbook is this one for pralines from Senator Allen J. Ellender of Louisiana. I understand it originally came from the Senator's mother in Terrebonne Parish—you can't get much closer to our New Orleans scene than that.

MAKES ABOUT 2 DOZEN 3-INCH CANDIES

2 cups sugar
1 cup dark or light brown sugar
1 stick (8 tablespoons) butter
1 cup milk

*2 tablespoons light or dark corn
syrup*
*4 cups (1 pound) pecan halves (if
large, break in half)*

In 3-quart saucepan bring all ingredients except pecans to boil. Simmer about 20 minutes, stirring occasionally. Add pecans and continue cooking until mixture forms soft ball when dropped into cold water (234°).

Stir well and drop by large spoonfuls on wax paper. When cool, store in airtight container until ready to serve. (The Senator's mother laid sheets of newspaper under the wax paper to help absorb heat.)

Note: For this party, you might prefer to make a more bite-sized, 1½- or 2-inch praline rather than the traditional 3-inch size.

DATE SQUARES

This is a slightly different version of a very good recipe from Jean Allen, a local friend.

MAKES 30 TO 36

1 cup sugar
2 eggs
½ cup flour
½ teaspoon baking powder

¼ teaspoon salt
1 cup pitted dates, chopped
1 cup chopped pecans

Beat sugar and eggs until fluffy. Add flour, baking powder and salt, and blend. Fold in the dates and nuts.

TO BAKE   PREHEAT OVEN TO 350°

Grease an 8-inch square pan. Spoon batter into pan and bake for 30 minutes. Remove from oven and cut into small squares.

25
A GALA
CHAMPAGNE EVENING

A very special party for 200 or so

CHAMPAGNE

GRAVLAX   SANDWICH   TOWER

PÂTÉ   MAISON

CEBICHE   SHRIMP   TOAST

DÉLICE   D'ORIENT

WATER   CHESTNUT   MEATBALLS   SAMOSAS

BEER   PUFFS   WITH   CRABMEAT

SHABU   SHABU   PAUL'S   BARBECUED   PORK

ARTICHOKE   SQUARES   SALAMI   ROLL   UPS

GALA   VEGETABLE   TERRINE

SNOWY   MARINATED   MUSHROOMS

FRENCH   SPICED   ONIONS

DILLED   SLICED   CUCUMBERS

MELTED   CAMEMBERT   WITH   ALMONDS

GORGONZOLA   CHEESE   ROLL

HOT   PEANUTS   BACON-WRAPPED   DATES

FRESH   FRUIT   IN   SEASON

CHOCOLATE   TRUFFLES

PETITE   BOURBON   CAKES

PRALINE   RUM   BALLS

PLATTERS   OF   LEMON   SQUARES,
THUMBPRINT   COOKIES
AND   PHYLLO   FRUIT   TARTS

OPEN   BAR   PUNCH   TABLE   COFFEE

A GALA CHAMPAGNE EVENING

Ideally a proper gala will spring naturally from the occasion being feted. A museum may be having a special exhibit, a music center a special performance, an ASPCA an animal show, and so on. But sometimes this is not the case: sometimes it is just time to have a dance or a party or perhaps a very special affair to thank someone—a faithful retiring president or board member, perhaps, or giant benefactor.

There are many successful ways to organize a gala. But first, certain basic questions must be considered, especially its central purpose and whether the emphasis is to be fund-raising or pure party.

In the case of the museum for which I have helped plan so many, we use our gala as a final celebration after our annual ballet benefit. Although the emphasis is on a gay party, we make no bones about its also being a money maker. In fact, we count on this post-ballet party to add at least a thousand dollars—often more—to our final take. We do this by almost doubling the cost of the ballet ticket for those attending the gala. Though I must add we also use the occasion to thank a number of nonmembers—and even a few of the less affluent members—who have helped us in special ways with the ballet or during the year. And our gala guest list always includes the ballet troupe members: it is a highlight of the evening when they arrive still flushed from their dancing and ready to enjoy the goodies.

The same bases must be touched for a gala as for other fund-raising parties: publicity, tickets, proper help, decorations, and good food and drink. However, for the purpose of this section we will limit the discussion to the role of the gala food and drink committee.

Since the gala will be a champagne affair, one of the first tasks is to arrange for the champagne. In Vermont, since we have the State Liquor Store system, donations or discounts from stores are not possible; in other states with private liquor merchants, this may be possible. (However—with luck—these costs are sometimes absorbed by individual donations.)

Planning for the gala food must also begin early. We first plan a tentative menu and then "invite" board members and other friends of the museum to contribute these foods or similar favorites; sometimes we mail recipes and ask that they be made. This process isn't difficult but it does take planning and follow-through: it's important to keep track of who is bringing what so that the food for the party will be nicely balanced, as well as ample—and good.

For a suggested menu I have outlined an ambitious buffet which can be brought out gradually over the course of the party, some of the dishes to be placed on buffet tables and others to be passed by young volunteers under the watchful eye of a professional overseer.

No doubt your organization will not stick solely to my menu: each organization's members have their own specialties and their own tastes. However, do insist that the initial display be eye-catching and with a good mix of soft and crisp, hot and cold, salty and bland, with most of the hors d'oeuvre bases touched (i.e., cheese, fish, chicken, meat, nuts, sweets, etc.). I hope you will try at least some of the recipes I have reserved for this gala section and will go through the index to find others that appeal to you; but most important, plan a menu that will work for you.

Depending on the final number of people expected, you may want two or three buffet tables: I find two usually works well; one is never enough. If your hall does not have an established bar area, you will need several sturdy tables for this purpose. Our gala is usually set up around three bars. In addition to a bar for the champagne (we offer champagne free in the early part of the evening to welcome the guests), we have another for a nonalcoholic punch and an open bar, offering wine and soft drinks as well as liquor, for those who would prefer these. Depending on the price of your tickets, you might charge for everything or offer champagne throughout the evening instead of cutting it off as we do. The open bar will require either a price list or a basket and sign suggesting donations. Different states and towns handle these matters in various ways. It is the responsibility of the gala committee to adhere to local restrictions and to obtain any necessary permits.

Whatever your choice of food, it should be elegant and as unusual as you can manage: people do like a change. And keep some surprises for later in the evening: it's always fun to have something new brought out occasionally as the evening winds along. At the beginning, I would feature the Gravlax (rather a lot of work, but a real conversation piece and, if you have time, fun to do), along with the Sandwich Tower and Pâté Maison. The Sandwich Tower adds a colorful touch and a nice vertical balance to the table, and the Pâté is a lovely basic one (though I have never yet worked with an organization that didn't have at least one pâté expert on its rolls).

These can then be surrounded by platters of the other food—all to be refilled or replaced as the guests clean them off (proper help in the kitchen will keep an eye on this). You'll want chafing dishes or Crock-Pots for the Water Chestnut Meatballs and the Shabu Shabu and a warming tray perhaps for the Samosas and Délice d'Orient. Then, toward the end of the evening, the sweets and coffee can be brought out, with bowls of fresh fruit in season.

Recipes for all the menu items follow here, except for the Camembert, the Samosas and a few of the sweets, which can be found in other parties throughout the book. Punch ideas can be found in the index.

Along with the food and drink for this special gala, attention must be given to the setting. It adds so much to have things attractively served and surrounded. Usually there will be a separate decorations committee that will tend to the flowers for the hall and for the tables, but it is important that the decor be coordinated with the food and what the gala committee has in mind. Beyond that, it is often possible to have either the kitchen professional or one of the members prepare special decorations for the hors d'oeuvre platters. Delicately shaped vegetables and edible flowers add a lovely touch and spell "special" to all there. If you possibly can, plan background music to enhance the setting even more, being sure it is designed for the occasion—pleasant but unobtrusive.

Preparing the food and drink—and the setting—for a lovely gala may seem like a horrendous task at times, but with careful planning and enough help (including a proper clean-up crew) it's amazing how smoothly it will go, each year growing easier and easier. Nonetheless be prepared for emergencies with extra fuses, extra ice, extra wine and boxes of crackers and cheeses that can be returned—just in case the power should blow, the ice should run out, your guests should be hungrier than you expect or one of your donors should let you down.

Two final notes. No matter how tiresome it may seem, be sure that someone on each of the committees keeps careful track of costs; this so you will know exactly what your profit and loss picture is, and also to help with even better planning in the future. General memos should be kept, too, on where things came from, who made what, what worked well and what, if anything, didn't—all this will help future committees immeasurably and will ensure better and better, and even more profitable, galas as the years go by.

And do—maybe above all—remember a quote from Ralph Waldo Emerson: "Nothing great was ever achieved without enthusiasm."

GRAVLAX

This is a tasty way to stretch fresh salmon a little further.

MAKES 12 TO 20 SERVINGS

2 bunches fresh dill, or a bit more, as needed
1 (3½- to 4-pound) piece salmon, preferably cut from the center
¼ cup kosher salt
¼ cup sugar

1 teaspoon coarsely ground white peppercorns
3 tablespoons Cognac (optional)
1 recipe Mustard-Dill Sauce (see below)

Trim any tough stems from the dill, rinse the tender portion and pat dry.

Bone the salmon piece or ask your fishmonger to do it for you: there should be 2 fillets of equal size and weight. Do not skin or rinse the fish; just pat it dry with paper toweling.

Combine the salt, sugar, pepper and optional Cognac and rub into the pink flesh of the salmon.

Spread ⅓ of the dill over the bottom of a flat dish. Add one of the salmon pieces, skin side down. Cover this with another ⅓ of the dill. Add the remaining piece of slamon, placing it sandwich-fashion over the dill, skin side up. Cover with the remaining dill and place a sturdy plate or small wooden plank over all. Top with a sizable weight and let stand in the refrigerator for about 48 hours, turning the "sandwich" every 12 hours and always re-covering it with the plate and weight.

To serve, slice very thin on the bias, like smoked salmon, and place on a square of dark Swedish bread—with a bowl of Mustard-Dill Sauce nearby.

Mustard-Dill Sauce

MAKES ABOUT 1½ CUPS

½ cup Dijon mustard
2 teaspoons dry mustard
⅔ cup vegetable oil
Juice of 1 small lemon

¼ cup sugar
½ cup chopped fresh dill
Salt
Freshly ground black pepper

In a mixing bowl, combine the two mustards. Gradually beat in the oil in a slow steady stream, whisking constantly until smooth and thick. Stir in the lemon juice, sugar and dill, and season with salt and pepper.

SANDWICH TOWER

I'm indebted to Peggy Watson for this party recipe.

Make or buy a good firm round sandwich loaf (5 inches across by 6 inches high is a good size). Cut the loaf into thin round slices, saving end pieces, and make individual sandwiches with fillings of homemade mayonnaise mixed with smoked salmon or smoked bluefish, crabmeat, deviled ham or your own favorite. A paste of minced onions, mushrooms, butter and flour, with or without a little puréed spinach, makes another good filling (the proportions and quantity according to taste and to what other fillings you are using). The fillings can be all the same or different.

Stack the sandwiches into a neat tower. Cut tower into wedges; number will depend on size of loaf. Use an end piece to make top for tower and decorate with a toothpick holding small pearl onions, olives or pickles.

Note: For a sweet version, marmalade or jam can be used for the filling, with or without cream or cottage cheese.

PÂTÉ MAISON

As pâtés go, this one is not overly difficult—and not overly rich.

SERVES 18 TO 20

1½ pounds twice ground beef	*½ cup Cognac*
1½ pounds twice ground pork	*1 tablespoon Worcestershire sauce*
2 eggs	*½ teaspoon pepper*
⅔ cup breadcrumbs	*1½ teaspoons salt*
⅔ cup milk	*½ teaspoon basil*
2 tablespoons chopped onion	*½ teaspoon thyme*
2 tablespoons butter	*14 to 16 bacon strips*

TO PREPARE PÂTÉ

If your butcher didn't grind the meat twice, be sure you do. Then place it and eggs in large bowl. In another bowl soak crumbs in milk and add to meat. Sauté onion in butter and add to meat with rest of ingredients, except for bacon. Poach a spoonful to taste; adjust seasoning and mix until very smooth.

TO SHAPE AND BAKE   PREHEAT OVEN TO 400°

Shape meat into 8-by-16-inch rectangle on foil. Wind bacon strips closely together around pâté. Seal foil and place pâté in baking dish. Bake for 1 hour;

open foil, reduce heat to 350° and bake another 35 minutes until bacon is browned and juices run yellow.

Remove from oven and cool. Rewrap in foil, and still in baking dish, weight pâté (a can or small brick works well, resting on plate or wood slab). Cool and refrigerate, still weighted, overnight. Remove weight, re-cover closely with foil and let ripen in fridge for at least several days.

CEBICHE

A popular Mexican dish varying in spiciness and kind of fish used—but always marinated in lime juice. This version comes from *The Cusines of Mexico* by Diane Kennedy.

MAKES 10 TO 12 APPETIZER-SIZED SERVINGS

1 pound fillets of mackerel or other oily fish

1 to 1½ cups lime juice, to cover fish

3 to 4 canned serrano or jalapeño chilies

¼ cup olive oil

2 to 4 tomatoes, skinned, seeded and chopped

½ teaspoon oregano

Salt to taste

Freshly ground pepper to taste

Slices of 1 avocado and 1 onion, for garnish (optional)

Coriander, for garnish (optional)

Cut the fish into small (½-inch) cubes and cover with lime juice. Marinate at least 5 or 6 hours, basting regularly; the fish should become opaque.

Drain chilies and chop, reserving the seeds and pickle juice. Add chopped chilies to fish, but go light as more can be added later if necessary. Then add olive oil, tomatoes and seasonings. Mix well and allow to season. Taste and add more chilies if wanted. (If you like things really hot, you can add the chili seeds, or some of them—but be careful.)

To serve, place the cebiche on one or more serving platters and garnish with avocado slices, onion rings and coriander as wanted (dried coriander is not so overpowering as chopped fresh). Serve with toothpicks and napkins.

Note: Another way to serve is to add marinated shrimp or scallops with or without strips of sweet red pepper.

SHRIMP TOAST

This shrimp tidbit comes from China, kindness of Hi Kyung Brandt.

MAKES 16 TO 20 SERVINGS

*½ pound shrimp, shelled and
  deveined
5 water chestnuts
1 teaspoon minced fresh ginger
1½ teaspoons cornstarch
1 tablespoon sherry*

*1 egg, lightly beaten
½ teaspoon salt
Pepper to taste
4 or 5 slices white bread
Oil for deep frying*

Mince together the shrimp and water chestnuts, and add ginger. Make paste of the cornstarch and sherry and add to the minced ingredients with the egg and salt and pepper. Blend well.

Trim off bread crusts. Spread shrimp mixture evenly over bread and cut each slice into quarters.

TO FRY   HEAT OIL TO SMOKING (375°)

Place bread, a few pieces at a time, shrimp side down on slotted spoon; then gently lower into oil. Reduce heat slightly and deep fry until bread is golden brown. Turn pieces over and fry a few seconds more.

Drain well on paper toweling before serving.

DÉLICE D'ORIENT

This tasty canapé is served at the Ritz-Carlton in Boston.

SERVES 20

*⅓ cup chutney
½ cup very finely chopped lean ham
20 bread rounds, 1 to 2 inches in
  diameter, toasted*

*3 tablespoons grated Parmesan
  cheese*

Coarsely chop chutney in blender, combine with ham and mix together well. Spread on toast rounds, sprinkle with cheese and broil under high heat until brown. Serve hot (a warming tray works well).

Note: You can make your own toast rounds if you choose, though I often use the Pepperidge Farm party rounds.

Adapted from *The Ritz-Carlton Cook Book and Guide to Home Entertaining* by Helen Ridley.

WATER CHESTNUT MEATBALLS

MAKES 5 TO 6 DOZEN

1 pound ground beef
1 pound ground sausage
4 cups soft breadcrumbs
2 (7-ounce) cans water chestnuts, chopped
1 cup milk

2 tablespoons soy sauce
1 small onion, minced
2 cloves, garlic, minced
1 recipe Hot Pepper Sauce (see below)

Combine all ingredients except sauce, mixing well. Form into balls the size of a walnut and set on lightly greased baking sheet.

TO BAKE   **PREHEAT OVEN TO 350°**

Place in oven for 15 minutes, turn over and bake another 10 or 15 minutes. Should be nicely browned. Taste one to test for doneness. When ready, serve warm in chafing dish or Crock-Pot covered with the Hot Pepper Sauce.
    If you like, these meatballs can be frozen.

Hot Pepper Sauce

AMPLE FOR 5 TO 6 DOZEN MEATBALLS

½ cup hot pepper jelly
½ cup hoisin sauce

½ cup water
¼ cup dry sherry

Mix ingredients together well in cooking pot. Simmer to meld; add to meatballs and mix gently.

BEER PUFFS WITH CRABMEAT

Although we are using crabmeat here, other fillings would work equally well with these puffs.

MAKES 60 TO 80 PUFFS

1 recipe Crabmeat Puff Filling (see below)

1 recipe Pâte à Chou (see page 399), substituting 1 cup beer for the water

First, following the recipe below, prepare the Crabmeat Filling and set aside.

Then, prepare the Pâte à Chou, using beer in place of the water. Once made, the dough is best used while still warm.

TO BAKE AND FILL PUFFS   **PREHEAT OVEN TO 450°**

Drop dough by teaspoonfuls 1 inch apart onto buttered baking sheet. Bake 10 minutes, then reduce heat to 350° and bake another 10 minutes, or until puffs are lightly browned and free from moisture.

Cool puffs, split and fill with Crabmeat Filling.

Note: The Beer Puffs for this combination can be made ahead and frozen. Then, shortly before serving, bring puffs to room temperature and fill with freshly made filling.

Crabmeat Puff Filling

AMPLE FOR 60 TO 80 PUFFS

1 (7-ounce) can crabmeat	*Freshly ground pepper to taste*
2 tablespoons sour cream	*Herbs of choice to taste*
2 to 3 teaspoons gin	

Mix together the crabmeat, sour cream and gin (the gin removes any tinny taste from the canned crabmeat); season and set aside until Beer Puffs are ready to fill.

SHABU SHABU
(JAPANESE FONDUE)

SERVES 20 OR MORE

3 (10-ounce) cans chicken broth	*12 scallions, cut into 2-inch lengths*
1 square dried Japanese sea kelp	*12 fresh mushrooms, sliced*
2 pounds chicken breasts, skinned, boned and thinly sliced into 1½-inch pieces	*24 spinach leaves, stems trimmed off*
	8 ounces yarn noodles, softened, or fine spaghetti, broken in short lengths (optional)
2 (4-ounce) cakes tofu, cut in quarters	
1½ heads Chinese cabbage, cut into 1½-inch pieces	

Bring broth to boil in fondue pot and add sea kelp. Simmer 3 minutes and remove kelp. When party is ready to begin place pot on serving table and keep broth boiling gently throughout.

Arrange chicken slices on platter with the tofu, cabbage, scallions, mushrooms, spinach and noodles or spaghetti, if used, on one or more additional platters.

Let guests serve themselves by taking piece of chicken, or the various vegetables, with a fondue fork or chopsticks, cooking it briefly in boiling liquid and then dipping it in either the Ginger or the Sesame Dipping Sauce below. The guests can then transfer the cooked bits to individual plates.

Be sure that someone is assigned the job of watching over the pot to replace the broth and various ingredients as needed.

Note: For a party this size, an electric fondue pot will prove far easier to work with; try to secure one.

Ginger Dipping Sauce

MAKES ABOUT 1 CUP

½ cup soy sauce
½ cup lemon juice or rice vinegar
2 tablespoons minced scallions, with tops

1 tablespoon finely grated fresh ginger
¼ teaspoon cayenne

Combine all ingredients, mixing well. Let stand, covered, at least an hour before serving.

Sesame Dipping Sauce

MAKES ABOUT 1 CUP

¼ cup sesame seeds
¼ cup soy sauce

¼ cup dashi (Japanese soup stock)
2 tablespoons rice vinegar

Toast sesame seeds in moderate (350°) oven 10 to 15 minutes, or until lightly browned (watch carefully); then grind (see Notes) and combine with remaining ingredients.

Let sauce season before serving.

Notes: Canned *dashi* can be found in specialty food shops and Japanese markets. The sesame seeds may be ground with a mortar or pestle or small hand grinder.

PAUL'S BARBECUED PORK

This is a variation of Chinese barbecued pork but lighter in flavor and served cold.

MAKES 100 SERVINGS

1 loin of pork, boned and rolled
1 cup soy sauce
¼ cup honey or maple syrup

1 teaspoon freshly ground pepper
½ cup red wine or dry sherry

Ask your butcher to prepare the pork. A whole loin should be cut into 3 or 4 equal rolls and tied with string.

Combine the remaining ingredients, mixing well, and pour over pork rolls. Marinate for at least an hour before cooking.

TO BROIL   **PREHEAT OVEN TO 350°**

Broil (3 to 4 inches below heat) for 30 to 45 minutes. Turn heat up for last 10 minutes to 450° and baste frequently. When done, cool and slice thinly. It can be either served right away or kept 2 or 3 days in the refrigerator.

To serve, set pork slices out on a platter with a basket of the thin-sliced party rye bread and bowls of hoisin sauce and assorted mustards. For easy passing, the pork could be served directly on the rye slices with a dab of one or the other toppings already added.

Note: In China, barbecued pork is dyed red, the color of happiness. The hoisin sauce will help achieve that result for this American version.

ARTICHOKE SQUARES

This recipe from Marjorie Baden is a little different—and good.

MAKES 60 TO 70 SMALL SQUARES

2 (6-ounce) jars marinated
artichokes, drained (oil reserved)
and thinly sliced
½ cup diced onion
4 eggs, beaten
½ cup water

¼ cup dry breadcrumbs
⅛ teaspoon oregano
½ teaspoon salt
⅛ teaspoon pepper
Dash Tabasco sauce
2 cups grated Cheddar cheese

Sauté onion in reserved artichoke oil; drain and discard oil. Combine eggs, water, breadcrumbs, oregano, salt, pepper and Tabasco. Add onions, cheese and artichokes; mix gently and spread in greased 9-by-13-inch baking pan.

TO BAKE   **PREHEAT OVEN TO 350°**

Bake 17 or 18 minutes. Remove from oven, cool slightly and cut into small squares.

Note: A doubled recipe, baked 30 minutes, can be served as a casserole.

SALAMI ROLL-UPS

This is one of many variations on the old salami and ham roll-ups I guess we have all made—or had our children make for us—for years.

MAKES 30 TO 40 CORNETS

6 ounces cream cheese, thinned with
    a little milk or cream
6 tablespoons sour cream

2 tablespoons horseradish
1 pound Genoa salami, sliced
Paprika, for garnish

Mix cream cheese, sour cream and horseradish together well.

Roll salami slices into little cornets. Fill with cream cheese mixture, holding together with tooth pick if necessary. Sprinkle lightly with paprika and chill. Serve on a tray with other small hors d'oeuvre.

GALA VEGETABLE TERRINE

This combination of a spinach-zucchini terrine with a carrot pâté with prunes is refreshingly different and pretty to serve. However, it does take time.

MAKES 5 TO 6 DOZEN MODEST-SIZED SLICES

2 pounds zucchini, trimmed and
    thinly sliced
2 bunches scallions, chopped, greens
    included
¼ cup olive oil
3 cloves garlic, chopped coarsely
1 (10-ounce) package frozen,
    chopped spinach, thawed
1 tablespoon tarragon
1 teaspoon dill weed

Dash cayenne
1 to 2 teaspoons salt
Several grindings black pepper
4 eggs, plus 2 whites for brushing
    layers
1 tablespoon bitters
1 cup dry breadcrumbs
1 recipe Carrot with Prunes Pâté
    (see below)
Butter for greasing terrines

In a covered skillet slowly sauté the zucchini and scallions in the olive oil about 15 minutes, stirring occasionally. Add garlic, turning up heat and stirring until all juices have evaporated. Scrape mixture into food processor or blender and set aside.

Squeeze all juice from spinach and add to zucchini mixture. Purée, add seasonings to taste and purée again briefly. Beat whole eggs and bitters together, and with motor running, slowly add to vegetable mixture, sprinkling in the breadcrumbs just at the end. Set mixture aside and prepare Carrot with Prunes Pâté.

TO FORM AND BAKE   PREHEAT OVEN TO 350°

Cut parchment or waxed paper to fit top and bottom of two 8-cup terrines. Butter molds, fit each with 1 piece paper and butter again. Spread ¼ zucchini-spinach mixture in each evenly, carrying carefully into the corners. Brush with beaten egg white.

Scoop ½ carrot pâté into each terrine, spreading it lightly over green mixture. Gently press a row of the stuffed prunes (5 or 6) into each terrine, then a row of the carrot halves; and brush carrot-prune layer with beaten egg white. Cover with remaining zucchini-spinach mixture pressing down well. Brush again with egg white and cover with buttered paper.

Cover molds and place in water bath. Bake 1½ hours or until a knife slid into center of each comes out clean. Uncover molds, turn heat off and let terrines cool in oven. When cool, remove molds from water bath and weight lightly with a 2-pound (or less) brick or can. Let set for about 3 hours; remove weight and paper, cover terrine and refrigerate for 1 to 2 days.

When ready to serve, turn terrines out onto platters and decorate with carrot and other vegetable flowers. Slice and serve with a basket of biscuits or small rye slices nearby.

Note: If each pâté slice is sliced again 3 or 4 ways, there will be ample cracker-sized portions.

Carrot with Prunes Pâté

This pâté also stands alone nicely but I especially like it as a colorful center for this Gala Vegetable Terrine.

**AMPLE FOR ONE 6-CUP TERRINE
OR CENTER LAYER FOR TWO 8-CUP TERRINES**

10 to 12 large pitted prunes (fewer for solo terrine)
½ to ¾ cup Madeira
½ teaspoon nutmeg
1 lemon slice
1¾ pounds carrots, ¼ left whole, ¾ shredded
3 tablespoons butter
1 large onion, chopped
3 cloves garlic, minced
1 pound mushrooms, chopped

Juice of ½ lemon, about 1½ tablespoons
Salt and pepper to taste
½ cup parsley leaves, chopped
1½ cups walnuts, ground
1 cup grated Parmesan cheese
½ cup breadcrumbs
½ teaspoon mace
½ teaspoon ginger
4 eggs
3 tablespoons heavy cream

Rinse the prunes and place in non-reactive pot with enough Madeira to cover. Cover pot and soak for 1 hour. Add ¼ teaspoon nutmeg and lemon slice, bring to simmer and cook gently for about 10 minutes. Drain, reserving the Madeira juice.

Cut the whole carrots in half lengthwise and cook in boiling water until barely tender. Set aside to cool.

Melt the butter in a large skillet, add chopped onion, cover and cook until soft and translucent. Add garlic, mushrooms, lemon juice, 2 tablespoons Madeira juice and salt and pepper; cover and simmer for 5 minutes or so to draw out mushroom juices. Uncover and cook, stirring often, until juices evaporate. Cool for 5 minutes or so and season with remaining nutmeg and parsley. Scrape into large mixing bowl; add shredded carrots, 1¼ cups ground nuts, cheese, breadcrumbs, mace and ginger. Beat eggs with 2 tablespoons cream, pour over carrot mixture and mix well.

Poach a spoonful to taste and adjust seasonings as needed (remembering that pâté served cold usually needs to be a little more highly seasoned).

Make a paste of the remaining ¼ cup walnuts with 1 tablespoon Madeira juice and remaining tablespoon heavy cream. Use this to stuff soaked prunes.

Then incorporate Carrot with Prunes Pâté into Gala Vegetable Terrine as directed above.

Note: If using a food processor to prepare the ingredients for this pâté, I find the best order is: nuts, cheese, onion, mushrooms, parsley and carrots.

SNOWY MARINATED MUSHROOMS

Start with fresh, white mushrooms, and this recipe will keep them that way.

MAKES 30 OR SO

½ cup white wine
½ cup white vinegar
¼ cup lemon juice
1 tablespoon chopped fresh
  tarragon, or 1 teaspoon dried

Salt and pepper to taste
1 tablespoon Calendula petals (2 to
  3 flowers) (optional)
1 pound medium mushrooms, fresh
  and white

Combine all but the mushrooms and either shake or mix well. (Be sure to taste and season accordingly; vinegars vary so it is often necessary to vary the seasonings accordingly.)

Put mushrooms in fairly deep serving dish. Pour marinade over mushrooms, cover with a plate and weight. Put in refrigerator to marinate, at least overnight.

When ready, drain and serve with cocktail picks close by.

Note: The strained marinade from the mushrooms can be kept almost indefinitely in the refrigerator and used again.

FRENCH SPICED ONIONS

This recipe derives from the French countryside near Nimes.

MAKES 24 TO 30 SERVINGS

1½ pounds very small onions,
  canned or blanched fresh
2 tablespoons butter
2 tablespoons oil
¾ cup consommé
¼ cup wine vinegar
¾ cup seedless raisins

3 tablespoons tomato paste
2 tablespoons brown sugar
½ teaspoon salt
⅛ teaspoon crushed red pepper
¼ teaspoon thyme
1 bay leaf
Generous grinding black pepper
  (3 turns)

In a skillet, brown onions on all sides in butter and 1 tablespoon oil. Onions should be in a single layer so you may need to do 2 lots; add extra butter if necessary.

Combine remaining ingredients in saucepan and simmer for several minutes, removing the bay leaf when done.

TO BAKE AND SERVE   PREHEAT OVEN TO 325°

Arrange browned onions close together in shallow baking dish and cover with sauce. Bake for about 1 hour or until tender; time will depend on the size of the onions. Cool and then chill in the sauce, keeping onions chilled until ready to serve. Serve in a colorful bowl with toothpicks nearby.

DILLED SLICED CUCUMBERS

To prepare, first peel and then score outside of cucumbers with a fork (this removes bitterness). Then slice thinly and put in a bowl with ice and salt. Scatter dill seed over cucumbers and chill for at least 2 hours. Drain, wash in cold water and shake to dry. Serve sprinkled with fresh dill and accompany with sour cream or Marie's Blue Cheese Dressing, one of my favorites (it's storebought but hard to beat).

MELTED CAMEMBERT WITH ALMONDS

Using well-ripened Camembert, remove top rind, heat gently and when thoroughly warm, sprinkle with slivered almonds.

GORGONZOLA CHEESE ROLL

MAKES 4 TO 5 CUPS

1 pound cream cheese
8 ounces finely grated
  medium-sharp Cheddar cheese
8 ounces Gorgonzola cheese

¼ teaspoon nutmeg
2 tablespoons port
½ cup pistachio nuts, ground

Mix all but nuts well in food processor or blender, shape into a log and chill. Then roll in ground nuts and keep chilled until ready to serve.
  Serve with plain water biscuits.

HOT PEANUTS

This is a nice change from the more traditional salted cocktail peanut.

SERVES 10 TO 20, OR MORE

3 to 4 tablespoons crushed red pepper
3 tablespoons olive oil
4 cloves garlic
1 (12-ounce) can unsalted cocktail peanuts

1 (12-ounce) can Spanish peanuts, paper shells left on
1 teaspoon salt
1 teaspoon chili powder

Heat red pepper in oil for 1 minute. Crush garlic and add to oil. Add peanuts. Cook mixture over medium heat for 5 minutes. Remove from heat; add salt and chili powder. Taste and correct seasoning as needed.

Drain on paper towels and keep tightly covered until ready to serve.

BACON-WRAPPED DATES

MAKES 48

48 blanched almonds
48 pitted dates
1 teaspoon salt
2 teaspoons freshly cracked white peppercorns

1 teaspoon freshly grated nutmeg
2 teaspoons dry mustard
1 cup Cognac or good brandy
24 slices bacon

Stuff almonds into dates. Put them in bowl with salt, pepper, nutmeg and mustard. Mix well. Add brandy and mix again. Allow to sit 2 to 3 hours, or longer.

Cut bacon slices in half and partially cook. Roll each bacon piece around marinated date and secure with toothpick.

TO BROIL   **SET BROILER AT 450°**

Broil about 10 minutes, turning once to brown on both sides. Drain on paper toweling and serve with toothpick in place.

CHOCOLATE TRUFFLES

A perfect ending to a large party where a little sweet accompanies the coffee. I almost always use a double boiler when I am working with chocolate: it's safer.

MAKES ABOUT 50

1⅔ cups cream
7 tablespoons sweet butter
1 pound semi-sweet chocolate, broken into pieces

2 tablespoons Kahlua or other coffee liqueur
Cocoa powder, for dusting (I prefer Droste's)

TO MIX

Put cream and butter into top of double boiler and heat gently over direct heat until butter melts. Then, stirring briskly, bring mixture to a boil. Remove from heat and add chocolate pieces, stirring until completely melted. If the mixture needs more heat, use pot as top of double boiler, and over hot water, stir until mixture thickens. Then add Kahlua, cover pot and refrigerate for at least 2 hours, stirring 2 or 3 times as the mixture hardens.

TO FORM TRUFFLES

Scoop up portions of chocolate mixture with a spoon and dust well with cocoa powder. Rub additional cocoa powder on hands and roll chocolate scoops to make balls; roll again in cocoa and refrigerate immediately. Keep cool until ready to serve.

PETITE BOURBON CAKES

For best results when making this recipe use straight bourbon (bourbon that is at least two years old and no less than 80 proof). Blended whiskey can be used but it lacks the character of the real thing.

MAKES 60 TO 80

4 cups finely ground almonds
1 cup fine dry breadcrumbs or cake crumbs
1½ cups golden raisins
12 eggs, separated

2 cups firmly packed light brown sugar, sifted
1 cup bourbon
Confectioners' sugar, for topping

In a bowl, mix together almonds, crumbs and raisins. In separate bowl, beat egg yolks and 1½ cups sifted brown sugar together until thick and light colored. In third bowl, beat egg whites until foamy, gradually adding remaining brown sugar. Continue beating whites until soft peaks form.

Alternately fold egg whites and nut-raisin mixture into egg yolk mixture; stir in bourbon.

TO BAKE   **PREHEAT OVEN TO 375°**

Line 1- or 1½-inch muffin tins with the little paper quiche or candy cups about ⅔ full with cake batter. Bake 10 minutes, or until a light golden brown.

Cool and then dust lightly with confectioners' sugar.

Note: These cakes can also be made in large muffin tins and served as tea or coffee cake with butter. In that case you should butter the tins.

PRALINE RUM BALLS

A pleasantly spiced and spiked sweet.

MAKES 60 BALLS

2 cups fine dry vanilla wafer, dry cookie or cake crumbs

2 cups sifted confectioners' sugar, plus extra for rolling

4 tablespoons Praline Powder (see below)

1 teaspoon cinnamon

1 teaspoon ground ginger

2 cups chopped pecans

4 tablespoons corn syrup (light or dark)

½ cup dark rum

Combine crumbs, 2 cups confectioners' sugar, Praline Powder, cinnamon, ginger and pecans. Mix well. Stir in corn syrup and rum. Dust hands with confectioners' sugar and shape dough into 1-inch balls. Roll balls in sifted confectioners' sugar and store refrigerated in covered jar until ready to serve.

Note: Brandy may be substituted for the rum in the same proportion.

Praline Powder

MAKES 1½ CUPS

1 cup sugar

¼ teaspoon cream of tartar

¾ cup blanched almonds

Lightly brush a jelly-roll pan or baking sheet with vegetable oil. Combine ingredients in heavy-duty saucepan and put over moderate heat. As sugar beings to melt, turn the mixture with metal spoon. When mixture is caramelized and a rich medium-caramel color, pour it onto jelly-roll pan. It will quickly set and become brittle.

When cool and hard, break into chunks small enough for electric blender. Pulverize in blender to a powdery consistency. Powder may be refrigerated indefinitely in screw-top jar.

Note: This powder is sometimes used to dust chocolate truffles or plain cakes and cupcakes and can be used as an ice cream topping.

LEMON SQUARES

The crust for these may be mixed by hand or in a food processor, and the filling made in a blender or food processor, as well as by hand.

MAKES 4 TO 6 DOZEN

2 cups flour, plus 4 tablespoons
½ cup confectioners' sugar, plus extra for dusting
2 sticks (½ pound) butter or margarine

4 eggs, lightly beaten
2 cups granulated sugar
6 tablespoons lemon juice
½ teaspoon baking powder

TO MAKE
AND BAKE CRUST   PREHEAT OVEN TO 300°

Mix 2 cups flour, confectioners' sugar and butter or margarine in pie-crust fashion. Press into 13-by-9-inch baking pan and bake 25 minutes.

TO TOP AND FINISH

While crust is baking, combine eggs, granulated sugar, lemon juice, 4 tablespoons flour and baking powder. When crust is ready, spread lemon mixture over crust and bake, still at 300°, another 25 minutes.

Cool and dust with confectioners' sugar.

Note: These squares are very rich so can be cut quite small to reach the higher yield.

BACK-UP BASICS
FOR THE
PARTY GIVER

DRESSINGS, DIPS, MARINADES AND SAUCES

This selection of Dressings, Dips, Marinades and Sauces will augment the many already given with the recipes. A new topping is often all a familiar hors d'oeuvre needs to give it a welcome new zest.

For a complete tally of all dressings, dips, marinades and sauces see their listings in the index.

BASIC VINAIGRETTE

When making Vinaigrette the quality of the vinegar is important, as is the relative proportion of oil to vinegar. Always remember to mix in the seasonings before the oil; they don't mix well otherwise.

MAKES ABOUT 1 CUP

1 tablespoon Dijon mustard
3 tablespoons wine vinegar (red or white)
1 teaspoon sugar
½ teaspoon salt

½ teaspoon freshly ground black pepper
Minced parsley and/or minced fresh chives, to taste
½ cup olive oil

Measure mustard into bowl. Whisk in vinegar, sugar, salt, pepper and herbs to taste. When well mixed, slowly whisk in olive oil until mixture is thoroughly blended. Adjust seasoning to taste as needed. Cover until ready to use.

Vinaigrette is best if made just before using, but this is often not possible. In that case, whisk again lightly just before serving.

Note: Although olive oil is surely best, I often use equal parts olive oil and *good quality* vegetable oil.

HOMEMADE MAYONNAISE

Mayonnaise need not be difficult. If you have a food processor use the recipes in your companion booklet. Add different seasonings according to the nature of the salad or mousse it will be used for, and of course always use fresh herbs when possible.

If you want a thinner or less rich dressing, thin it with sour cream before adding the seasonings and herbs. This is an especially useful idea for dressings to be used with meat or fish salads which are to be served outside.

CLASSIC MAYONNAISE

Though I make a number of mayonnaises, I come back to this one and use the fresh herbs rather than the dried whenever I can.

MAKES 1½ TO 2 CUPS

2 egg yolks	*Salt*
1 tablespoon Dijon mustard	*Freshly ground black pepper*
1½ cups oil, more or less	*1½ tablespoons fresh chives, chervil*
1 to 2 tablespoons wine vinegar or	*or parsley, minced, or 1*
lemon juice	*teaspoon dried (optional)*

Put egg yolks and mustard in warm bowl and mix with a whisk. Then put the bowl over boiling water and continue to beat for 8 or 9 seconds to lightly poach the egg yolks with the mustard; you will feel a slight difference—it will be smooth and a little sticky.

Remove from steam and beat in the oil, a teaspoonful at a time. When mixture is creamy, add more oil, again a little at a time, until about ¾ cup oil is gone and mayonnaise is saturated. Bring vinegar or lemon juice to boil and add (this will give mixture more capacity to absorb oil). When mayonnaise becomes clearer and creamier, add more oil, beating constantly. Then season with salt and pepper, and the herbs, if desired.

This mayonnaise will keep several weeks if properly stored in fridge.

Note: For a truly green mayonnaise, increase the amount of chives, chervil and parsley twofold or more.

LEMON-GARLIC MAYONNAISE

MAKES ABOUT 3 CUPS

1 whole egg, plus 2 egg yolks
¼ to ½ cup fresh lemon juice
1 teaspoon sugar
Salt and freshly ground pepper to taste

6 to 8 large cloves garlic, peeled and chopped (see Note)
1 ¼ cups best-quality olive oil
1 cup vegetable oil

Combine the whole egg, egg yolks and ¼ cup lemon juice and sugar in a blender or food processor (fitted with steel blade). Season to taste and blend for 1 minute.

Add the garlic, and with motor running add the oils in a steady stream until all of the oil is incorporated. Scrape sides of container and correct seasoning, adding more lemon juice or sugar if wanted (I usually do).

Store, covered, in the refrigerator until ready to use.

Note: The matter of how much garlic is a matter of discretion as well as personal taste. Not only does the size of the garlic cloves vary, its pungency does as well. You might want to start easy and work up from there.

GARLIC MAYONNAISE

Known as *aïoli* (pronounced *eye-oh-lee*) in southern France, this dressing has a strong garlic base. Although traditionally made with a mortar and pestle, an electric beater works well (a food processor tends to make the result too "gluey").

MAKES 1 CUP

1 (1-inch-thick) slice French bread, crust removed
2 tablespoons wine vinegar
6 large cloves garlic

1 teaspoon salt, plus or minus
2 egg yolks
½ cup olive oil
½ cup vegetable oil

Soak slice of bread with vinegar in quart mixing bowl; then mash to paste, squeezing out excess vinegar.

Mash garlic to a pulp with pinch of salt (fresh garlic is easy to mash).

Add egg yolks and garlic paste to bread and mix well. Then dribble oil drop by drop while whisking constantly (putting the bowl on a wet potholder or dish towel helps keep it stationary to free both hands for whisking and pouring). As the dressing thickens, the oil may be added more quickly. Season to taste with remaining salt.

Refrigerate. Can be stored in fridge for several days.

EGGLESS HERB MAYONNAISE

This mayonnaise is an excellent recipe, especially for non-egg eaters. It is most easily made with a food processor but can be made by hand.

MAKES 1½ CUPS

3 tablespoons Dijon mustard
1 tablespoon good wine vinegar
2 tablespoons water
1 cup oil (½ olive and ½ vegetable)
2 tablespoons cold evaporated milk
Handful parsley sprigs, washed and well-dried

Dozen or so large fresh basil leaves, or 1 teaspoon dried tarragon
½ teaspoon salt
Freshly ground pepper
1 teaspoon capers, well-drained

In food processor blend mustard, vinegar and water. Beat in oil through pour spout in thin stream, alternating each 4 to 5 tablespoons oil with drops of cold milk (this stabilizes emulsion of oil and mustard). When all of oil and milk is added, scrape sides of bowl and add herbs. Beat another 8 to 10 seconds until all is incorporated. Add seasoning, taste and correct as necessary. Lastly, add capers, stirring in gently.

To make by hand, beat oil and milk gradually into mustard and vinegar, omitting water. Add chopped herbs and capers at end. Should sauce become too thick or begin to separate, stir in a small piece of ice.

This dressing may be stored up to a week in the refrigerator. If it should thicken, stir in a few drops of lemon juice or water.

Note: If a plain eggless mayonnaise is wanted, simply omit the herbs.

LOW-CAL MAYONNAISE

This may not save many calories but it will save some. Be sure to have the ingredients at room temperature.

MAKES 1½ CUPS

2 egg yolks
½ teaspoon prepared mustard
1 teaspoon lemon juice, or more to
   taste
½ teaspoon salt

1 to 1½ cups polyunsaturated oil
White pepper to taste
Dash Tabasco sauce to taste
(optional)

Beat the egg yolks lightly with the mustard and lemon juice; add salt. Then slowly add oil, a few drops at a time, continuing to whisk the egg mixture and waiting for egg mixture to absorb each addition of oil before adding more (after ½ cup oil has been beaten in, amounts added can be increased). Continue process until no more than 1½ cups of oil have been added (eggs will only absorb so much oil and of course vary in size; too much oil will make mayonnaise too thin). Taste and add more lemon juice (or vinegar if you prefer) and seasonings as wanted.

   Scrape mayonnaise into bowl, cover tightly and refrigerate until needed.

Note: If mayonnaise should curdle, warm a clean bowl. Put in 1 egg yolk and 1 teaspoon mustard and beat. Then slowly add in 1 tablespoon curdled dressing and then slowly the rest.

LOW-FAT COTTAGE CHEESE DRESSING OR DIP

MAKES ABOUT 1½ CUPS

1 cup low-fat cottage cheese
4 tablespoons milk
2 tablespoons lemon juice

2 tablespoons mayonnaise
2 tablespoons minced onion

Blend together the cottage cheese, milk and lemon juice. Then blend in the mayonnaise and onion.

   Refrigerate until ready to serve.

Note: Fresh herbs may be added at will.

Variation: Two tablespoons blue cheese and 1 tablespoon Worcestershire sauce may be substituted for the mayonnaise and onion.

DILL AND SOUR CREAM DRESSING OR DIP

MAKES ABOUT 1¼ CUPS

1 cup sour cream
2 teaspoons lime juice
Salt
Freshly ground white pepper

1 teaspoon Worcestershire sauce
2 to 3 tablespoons finely chopped
  fresh dill

In a small mixing bowl, combine the sour cream and lime juice and season with salt and pepper. Add the Worcestershire and dill and blend well. Chill for several hours before serving.

MILK AND GARLIC DRESSING

A light, yet tasty dressing.

MAKES ABOUT 2 CUPS

1 cup salad oil
½ cup milk
⅓ cup white wine vinegar
1 teaspoon sugar

1 teaspoon salt
1 teaspoon pepper
2 or 3 cloves garlic, finely chopped,
  to taste

Mix all together well and allow to blend. If you prefer a bland dressing, go light on the garlic.

BASIL DRESSING

This versatile dressing may also be used as a dip for various vegetable platters.

MAKES ABOUT 1½ CUPS

¼ cup wine or cider vinegar
3 tablespoons chopped fresh basil
  (do not use dried)

4 tablespoons chopped parsley
Salt and pepper to taste
1 cup oil (½ olive and ½ vegetable)

Mix vinegar and seasonings well. Then gradually add oil, stirring well. This dressing may be prepared ahead, but shake well before using.

Note: This dressing may be kept well covered in the refrigerator. However, before using again, I like to strain any leftover dressing to take out the old herbs (they tend to turn dark). I then add fresh ones.

HERB DIP WITH CALENDULA PETALS

This dip can be used on the thin side as a dip for crudités or thicker as a filling for salami coronets or small creampuffs.

MAKES ABOUT 1½ CUPS

1 (8-ounce) package cream cheese
2 tablespoons sour or heavy cream
1 tablespoon fresh summer savory, or 1 teaspoon dried
1 tablespoon fresh thyme, or 1

teaspoon dried
2 tablespoons calendula petals (optional)
1 to 2 twists freshly ground black pepper

Beat all together until fluffy.

Note: This recipe is only a base. Feel free to substitute your favorite herbs and flavors at will.

CHUTNEY DRESSING

MAKES 2 CUPS

1 teaspoon curry powder
1 tablespoon lemon juice
3 tablespoons tomato catsup

3 tablespoons purée of chutney (whirled in blender or forced through sieve)
1½ cups mayonnaise

Combine curry powder and lemon juice to make paste. Add catsup and chutney. When well mixed, add mayonnaise and blend all together well.
    Store, covered, in refrigerator.

Note: Using half yogurt, half mayonnaise will make a less rich dressing and a good dip.

CAPER-MUSTARD DRESSING

This is the dressing suggested for putting together the Savory Sandwich Loaf on page 25, but it would work equally as well as a dressing for any of the cold smoked fish recipes.

MAKES ABOUT 1 CUP

6 tablespoons mayonnaise
3 tablespoons capers, drained
2 tablespoons Dijon mustard
2 teaspoons vinegar

2 teaspoons Worcestershire sauce
1 teaspoon dried thyme, or 1
    tablespoon chopped fresh

Blend all ingredients together well in a small bowl or in your blender or food processor. Any unused dressing can be safely stored, tightly covered, in the refrigerator for several weeks.

POPPY SEED DRESSING

The poppy seeds add a nice subtle crunch to this flavorful dressing.

MAKES 1½ CUPS

¼ cup coarsely chopped onion
⅓ cup red wine vinegar
2 tablespoons honey
1 teaspoon dry mustard

½ teaspoon salt
1 cup vegetable oil
2 tablespoons poppy seeds

In a food processor or blender, purée the onion. Add the vinegar, honey, mustard and salt, and blend well. Continue to blend, adding the oil in a slow steady stream. Remove from the processor and stir in the poppy seeds.

    The dressing may be stored in a sealed container in the refrigerator for up to 2 weeks.

Note: A little of this dressing blended into a few dollops of cream cheese or yogurt makes an excellent last-minute dip.

YOGURT DRESSING OR DIP

This is only one of many yogurt dips and dressings. Modify to taste with various seasonings and fresh herbs.

MAKES ABOUT 1 CUP

1 cup yogurt	*½ teaspoon salt*
1 teaspoon wine vinegar	*½ teaspoon sugar*
½ teaspoon minced garlic	*½ teaspoon oregano*

Mix all together well and keep chilled until served.

Note: Using half sour cream, half yogurt will give a thicker and richer dip. For a different taste, cumin or coriander can be substituted for the oregano, and in summer I like to use calendula petals (straight from the plant).

GREEN YOGURT DRESSING

If you must, for this dressing substitute 1 teaspoon dried herbs for 2 to 3 tablespoons fresh. You can use the Classic Mayonnaise from this section or Hellmann's.

MAKES ABOUT 3 CUPS

2 cups yogurt	*1 tablespoon fresh chopped tarragon*
1 cup prepared mayonnaise	*1 clove garlic, minced*
1 to 2 tablespoons fresh chopped basil	*6 or so sprigs parsley, finely chopped*
1 tablespoon fresh chopped dill	*Salt and pepper to taste*

Mix or blend all ingredients together well. Serve as a dressing for lettuce, spinach or cucumber salad.

Note: This dressing is far superior if made with fresh herbs.

BLUE CHEESE SPREAD OR DIP

MAKES ABOUT 5 CUPS

2 pounds cream cheese, softened	*1 cup ground pecans*
¼ pound domestic blue cheese	*Black pepper to taste*

Mix all together well (I use a food processor). Transfer to bowl and let meld for several hours before serving.
   Add sour cream to make a good consistency for dipping.

ANNE'S CUCUMBER DIP

A light, refreshing dip—simple and easy to make.

MAKES 2 TO 3 CUPS

1 (3-ounce) package cream cheese,
softened
3 cucumbers, peeled, seeded and
finely chopped
1½ onions, finely chopped

Juice of 1 lemon, or more to taste
Salt and freshly ground black
pepper to taste
1 cup sour cream, more or less

Mix cheese, cucumbers, onions and lemon juice together well. Add salt and pepper to taste. Thin with sour cream to make a good consistency for dipping, adding a small amount at a time.

Leftover dip can be kept safely in refrigerator for several weeks, thinning with more sour cream as needed before serving.

FETA WALNUT DIP

MAKES 2 ¾ CUPS

1 cup crumbled feta cheese
2 tablespoons olive oil
½ cup milk

1 cup chopped walnuts
Dash cayenne
1 teaspoon paprika

Soak feta in water for an hour or 2 to partially desalt. Combine in blender 1 tablespoon oil, 3 tablespoons milk, ⅓ cup feta and ⅓ cup walnuts, and blend, first on low then medium speed. While the blender is still running on medium speed, add remaining ingredients and blend to a paste. Remove, and chill.

Serve with raw vegetables, crackers or pita bread.

SARDINE DIP

MAKES ABOUT 2 CUPS

1 (8-ounce) package cream cheese,
softened
1 (3-ounce) package boneless
sardines, drained and mashed

1 tablespoon chopped chives
2 tablespoons chopped parsley
About ½ cup light cream
Salt and pepper to taste.

In a bowl, mash cream cheese until soft and fluffy. Stir in sardines, chives and parsley. Gradually beat in cream until mixture is light and fluffy—the consistency of thick whipped cream. Season to taste and serve as soon as possible.

HERBED WHITE-WINE MARINADE

This is especially nice for chicken and fish.

MAKES ABOUT 1½ CUPS

1 cup minced onions
3 cloves garlic, minced
3 tablespoons olive oil
¼ cup tarragon vinegar
1 cup dry white wine
1 tablespoon fresh thyme, or 1
  teaspoon dried

1 tablespoon fresh rosemary, or 1
  teaspoon dried
1 bay leaf
6 parsley sprigs, chopped fine
6 peppercorns

In a stainless-steel or enameled saucepan over moderate heat, cook the onions and garlic in the olive oil, stirring until the onions are softened. Add the tarragon vinegar and cook over moderately high heat until the liquid is reduced by half. Add the wine and seasonings and bring to a boil. Then simmer for 5 minutes. Let the marinade cool in the pan and then transfer to a ceramic or glass dish and keep in refrigerator until needed.

Note: As always, fresh herbs (when available) make the better result. With the vegetable matter strained out, marinade can be safely kept in the refrigerator for as long as 3 months.

CANTONESE MARINADE

I like this as a marinade for thinly sliced pork strips. Let the strips soak at least several hours; overnight is even better. Then, while cooking, glaze with the Cantonese Glaze following.

MAKES ABOUT 1½ CUPS

2 teaspoons minced garlic
3 tablespoons maple syrup
5 tablespoons black soy sauce

⅓ cup hoisin sauce
½ cup pale dry sherry
2 tablespoons smooth bean paste

Mix all ingredients together well and pour over meat, basting frequently. Then drain before cooking.

Cantonese Glaze

MAKES ABOUT ⅓ CUP

2 tablespoons maple syrup   3 tablespoons thin soy sauce
2 teaspoons sesame seed oil

Mix ingredients well and baste frequently throughout cooking.

GINGER-SOY MARINADE

This marinade is particularly good for chicken and pork and makes a good teriyaki sauce.

MAKES ABOUT 1½ CUPS

½ cup soy sauce   1 clove garlic, mashed to a paste
⅓ cup honey or pure maple syrup   1 teaspoon peeled and grated fresh
⅓ cup medium-dry sherry   ginger

Mix all ingredients together well in a ceramic bowl and pour over meat, basting at intervals.

To reuse, strain out garlic and ginger pieces. Put in a glass jar and store in the refrigerator.

Note: Whereas most marinades require overnight soaking, this one is authoritative enough to give chicken or pork a good flavor in only an hour or so.

TERIYAKI SAUCE

Especially nice for chicken and pork but also good for steak, lamb and shrimp.

MAKES ABOUT 1 QUART

½ teaspoon dry mustard   1 pint pineapple juice
1 tablespoon ground ginger   1 pint soy sauce
1 tablespoon garlic powder

Mix all together well and let stand. Use as a marinade for a minimum of 24 hours; longer is better.

Refrigerated, this marinade will keep almost indefinitely.

QUICK TOMATO SAUCE

MAKES ABOUT 1⅓ CUPS

5 tablespoons olive oil
1 tablespoon minced shallots
½ cup tomato paste
1⅓ cups chicken broth or water
1 bay leaf

2 teaspoons mixed herbs (see Note below)
Salt to taste
Freshly ground pepper to taste
Freshly grated nutmeg to taste

Heat the olive oil in a medium-sized saucepan. Add the shallots and sauté gently for about 1 minute. Stir in the tomato paste, the liquid and herbs, and season lightly. Simmer for 12 to 15 minutes, stirring frequently. Remove bay leaf and correct seasoning as needed.

This sauce can be stored in the refrigerator for 2 to 3 days (or even longer if water rather than chicken broth is used), or for several weeks in the freezer.

Note: For the mixed herbs in this recipe, I prefer to use what is commonly known as *herbes de Provence*—a combination of thyme, oregano, marjoram and savory ground with a small amount of bay leaf (fresh if available, but dried will work fine).

FRESH TOMATO SAUCE

Use a sieve or food mill to process this sauce; a food processor or blender will incorporate the tomato fibers and stringy pulp into the sauce.

MAKES 1½ CUPS

½ medium yellow onion, coarsely chopped
2 tablespoons olive oil
1 pound fresh, ripe plum tomatoes, peeled and halved, or 1 (16 ounce) can Italian plum tomatoes

¼ teaspoon dried oregano
1 tablespoon minced fresh basil
Salt
Freshly ground black pepper
¼ teaspoon sugar
1 tablespoon butter, softened

In a medium saucepan, sauté the onion in oil until softened, about 5 minutes. Add the tomatoes, oregano, basil, salt and pepper and sugar to taste, and simmer, partially covered for about 30 minutes. (If tomatoes are not ripe enough, you may need to add a little water. If using canned, add the tomatoes and their juice.)

Pass the mixture through a sieve or food mill fitted with a fine disk. While the sauce is still warm, stir in the softened butter and blend until melted.

Note: This sauce may be made several days ahead and kept in the refrigerator. It also freezes well, keeping several months.

ROSY CREAM SAUCE

MAKES ABOUT 1¼ CUPS

1 cup sour cream
½ cup tomatoes, peeled, seeded,
*   drained and chopped coarse*

1 tablespoon bitters
Salt and pepper to taste

Combine all ingredients in a blender or by hand until smooth.

Note: This sauce may be prepared a day or two ahead and then whisked just prior to serving.

RÉMOULADE SAUCE

For this sauce, finely chop all the ingredients.

MAKES ABOUT 1 PINT

3 tablespoons chopped sour pickles
2 tablespoons chopped capers
1 tablespoon each chopped onion,

fresh parsley and, if available,
fresh tarragon
1½ cups mayonnaise

Combine all ingredients well and store in refrigerator until needed.

Note: Depending on the mayonnaise used and your particular taste, you might want to add a little mustard.

Adapted from *The Ritz-Carlton Cook Book and Guide to Home Entertaining* by Helen Ridley.

SHALLOT SEAFOOD SAUCE

This recipe makes an excellent sauce for oysters, but it also does nicely for other seafood.

MAKES ABOUT 1 CUP

½ cup red wine vinegar
½ cup tarragon vinegar
2 shallots, finely chopped or minced
Pinch sea salt

Sprinkling coarsely ground fresh
*   black pepper*
Dash Tabasco sauce

Combine all ingredients and mix thoroughly. Let sauce season before serving.

PLUM, OR DUCK, SAUCE

This is a very good plum sauce which came to me from Florence Lin during a wonderful series of Chinese cooking classes at New York's China Institute.

MAKES ABOUT 1 CUP

¼ cup stewed plum sauce or plum jam
¼ cup apricot preserves

¼ cup applesauce
¼ cup kumquat marmalade
1 tablespoon chili sauce

Mix well together and let blend for several days.

SZECHWAN HOT SAUCE

MAKES ½ CUP

½ cup vegetable oil
2 tablespoons cayenne

½ teaspoon Szechwan peppercorns, roasted and ground

Mix ingredients in covered jar and let sit for a week.

OREBRO SAFFRON SAUCE

This lovely sauce is a wonderful plus for most fish dishes. It adds delightful taste, velvety texture and a warm yellow color. Serve warm with terrines, hot over hot main dishes.

MAKES 1 CUP

½ cup fish stock or Court Bouillon (see recipe, page 398)
½ cup heavy cream
½ cup white wine

Large pinch powdered saffron
Salt and pepper to taste
1 stick (8 tablespoons) butter, diced

In saucepan, boil together fish stock or Court Bouillon, cream, wine and saffron until reduced by half. Taste; if more saffron is desired, add during this reduction. Season lightly with salt and pepper, remove from heat and cool for ½ minute. Then whisk in butter, a few pieces at a time, until sauce is thick and velvety.

Note: Do not plan to prepare this sauce ahead completely: reheating after butter is added will destroy its consistency. It can be prepared to the point of adding butter; then, just before serving, reheat sauce and add the butter. This last step takes only a minute or so.

COURT BOUILLON

This will do nicely for the recipes calling for court bouillon.

MAKES 2 ½ CUPS

1 pound fish bones and trimmings
1 medium carrot, sliced
1 medium onion, sliced
2 tablespoons butter
Bouquet garni of thyme, ½ bay
leaf, parsley and celery stalk

2 cups dry white wine
Salt
Freshly ground black pepper

Clean and coarsely chop the fish trimmings.

In heavy pot, sauté carrot and onion in butter for 5 minutes. Add fish bones and, bouquet garni, wine and 4 cups water, and boil for 25 minutes.

Strain, return to saucepan, and reduce to 2½ cups, or less if you want even stronger flavor. Taste and season with salt and pepper.

This Court Bouillon can be kept refrigerated for several days or can be frozen.

Note: Refreshed bottled clam juice can be used as a substitute for court bouillon if necessary. Simply bring clam juice to boil with bouquet garni, as above, and a little white wine if appropriate to recipe.

MOCK CRÈME FRAÎCHE

This is a simple crème fraîche which can be made in a food processor, blender or by hand.

MAKES 1 ⅓ CUPS

⅓ cup buttermilk

1 cup heavy cream

Blend liquids together well (in a processor about 3 seconds, using the metal blade). Put into bowl and let stand in a warm place until thickened, about 24 hours. Mix well again and store in covered jar in refrigerator until ready to use.

BASIC PASTRIES

I suppose there are as many pastries as there are famous pastry chefs, but for the purposes of this book I am including only the basic recipes you will need to complete certain of the recipes in the book and that every seasoned party giver should have at hand—a *pâte à chou* for all sorts of puffs; a *pâte brisée* for tarts, turnovers and quiches, among other things; a puff pastry, a *pâté en croûte* pastry and a firm cream cheese pastry, plus a favorite pie dough—and a few alternatives I can't resist sharing, including a very nice pastry cream and a dorure.

Some of the party recipes are self-contained with their pastry recipes right at hand; others refer you to the proper reference page. A complete list of all pastry recipes appears in the index.

I don't consider myself a master pastry maker but I have found a few things that seem to make it easier: work as quickly as possible (when hands get hot this spoils pastry); keep the ingredients as cold as possible (one reason why rolling on marble works so well); roll between sheets of wax paper (cuts down on contact and mess), and use a dusting can for sprinkling flour (easier and neater). Maybe most important: don't let it scare you; practice makes perfect!

PÂTE À CHOU

This is an excellently versatile pastry for all sorts of puffs. With slightly different seasoning it can become cream puffs, cheese puffs, shrimp puffs, even dumplings or gnocchi.

MAKES ENOUGH FOR ABOUT 5 DOZEN LITTLE OR 2 DOZEN MEDIUM PUFFS

1 cup water
1 stick (8 tablespoons) sweet butter, cut into pieces

¼ teaspoon salt
1 cup flour
3 to 5 large eggs

In heavy saucepan, bring water, butter and salt to boil over high heat. Reduce heat to moderate, add flour all at once and beat with wooden paddle until mixture leaves sides of pan and forms ball.

Transfer mixture to bowl, and with electric mixer beat in 3 of the eggs, 1 at a time, beating well each time. The batter should be stiff enough to hold soft peaks. If necessary, thin batter further by adding additional eggs 1 at a time, teaspoonful by teaspoonful, beating each lightly before adding. Dough should be shiny.

The dough should be used while still warm; it stiffens as it cools and gets hard to handle.

Pâte â Chou can be frozen. To use, bring to room temperature and then heat over hot water until pastry is warm, not hot, through: if too hot, pastry may not puff properly.

Note: This pastry can be varied to fit the purpose. For puffs to be filled with such savories as shrimp, ham, cheese and the like, you might want a little spicier flavor: simply add a large pinch of pepper and perhaps a small pinch of nutmeg or other seasoning of your choice. For a sweeter, dessert-type puff, omit the salt and add a teaspoon of sugar in its place.

PUFF PASTRY

This is the puff pastry I like to make in my food processor. If your processor is small, make it in two batches.

MAKES 2 ½ POUNDS

1 pound butter	*1 teaspoon salt*
1 pound flour	*1 cup ice water*

Cut the butter into tablespoon-sized pieces and distribute evenly around processor bowl. Cover the butter with the flour and salt. Process by pulsing about 15 times—the butter should be in small well-floured pieces. Add the ice water in 3 lots, pulsing the processor with each addition. The pastry should then resemble crumbs.

Turn pastry out on floured pastry cloth and with floured hands gather the pastry into rough rectangle. Then roll out with floured rolling pin into a rectangle whose width is half its length. Do not allow the butter to show through the flour; pat more flour over any visible butter spots.

Fold the pastry in thirds making 3 layers. Turn so that the open end is facing you and roll out again to a rectangle and again fold in thirds. Wrap and chill for 30 minutes.

Repeat the folding and turning process four more times, chilling the pastry at least 30 minutes between each folding.

The pastry is now ready to use.

PÂTE BRISÉE

This is a good basic French pastry dough for pies, tarts, quiches and turnovers. Sometimes it seems every chef has his or her own favorite (or favorites). This is one of several I use.

AMPLE FOR AN 8- TO 10-INCH TART SHELL OR, DEPENDING ON SIZE, 1 TO 1½ DOZEN INDIVIDUAL TARTLETS

1½ cups flour
6 tablespoons cold sweet butter, cut into bits
2 tablespoons cold vegetable shortening

¼ teaspoon salt
3 tablespoons ice water

In a large bowl, blend the flour, butter, vegetable shortening and salt until mixture resembles meal. Add ice water and toss until water is completely incorporated. Form the dough into ball and knead lightly with heel of hand against smooth surface for a few seconds (this to distribute fat evenly). Again form dough into ball and dust with flour; wrap in wax paper and chill at least an hour before using.

Note: This dough may be frozen and then used later as needed. This is good to know if you want to double the recipe: use one half and save the other.

RICH TART PASTRY

This is an excellent tart pastry from Paula Peck.

MAKES 1 (9-INCH) TART OR 2 DOZEN TARTLET SHELLS

2 cups sifted flour
3 tablespoons sugar
1½ sticks (12 tablespoons) butter, at room temperature

½ teaspoon salt
2 teaspoons grated lemon rind
3 hard-cooked egg yolks, mashed
2 raw egg yolks

Place flour in a bowl. Make well in the center. Add all ingredients to well. (Butter should not be chilled, nor soft enough to be oily.)

With fingertips, make a paste of center ingredients, gradually incorporating flour to form a smooth, firm ball of dough. Work quickly so butter does not become oily. When sides of bowl are left clean, the pastry is finished. Wrap it in wax paper and chill until firm enough to roll.

When time to roll, roll between sheets of wax paper.

Note: To make a less fragile and crisper pastry, substitute 2 egg whites for the raw egg yolks.

CREAM CHEESE PASTRY

This is an alternative cream cheese pastry using white flour (my favorite is the whole wheat version I use for the Cocktail Quiches on page 205). It is also firm enough to hold its shape nicely.

MAKES AMPLE FOR 30 (2-INCH) TURNOVERS OR SINGLE CRUST FOR A 9-INCH PIE

1 cup sifted flour
1 stick (8 tablespoons) butter or margarine

1 (3-ounce) package cream cheese

Place flour in bowl and work in butter or margarine and cream cheese with pastry blender or fingers. Form into a roll when well blended. Wrap in wax paper and chill several hours or overnight until stiff enough to roll out.

Note: This pastry can be easily assembled in electric mixer, adding flour last. If using a food processor, pulse butter and cream cheese. Then slowly add flour until a ball is formed.

MAX'S PASTRY

This is a "never-fail" all-purpose pastry recipe for use in the food processor. Note that the salt is replaced by sugar for a dessert pastry. This is a *pâte brisée* type pastry and especially nice for tarts, quiches and turnovers. Note, too, that it uses no eggs—nice when baking for non-egg eaters.

MAKES AMPLE FOR 1 (8- TO 10-INCH) TART SHELL OR 36 INDIVIDUAL TARTLET SHELLS

1½ cups flour
Pinch salt (1 tablespoon sugar for dessert pastry)
1 stick (8 tablespoons) sweet butter, in 1-ounce chunks

1 tablespoon cold Crisco or other vegetable shortening
2½ to 3 tablespoons ice water

Put flour and salt or sugar into food processor bowl fitted with steel blade. Add butter chunks and shortening. Process until mixture resembles cornmeal. With machine running, add ice water until mixture forms ball (approximately 50 pulses).

Wrap in plastic wrap and chill for at least an hour before using.

Note: This dough can also be made and then frozen until needed.

ANGELA'S SWEET PASTRY DOUGH

A young baker of my acquaintance uses this combination when she wants a slightly sweeter *pâte brisée.* You might like to try it.

MAKES 45 (2-INCH) INDIVIDUAL SHELLS OR 15 (4½-INCH) TART SHELLS

2½ cups flour
2 sticks (½ pound) butter or ⅗ margarine to ⅖ butter, softened and cut into 1-inch chunks (see Note below)

½ cup sugar
1 egg, beaten
1 teaspoon vanilla

Blend flour, shortening/butter, sugar and egg together, blending well (in food processor this can all be done at once). Add vanilla and blend again quickly. Form dough into ball (processor will do this for you) and proceed as with other dough.

Note: I find the Country Morning margarine/butter blend works well for this if you want to cut down on the butter a bit.

PASTRY FOR PÂTÉ EN CROÛTE

This is a sturdy pastry as it must hold up well. At the same time it must be flexible enough to wrap easily without cracking.

AMPLE FOR A LARGE PÂTÉ

4 cups flour
1 teaspoon salt
10 tablespoons butter or lard, chilled and cubed

2 small eggs, chilled
7 tablespoons cold water (approximately)

Sift the flour and salt together in a large mixing bowl. Add the butter or lard and cut into flour with a knife until the mixture has the consistency of bread crumbs. (Or combine flour, salt and butter in the bowl of a food processor and use on/off switch to cut fat into flour.) Add the eggs to the mixture and work with a fork (or on/off switch of processor) until incorporated into flour. Add cold water, one tablespoon at a time, blending with a fork (or processor blade) until mixture begins to stick together. (Do not allow dough to form a ball as it overworks the gluten in the flour and toughens the pastry.

Gather the dough into a ball. On a lightly floured pastry board or marble slab, knead the dough lightly with the heel of the hand, pushing dough down and away from you gently about 6 times. (This blending of fat and flour is called *briser,* to break, in French.) Again gather the dough into a ball, wrap in plastic wrap and chill for at least 1 hour before rolling out. Dough will keep in the refrigerator for several days.

LARD PASTRY DOUGH

An excellent lard pastry dough.

MAKES AMPLE FOR 8- OR 9-INCH PIE

2 cups flour	*1 teaspoon salt*
4 tablespoons lard, chilled and cut into bits	*¼ to ⅓ cup ice water*
3 tablespoons cold sweet butter, cut into bits	

In a large bowl blend the flour, lard, butter and salt until the mixture resembles meal. Gradually add enough ice water to form a dough, tossing until the water is fully incorporated. Form the dough into a ball, flatten slightly and chill, wrapped in wax paper, for at least 1 hour before using.

ANGELA'S PIE DOUGH

This is another of Angela's good recipes. She is such a wonderful baker that I share it with you. Lard makes the best pie dough. You'll need to increase her amounts if you have a large pie in mind.

MAKES 12 TO 15 PETITE SHELLS OR 1 (10-INCH) PIE CRUST

1 cup flour	*2 to 4 tablespoons water*
⅓ cup shortening (lard preferred)	*Pinch salt*

Blend all together well and chill slightly before rolling out.

FILLINGS AND FROSTINGS

PASTRY CREAM

This pastry cream, from Dione Lucas, is the one I usually use.

**ENOUGH FOR 1 (10-INCH) TART OR
12 (3¼-INCH) TARTLETS**

*1 whole egg, plus 1 yolk and 2
    whites*
3 tablespoons flour
3 tablespoons sugar
Tiny pinch salt

*2 tablespoons (2 envelopes)
    unflavored gelatin*
1 cup milk
1 cup heavy cream, whipped

Put whole egg and extra yolk in bowl with flour, sugar and salt. Beat with wire whisk until mixture is well blended and frothy. Stir in gelatin.

Bring milk to boil in small pan. Slowly pour into egg mixture, stirring. Transfer whole mixture to saucepan and heat over low heat, stirring with wooden spoon until it thickens. Immediately remove from heat, put over bowl of ice and continue to stir until mixture cools a bit.

Beat egg whites to soft peaks and stir into pastry cream. Then gradually, spoonful by spoonful, beat mixture into the whipped cream. If runny, chances are milk wasn't boiling (use as sauce and start over).

Variation: For cream puffs or eclairs one of my favorite variations is to add about 2 tablespoons Framboise (raspberry brandy) to the Pastry Cream (at the very end) and then use another 2 tablespoons Framboise, blended over low heat with 1 cup currant jelly, as a glaze.

DORURE

A sealant used to brush or seal certain pastries.

MAKES SMALL AMOUNT

1 egg yolk　　　　　　　　　　*1 tablespoon milk or water*

Blend together well and apply with pastry brush as recipe requires. Recipe may be doubled or more for large baking chores.

MOCHA BUTTER CREAM

ENOUGH TO FILL ABOUT 25 SMALL CORNETS OR TO FROST 12 CUPCAKES

2 egg yolks　　　　　　　　　　*1½ tablespoons rum, preferably*
⅔ cup confectioners' sugar　　　　*dark*
2 tablespoons powdered instant coffee　*1 stick (8 tablespoons) sweet butter*

Put the egg yolks into a heatproof (nonaluminum) bowl. Gradually add the sugar, beating until the mixture is a pale creamy yellow. Set the bowl over simmering water and continue to beat until the mixture has thickened and is sticky. Dissolve the instant coffee in the rum. Blend thoroughly into the egg mixture and remove from heat. Add the butter by bits, waiting until each piece has been thoroughly incorporated before adding the next. Refrigerate to firm the cream, but not enough to harden it completely.

ORANGE BUTTER CREAM

ENOUGH TO FILL ABOUT 25 SMALL CORNETS OR TO FROST 12 CUPCAKES

1 large thick-skinned orange　　　*2 to 3 tablespoons orange liqueur*
2 egg yolks　　　　　　　　　　*or Benedictine*
¼ cup confectioners' sugar
1 stick (8 tablespoons) sweet butter,
softened

Grate the orange peel into a bowl (be sure to grate only the orange portion; the white will be bitter). Add the egg yolks. Then add the sugar in small quantities, beating until the mixture is a pale creamy yellow.

Blend in the butter. Finish the cream by adding the orange liqueur or Benedictine—and wait for the lovely aroma! Refrigerate to firm.

CHOCOLATE BUTTER CREAM

ENOUGH TO FILL ABOUT 25 SMALL CORNETS OR CUPCAKES

5 ounces German's sweet chocolate, broken into small pieces
3 tablespoons strong coffee

5 tablespoons sweet butter
2 tablespoons orange liqueur or Benedictine

Put the chocolate and the coffee in the top of a double boiler, set over simmering water, and stir until smooth. Remove from heat and stir in the butter by bits, waiting until each piece of butter has been thoroughly incorporated before adding the next. Add the liqueur and refrigerate to firm.

A FEW MORE PUNCHES

I guess the White Wine Fruit Punch in the Country Wedding party is my favorite all-round punch. That is certainly the one I use most, but of course it doesn't serve for every occasion. Though you will have found other suggestions—for both alcoholic and nonalcoholic beverages—as you have made your way through the book (see the index for a complete listing), here are a few more you might like to try.

WATERMELON PUNCH

This is a lovely refreshing punch with a subtle combination of flavors. When served in the watermelon shell, it makes an attractive centerpiece.

MAKES 28 (4-OUNCE) SERVINGS

1 large watermelon	*2 quarts limeade, made fresh or*
2 cups melon balls	*from frozen concentrate*
	1 quart vodka

Cut a thick slice horizontally from the top of the watermelon. Scoop out at least 2 cups melon balls, or make up a combination of watermelon, cantaloupe and honeydew—especially nice, and more colorful. Scoop out remaining melon meat and reserve. Refrigerate the melon shell and balls.

Press the reserved melon meat through cheesecloth until you have 2 cups juice. Combine juice, limeade and vodka, and chill.

When ready to serve, place watermelon shell (it's fun to serate the edge —jagged-tooth fashion—all the way around if you have time) in a large tray or bowl of crushed ice. Pour vodka mixture into shell over large block of ice and add melon balls.

CRANAPPLE PUNCH

Another refreshing punch with just enough spice to give it a nice zip. If you prefer, a bottle of a good moderately priced red burgundy could do no harm.

SERVES 25 TO 30

1 quart cranapple juice
1 (10-ounce) can frozen lemonade
Dash cinnamon

Dash allspice
1 quart ginger ale

Mix the fruit juice, lemonade and spices well over the ice in your punch bowl, adding the ginger ale just prior to serving.

MIMOSA PUNCH

MAKES 3 ½ QUARTS

6 cups freshly squeezed orange juice, chilled
1½ cups orange liqueur
2 bottles (25.4 ounces) Champagne,

sparkling Blanc de blanc or other sparkling white wine
Orange slices
Strawberries

In a large punch bowl, combine the orange juice and the liqueur. Pour in the Champagne and float the orange slices and strawberries on top. Serve immediately.

HARVARD '45 MILK PUNCH

This milk punch makes an excellent switch from the sometimes just too sweet and too rich eggnog. This one—which can be spiked up or down to your taste —is especially good late Christmas morn. Somehow the wrapping paper doesn't rattle quite so fiercely with a glass of this in your hand.

MAKES 2 TO 3 QUARTS

2 quarts milk
1 pint coffee ice cream
Sugar to taste

2 parts bourbon to 1 part rum
Freshly grated nutmeg

Mix the first 4 ingredients in the order given. This can be done by hand or in a blender bit by bit. The liquor to be added is to your taste, keeping the proportions as given here. The punch should be smooth and pale cream in color. Sprinkle with nutmeg when ready to serve.

Note: I have used blended whiskey instead of bourbon and no one seemed the wiser.

FISH HOUSE PUNCH

This is an old recipe written out in wineglasses rather than ounces or cups. A wineglass is approximately 2 ounces.

AMPLE FOR 8

2 tablespoons bitters
2½ wineglasses lemon juice
4 tablespoons Simple Syrup (see
  below)
4 wineglasses peach brandy
4 wineglasses Cognac

2 wineglasses rum
3 pints cold water
Mix together well in order given
and pour over ice block. Serve
promptly.

Note: To make simple syrup, combine 2 parts water with 1 part sugar and boil for 2 minutes. Some newer recipes for this punch replace the tap water with sparkling water.

YANKEE EGGNOG

This is a delicious eggnog which comes to me from one of our Vermont friends—and from his forebears before him. In Vermont we age it a bit in a handy snowbank. If you must, I suppose a refrigerator would do as well.

MAKES ABOUT 2 GALLONS

1½ dozen eggs, separated
1½ boxes confectioners' sugar, or
  less to taste
½ gallon whiskey
½ gallon milk

1½ quarts light cream
⅘ quart (7.5 litres) light rum
1½ teaspoons salt
Freshly grated nutmeg, for dusting
  (optional)

Beat egg yolks very well, and then, in order, slowly add sugar, ¾ of the whiskey, milk, cream and rum. Mix well and add remaining whiskey to taste (it will strengthen with age). Beat salt and egg whites together until stiff and combine with whiskey-rum mixture.

Age, chilled, at least a week before serving. To serve, dust with nutmeg if desired.

Note: If you are expecting to do a fair amount of holiday entertaining, make several batches of this at once. It will keep beautifully throughout the entire holiday season—just be sure to keep it chilled. By the same token, if even this is too much, the recipe can easily be halved.

GLÖGG

Just "the right stuff" for a dark, dank day's gathering or December 14th (St. Cecilia's Day).

MAKES 1 GALLON

2 cups water
1½ cups sugar, carmelized
Spice bag of 5 allspice, 9 or 10 cloves, 1 piece fresh ginger, 2 or 3 bay leaves (or mixture of your choice)
1 cup raisins
Peeling of one orange
Several cinnamon sticks
1 gallon everyday good red wine
Cognac or whiskey to taste
¼ cup blanched almonds (optional)

Heat water and slowly add carmelized sugar. Add spice bag and simmer mixture at least 30 minutes. Add raisins and simmer another 20 minutes. Add orange peel and cinnamon sticks, simmer again another 5 or 10 minutes. Add wine and simmer slowly about 15 minutes before serving. Taste before serving, and, if wanted, add Cognac or whiskey to taste for smoothness.

Serve in punch cups, with a few raisins and, if you like, blanched almonds at the bottom of each glass.

A FEW WORDS ON CHEESE

Cheese plays such an important role in party planning and hors d'oeuvre making I didn't want to end this book without a little supplementary information on the cheeses I have used in the recipes for the party menus and recommended for the various cheese platters. Here is a little background on the purchase, care and serving of selected cheeses—both those given in the book and a few other favorites of mine you might want to try. Following that is a listing of many cheeses by type and origin.

For those readers particularly interested there are a number of good books on cheese. I have found Barbara Ensrud's 1981 *Pocket Guide to Cheese* and Vivienne Marquis' and Patricia Haskell's somewhat earlier *The Cheese Book* especially useful. (The "Type and Origin" listing here is in large part drawn from one in *The Dione Lucas Book of French Cooking*—an excellent book in many directions.)

As Clifton Fadiman once said, "Cheese is milk's leap toward immortality." Get on your seven-league boots and enjoy!

Purchasing. Although many cheeses come already packaged, most cheese shops and many special cheese departments in other stores keep cheese wheels and wedges from which you can sample before buying. Unless you know clearly what you want, look for one of these stores so you can sample new varieties before purchasing. And even if you do know, it often pays to sample first. Goat cheeses, for instance, are quite different: unless you know them well, it is important to taste them before buying. Roquefort is another example: it comes in varying degrees of saltiness, so again tasting is most helpful.

As you consider the cheeses check the packages or rinds to see what type you are looking at and to ascertain its country of origin. Don't buy anything that doesn't look attractive to you. It isn't just aesthetics: usually cheeses that look good are good. Cheddar and other firm cheeses, for instance, need not appear moist but if they are heavily cracked or show white flecks skip them. Roquefort, on the other hand, should appear moist and should not be gray or show blackish streaks. The soft cheeses should feel pleasantly plump.

Camembert and Brie should fill their wooden boxes and be flat on top, not concave, and of course should be soft, white and glossy. With all these, if you have a good cheesemonger his or her advice can be a great help.

When experimenting buy small amounts so you can try the cheeses out in the privacy of your own kitchen before incurring the expense of a large piece. And no matter what cheese you choose be sure it is well wrapped before you take it from the store. Don't buy cheeses that have not been kept covered with a tight plastic film or from a case where strong and mild cheeses are kept side by side or near other strong foods.

Storing. Most newly purchased cheese should be kept wrapped in the refrigerator. Hard cheeses will keep longer than soft but both will keep well, at least for a while, if properly wrapped, especially if the wrapping paper is changed often. Rewrap most freshly purchased cheese in plastic wrap and then aluminum foil and keep it refrigerated. (To ensure freshness, some people keep cheeses wrapped in a cloth dampened with a solution of ½ cup water, 1 teaspoon vinegar and ½ teaspoon salt. I have never done this; perhaps we eat it too quickly.)

Blues are different: they require air. Wrap them in a damp cloth and cover them with a dome of some sort. This will keep them moist and still allow air to circulate.

Whole soft cheeses should stay in their containers until shortly before serving. They should be eaten as soon as possible: even refrigeration, though it will help, will not hold them from ripening.

The double and triple cream cheeses hold well. The high cream content seems to make the difference.

And do remember: don't panic if a little mold appears on your cheese; it is quite harmless and can be simply scraped away.

Freezing. Some cheese freezes well (for instance, I have had good success with Brie, Cheddar and Parmesan). Others do not. Still others freeze well when cooked, for example in a quiche Lorraine or cheese sauce. If there is any chance you expect to have leftover cheese to freeze, ask your cheese merchant whether or not the particular type you wish to buy will freeze successfully.

Serving. No matter which cheeses you select, they should be served attractively and with attention to what complements them. Since most cheeses contain a good deal of salt, most blend well with the plain unsalted crackers: I especially like Bremner, Jacobs and others of the water biscuits, but thinly sliced French and Italian breads are good too. The highly flavored cheeses, such as Roquefort, herbed Boursin, and Danish blue, match well with a Russian black bread or a good pumpernickel. Fresh fruit is another excellent accompaniment.

If serving cheese on a cheese board or marble serving tray, fresh grape leaves or oak leaves in season add an attractive touch—and of course strawberries and the triple cream cheeses are made for each other.

Some Popular Cheeses by Type and Origin

Type	Name	Current Origin
Hard (firm/almost brittle)	Parmesan	Italy: Parmigiano
	Cheddar	U.S.A.: Vermont, Wisconsin and other states
		Canada (Black Diamond)
		England: many locales
	Monterey Jack	U.S.A.: California
Firm (solid but not crumbly or brittle)	Comté (Gruyère)	France: Jura
	Beaufort	France: Savoy
	Edam	Holland: north
	Gouda	Holland: south
	Provolone	Italy: Palermo
Blue (firm to creamy, with blue fissures)	Roquefort	France: Aveyron
	Bleu de Bresse	France: Lyon
	Gorgonzola	Italy: Cremona
	Stilton	England
Semisoft (soft but not runny)	Port du Salut	France: Mayenne
	Morbier	France: Franche-Comté
	Munster	France: Alsace
	Reblochon	France: Savoy
	Fontina	Italy: Val d'Aosta

Type	Name	Current Origin
Soft (creamy or runny)	Brie	France: Meaux
	Camembert	France: Normandy
	Pont l'Évêque	France: Normandy
	Vacherin Mont d'Or	Switzerland: Fribourg, Vaud

FRESH CHEESES

Type	Name	Current Origin
Simple cream (less than 50 percent fat)	Ricotta	Italy and U.S.A.
	Mozzarella	Italy and U.S.A.
	Cottage and Pot Cheese	U.S.A.
Double cream (60 percent fat)	Chèvre Ste. Maure*	France
	St. Marcellin*	France
	Caprice des Dieux	France
Triple cream (75 percent fat)	Brillat-Savarin	France
	Explorateur	France
	Boursault	France
	Boursin	France
	Rondelé	U.S.A.
Chèvre (goat)	Montrachet	France: Burgundy
	Bucheron	France: Poitou

*All or partial goat cheese.

ALL ABOUT NUTS—OR ALMOST

I have used nuts so often in this book—both in recipes and as side dishes—I wanted to share some further background on these tasty bites. I hope it will be helpful.

Equivalents

> 5½ ounces nutmeats equal approximately 1 cup.
> 1 pound nutmeats equals 4 cups coarsely ground.
> 1 pound nuts in shells equals ½ pound shelled nuts.
>
> *Almonds:* ⅘ pound unshelled equals 1 cup chopped.
>
> *Peanuts:* 1½ pounds unshelled equal 3 cups chopped.
>
> *Pecans:* 2½ pounds unshelled equal 3 cups chopped.
>
> *Walnuts:* 2½ pounds unshelled equal 4 cups chopped.

Miscellany

Nuts in shells should keep up to 6 months. Shelled nuts should be kept frozen if not used fairly quickly.

Nuts slice and shred best when warm and moist.

If pecan shells are hard to crack, pour boiling water over them first; then cool.

Do not use meat grinder for nuts: result will be mushy and greasy instead of dry and crunchy.

TO BLANCH
> *Almonds, pistachios and English walnuts:* Shell and cover with boiling water. Let stand 2 minutes; drain. Put in cold water; drain again. Rub off skins and dry thoroughly.

Filberts: Same as above, only let stand 6 minutes. Remove skins with sharp knife.

Brazil nuts: Heat thoroughly in slow oven before cracking. Then proceed as for almonds.

Butternuts: Cover whole nuts with boiling water. Let stand 10 minutes and proceed as for almonds.

TO TOAST

Use blanched almonds and filberts; raw peanuts, with skins removed; whole pecan and walnut meats. For each cup nuts, heat ½ cup olive oil or butter in small frying pan. Put nuts in pan to cover bottom and stir until brown. Remove with slotted spoon and drain on brown paper. Avoid cooking too long; nuts will darken.

TO SALT

Sprinkle toasted nuts while hot.

PEELING CHESTNUTS

Chestnuts can be peeled day before using, but do not use any with dark spots on the meat. On rounded sides of each nut, with small sharp paring (or chestnut) knife, make a long X cut deep enough to go through outer covering and underneath brown skin. Cover with water and slowly bring to boil (takes about 15 to 20 minutes). When water begins to boil, remove from heat, keeping nuts in hot water. Test one, holding with potholder; peel and shell should slip off easily. Keep nuts in hot water until their turn to be peeled. If some are difficult, boil an additional few minutes.

A NEAT NUT TRICK

For salad dressing, soak fresh walnuts in walnut or vegetable oil prior to making dressing; drain nuts, using oil to make dressing and adding nuts to salad when ready.

HOW MUCH FOR HOW MANY

GUIDELINES FOR 100 PEOPLE

Knowing what quantities to plan for large parties can be difficult, especially as so few of us have experience with this type of food preparation except on rare occasions. Perhaps this partial listing taken in part from *The Fannie Farmer Cookbook* and in part from experience will help. I hope so. The meat, vegetable and fruit amounts are for main portions; using these foods for hors d'oeuvre purposes will stretch them considerably further.

Foodstuff	*Amount Needed*
Coffee	2½ pounds
Tea	½ pound
Coffee cream	6 pints
Whipped cream	2 quarts
Butter	2 pounds, cut in squares
Ice cream	3 gallons
Meatloaf	18 pounds
Roast pork	30 pounds
Roast beef or veal	40 pounds
Roast chicken or turkey	60 pounds
Baked ham	30 pounds
Potatoes	35 pounds
Salad dressing	2 quarts
Peas (frozen)	10 (10-ounce) packages
(canned)	3 No. 10 cans
Apples (for applesauce)	2 pecks
Applesauce (canned)	3 No. 10 cans

OTHER HANDY GUIDELINES

12-pound ham serves 20.
20-pound turkey (or equal amount chicken) serves 20 generously.
4 pounds chicken equal 4 cups diced chicken.
1 gallon ice cream equals 30 scoop-sized portions.
12 quarts punch equal 96 glasses punch.
1 gallon punch serves 20.

HIRING A CATERER

These are important points to keep in mind when making use of a caterer to ensure no misunderstandings—and a good party!

It's important first, of course, to find a good caterer. Word of mouth is most helpful, but failing that, call the local paper, clubs, churches, etc. You want to be sure the caterer knows and serves good food and is dependable.

The arrangements will vary with the occasion but they should be clear no matter how small or large a party you are hiring for. If at all possible, arrange a personal interview beforehand and meet in the space where the party will be given so specific plans can be laid. You should expect to pay for this interview even if the arrangements don't work out. In most cases, a contract is wise; expect to pay up to 50 percent in advance against costs for food, etc. It should be made clear just what service is involved (a bartender is a must for 25 or more, etc.), whether someone will be provided to clean up, and just what equipment is included.

Remember that a relationship with a good caterer is much like a family relationship. Although caterers are experts, they should also be willing, and even anxious, to try to accommodate your suggestions. So don't hesitate to ask for special dishes or that the caterer meet any special dietary requirements. Caterers want to please too.

If your life leads you to be involved with frequent catering, it is a good idea to keep some sort of record of each occasion—making note of the caterer, the arrangements, and rating the various dishes served. You will find this a handy file to have.

INDEX

A

Almond(s):
    french-fried, 252
    orange dip, 283
Anchovies, Swedish, 330
Angela's Pie Dough, 404
Angela's Sweet Pastry Dough, 403
Apple:
    and blueberry tart, 121
    cake, 312
    crisp, 114
    and date tea loaf, 93
    filling for phyllo tarts, 310
Applesauce Wedding Cake, 151
Apricot(s):
    filling for phyllo tarts, 310
    pecan bread, 100
    stuffed, fresh, 72
    walnut bars, 82
Artichoke Squares, 371
Asparagus and Ham Rolls, 331
Aspic, tomato, 113
Avocado:
    dip, 211
    dip, curried, 226
    guacamole, 133
    soup, cold, 43

B

Baba Ghanoush, 69
Bacon:
    water chestnuts in, 109
    wrapped dates, 377
Baklava, 179

Balls:
    blue cheese, 221
    bourbon, 196
    broccoli, 118
    codfish, 319
    codfish, spicy, 222
    date, 75
    potato, spicy, 224
    praline rum, 379
    shrimp and crabmeat, curried, 211
    Viennese, 343
Banana Raita, 60
Barbecued pork, Paul's, 371
Barbecues, 116, 119–120
Bars. See Cookies and Bars
Basil dressing, 388
Bean soup, black, 30
Beard's (James) Shrimp Sauce, 273
Béarnaise Sauce, 274
Bed Book of Eating and Drinking, The
    (Wright), 255
Beef:
    chipped, in Swedish rye round, 209
    fondue, 127
    in pâté maison, 365
    taco filling, 135
    tenderloin, 273
    tenderloin, and French bread dip, 356
    tourtière, with pork, 163
    in water chestnut meatballs, 368
Beer, 41
Beer Puffs with Crabmeat, 368
Beignets, French, 357
Belgian endive, platter with peapods and
    tomatoes, 191

Benne Chicken Fingers, 191
Biscuits:
    beaten, tiny, 189
    ham and cheese, 306
    hot, with herbed butter, 113
    Nancy Drews, 15
    water, 413
Black bean soup, Senate, 30
Blanching, of nuts, 416
Bloody Marys, 35, 36
Blue cheese, 413, 414
    ball, 221
    dip, 133
    spread or dip, 391
Blueberry:
    and apple tart, 121
    muffins, 39
Bluefish Mousse, 283
Bolillos, 49
Bouchée:
    crabmeat, 193
    lobster, 192
    lobster mousse, 274
Bouillon, Court, 398
Bourbon:
    balls, 196
    cakes, petite, 378
Boursin, 146
Box:
    breakfast, 298, 301, 312–314
    lunch, 297, 299–312
Bread:
    apricot-pecan, 100
    biscuits, beaten, 189
    for cheese, 413
    Greek Christmas, 177
    lemon, 99
    pumpkin, 31
    rings, sweet, Greek, 176
    sticks, cinnamon, 101
    Swedish coffee, 334
Breakfast: boxed, 298, 301, 312–314
    Southwestern Sporting, 34, 41–50
Bridge Nibbles, 353
Broccoli:
    balls, 118
    mousse, 149
    and scallop terrine, 10
Brown bag:
    breakfasts, 298, 301, 312–314
    lunches, 297, 299–312

Brownies:
    butterscotch, 32
    chocolate, 122
Brunch, 35–36, 41
    New England Sunday, 33, 35–40
    Southwestern Sporting Breakfast, 34,
    41–50
Buffet, for gala champagne evening,
    359–380
Burgundy Sauce, 355
Bus meals, 301–302
Butter:
    cookies, 150
    herbed, 113
Buttercream:
    chocolate, 407
    mocha, 406
    orange, 406
Butterscotch Brownies, 32

C

Café Brûlot, 255
Cake:
    apple, 312
    beignets, French, 357
    bourbon, petite, 378
    cheese, Lillian's, 115
    cheese, miniature, 235
    chocolate, one-pan, 27
    fruit, Kitty's, 311
    poppyseed, 73
    pound, old-fashioned, 197
    Queen Mother, 252
    Scot's Seed, 94
    sponge, Ritz, 236
Cakes, wedding:
    applesauce, 151
    Gramercy Park, 264
    guidelines for, 153–154
    Heidi's Victorian, 280
    Jonathan's Dream, 276
    old-fashioned daisy, 286
Calendula petals:
    in herb dip, 389
    in yogurt dressing or dip, 390
Camembert, melted with almonds, 376
Candies:
    praline rum balls, 379
    pralines, Creole, 357
Cantonese Marinade, 393

Caper and Mustard Dressing, 390
Caponata, 68
Cardamom Cookies, 83
Caribou (alcool), 159
Carolina Eggnog, 186
Carolina Whiskey Nutcake, 198
Carrots:
    gingered, 57
    with prunes pâté, 374
Casserole, zucchini, 112
Cassis Sherbet, 288
Caterers, hiring, 419
Caviar:
    and egg dip, 329
    and pâté pie, 212
    pie, 190
Cebiche, 366
Celery hearts, marinated, 174
Champagne, 361, 362
    chicken in, 284
    party, 359–380
Cheddar cheese, in gorgonzola cheese
    roll, 376
Cheese:
    boursin, 146
    cake. *See* Cheese cake
    crescents, 73
    Edam, stuffed, 323
    Feta, 166
    fingers, sesame, 117
    and ham biscuits, 306
    Kasseri, 166
    and pistachio roll, 110
    puffs, hot, 12
    roll, gorgonzola, 376
    roll, paprika, 109
    and spinach triangles (Tiropitas), 169
    straws, Williamsburg, 187
    See also Cream cheese; Dips;
    Dressings
Cheese, about, 412–415
    freezing, 413
    purchasing, 412–413
    serving, 413
    soft, 413
    storing, 413
    type and origin listing, 414–415
Cheese Book, The (Marquis; Haskell), 412
Cheese cake:
    Lillian's, 115
    miniature, 235

Cherry, filling for phyllo tarts, 310
Cherry tomatoes, stuffed with crab or tuna
    mousse, 70
Chestnuts, 417
Chicago Cucumber Soup, 119
Chick peas, in Hummus, 71
Chicken:
    barbecued, 119, 120
    in champagne, 284
    filling, in spring rolls, 307
    fingers, Benne, 191
    fondue, 127
    marinated strips, 58
    salad with sesame and pasta, 306
    southern baked, 111
    wings, cocktail, 263
    wings, fruited, 224
Children's parties, 125–126
Chile-Queso Squares, 44
Chili con Queso, 81
Chili sauces, 135–136
Chimichangas, 46
Chinese:
    hot-sour soup, 302
    meatballs, 321
    spiced nuts, 28
    spring rolls with shrimp and chicken
    filling, 307
    sweet nuts, 13
Chocolate:
    brownies, 122
    butter cream, 407
    cake, one-pan, 27
    chip and oatmeal cookies, 310
    diamonds, 345
    éclair filling, 346
    truffles, 378
Chowder:
    clam, 29
    corn, 111
Chutney, 60
    and curry spread, 14
    dressing, 389
Christmas Eve party, 157, 159–165
Cider, hot, 84
Cinnamon:
    sticks (bread), 101
    toast, 234
Clam(s):
    Borofsky, with mushrooms, 223
    chowder Zelda, 29

Clam(s) *(Continued)*
    and oyster raw bar, 353
    spread, hot, 323
Cocktail party, 201–215
Cocktail sauce:
    raw bar, 354
    Ritz, 223
Codfish:
    balls, 319
    balls, spicy, 222
Compote, baked fruit, 40
Connoisseurs' Handbook of California Wines,
    The (Olken; Singer; Roby), 337
Cookies and Bars:
    apricot walnut, 82
    brownies, chocolate, 122
    butter, 150
    cardamom, 83
    date squares, 358
    Ellen's thumbprint, 256
    Florentines, 254
    ginger, old-fashioned, 82
    Giu Ma Bang, 255
    hazelnut meringue, 234
    hermits, Helene's, 248
    Koulourakia, 176
    Kourambiedes, 175
    lemon squares, 380
    oatmeal chocolate chip, 310
    pecan Tasjes, 227
    pirouettes, 342
    raisin delights, 275
    raspberry rings, 341
    sand tarts, 341
    shortbread, Scotch, 95
    spritz, 214
    toffee, English, 226
Cooking Texas Style (Wagner; Marquez),
    131
Corn:
    chowder, 111
    dogs, 49
    on the cob, roasted, 119, 120
    sticks, 242
Cornets de Jambon, 13
Cornish Pasties, 304
Cottage cheese, dressing or dip, 387
Court Bouillon, 398
Couscous, in Tabbouleh, 70
Crab(meat):
    in beer puffs, 368
    bouchée, 193

    mousse, 70
    quiche filling, 206
    and shrimp balls, curried, 211
Crackers, 413
    Ritz, in hot clam spread, 323
Craftsbury Inn Lemon Rice, 286
Cranapple Punch, 409
Crawfish Boil, Creole, 355
Cream:
    Devonshire, 103
    pastry, 405
Cream cheese:
    about, 413, 415
    in gorgonzola cheese roll, 376
    pastry, 402
    tomatoes stuffed with, 331
Crème Fraîche, mock, 398
Creole cooking, 351, 352, 355, 357
Crescents, cheese, 73
Cretons, 161
Crudités, 67
    with egg caviar dip, 329
Cucumber(s):
    dilled, sliced, 376
    dip, Anne's, 392
    Raita, 60
    sandwiches, 97
    slices, devilish, 234
    soup, Chicago, 119
Curry(ied):
    avocado dip, 226
    and chutney spread, 14
    eggs stuffed with, 146
    lamb, 59
    party, 51–62
    shrimp and crabmeat balls, 211
Custard:
    classic soft, 102
    lemon, tarts, 179

D

Date(s):
    and apple tea loaf, 93
    bacon-wrapped, 377
    balls, 75
    balls, baked, 31
    squares, 358
    stuffed, 228
Delice d'Orient, 367
Deviled Eggs Platter, 68
Devonshire Cream, 103

Dill(ed):
    cucumbers, 376
    in Gravlax with mustard-dill sauce, 363
    and sour cream dressing or dip, 388
Dione Lucas Book of French Cooking, The, 412
Dip:
    avocado, curried, 226
    Baba Ghanoush, 69
    blue cheese, 133, 391
    chili con queso, 81
    cottage cheese, low-fat, 387
    cucumber, Anne's, 392
    dill and sour cream, 388
    egg caviar, 329
    feta walnut, 392
    French bread, for beef tenderloin, 356
    Gado Gado Sauce, 67
    ginger scallion, 321
    guacamole, 133
    herb, with calendula petals, 389
    Hummus, 71
    mustard-oil, 309
    orange-almond, 283
    sardine, 392
    seviche avocado, 211
    seviche tomato, 210
    spinach, 321
    Skordalia, 172
    Tarama Salata Lianide, 173
    Taramasalata, 173
    yogurt, 390
Dolmades, 171
Dorure, 406
Dove, breast on wild rice, 194
Dressing(s):
    basil, 388
    caper-mustard, 390
    chutney, 389
    cottage cheese, low-fat, 387
    dill and sour cream, 388
    Louis, 207
    mayonnaise, classic, 384
    mayonnaise, eggless herb, 386
    mayonnaise, garlic, 385
    mayonnaise, homemade, 384
    mayonnaise, lemon-garlic, 385
    mayonnaise, low-cal, 386
    milk and garlic, 388

    nuts in, 417
    poppy seed, 390
    vinaigrette, 383
    yogurt, 390
    yogurt, green, 391
Duck breast, in casserole, 194
Duck Sauce, 397

E

Éclairs, miniature, 346
Edam cheese, stuffed, 323
Egg(s):
    and caviar dip, 329
    in chile-queso squares, 44
    curry-stuffed, 146
    deviled, platter, 68
    hard-boiling, 68
    Huevos Rancheros, 45
    scrambled, cold, 313
Eggnog:
    Carolina, 186
    Yankee, 410
Eggplant:
    Baba Ghanoush, 69
    caponata, 68
Ellen's Thumbprint Cookies, 256
Endive, Belgian, platter with peapods and tomatoes, 191
English Toffee Bars, 226
Equivalents, for nuts, 416

F

Fannie Farmer Cookbook, The, 418
Farm Wife's Head Cheese, 163
Feta cheese, and walnut dip, 392
Figs, nut-stuffed, 180
Fine Arts Cookbook, The, 240
Fish:
    cebiche, 366
    Kedgeree, 37
    orebro saffron sauce for, 397
Fish House Punch, 410
Florentines, 254
Fondue, 125–127
    Shabu Shabu, 369
Four Great Southern Cooks, 188
Frankfurters. *See* Hot dogs
French Beignets, 357
French bread dip, for beef tenderloin, 356

From Julia Child's Kitchen, 68
Frostings:
    chocolate buttercream, 407
    mocha butter cream, 406
    orange butter cream, 406
Fruit, 251
    cake, Kitty's, 311
    compote, baked, 40
    and maple shrub, 256
    phyllo triangles, 214
    punch, Sangria-style, 132
    punch, white wine, 155
    salad melon basket, 136
    tarts, phyllo, 309
Fund-raising parties, 291–295, 299–302,
    317–318, 327–329, 337–340, 351–353,
    361–363

G

Gado Gado Sauce, 67
Game dishes, 194
Garam Masala, 54
Gazpacho, 118
German pancakes, 37
Ginger:
    cookies, old-fashioned, 82
    dipping sauce, 370
    ice cream, 62
    meatballs, 221
    and scallion dip, 321
    soy marinade, 394
    vegetables, 57
Giu Ma Bang Cookies, 255
Glaze, dorure, 406
Glögg, punch, 411
Goat cheeses, 415
Good Food from Mexico (Mulvery; Alvarez),
    131
Gorgonzola Cheese Roll, 376
Grace's Curry and Chutney Spread,
    14
*Grand Central Oyster Bar & Restaurant
    Seafood Cookbook,* 354
Grand Opening party, 217–228
Grape juice, and rhubarb punch, 228
Gravlax, 363
Greek party, 158, 166–180
Green Soup, 303
Green Yogurt Dressing, 391
Grills, 119
Guacamole, 133

H

Ham:
    and asparagus rolls, 331
    baked country-style, 147
    and cheese biscuits, 306
    cornets de jambon, 13
    in delice d'orient, canapé, 367
    deviled, in cucumbers, 234
    southern-style, Smithfield, 185, 188
    and spinach filling for quiche, 206
    and veal pâté en croûte, 243
Hard Sauce, 197
Harvard '45 Milk Punch, 409
Harvest, 65–66
Hazelnut Meringue Cookies, 234
Head Cheese, Farm Wife's, 163
Heide's Victorian Wedding Cake, 280
Helene's Hermits, 248
Herb:
    dip, with calendula petals, 389
    terrine, 24
    white wine marinade, 393
Hermits, Helene's, 248
Herring:
    gourmet, 330
    kippered, 96
    pickled salt, 320
Hibachi, 119
Hollandaise, 240
Hot dogs:
    baby, in blanket, 108
    corn dogs, 49
Hot Sauce, 136
    Szechwan, 397
Hot-Sour Soup, 302
Huevos Rancheros, 45
Hummus, 71
Hush Puppies, 43
Hush Puppy Balls, 44

I

Ice cream, ginger, 62
Indian food, curry party, 51–62
Invitation to Indian Cooking, An (Jaffrey),
    54

J

Jalapeño peppers, 136
Jambon, cornets de, 13

Japanese fondue, Shabu Shabu, 369
Jazz party, 349–358
Jelly, hot pepper, 188
Jonathan's Dream Wedding Cake, 276
Joy of Cooking, The (Rombauer; Becker),
  240, 354

K

Kasseri cheese, 166
Kedgeree, 37
Keftedes, 170
Kidney (lamb or beef), and steak pie,
  95
Kidneys (pork), in cretons, 161
Kielbasa, with barbecue sauce, 145
Kippered Herring, 96
Kirsch Sorbet, 267
Kitty's Fruitcake, 311
Koulourakia, 176
Kourambiedes, 175
Kumquats, and lichee nuts, marinated,
  227

L

Ladies' Aid Cookbook, The (Vaughan), 103
Lamb Curry, 59
Lard Pastry Dough, 404
Lemon:
    bread, 99
    cheese tarts, 195
    custard tarts, 178
    puffs, 213
    rice, Craftsbury Inn, 286
    sherbet, 287
    squares, 380
Lentil Salad, 148
Lichee nuts, and kumquats, marinated,
  227
Lillian's Cheese Cake, 115
Loaf:
    savory sandwich, 25
    tea, apple and date, 93
    tea, apricot-pecan bread, 100
    tea, lemon bread, 99
Lobster:
    mousse bouchées, 274
    salad bouchées, 192
Lorene's Swedish Coffee Bread, 334
Louis Dressing, 207
Low-cal mayonnaise, 386

Lumpfish roe, in caviar pie, 190
Lunch, boxed, 297, 299–312

M

Maple:
    fruit shrub, 256
    syrup pie, 164
Marinade(s), 393–394
    Cantonese, 393
    ginger-soy, 394
    herbed white-wine, 393
Marinated:
    Greek olives, 175
    lichee nuts and kumquats, 227
    mushrooms, 12, 375
    mushrooms, Greek-style, 174
    onions, 174
    sausages and peppers, 314
Max's Pastry, 402
Mayonnaise:
    classic, 384
    eggless, herb, 386
    garlic, 385
    homemade, 384
    lemon-garlic, 385
    low-cal, 386
Meatballs:
    Chinoise, 321
    ginger, 221
    Keftedes, 170
    paprika, 144
    Swedish, 332
    water chestnut, 368
Meats, barbecuing, 116, 119–120
Melon:
    fruit salad in basket, 136
    and prosciutto, 262
Meringue cookies, hazelnut, 234
Mexican recipes, 41–50, 129–137
Milk and Garlic Dressing, 388
Mimosa Punch, 409
Mince Tarts, hot, 196
Mocha Butter Cream, 406
Montreal Pâté de Maison, 161
Mousse:
    bluefish, 283
    broccoli, 149
    crab or tuna, 70
    lobster bouchées, 274
    salmon, 92
Muffins, blueberry, 39

Mulled wine, 84
Museum openings, 217–228
Mushroom(s):
    herb-stuffed, broiled, 80
    marinated, 12, 375
    marinated, Greek-style, 174
    nonpareil, 28
    tartlets, 232
Mustard:
    and caper dressing, 390
    dill sauce, 364
    and oil dip, 309

N

Nachos, 81
Nancy Drews, 15
New England Sunday Brunch, 33,
    35–40
Nutcake, Carolina whiskey, 198
Nuts, 416–417
    and bolts, 126
    Chinese spiced, 28
    Chinese sweet, 13
    pecans, spiced, 187

O

Oatmeal Chocolate Chip Cookies, 310
Olives, marinated Greek, 175
Onion(s):
    marinated, 174
    roasted, 119, 120
    shells, stuffed, 333
    spiced, French, 375
    tart, 79
Orange:
    almond dip, 283
    butter cream, 406
Orbec Sauce, 245
Oysters, 160
    and clam raw bar, 353
    creamed, 95

P

Pancakes, German, 37
Papaya, Turkey and Walnut Salad, 241
Paprika:
    cheese roll, 109
    meatballs, 144
Party mixes, 126

Pasta:
    and pepper salad, 149
    salad, 26
    and sesame chicken salad, 306
Pasties, Cornish, 304
Pastries:
    all-purpose, Max's, 402
    basic, 399–404
    cheese crescents, 73
    chocolate diamonds, 345
    cream cheese, 402
    cream filling, 405
    dorure, glaze, 406
    dough, Angela's sweet, 403
    eclairs, miniature, 346
    French beignets, 357
    lard dough, 404
    lemon chess tarts, 195
    lemon puffs, 213
    pâte à chou, 399
    pâte brisée, 401
    pâté en croûte, 403
    phyllo fruit triangles, 214
    pie dough, Angela's, 404
    puff, 400
    puffs, beer with crabmeat, 368
    Puits d'Amour, 266
    sesame-cheese fingers, 117
    tarts, rich, 401
    Viennese balls, 343
Pâté, 9, 160
    carrot with prunes, 374
    and caviar pie, 212
    chicken liver, porkless, 29
    en croûte, decorating, 246–247
    en croûte, pastry for, 403
    ham and veal, en croûte, 243
    maison, 365
    de maison, Montreal, 161
Pâte à Chou, 399
Pâte Brisée, 401
Paul's Barbecued Pork, 371
Peanuts, hot, 377
Peapods, Chinese, in platter with endive
    and tomatoes, 191
Pear Sherbet, 61
Pecan(s):
    spiced, 187
    Tasjes, cookies, 227
Pepper(s):
    hot, sauce for meatballs, 368
    hot chili, 135–136

marinated with sausages, 314
and pasta salad, 149
with sweet and hot sausages, 322
Petit Fours, chocolate diamonds, 345
Phyllo:
in baklava, 179
fruit tarts, 309
fruit triangles, 214
in tiropitas, 169
Pickled Salt Herring, 320
Picnics, 17–32
Pie(s):
caviar, 190
Cornish Pasties, 304
dough, Angela's, 404
maple syrup (tarte au sirop d'erable),
164
pâté and caviar, 212
steak and kidney, 95
Pirouettes, 342
Pistachio and Cheese Roll, 110
Plum Sauces, 309, 397
Pocket Encyclopedia of Wine (Johnson), 338
Pocket Guide to Cheese (Ensrud), 412
Poppyseed:
cake, 73
dressing, 390
Pork:
barbecued, Paul's, 371
in cretons, 161
in pâté maison, 365
teriyaki, 208
tourtière, 162
tourtière, with beef, 163
Potato(es):
balls, spicy, 224
chips, Pennsylvania Dutch-style, 131
new, baby, baked à la mode, 212
salad, 147
skin, chips or boats, 225
Pound cake, old-fashioned, 197
Praline(s):
Creole, 357
rum balls, 379
Preview party, 325–334
Price's (Vincent) Bloody Marys, 36
Prosciutto with Melon, 262
Prunes with Carrot Pâté, 374
Publicity, 293
Puff pastry, 400
Puffs, beer with crabmeat, 368
Puits d'Amour, 266

Pumpernickel and Spinach Loaf, 209
Pumpkin Bread, 31
Punch(es), 408–411
cranapple, 409
Fish House, 410
fruit, sangria-style, 132
glögg, 411
Harvard '45 Milk, 409
mimosa, 409
rhubarb, 267
rhubarb-grape juice, 228
strawberry rhubarb, 156
watermelon, 408
white wine fruit, 155
Yankee eggnog, 410
Putting Food By (Greene), 163

Q

Quail Marinated in Wine Sauce, 194
Quantities for 100 people, listed, 418
Queen Mother Cake, 252
Quiche, cocktail, 205

R

Raisin Delights, 275
Raita:
banana, 60
cucumber, 60
Raspberry Rings, 341
Raw Bar, oyster and clam, 353
Reception party, 217–228
Regional Cuisines of Greece, The, 167
Rémoulade Sauce, 396
Retsina, 168
Réveillon de Noël, 157, 159–165
Rhubarb:
and grape juice punch, 228
punch, 267
rolls, 38
and strawberry punch, 156
Rice, lemon, Craftsbury Inn, 286
Ritz crackers, in hot clam spread, 323
Ritz Sponge Cake, 236
Roasting, vegetables, 119, 120
Rolls:
Bolillos, 49
cheese and pistachio, 110
paprika cheese, 109
rhubarb, 38
salami, 372

Rolls *(Continued)*
   spring, with shrimp and chicken
   filling, 307
   watercress, 98
Rum balls, praline, 379
Rutabaga, gingered, 57

S

Saffron Sauce, orebro, 397
Salad:
   lentil, 148
   lobster bouchées, 192
   pasta, 26
   pepper pasta, 149
   potato, 147
   sesame chicken pasta, 306
   turkey, papaya and walnut, 241
Salad dressings. *See* Dressings
Salami Roll-ups, 372
Salmon:
   Gravlax, 363
   Kedgeree, 37
   mousse, 92
   smoked, tea sandwiches, 98
   smoked, with lemon and capers, 262
Salon, old-fashioned, 229–236
Salsa Picante, 135
Samosas with Sookhe Aloo Filling, 54
Sand Tarts, 341
Sandwich(es):
   cucumber, 97
   loaf, 25
   smoked salmon, 98
   tower, 365
   watercress rolls, 98
   Westphalian squares, 318
Sangria, 41, 42
Sardine Dip, 392
Sauce(s):
   Béarnaise, 274
   burgundy for raw bar, 355
   cocktail, for raw bar, 354
   cocktail, Ritz, 223
   cream, rosy, 396
   duck, 397
   fondue, 127
   Gado Gado, 67
   ginger dipping, 370
   hard, 197
   Hollandaise, 240
   hot, 136

hot pepper, for meatballs, 368
mustard-dill, for gravlax, 364
Orbec, for pâté, 245
Orebro saffron, 397
plum, 309, 397
Rémoulade, 396
salsa picante, 135
sesame dipping, 370
shallot seafood, 396
shrimp, James Beard's, 273
skordalia, 172
sorrel, 284
Szechwan, hot, 397
Teriyaki, 394
tomato, fresh, 395
tomato, quick, 395
Sausage(s):
   kielbasa with barbecue sauce, 145
   marinated with peppers, 314
   sweet and hot, with peppers, 322
   in water chestnut meatballs, 368
Scallion and Ginger Dip, 321
Scallop(s):
   and broccoli terrine, 10
   in Seviche, bay, 210
   in Seviche, sea, 77
Scones, 93
Scotch Shortbread, 95
Scot's Seed Cake, 94
Screwdrivers, 35, 36
Seafood:
   fondue, 127
   sauce, shallot, 396
Seed Cake, Scot's, 94
Senate Black Bean Soup, 30
Serrano peppers, 135–136
Sesame:
   and cheese fingers, 117
   chicken and pasta salad, 306
   dipping sauce, 370
   seed cookies, Giu Ma Bang, 255
Seviche:
   Meeting House Lane, 210
   scallop, 77
Shabu Shabu, 369
Shallot Sauce, for seafood, 396
Shellfish, raw bar, 353
Sherbet:
   cassis, 288
   lemon, 287
   pear, 61
   watermelon, 257

Shortbread, Scotch, 95
Shrimp:
    chilled, 272
    and crabmeat balls, curried, 211
    in Creole crawfish boil, 355
    filling for spring rolls, 307
    jumbo, Indian, 57
    with Louis dressing, 207
    toast, 367
Sika Gemista, 180
Skordalia, 172
Sorbet, Kirsch, 267
Sorrel Sauce, 284
Soup:
    avocado, cold, 43
    black bean, Senate, 30
    clam chowder Zelda, 29
    corn chowder, 111
    cucumber, Chicago, 119
    Gazpacho, 118
    green, 303
    hot-sour, 302
    tomato and yogurt, chilled, 304
    zucchini, 303
Sour cream, and dill dressing or dip, 388
Southern Thanksgiving party, 183–199
Southwestern Sporting Breakfast, 34,
    41–50
Soy and Ginger Marinade, 394
Spinach:
    brownies, 78
    dip with Swedish rye round, 321
    and ham filling for quiche, 206
    pumpernickel loaf, 209
    Tiropitas, 169
    in vegetable terrine, 372
Sponge Cake, Ritz, 236
Spread:
    blue cheese, 391
    clam, hot, 323
    curry and chutney, 14
    Tarama Salata Lianide, 173
    Taramasalata, 173
Spring rolls, with shrimp and chicken
    filling, 307
Spritz Cookies, 214
Squares:
    artichoke, 371
    lemon, 380
Squash blossoms, fried, 72
Steak:
    barbecued, 119, 120

and kidney pie, 95
    tartare, 263
Strawberry:
    cream tart, 101
    and rhubarb punch, 156
Swedish:
    anchovies, 330
    coffee bread, 334
    meatballs, 332
    rye, chipped beef in, 209
    rye, with spinach dip, 321
Sweet potatoes, roasted, 119, 120
Szechwan Hot Sauce, 397

T

Tabbouleh, 70
Taco:
    fillings, 135–136
    shells, 134
Tarama Salata Lianide, 173
Taramasalata, 173
Tart(s):
    blueberry-apple, 121
    lemon chess, 195
    lemon custard, 178
    mince, hot, 196
    onion, 79
    pastry, Max's, 402
    pastry, rich, 401
    phyllo fruit, 309
    au sirop d'erable, 164
    strawberry cream, 101
Tartare, steak, 263
Tartlets, mushroom, 232
Tasjes (pecan cookies), 227
Tea, 87–91
    afternoon, 86, 88–89, 97–104
    brewing, 91
    high, 85, 87–88, 92–96
    iced, 91
    iced, spicy, 103
    varieties of, 90
Tea loaf:
    apple and date, 93
    apricot-pecan bread, 100
    lemon bread, 99
Teenagers' parties, 131–132
Tequila Sunrises, 41, 42
Teriyaki:
    pork, 208
    sauce, 394

Terrine:
    broccoli-scallop, 10
    fresh herb, 24
    vegetable, 372
Tex-Mex, 41–50, 129–137
Thanksgiving party, Southern, 183–199
Tiropitas, 169
Toast:
    cinnamon, 234
    shrimp, 367
Toasting, of nuts, 417
Toffee bars, English, 226
Tomato(es):
    aspic, 113
    cherry, stuffed with crab or tuna
    mousse, 70
    cream sauce, 396
    dip, 210
    plum, peapods and endive platter,
    191
    sauce, fresh, 395
    sauce, quick, 395
    stuffed à la Amy, 312
    stuffed with cream cheese and
    consommé, 331
    and yogurt soup, chilled, 304
Torte, Trinidad, 253
Tortillas, 134
    Chimichangas, 46
    corn, 47
    flour, 48
Tourtières, 160
    pork, 162
    pork and beef, 163
Trinidad Torte, 253
Truffles, chocolate, 378
Tuna Mousse, 70
Turkey Papaya and Walnut Salad, 241
Turnips, gingered, 57

V

Vanilla, eclair filling, 346
Veal:
    and ham pâté en croûte, 243
    onion shells stuffed with, 333
Vegetable(s):
    crudités, 67
    crudités with egg caviar dip, 329
    fondue, 127
    gingered, 57
    roasting of, 119, 120
    terrine, 372
Vegetarian meals, 63–84
Vermont: A Collection of Outstanding Recipes,
  78
Victory Garden Cookbook (Morash), 226
Viennese Balls, 343
Vinaigrette, 383
Vine leaves:
    stuffed, hot, 171
    stuffed, with mint and rice, 21

W

Walnuts:
    Chinese sweet nuts, 13
    and feta dip, 392
    and turkey and papaya salad, 241
Water chestnuts:
    in bacon, 109
    in meatballs, 368
Watercress Rolls, 98
Watermelon:
    punch, 408
    sherbet, 257
Wedding cakes:
    Gramercy Park, 264
    Guidelines for, 153–154
    Heidi's Victorian, 280
    Jonathan's Dream, 276
    old-fashioned daisy, 286
Weddings:
    afternoon, elegant, 269, 271–280
    candlelight supper, 270, 281–288
    country, 139–156
    winter, 259–268
Westphalian Squares, 318
Wheat, in Tabbouleh, 70
Whiskey, in Carolina nutcake, 198
White wine. *See* Wine, white
Williamsburg Cheese Straws, 187
Wine(s):
    about, 337–339
    care and handling of, 340
    Greek, 167, 168
    mulled, 84
    sparkling, 339
    tasting party, 335–347
Wine, white:
    fruit punch, 155
    herbed marinade, 393

Y

Yankee Eggnog, 410
Yogurt:
    dressing, green, 391
    dressing or dip, 390
    and tomato soup, chilled, 304

Z

Zucchini:
    casserole, 112
    gingered, 57
    soup, cold, 303
    in vegetable terrine, 372